At the Decisive Point in the Sinai

Foreign Military Studies

History is replete with examples of notable military campaigns and exceptional military leaders and theorists. Military professionals and students of the art and science of war cannot afford to ignore these sources of knowledge or limit their studies to the history of the US armed forces. This series features original works, translations, and reprints of classics outside the American canon that promote a deeper understanding of international military theory and practice.

The Institute for Advanced Military Thinking (IAMT) was formed by retired senior officers of the Israel Defense Forces to serve as a bridge between the theories and policies of the academic world and the doctrine, training, and other preparations required for field operations. The IAMT applies this approach across the full spectrum of future land warfare by:

- initiating and supporting joint discussions regarding the historical lessons offered by land warfare in the Middle East;
- encouraging innovative thinking and open debate about current critical defense issues;
- supporting decision makers as they prepare for future challenges.

Series Editors: Roger Cirillo and Gideon Avidor

An AUSA Book

AT THE DECISIVE POINT IN THE SINAI

Generalship in the Yom Kippur War

General Jacob Even, IDF (Ret.),
and
Colonel Simcha B. Maoz, IDF (Ret.)

Translated by Simcha B. Maoz and Moshe Tlamim

Originally published in Hebrew by Modan Publishing House, Ltd., Maarachot (IDF Publishers).

Scholarly publisher for the Commonwealth,
serving Bellarmine University, Berea College, Centre College of Kentucky, Eastern Kentucky University, The Filson Historical Society, Georgetown College, Kentucky Historical Society, Kentucky State University, Morehead State University, Murray State University, Northern Kentucky University, Transylvania University, University of Kentucky, University of Louisville, and Western Kentucky University.

Editorial and Sales Offices: The University Press of Kentucky
663 South Limestone Street, Lexington, Kentucky 40508-4008
www.kentuckypress.com

Cataloging-in-Publication data is available from the Library of Congress.

ISBN 978-0-8131-6955-2 (hardcover : alk. paper)
ISBN 978-0-8131-6957-6 (epub)
ISBN 978-0-8131-6956-9 (pdf)

This book is printed on acid-free paper meeting
the requirements of the American National Standard
for Permanence in Paper for Printed Library Materials.

Manufactured in the United States of America.

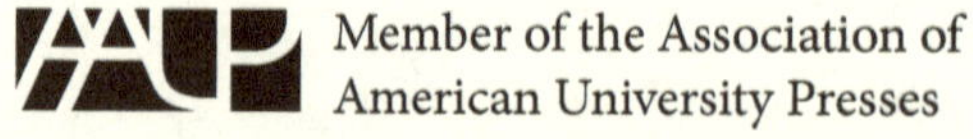

Contents

Foreword

Unlike other works on generalship at the strategic level, such as Eliot A. Cohen's *The Supreme Command,* this book focuses on generalship at the senior field command level, that is, the division commander and his team. It is the story of generalship as it was revealed on the battlefield in Major General Ariel Sharon's 143rd Division in the Yom Kippur War.

The authors, Major General (Res.) Jacob Even and Colonel (Res.) Simcha Maoz relate the heroic events that they played a major role in. General Even was the deputy commander of the 143rd Division and Colonel Maoz his assistant. Their involvement in the war is the source of the book's authority, but the story is not about their personal experiences; instead, it describes the war from the view of senior officers who were partners in the generalship of their commander, Major General Ariel Sharon.

I have purposely chosen the word *story* rather than *research* because a good story is more powerful than meticulously detailed historical research that describes precisely what happened without delving into the depth of the story or teaching what could have happened. Cognizant of their duty to future generations of commanders, the authors wish to present their concept of the Yom Kippur War in order to instruct a younger generation of senior field commanders in the essence of their responsibility and the degree to which a military operation's fortune rests on their shoulders.

As a matter of principle, a division commander in all armies carries the rank of major general. It is not only his formal position in the military hierarchy that determines this rank but also the unique function he fulfills as one who is required to stand at the point of interface between the tactical dimensions of war and its operational and strategic dimensions. By dint of his professional wisdom, prestige, and leadership authority, which also determine the specific gravity of his opinions and recommendations for the political level, a division commander serves as an intermediary point between the view of war as a mosaic of microevents and the broader perspective of it as a macroevent.

It is generally considered, and occasionally even taught, that the supreme strategic level issues orders outlining what to do and leaves to the operational level the responsibility of deciding how to do it. But a close familiarity with the development of the war teaches how often the exact opposite happens. A person who knows how to do something and believes in his ability to get it done can convince the commanding level in a critical discussion as to what (it) must (order) to be done. Sharon's struggle to realize the idea of crossing the Suez Canal is a perfect example of this. The crossing battle was the climax of the Yom Kippur War, and this book describes the development of the war from the perspective of Sharon's division and the unfolding events that led to this climax. We can also learn a great deal from the initial chaotic days of the war and difficulties of the defensive campaign.

The First Days of the War: The Defensive Campaign

The book clearly and critically describes the depth of operational surprise in the October 8–9 battles. This surprise is revealed as even greater than the intelligence failure in not warning of the outbreak of war. The tactical results of the battles between the IDF and Egyptian forces in the first days created the vertiginous shock that stemmed from our forces' operational concept and fighting method, both of which proved incompatible with and mistakenly built for coping with the Egyptian concept of operations, one based on a broad mass of infantry saturated with antitank missiles. Much has been written on how the Israeli battalions and companies adapted to the new and unexpected phenomenon. But this book uniquely focuses on the way in which the division level dealt with the challenge: the division commander's struggle to maintain the offensive initiative within the defensive framework, especially on October 9, and the way in which the division stabilized the defensive line in the Hamadia-Kishuf sector, an invaluable achievement in the defensive battle that later forged the conditions for the counterattack, otherwise known as *the crossing battle.*

The Transition from Defense to Offense

When did the defensive period end? Were conditions created for the transition to the offensive?

These questions, like operational and strategic questions, do not and cannot have a textbook solution. They demand judgment that is focused on the context of the events. They are exactly the type of questions that the commanding general has to deal with and the commanders of the campaign have to decide. The web of anxieties and uncertainties that characterized the idea of the canal crossing is an example that provides inspiration for an in-depth study of the main role that the division commander has in contributing to the crystallization of such fateful decisions at both the General Staff and the political levels.

The Crossing Battle: Why?

At the heart of the ability to decide on an action is an intelligent questioning of the reason for the action. In making the crucial decision in the offensive campaign, "What for?" or "For what purpose?" is the key question whose clarification involves a penetrating analysis in order to decide on the campaign's timing, direction, and finish lines. The book highlights the dilemma of waiting for the Egyptian divisions to cross the canal before October 14 and the question of their possible renewal of the offensive. These fluctuations in the dynamics of the war demand a one-time decision on the nature and rationale of the developing intentions and the formulation of a plan that the division commander prepares for and exploits to his advantage.

No redeeming procedure exists for dealing with the pressure that accompanies these questions. To the general at the field level—that is, a division commander—who believes in his capabilities, this discussion offers a vital influence that stems from his authority, which is anchored in his presence, in his connection with actual battle and its friction, and his close familiarity with the fighting abilities of his subordinates, commanders and soldiers alike.

Thus, we see that the test of a division commander relates not only to his authority over his subordinates but also to his ability to influence the levels above him.

Generalship and Friction with the Superiors

Sharon's struggle to convince others of his view and put his idea into action is unprecedented in Israel's battlefield heritage. Some have criticized Sharon for the way in which he conducted this struggle and refer to him as a figure in *the war of the generals* in the post–Yom Kippur War period.

But the opposite can also be argued. I found in this story the expression of the personal strength required of a senior field commander to convince his superiors of the merit of his ideas.

By its nature, generalship seems to include the creation of friction-laden situations among the division commanders engaged in the campaign as well as between the division commanders and the superior level. This was reflected in the abrasive tension between Sharon and Haim Bar-Lev, the front commander, regarding the ongoing transfer of forces across the canal and maximizing the crossing's potential before the access routes were firmly secured and a permanent bridge erected. This case is also enlightening in that Sharon's concept is exactly what was needed. On the other hand, Bar-Lev's cautious stance and his decision to delay the continued crossing until the bridge was secured were later found to be correct in light of the difficulties involved in bridge construction under sustained, devastating artillery shelling. But, without Sharon's dauntless handling of the situation and the devoted work of his subordinates (headed by the deputy division commander), the crossing would not have taken place or the bridge have been completed. Viewing the events from the vantage point of hindsight as a paradigm of contrast and symmetry between Sharon and Bar-Lev sheds light on the pertinent conflict between senior commanders regarding the conduct of the war and is, in itself, a lesson well worth learning.

The Impact of Commanding from Up Front

Sharon's presence on the battlefield and his influence on the fighting underscored more than anything else the beginning of the crossing battle on the first night of Operation Stouthearted Men (October 15–16). Two crucial decisions should be credited to Sharon:

1. His determination that night not to postpone the start of the crossing campaign despite the vexatious obstacles involved in moving the rafts and the roller bridge forward to the crossing area.
2. His unequivocal decision to send Dani Matt's paratrooper brigade to the bridgehead despite the fog of battle surrounding Amnon Reshef's 14th Tank Brigade's ferocious, costly fighting to establish a corridor to the crossing point.

The 143rd Division bore the fate of the campaign and the nation on its shoulders that night. The talmudic sages say of such a condition: "There are those who buy their world in a single hour." This is the story of the heroism displayed by an entire division whose men and officers selflessly lived up to the trust of the division commander that they would successfully fulfill whatever mission he assigned them.

That night was the start of the crossing battle. It was one of many long nights during the war, but it was without doubt a climax, the buildup to which is excellently described in this book—from the moment the division's brigades organized for defense on October 7, through the October 8–9 battles, to the crystallization of the crossing idea as the turning point from defense to offense.

The Role of the Deputy Division Commander

Major General (Res.) Jacob Even tells the whole story of the division's fighting and his own story as deputy division commander beginning with the organization at the division's emergency storage facilities, continuing with the lengthy coordination and operational transportation of the division from its camps between Beersheba and Tel Aviv to the Suez Canal front, and culminating with his role as commander—assigned by the division commander—of important elements of the division's battle. His story reflects the duty of a deputy division commander, the right-hand man of the division commander, not only as his potential replacement, but also as an authoritative commander, a partner in making key decisions, capable of taking responsibility and relieving the commander of some of his burdens. The manner in which Even commanded the battles from his FCP on October 8–9 is a preeminently instructive example of responsibility sharing by a division commander and his deputy. The high point of his role in the crossing battle was his personal responsibility for bringing the rafts and roller bridge to the canal, launching and assembling the bridges, and organizing the "Yard" (see chapter 9) as the bottleneck through which the divisions crossed the canal under uninterrupted artillery fire. His personal story must be compulsory reading for all senior field commanders and their deputies.

Generalship in war is different in essence from managing a production line. War is a multidimensional event in which senior field commanders must order a great number of troops and a vast array of weapons in a constantly changing environment that is generally intractable to concentrated control. Such a condition demands of the general the skill of a ship captain who, with his crew, is responsible for capitalizing on the wind for his needs, fully aware that he has no control over it but that he is still able to exploit the force to his advantage. The story of the Yom Kippur War as it was led by commanders who faced the test of generalship can and needs to serve as a standard for the next generation of commanders to aspire to. It is they who are preparing for new tests that will demand the highest level of generalship.

This book is an invaluable source of inspiration to the IDF's senior combat commanders who are preparing for the coming challenges.

Major General Gershon Hacohen
Commander, IDF Colleges
Commander, Northern Corps
November 2011

Abbreviations

APC	armored personnel carrier
CoGS	chief of General Staff
CoS	chief of staff
FCP	forward command post
IAF	Israeli air force
IDF	Israel defense forces
MARSHAL	Sharem el-Sheikh Military District
MI	military intelligence
SAM	surface-to-air missile

Authors' Note

> Cato the Elder, who often served as commander of Rome's armies and always emerged victorious, believed that he could better serve his country if he wrote on military matters instead of his personal exploits on the battlefield since the results of heroic acts pass away whereas writing for the good of the public is of lasting benefit. (Vegetius, *De re militari*)

Raison d'être

This book is not history for history's sake but a study of generalship—the art of command at the highest levels. Its target audience is the senior political-security level in Israel, among them members of the General Staff, corps, division, and brigade commanders and officers designated for or aspiring to reach this elite group, and the reader who wishes to gain a deep understanding of the issues facing this group and the manner in which the challenges created by these issues are—or should be—dealt with.

It was not our intention to present a systematic doctrine via scholarly lectures, dogmatic sermons, or the regurgitation—manifest or disguised—from the vast literature on this subject. Instead, we chose to describe, and occasionally express our opinion on, specific events on the Suez Canal front during the Yom Kippur War, with a focus on the IDF's southern front headquarters, the IDF General Staff, and the divisions that fought in the Suez Canal theater, particularly in the Egyptian Second Army sector, because of the essence of generalship that can be learned from them. In this field, like any other, the most powerful and reliable tool for gaining a penetrating understanding is strategic and operational failure. The lessons of success are often illusory and misleading and always vague and deceptive; the lessons of failure, however, are always sharp, reliable, and clear if we take the pains to derive them wisely and honestly. We wish, then, to focus on the mistakes but not necessarily on their perpetrators.

The Israeli government appointed the Winograd Commission in the wake of the blunders made in the Second Lebanon War (2006) at the General Staff and other senior command levels, especially regarding the ground forces. Following the commission's findings, the CoGS, the commanding general of the Northern Command, and four division commanders, who had been tasked with crushing a few thousand Shiite guerrillas in South Lebanon, either left the IDF or had their careers blocked. Later, the deputy CoGS and the commander of the Israeli navy fell victims of the wartime debacle, despite the attempts to blur the fact. Furthermore, the prime minister and the defense minister also paid the price for the fiasco with their political heads. In this case, just as in the post–Yom Kippur War period, the government failed to appoint a regular major general as CoGS but instead turned to a recently retired general for this position—Major General (Res.) Gabi Ashkenazi.

The First Lebanon War (Operation Peace for Galilee) (1982–1985) ended without the dismissal of the top brass (if we exclude the recommendations of the official commission of inquiry that investigated the Sabra and Shatila events) despite its poor performance in the war, but the following excerpt sheds light on the flaws in IDF generalship at the high command level: "The war revealed inconceivable weakness and the total absence of generalship at the large formation, regional command, and the General Staff level" (Wald 1987, 76).

The Agranat Commission, which was appointed six weeks after the Yom Kippur War (November 1973), examined only the first three days of fighting, which were sufficient for it to recommend sacking the CoGS, the chief of MI, the general of the Southern Command, and several of their assistants. It should also be noted that, when a replacement for the CoGS had to be found, none of the IDF generals who fought in the war was deemed worthy of this role, and the government picked Major General Mordechai Gur, who had been the IDF military attaché in Washington during the war.

One common feature links these three points in time: the lengthy absence of competent generalship at the senior level. From the War of Attrition (1967–1970) until the present, every war has exposed the open secret that the IDF's weakest link is its senior command. Unless effective steps are taken to rectify this frightening flaw, the danger inherent in it will put the country and the lives of its citizens and soldiers at great risk in the next war. Internalizing the lessons to be taken away from the book is one of these steps. We wish to emphasize: the opinions and assessments in it are largely ours alone; if an opinion is presented that is not ours, we will make explicit note of it. In conclusion, regarding the motive for writing this book, we quote from the preface to Major General J. F. C. Fuller's groundbreaking work *The Conduct of War:*

> There are many manuals on war, and although I am no great lover of official textbooks, when I had written this book it occurred to me that there was ample room for one which should head the list—namely on "The Conduct of War". It should be written for both statesmen and soldiers, and be made compulsory reading. With advantage it might be divided into two parts: "How to Conduct a War" and "How not to

> Conduct a War"; for the second part, as this book will show, there is a superabundance of raw materials. (Fuller 1961, 14).

Methodology

As stated, this book is not a historical study even if it might be perceived as such. We therefore felt it unnecessary to embellish it with unnecessary academic apparatus. Nevertheless, we have presented the reader with a list of the sources that helped us describe and analyze events and situations that we were not witness to.

The journalist Eitan Haber (2010), who was the late Yitzhak Rabin's senior adviser and bureau chief at the time, says:

> Historians tend to accord supreme and exclusive importance to papers; documents are the lifeblood and oxygen of their research. Without records, documentation, and especially protocols they have nothing. . . . Until [I] happened to serve as a public servant [I] too thought that protocols . . . were priceless. Like many others, [I] became enamored with documents. Well, it's all bullshit. Protocols are evidence of practically nothing.

We would unhesitatingly add the above-mentioned Anglo-Saxon expletive to the rest of the so-called historical sources in the historian's quiver—including war diaries, testimonies given under various circumstances, texts from wireless transmissions, lectures by senior commanders before military and other forums, memoirs brimming with alibis and self-aggrandizement and whatnot, all of which only reinforce what has already been stated (by Uri Avnery, a journalist and political activist, on Moshe Timor's radio program *Shishi Shabat*, Reshet Beit, October 2, 2010)—that "every document is a forgery." To the truth seekers among us, let us say that one photograph often lies better than a thousand words.

Momentous decisions are made and crucial matters finalized between two or three interested parties in the strangest of places, in chance meetings without witnesses, without leaving a trace of paper confirmation. The official documents, radio transmissions, memoirs, expert and erudite analyses, and even photographs are designed first and foremost to create a false presentation and camouflage the real proceedings that led to historic results.

Not only is the raw material available to the professional historian, by its nature, fragmentary and impaired, but the process of rendering it into a historical work also recalls the axiom of the Israeli historian and journalist Tom Segev

(2010): "History is fundamentally a political profession." The facts on which the historian chooses to base the history are solely his interpretation of events that he expects us to believe occurred. The interpretation reflects his skill and acumen in connecting them to the political and social views and personal interests that guide him.

The only tool that can light the way to some kind of understanding of past events and identify processes that may have led to them is intelligent speculation, which, indeed, we have been unsparing in applying to an issue that has many documents relating to it but none contributing so much as one iota of truth to its clarification. We have subjected our speculation to the critique of pure reason; we employed it, when possible, guided by the rule from the field of statistics known as *the principle of maximum likelihood* (an analytic technique in the field of statistical inference that enables identifying which hypothesis among several is most likely to explain a certain phenomenon). This principle determines the path for speculation, provides it with a logical framework, and brings it as close as possible to what is most acceptable even if this is not a foolproof guide to the truth. After all: "What is truth?" (Pontius Pilate's immortal question [John 18:38]).

Why the Suez Canal Zone?

We chose to focus on the events of the Suez Canal front for two main reasons:

1. The war on the southern front was the IDF's most intensive. The moves in it were unique in IDF history, and the failures on this front, like some of the victories, hold lessons and insights that are invaluable to this book.
2. We served in Ariel Sharon's 143rd Division. Even was deputy division commander, and Maoz was one of his staff officers. We played an active role in some of the key events and were witnesses to others. We knew personally the main generals discussed herein—from the CoGS and his deputy down the rungs.

1

The Order and the Division

From Call-Up to Assembly

The Order

In the first week of October 1973, despite wishful thinking, fear was rising in the highest political and military levels that war was about to erupt on the Golan Heights and Suez Canal. By the end of the week, the IDF took critical steps, such as declaring a "C"-level alert (preparing for the mobilization of the reservists), calling up auxiliary air force units, reinforcing the northern front with armor and artillery, and issuing warnings at various levels to prepare for blocking battles and a general mobilization. These steps were carried out under the fading hope that the approaching war was only a bad dream that could be averted by dint of MI's concept, which the political and military elite accepted, regarding the necessary conditions for the outbreak of war between Israel and the Arab states. According to this concept, Syria would not go to war without Egypt, and Egypt would not go to war until it obtained long-range weapons capable of reaching Israel's heartland. This concept was the antithesis of the biblical sage's twenty-three-hundred-year-old advice: "Better is the sight of the eyes than the wandering of the desire" (Eccles. 6:9).

In the early morning of Yom Kippur (the Day of Atonement, the holiest day in the Jewish calendar), October 6, 1973, the uncertainty abruptly ended. At approximately 0400, the political and military decision makers realized that war would erupt that day. In the five hours that had passed since the CoGS, Lieutenant General David ("Dado") Elazar, and the defense minister, Moshe Dayan, learned that war was imminent, the two had been bickering over the scale of mobilization. At 0900, Prime Minister Golda Meir gave the CoGS the green light to call up two divisions immediately. Elazar mobilized the 143rd Armored Division for the southern front and the 146th Division to serve as the General Staff's reserve force. Twenty minutes later, the prime minister approved a full-scale call-up.

The 143rd Division

In the 1967 Six-Day War, the 31st Provisional Division had fought under the command of Major General Avraham Yoffe in Sinai's central axis, where it captured the Gidi and Mitla Passes and reached the Suez Canal in the Port Fuad area. In January 1972, the 31st became the permanent 143rd Division. The general of the Southern Command in this period was Major General Ariel Sharon. In mid-July 1973, Sharon ended his tenure in the Southern Command, apparently unwillingly, and retired from the IDF, diving headfirst into the political arena. His replacement was Shmuel Gonen, who only a year earlier, in May 1972, had been promoted to major general. Despite the CoGS's opposition, Dayan named Major General (Res.) Ariel Sharon commander of the 143rd. By doing so, he rectified to a degree his consent to appoint Gonen commander of the Southern Command. As commander of the 143rd, Sharon insisted on Colonel Jacob ("Jacky") Even as his deputy. Even's armor experience included several key roles, such as commander of the 520th Armored Brigade in Yoffe's division in the Six-Day War, commander of the Armor School, and commander of the 7th Tank Brigade in the War of Attrition (1969–1970). Sharon needed Even's professionalism, experience, and proven ability as commander of large-scale armor units. The 143rd was a reservist division. Many of its men and officers were veterans of the Six-Day War and the War of Attrition and as such were familiar with the areas east of the canal.

On October 6, the division consisted of the 421st Tank Brigade under the command of Colonel Haim Erez, the 600th Tank Brigade under the command of Colonel Tuvia Raviv, and the 875th Mechanized Brigade (formerly the 8th Brigade) under the command of Colonel Aryeh Dayan. On the following day, while the division was heading to the canal, the Southern Command requisitioned the 875th and annexed it to the 252nd Division (also known as the Sinai Division) under the command of Major General Avraham ("Albert") Mandler. In its place, and on the same day, the 143rd received the 14th Tank Brigade, a regular army brigade, under the command of Colonel Amnon Reshef, which, since the start of the war, had been part of the Sinai Division fighting in the canal area. The 143rd—especially after the departure of the 875th (with its forty-five Sherman tanks) and the entry of the 14th Brigade, which was made up entirely of Patton ("Magach") tanks, the IDF's newest model—gave the Magach M60A1 tanks, the most advanced Magach model, to the 600th Brigade and the 87th Reconnaissance Battalion.

The level of manpower and the main armored combat vehicles greatly assisted the division's commanders in their efforts. Many of the men and officers were young in age but already combat experienced. Many had served in the 79th Tank Battalion, which Colonel Even had established as the IDF's first Magach tank battalion (equipped with Patton M48s and M60s). Many of the battalion's men and officers who were serving in the 143rd had grown to maturity under Colonel Even's tutelage. His acquaintance with most of them and his appreciation of their capabilities proved invaluable in working with them. Of no less importance was the fact that they recognized him as a leader and an educator of officers and soldiers and knew what to expect of him as a field commander and what he would demand of them. As Even remembers:

> When I assumed my position in the 143rd Division, no one thought that war was imminent, but as soon as I arrived I assembled all the division's officers and made it clear: "We're preparing the division for war." No one raised a brow. They all understood exactly what I meant: the division's command intended to prepare the division for war in all earnestness. As a first step, every element of combat preparation was examined: the division's operational plans, ammunition, equipment, vehicle outfitting, training level, manpower, and so forth. Next, work plans were drawn up. The level of the division and brigade staffs was very high. Their excellence stemmed from the fact that most of the officers, and first and foremost the division CoS, Colonel Gideon Altshuler, were experienced career officers with superb reputations. The core senior command consisted entirely of career officers. I was acquainted with most of them, both the career officers and the reservists, from my service in the armored corps and the 79th Battalion over the years.

(For details of the division's order of battle and main officer roles, see appendix A.)

Shortly after 1400, the Southern Command informed the division's headquarters that the Egyptian army was crossing the canal in large force and overwhelming the Israeli strongholds on the Bar-Lev Line. The report stunned the division's headquarters. "Had the Egyptians gone mad?" Everyone was convinced that the IDF would crush the invaders, as Haim Bar-Lev once said, "fast, hard, and elegantly," in a kind of repeat performance of the IDF's victory in the Six-Day War. It should be noted that, on October 6, the upper echelons of the government and the IDF were still unaware of the Egyptian army's superlative antitank capability, its infantry's excellent training and courage, to what degree the IAF was neutralized, the limitations of Israel's regular army, and the extent to which Israeli armor's combat doctrine was already obsolete. Added to the magnitude of the surprise were the deficiencies in the IDF high command.

Now, years after the war, it is clear beyond the shadow of a doubt that the myth of the October 6 surprise cannot excuse the IDF's blunders in the first three days of the fighting. The only surprise that the senior commanders of the division felt on hearing the reports of the two-front attack was that the Egyptians and Syrians had initiated an act of suicide. No one in the division doubted for a moment that the IDF would expedite the enemy in accomplishing its self-destruction. And this is where the IDF was caught by surprise.

The Call-Up

After the Southern Command headquarters issued alerts in the morning, the division's headquarters and brigades began feverishly preparing for a general mobilization. When the call-up order arrived at approximately 0930, the mobilization network went into high gear. Because the entire broadcast system and communications network in Israel was shut down on Yom Kippur, a covert call-up was decided on. Yom Kippur made it very easy to employ this system.

After the war, Egyptian president Anwar Sadat boasted in his autobiography and on countless other occasions that the goal of Egypt's war initiative was to shatter Israel's security doctrine. At the basis of the doctrine stood the IDF's structure as a reservist-based army that mobilizes regardless of the nature, aims, and initial conditions of the war. From this fundamental principle, Israel's national security doctrine derived the rest of its concepts, such as a short war—that is, quickly transferring the fighting onto enemy territory—or relying on special force elements such as the IAF and MI.

The decision of Sadat and Syria's president Hafez al-Assad to launch the war on Yom Kippur, the day when the Israeli media were shut down, was undoubtedly designed to hurt the IDF's ability to mobilize the reservists rapidly and efficiently. (In his memoirs, the Egyptian CoGS, Major General Saad el-Shazly, explained that the choice of Yom Kippur for D-day was because of its historical-symbolic meaning for Muslims the world over.) But this reveals the Egyptian planners' total lack of understanding of the way Israeli Jews observe this particular holy day. On Yom Kippur, the Israeli media are shut off and thus are useless for calling up the reservists, at least in the initial stages. But, by the same token, the main elements needed for rapid mobilization are at the height of availability: most Israeli Jews are at home or in neighborhood synagogues. Military and civilian vehicles designated for military purposes or the call-up are located in their regular parking places, telecommunications systems are open, and the road networks are empty of traffic. Once the General Staff signals the mobilization, it is not long before the reservists reach their assembly areas on the front. The bulk of the time is devoted to the arrival of the reservists in the emergency storage depots, converting civilians into military units, and getting them to the assembly areas. This part of the mobilization is significantly shortened if the road networks are open and the vehicles designated for requisitioning or use during the mobilization can be obtained quickly. Good weather also plays a part in speeding up the mobilization and deployment.

Regarding the reservists' call-up, the enemy planners also made a major mistake. Theoretically, a public call-up is immediate: all the reservists, no matter where they are, simultaneously receive the order to report for duty, and very little time is needed to complete the process. But the covert mobilization system—largely based on the mass communications phenomenon of the exponential spread of information in a population—is also able to reach hundreds of thousands of men within one to two hours and have them report to active duty. The enemy planners failed to understand the tremendous power inherent in the swift spread of this geometric line and thought that the silenced media would lead to a slower mobilization. In reality, the mobilization and transportation of the men from their homes to their bases proceeded very quickly. The reservists began streaming into the emergency storage depots almost immediately after the start of the call-up. The slow rate of call-up that the enemy planners expected when selecting Yom Kippur as D-day was far outweighed by the advantages that the conditions of the holy day gave to the mobilization. As a result, the first armor units arrived at the southern front in less than twenty-four hours from the outbreak of war (much more quickly than such units arrived at the northern front). That Yom Kippur was D-day for the joint Egyptian-Syrian attack was a key factor in this phenomenal achievement.

The Egyptian General Staff, like its Israeli counterpart, estimated that the IDF would need at least forty-eight hours to transfer its reservists to the front. The Egyptian and Syrian General Staffs were obviously surprised to discover Israeli armored reservist divisions facing them on the front a full day before expected. There was room for the IDF to consider exploiting the enemy's surprise by immediately launching massive, determined counterattacks in the north and the south.

Two main conclusions can be drawn:

1. The Egyptian army did not shatter the Israeli combat doctrine. On the contrary, that doctrine, which was based on the full-scale call-up of the reservists and their deployment to the front in great strength and with record-breaking speed, is what eventually caused the Egyptian and Syrian armies' defeat and forced Sadat to seek, on his knees, first a cease-fire and then peace with Israel.
2. The balance of gain and loss between the Egypt and Syria, on the one hand, and Israel, on the other, that resulted from the enemy having decided on Yom Kippur as D-day proves for the umpteenth time the maxim, "The

> best is the enemy of the good." Perhaps this maxim should be adopted as a principle of war.

Most of the division's reservists received their call-up orders and reported to the emergency storage depots in the initial hours of hostilities. The rest of the day in the mobilization centers was spent mustering the perennial latecomers. By midnight, all the mobilization centers were closed. The organization of the units and divisions at the emergency storage depots was generally administered quickly and efficiently. Although foul-ups did occur, some of them disastrous, in equipping and preparing the troops and combat vehicles, they were miniscule in comparison to the chaos that had characterized the mobilization six years earlier at the state of the Six-Day War. After both wars, one heard the complaints of those who focused only on the chaos in the emergency storage depots. Such criticism is an annoying ritual that is better left to psychological and sociological studies than to the IDF. The undeniable fact is that, in October 1973, the IDF did not have three weeks' advance notice to organize for war, as it had in 1967. Nevertheless, within one day, it succeeded in deploying seven or eight combat-ready armored and infantry divisions on two fronts. Despite the tears and lamentations over the chaos in the emergency storage depots, this was an achievement without parallel in the annals of military history.

Colonel Even recalled:

> The division of labor at this stage between Arik [Sharon] and me characterized what was expected of a commander of his rank and his deputy. As the overall commander, Arik devoted all his mental and physical energy and time to learning the operational data on the front as they were happening, analyzing them, and piecing together a situation picture in the attempt to assess the future and formulate decisions that would be carried out. This was an evolving intellectual effort for him, given the kaleidoscopic events on the canal front that demanded continuous information collecting and reassessing the constantly changing situation. I saw my role as getting the division ready so that Sharon would be free to devote all his time, energy, and mental resources toward fulfilling his immediate role as the designer of the future. Together with the division's staff officers and brigade and unit commanders, and in coordination with the division commander, I assumed responsibility for overseeing the division's mobilization.

Sharon remained at the division's base at Sde Teiman (on the outskirts of Beersheba) at the start of the call-up, where he was constantly updated on the mobilization's progress. While he infused the effort with his personal authority and tenacity, he also dealt with matters that he deemed crucial for managing the division in the following days. Around noon, he moved to the Southern Command's headquarters, which had still not advanced to its command and control center at Um Hashiba in northwest Sinai. After being updated and gleaning what he could of the ground situation—which was very little, the information with which he was provided being extremely confused and mostly unreliable—he returned to Sde Teiman, updated his deputy, brigade commanders, and staff on events at the front, and outlined his view of the situation, all the while being regularly updated on the progress of the division's mobilization and organization. At this stage, he understood the Southern Command's intention to deploy the 143rd Division in the central sector of the canal front, somewhere between al-Balah Island in the north and the Botzer stronghold area in the south.

Assembly

On the evening of October 6, it seemed that several tank units would be equipped and ready to move out within a matter of hours and that other units—companies and battalions—would follow suit throughout the night. In line with Sharon's instructions, Even issued the following orders to the division's staff and brigades:

> Tank transporters will no longer carry Magach [M-48] tanks to the front as the initial deployment plan envisioned. Starting now the tanks will travel to the front on their tracks. Only the 875th Mechanized Brigade will send some of their Shermans to the front on transporters.
>
> Since we can't wait until the battalions and brigades are completely organized, every combat-ready company will immediately move out to the Suez Canal as soon as its tanks are manned, armed, and equipped in accordance with standing operation procedure. Every company will proceed to the front as an operational unit under the command of its officers.

Before moving out, the companies were briefed on their routes and final destination, as Sharon had conveyed them to the deputy division commander, brigade commanders, and division staff, as well as on traffic control points, maintenance, refueling, and communications procedures. Instructions were given regarding conduct and response in operational situations such as aerial attacks and ambushes. At midnight, the first companies pulled out. Before dawn, Sharon also set out to the west at the head of a convoy containing his FCP and the main elements of division headquarters. Even remained at Sde Teiman to make sure that the mobilization and organization continued at an accelerated pace, to solve sundry problems that always crop up in such an effort, and to push more units to the front as soon as they were ready.

It is not our intention to rehash all that has been said and written about the advantages and disadvantages (mostly advantages) of moving tanks on their tracks rather than on transporters. Nonetheless, an often-misconstrued point must be emphasized. While moving great distances from emergency storage depots, some tanks will always get stuck on the roadside because of mechanical breakdowns. This is the reality of equipment in storage. The majority of people attribute this phenomenon to the necessary evil of deploying tanks on their tracks, but the truth is that it should be attributed to their credit. Better that the tank, which will eventually break down after a certain number of hours of movement on its tracks no matter what the conditions are, should grind to a halt in our territory and be salvaged, repaired, and returned to service than during battle, when getting stuck because of a technical malfunction renders it a sitting duck. The fate of an inert tank on the battlefield is a foregone conclusion.

Sharon reached the 252nd Division's headquarters at Refidim on the morning of October 7 and stayed there to receive updates, form a picture of the events, and draw up plans for dealing with the situation. Despite the inflow of information, the accompanying noise, confusion, and unreliability of the data prevented him from understanding what was actually happening at the front and stymied his attempts to assess the situation, plan the division's deployment, and organize a counterattack. He reached Tassa at noon and immediately set out to observe the area and obtain a firsthand impression of the ground situation. True to his command style, he focused on developing an attack. But, at this stage, Gonen was mainly concerned that the Egyptians would exploit their success and move large forces to the junctions and areas dominating Artillery Road and even Lateral Road, especially in the direction of Tassa. Thus, he ordered Sharon to set up his headquarters in Tassa, deploy his division there when it arrived, organize for defense, and secure the area especially in the north and west. As day broke on October 7, most of the 143rd Division's units were heading toward the canal. Colonel Even left the task of completing the mobilization and pushing the rest of the division to the front to one of staff officers and set out for Tassa, arriving there at noon. Most of the division's units were already pouring in and deploying in the vicinity.

The 14th Brigade's commander, Colonel Amnon Reshef, arrived at 1400. His brigade had been fighting continuously in the central sector since the previous day and was being mauled. Reshef explained to Sharon his brigade's fighting on the previous day and its casualty rate (roughly 75–80 percent of the initial force). Sharon informed Reshef that the 143rd Division had been given responsibility for the central sector (from al-Balah Island in the north to the Botzer stronghold in the south) and that the 14th Brigade was now part of the 143rd.

By noon, most the division's units had assembled in their designated areas in the Tassa vicinity. According to plans, the 421st Brigade was deployed on Artillery Road and Lateral Road junctions with Spontani Road, about fifteen to twenty kilometers north and northwest of Tassa. The 600th Brigade was positioned about five kilometers west of Tassa on the Talisman (Tassa-Ismailia) axis, and what remained of the 14th Brigade, together with the 87th Reconnaissance Battalion, secured Akavish Road, about ten to fifteen kilometers southwest of Tassa (at the Yukon and Hamadia localities).

The Bar-Lev Line and the Strongholds

When the Egyptians launched the canal crossing, the Bar-Lev Line, the purported obstacle in their way, numbered only fifteen manned strongholds of the original thirty. Four of them were in the 143rd's sector: from north to south, Hezayon, Purkan, Matzmed, and Leklkan. Much has been said and written about the Bar-Lev Line and its strongholds, and it is not our intention to regurgitate the pros and cons. Nevertheless, a number of points will be noted given the tragic fate of the line during the war. The Bar-Lev Line was not built to defend the canal line from a massive attack such as the one the Egyptians launched at the start of the Yom Kippur War. Its real purpose was to demonstrate Israeli control of Sinai and Israeli presence on the eastern bank of the Suez Canal, that is, to serve as a kind of casus belli—a trip wire as it were—if the Egyptians dared to cross the canal with the intent of capturing territory (as opposed to carrying out a raid).

For reasons that were neither military nor professional, the strongholds on the Bar-Lev Line were assigned additional tasks, such as warning of preparations for a canal crossing and crossing attempts, protecting the soldiers in the strongholds, and integrating the strongholds in the defense of the waterline. Naturally, these tasks did not stand up to any test or to reason, truth, intellectual honesty, military professionalism, or achievability. The only role they served was to flaunt Israel's presence and strength and display contempt in the Egyptians' face. To accomplish this task, Israel was prepared to throw billions of dollars to the wind and abandon hundreds of IDF soldiers to death and captivity.

The Bar-Lev Line's contribution to Israel's security was not only negligible; it was plain negative. Its structure with its five hundred soldiers lacked any logic. It served as easy prey for the Egyptian army, which was able to allocate the necessary resources for its capture without detracting one iota from its main missions. The construction of the Bar-Lev Line provided the Egyptians with a target of the highest political, moral, and propaganda significance that could be swiftly won at no cost. Operationally, the Egyptian army could cross the canal at any point and deploy where it wished, without the need to attack the strongholds. In fact, it could even ignore them temporarily. But, given the enormous significance, which went beyond military exigencies, of liquidating the Bar-Lev Line, the Egyptian army began demolishing it as soon as it crossed the canal. In less than seventy-two hours, Egyptian flags were flying over most of the strongholds, hundreds of soldiers were dead (some massacred), wounded, or missing or taken prisoner.

From a purely military point of view, the line had been a liability; its contribution to blocking the Egyptian invasion was demonstratively counterproductive. It had not been built for this from the start—therefore it did not prove a disappointment in the conceptual sense. Its nugatory contribution to the canal crossing is illustrated by the amazing fact that the Egyptian army incurred only 208 casualties! Furthermore, the Bar-Lev Line was not even capable of defending itself, and the need of point defense for each and every stronghold when the Egyptians crossed immediately rendered them a heavy liability on the Southern Command's limited resources. A huge number of armored commanders and tank crews were killed and wounded, excluding the stronghold troops themselves, in the failed attempts to defend the line and link up with strongholds; hundreds of armored combat vehicles were destroyed or incapacitated, and the force that was left to the Southern Command for Sinai's defense was catastrophically weakened. The Egyptians had an indirect reason, but a good one from a military point of view, for attacking the Bar-Lev Line. Israeli armor tactics for linking up with the strongholds—which the Egyptians had precise knowledge of—enabled their infantry to determine exactly where to set up ambushes to knock out the Israeli tanks racing to link up with the strongholds.

All this intelligence was, or should have been, known to and understood by the defense minister, the CoGS, and the Southern Command general. These men were expected to know—and probably did know—that at H-hour plus one minute the role of the Bar-Lev Line strongholds would be over. Even if the Southern Command had prepared for this scenario according to the "Dovecote" operational plan, it would have been impossible with the means available, the armored tactics at the time, and the lack of air support to prevent the Egyptian army from crossing the canal and seizing territory. The CoGS and the general of the Southern Command were duty bound to order the immediate evacuation of the strongholds. Neither the political nor the military circumstances left room for any other option.

The fact is that no one in the security and military elite gave a direct, unequivocal order in time to withdraw from the strongholds. On a few occasions, the defense minister spoke with the CoGS or the general of the Southern Command and nudged them to evacuate the strongholds, but he made sure to mention that this was a "ministerial" recommendation. Since the CoGS could not ignore Dayan's stubborn recommendations, he contacted Gonen on different occasions and gave him permission to evacuate the strongholds "if it wouldn't split the forces," or "if it was possible," or "if there's pressure," or if, or if, but a straightforward, explicit order never came. Gonen, whose subordinates also pressed him to evacuate the strongholds, chose, for obvious reasons, to ignore all the so-called pressures and vacillations and leave the troops in the strongholds to deal with their fate alone.

The question remains, Why was a clear-cut order not issued? In our opinion, the reason is linked to the raison d'être of the Bar-Lev Line, which was supposed to project Israel's strength and determination not to cede one inch of territory to the Egyptians. The Egyptians interpreted the line's fall as a magnificent triumph, while Israel, caught by surprise, felt it a humiliating, excruciating blow (especially with the approach of parliamentary elections). Dayan's tenuous position in Golda Meir's government prevented him from ordering the strongholds evacuated; the only weapon in his arsenal was the clever trick of offering ministerial advice. The CoGS was unwilling to take responsibility and give the crucial order because of its national and political ramifications, especially if the possibility remained of destroying the Egyptian bridgeheads and retaking the line (an idea that Dayan realized was out of the question).

The fate of the strongholds was apparently not in the forefront of the general of the Southern Command's mind. Still reeling from the shock of events on the canal and their possible impact on the direction of the war and his own reputation, Gonen seems to have focused all his intellectual and psychological faculties on one overriding issue: how to achieve a dazzling, lightning-fast victory that would erase the shame and crushing defeat that had befallen his command. The order to evacuate the strongholds would be interpreted—above all by himself but also by the IDF, the government, and the citizens of Israel—as an admission of his failure and the trouncing of the IDF. In war, as in a stock market crash, you haven't lost until you've sold.

On October 7, some of the strongholds could have been evacuated despite their encirclement, but Gonen believed, solely on the basis of wishful thinking, that the following day would bring him a decisive victory. Then it would be possible not only to cross the canal but also to link up with the strongholds and man them anew. Thus, the ignominy of their capture would be atoned for, and he would be forgiven for the unbearable losses to his men. Gonen viewed the next day's counterattack as the capstone of the war, and, in his burning desire to concentrate all the Southern Command's forces on that effort, he refused to listen to any idea about trickling forces into other missions, such as evacuating the strongholds before they were captured. As he saw it, either the following day would be crowned with glory, and everything would return to its previous condition, and he would be forgiven, or it would end in abysmal defeat, in which case the fate of the strongholds would make little difference.

Thus, during the afternoon of October 7, while Sharon urged Gonen several times to allow him to rescue the strongholds in his sector, the latter remained silent or denied him permission. When Sharon turned to Dayan on the same matter, after realizing that Gonen was failing in his responsibility toward his men, Dayan had nothing to say except suggest that Sharon broach the matter in the Southern Command meeting that evening. Thus, for political and personal reasons, and against all common sense and standards of professional military leadership, responsibility, and ethical conduct, the strongholds were left to fend for themselves. In the wake of the October 8 debacle, the division commanders performed rescue missions on their own initiative in the strongholds in their sectors where troops were still alive. This is what the defense minister, the CoGS, and the general of the Southern Command had declined to do.

2

The IDF's "Day of Infamy"

There is no work, nor device, nor knowledge, nor wisdom. (Eccles. 9:10)

At noon on October 7, the General Staff and the commanding general of the Southern Command, General Gonen, already knew that the 162nd Tank Division, under the command of Major General Avraham ("Bren") Adan, and the 143rd Tank Division, under the command of Major General Ariel ("Arik") Sharon (Ret.), would join up in the evening with the 252nd Division, which had lost the lion's share of its strength the day before. Prior to the divisions' arrival, the sectors were reallocated: the 162nd was assigned the northern sector, the 143rd the central sector, and the 252nd, reinforced with the 875th Mechanized Brigade, the southern sector.

Of the three divisions, the 143rd's order of battle (the manner in which military forces are organized, disposed, maneuvered, and supplied) was the most battle ready. By evening, two tank brigades (Colonel Tuvia Raviv's 600th Brigade and Colonel Haim Erez's 421st Brigade) and the 87th Reconnaissance Battalion under the command of Lieutenant Colonel Bentzi Carmeli were deployed in the Tassa area for a total of over two hundred Magachs. Division headquarters were set up at Tassa. Also that day, the 14th Armored Brigade became attached to Sharon's division. As part of the 252nd Division, the 14th had been fighting since the start of the war. Now it came to the 143rd Division with only twenty operable tanks. During the night of October 7–8, more tanks were repaired, and, by morning, the brigade had about forty combat-ready tanks. At daybreak, the division deployed in its sector with nearly 250 tanks and prepared for battle.

As stated, the 143rd's commander, General Sharon, reached the sector at noon, October 7. After a futile attempt at the 252nd's headquarters in Refidim (Bir Gafgafa) to be updated on the situation at the front, he went to the area to observe it with his own eyes and soon gained the following insights:

- As of now, the Egyptian bridgeheads east of the canal are vulnerable to a concentrated and determined attack given their lack of depth and the absence of organized defense and armor.

- IDF divisions will be without almost any artillery or armored infantry until the evening of October 8.
- Egyptian infantrymen are heavily equipped with antitank weapons capable of reaching all ranges and are adept in their use. The Egyptians have organized their army and developed a new fighting doctrine capable of dealing with Israeli armored assaults; they have also devised effective antiaircraft fighting techniques that have minimized, if not completely neutralized, the IAF's intervention in ground battles on the canal front. The Egyptian infantry has met the challenge of the IDF armor at the bridgeheads very successfully, as the last twenty-four hours have shown.
- Given the present operational situation and what can be expected in the near future, the Bar-Lev Line strongholds are inconsequential. The failure to evacuate them immediately has put their troops at the needless risk of being wounded, captured, or killed.

Sharon came to the conclusion that the two divisions that just arrived should be ordered to launch a coordinated attack against the Egyptian Second Army's bridgehead with the aim of destroying it that very night and, if possible, cross the canal in the northern sector, where, he believed, crossing equipment had been prepared. This attack was designed to thwart the Egyptian effort and end the war with an Israeli victory. This idea expresses operational thinking that takes the balance of forces in the field into account and applies the main principles of war and Israel's security doctrine. Nevertheless, it should be noted that Sharon still viewed the division as the paramount combat formation. He did not envision an attack by a multidivision force—a *corps*—led by a single commander and made up of staff (or at least a corps-level forward command post), joint control mechanisms, organic assistance and support forces, reserves, and so forth. In effect, he proposed two coordinated, simultaneous division attacks in the same locale with one strategic goal and complementary operational objectives derived from it, but this was still not a single unified operational body for the maximum exploitation of strength. The Egyptians, on the other hand, had progressed further by establishing two corps (armies) for fighting in two separate theaters on the front.

In the early afternoon, Sharon presented his ideas to Gonen and the CoGS. The CoGS may have been inclined to veto anything that Sharon suggested, or he may have believed the IDF incapable of executing Sharon's plan. Whatever the reason, he categorically rejected Sharon's idea, and Gonen followed suit. But the seed had been planted. When an officer of Sharon's rank and status broaches an operational issue, rejecting it out of hand can come at a costly price, especially when the CoGS, Gonen, and the other brigade commanders in the south obviously supported a swift counterattack. Thus, on October 7, the CoGS, too, realized the need for a counterattack, but one that was utterly different from Sharon's. Throughout the day, he cooked up a north-to-south "rolling" attack for the following day in the Second Army bridgehead area from Kantara in the north to Deversoir in the south. The underlying concept was a mishmash of facts (some inaccurate), assumptions, ideologies, outdated military doctrines, and wishful thinking wrapped in exaggerated misgivings and discretion that stemmed from the previous day's trauma and a faulty assessment of the enemy's intentions and plans.

The following factors influenced the CoGS's operational idea:

- Belief in the armored division as the ultimate operational force, one above which organized military field strength—a corps—was unimaginable.
- Misconstruing the previous day's events regarding the Egyptian army's antitank tactics; and the belief that a broad deployment armored assault would batter the Egyptian army and force it off the battlefield. This myth had penetrated the IDF commanders' consciousness after their lightning victories in the 1956 Sinai Campaign and the Six-Day War and remained an idée fixe even after the Egyptian infantry had pulverized the 252nd Division on October 6. The initial fighting in Sinai illustrates how, in each clash, IDF field commanders desperately sought indications of the enemy's collapse and reveled in the discovery of every hint of one as though it were priceless booty until it painfully dawned on them that it was only a desert mirage.
- The mistaken belief that Egypt's war aim was no less than the capture of Tel Aviv. The CoGS stated this every time he had to diverge from being overly cautious.
- Groundless optimism, which was the result of sloppy staff work at the General Staff and the Southern Command, regarding the balance of armored forces.
- Disregard of the principle of mass concentration, which made mincemeat of IDF armor from the moment the war broke out.
- The high command's difficulty in overcoming the shock and fear for the fate of both Israel and their personal reputations as a result of the circumstances in which the war erupted and the events up to this point.

General Elazar's Orders

At approximately 1900, the CoGS arrived at the Southern Command's FCP at Um Hashiba to discuss the situation with Gonen and the division commanders and lay out his plan for the next day's counterattack. The division commanders present were Adan, Kalman Magen, who commanded the semi-independent division known as "Force Tiger" ("Namer") in the northern sector, and Mandler, the 252nd's commander. For some reason, the Southern Command failed to bring Sharon to the meeting in time. When it finally flew him to Um Hashiba, the meeting was already over. Sharon exchanged a few words with the testy and preoccupied CoGS, who was hurrying to board his helicopter. Gonen updated Sharon on the command's plans for the next day and his division's assignments. For years, Sharon would avow that he missed the meeting because of Gonen's machinations, perhaps with the CoGS's blessing. Although his absence was of major consequence in view of the following day's events, it is not known whether the cause was ever seriously investigated or anyone was called to account.

Gonen, who was eager to make a move that would obliterate the nightmare of his failures, proposed—in the spirit of the absent Sharon—that two divisions, Sharon's and Adan's, attack simultaneously the two Egyptian armies that very night and that each division cross the canal in its respective sector the next day and engage the enemy on both banks. This plan, which shows that Gonen had not grasped the main concepts of Sharon's proposal—force concentration in one sector; unity of time and place in the attack—was rejected by the CoGS because it was "too pretentious." Gonen's plan suffered from limited goals, dimensions, and benefit and reflected one cardinal principle: it guaranteed the survival of the Southern Command's forces. From this principle, the following features of the CoGS's plan become clear:

- Employing minimum fighting force in each time slot.
- Foregoing the idea of defeating the Egyptian army. Combing no-man's-land between the main Egyptian force and the Southern Command's forces, where the primary goal—which became clear, even if not formally stated—was to demonstrate initiative and aggressiveness and destroy Egyptian units and individuals whose bad luck put them in harm's way.
- Maintaining a safe distance between the attacking force and the enemy's deadly antitank positions on the canal.

Given these features, the plan for the counterattack envisioned the following:

- At each time slot only one division would attack while the two others blocked the sector and remained in reserve.
- The 162nd Division would launch a daylight attack moving south from the Kantara area while maintaining a safe distance of three kilometers east of the waterline and preparing for contact with the enemy west of Artil-

lery Road in the east. As the division moved in a southerly direction to the Matzmed stronghold area, it would engage Egyptian infantry and armor forces that had shifted west from their waterline localities into the area where the division was moving.

- At this point, the 252nd Division would commence blocking operations in its sector, and the 143rd Division would deploy on the vital areas on Artillery Road to block an enemy advance, serve as a reserve for the attacking division, and, if necessary, assist it.
- As long as the 162nd was engaged in combat, the 143rd would be on standby. If, and only if, the 162nd's attack succeeded, then the 143rd—with the CoGS's permission—would attack the Third Army's bridgeheads in the same way that the 162nd did, that is, by rolling them back from north to south. At this stage, the 162nd would continue blocking in its sector—from Matzmed to the north—and the 252nd would serve as the 143rd's reserve force.
- The CoGS did not veto the capture of Egyptian bridges and the passage on them to the western bank; nevertheless, it was obvious that he doubted that such an operation would succeed.

After the dialogue of the deaf with the CoGS, Sharon received the next day's marching orders from Gonen. According to Sharon, the orders stated:

- The 162nd Division attacks the Second Army sector in the Kantara area and south to the Matzmed locale. It then proceeds from north to south in the area west of Artillery Road, keeping a distance of three kilometers east of the waterline to avoid antitank missiles from the Egyptian ramps along the canal.
- At dawn, the 143rd Division deploys in the area north of Tassa and prepares to attack the Second Army's bridgeheads from the southeast to the northwest in order to complete the 162nd's attack. The 143rd will attack only after permission is granted by the Southern Command, which can be expected on the morning of October 8.
- Nothing was mentioned regarding the evacuation of the strongholds, though it was understood that, if the 143rd's mission succeeded, its forces would link up with the strongholds in its sector before they were captured.

In his testimony before the Agranat Commission, Sharon stated that, in effect, he was assigned responsibility for planning the attack west of the two main roads. The 421st and 14th Brigades would attack from the Havraga area and south of it toward the Firdan Bridge, and the 600th Brigade with the 87th

Reconnaissance Battalion would attack from the Akavish Road area toward Ismailia. The attack was supposed to develop at 0600 the next day (October 8) but required the Southern Command's approval. It was intended to be under way at the same time that the 162nd was attacking from north to south. Sharon was also told that while the attack was in progress he could link up with the strongholds. Gonen's instructions ran counter to the CoGS's plan that had been agreed on at Um Hashiba. Deviations like this—of which the CoGS was unaware or the full significance of which he failed to comprehend—created a continuous breakdown in communications between the CoGS and Gonen from the outset of the operation and had a decisive impact on the counterattack's failure.

Sharon's answer to the question of the commission member Lieutenant General Haim Laskov (Ret.) was that the warning order for the move south and the attack against the Third Army was first given to him on October 8 "before noon." He immediately corrected himself and said that the order was given to him "on the morning of October 8." In reality, during Gonen's conversation with Sharon, and in later conversations between the Southern Command staff officers and the division's staff officers, the warning orders were conveyed to the 143rd on three occasions between 0430 and 0630, October 8.

During his testimony, Sharon clarified the following points:

- Given the time and space estimate, he (apparently) realized that the two attacks were planned for the same area—his and the 162nd's—but were not intended to take place simultaneously. He further stated that he was not told anything about a joint action, one division's attack conditional on the other's.
- The counterattack's objective was sufficiently clear to him. At first he told the commission that, on the basis of his understanding of the mission, he drew the conclusion that the aim of the 162nd's counterattack was to destroy the Egyptian bridgeheads. But, when presented with the absurdity of this goal, given the injunction against moving toward or approaching the waterline, he corrected his earlier testimony and said that he "wouldn't [call] it the total destruction of the Egyptian foothold": "Let's call it reducing the Egyptian foothold to a very limited area and rescuing the strongholds."

Sharon returned to his headquarters at Tassa after midnight (October 8) and summoned his deputy and the division's intelligence officer, Colonel Yehoshua Sagi, to plan the division's deployment and the brigades' missions. As the hour for the attack drew near, the division spread out along Artillery Road with the

421st Brigade deployed in the dominating area (code name Havraga) on Artillery Road in the northern part of the division's sector, about twenty kilometers northwest of Tassa and the same distance northeast of Ismailia; the 14th Brigade holding Nozel, the areas overlooking the Talisman-Futon Junction (code name Makhshir and Hamutal), and the dominating areas southwest of Nozel and south of the Talisman (Tassa-Ismailia) axis; the 600th Brigade holding the vital areas on Akavish Road and the Kishuf fortification; and the 87th Reconnaissance Battalion in position between Akavish Road and Makhshir.

The 600th Brigade and the reconnaissance battalion, which were deployed in the southern part of the sector, functioned as an autonomous division force under Colonel Even. Sharon and his FCP established themselves in the northern part of the sector, in the 421st's area. Thus, the division was fanned out along thirty kilometers on all the vital junctions and dominating areas on Artillery Road and vicinity, with the division commander and his FCP positioned on the northern flank of the force that would be attacking directly west with two brigades.

Sharon gave his deputy, Colonel Even, twofold responsibility:

1. If the division attacked in the morning, Even would take command of the southern attack axis—from Akavish Road toward Ismailia.
2. The Akavish Road and Kishuf area in the sector's south would be essential in the battle. Its ridges dominated the Tassa-Deversoir axis (Akavish Road) that even at this stage Sharon visualized as the route the forces and canal-bridging equipment would travel on when the time came. The enemy's capture of Akavish Road and Kishuf would endanger and perhaps even scuttle the canal crossing. Securing this area would block the enemy's approach to the Yukon compound, where the crossing and bridging equipment was concentrated, and to the road to Tassa, the sector's nerve center. While Sharon was setting up the FCP to enable him to control events as effectively as possible, he ordered Even to ensure that the IDF's potentially decisive battle of the war, which depended on crossing the canal, would not be disrupted or foiled. Even's force, the 600th Brigade and the 87th Reconnaissance Battalion, was tasked with making sure that Akavish Road and Kishuf remained in the division's hands.

In building the division's command and control layout, Sharon's unique generalship came to the fore: a concentrated effort to achieve immediate control at the expected decisive point in the fighting zone; strategic thinking that looked beyond the immediate contingencies to the crucial stages of the war in Sinai; concern for the critical conditions needed to execute his moves; and maximum use of his deputy as his "extended personality."

The 143rd in Combat Operations on the Morning of October 8

Today we know that the CoGS erred in his assessment that the Egyptian army's ultimate goal was Tel Aviv. Its goal—as Sharon correctly estimated—was limited to capturing and entrenching itself in areas between the canal and Artillery Road. Furthermore, in the first two days of the war, it had not accomplished its missions yet. The Second Army's bridgehead was still shallow on the evening of October 7, mostly limited to a narrow area west of Lexicon Road, and slightly deeper in the southern part of the sector. The transfer of the Egyptian armored divisions had stalled on the first day partially due to IAF hits on the bridges.

On the night of October 7–8, hundreds of Egyptian tanks entered Sinai. By dawn, the Egyptians had seven to eight hundred tanks of various models on the eastern bank, most of them in the Second Army sector. Saad el-Shazly, the Egyptian CoGS, claims that, on the morning of October 8, Egypt had one thousand tanks in Sinai, about half of them T-54/55s, approximately two hundred T-62s, and three hundred antiquated, thinly armored, and poorly armed T-34s and amphibious tanks.

As daylight approached, the two Egyptian armies were ordered to reach their final destinations on Artillery Road. Armored units moved east from their narrow bridgehead to seize key areas in the sector and on Artillery Road and secure them until the infantry arrived. Parallel to this, the 143rd's forces headed to their assigned areas. The 600th Brigade and the reconnaissance battalion reached their positions at Akavish Road and Kishuf and the area north of Akavish Road at around 0500. Even before they arrived, the Egyptians had begun shelling them, and the fire continued as the brigade and the battalion moved into position. Egyptian armor was soon spotted rumbling toward Akavish Road from Missouri in the west and Makhshir in the north. The brigade opened fire, knocking out several enemy tanks, and the attack ground to a halt. Throughout the morning, Egyptian armor and infantry could be seen feeling their way toward Akavish Road and trying to retain their hold on parts of Makhshir (north of Akavish Road) and Televizia (west of it). Sporadic clashes flared up at Akavish Road and to the north that ended with the enemy's tanks destroyed and Israeli losses minimal. In the final tally, the enemy's stubborn groping toward the Akavish Road and Kishuf localities did not gain the desired results, and this critical area remained in the 143rd's hands.

"The wind goeth south . . . and returneth again according to its circuits" (Eccles. 1:6)

Just after 0600, Sharon was told that his attack, which was planned for 0600, had not been approved and that the 143rd would commence blocking operations in its sector. It would also serve as a reserve force for Adan's division, which would attack in the morning, and would be ready to drive south to attack the Third Army when ordered to. At 0800, the 162nd began the attack. According to Adan, his order of battle consisted of three brigades: the 217th under the command of Natan Nir (less the 126th Battalion, which remained in Baluza), the 460th Brigade under the command of Gabi Amir, and the 500th Brigade led by Colonel Aryeh Keren, for a total of 180 battle-ready tanks. The historian Lieutenant Colonel (Res.) Elhanan Oren wrote in 2004 that the 162nd had 175 tanks. The division launched the battle with only 150 tanks (one of the 217th Brigade's battalions, it will be recalled, had been transferred to Force Tiger). In other words, the 162nd set out to battle with roughly half the tank force of an armored division or, to put it differently, with the order of battle of one reinforced tank brigade. The division's armored infantry units had not left their bases in Israel yet, and the artillery group would arrive only in the evening. By way of comparison, the 143rd, which was protecting 162nd's flank and serving as its reserve force, had approximately 240 tanks.

It is not our intention to relate in detail the 162nd's moves, achievements, and deficiencies. Only the main points of its performance will be noted. At the outset, we can say that, until noon October 8, the division accomplished none of its assignments. It failed to launch a division or brigade attack. The 19th Battalion/460th Brigade carried out the only attack before noon, engaging the enemy in the Firdan Bridge area on the deputy brigade commander's initiative and without permission of the division commander or brigade commander and without supporting fire from either. It attacked from east to west in the direction of the canal. The enemy broke the attack about three kilometers from the waterline. The battalion was hit hard and withdrew, leaving seven tanks on the battlefield, and limping to the rear. Most of the vehicles that were not abandoned were damaged, the battalion commander, Lieutenant Colonel Haim Adini, was wounded, and most of the officers and crews were dead, wounded, missing, or captured.

The division's reports to the Southern Command and the command's reports to the General Staff were muddled and imprecise, characterized by a surfeit of wishful thinking and the tendency to tell the listener what he wanted to hear, by the listener's propensity to interpret what was said to mean what he wished to hear, by obeying before really understanding what was meant, and by superfluous noncommittal statements. These reports contributed to the original plan's collapse, the division's heavy losses, and the failure to carry out the mission.

Almost as soon as the attack began, the Southern Command sent the division on missions that had nothing to do with the previous night's plan. The drastic changes in the directions of movements and in the attack itself (from what the CoGS had dictated) precluded the division's chances of accomplishing anything worthwhile while causing it heavy casualties and great loss of weapons.

The conduct of the division and its brigades was characterized by deficiencies in the control of the forces, apathy, and the inability—or lack of will—to concentrate the division's strength in a coordinated, advantageous move. Starting in the late morning, the division's situation soon became precarious owing to the Egyptians' growing initiative in defensive battles and local counterattacks.

Gonen, whose heart was set on smashing the two bridgeheads as quickly as possible, crossing the canal at various points, winning the war with a "whizz-bang," and thus blotting out the sense of failure and panic that had seized him the previous two days, believed Adan's reports, justifiably or not, that the 162nd was on the verge of victory. He wasted none of his valuable time confirming the reports' accuracy. Typical of his conduct that day, he requested the CoGS's approval to pull the 143rd Division out of its current positions opposite the Second Army and dispatch it south to the Third Army's bridgeheads, an eighty-kilometer journey. As was his wont, Elazar gave the green light.

At 1045, Gonen contacted Sharon, updated him on the (purported) successes of the 162nd, and impressed on him the need to exploit this victory and destroy the Third Army's bridgeheads. He ordered Sharon to take his entire division out of its position along Artillery Road and the areas overlooking Akavish Road and travel as fast as lightning on Lateral Road to the Gidi area (afterward, the order would be revised, and Sharon would be ordered to reach Mitla). While the division was in transit, Sharon received more orders relating to the bridgehead attack. Gonen's idea was for the 143rd to roll over the bridgehead from south to north (as opposed to the CoGS's plan), capture an Egyptian bridge (or two), and use it (or them) to cross the canal with a reinforced brigade and advance approximately twenty kilometers west inside Egypt proper.

Sharon was in the field and aware that Adan's gains were far from what Gonen imagined—as far as east is from west—and that the 162nd was in desperate straits. But Sharon's efforts to get Gonen to see his misperception of the battlefield and rescind the order for the entire 143rd Division to leave its positions and head south were answered with a blunt threat of immediate removal from command if he did not start out at once.

Gonen was so convinced that Adan's division was fulfilling its assignment and so determined to throw the full weight of the 143rd against the Third Army's bridgehead and then cross the canal that he saw no need in ordering replacement procedures to protect the 162nd's suddenly exposed flanks once the 143rd vacated its positions. According to his understanding of the situation, with the 162nd's success, its area of activity would be protected as the 143rd gradually decamped: the 421st Brigade, the northernmost brigade, would leave first, then the 14th Brigade, which was in the sector's center, and finally the sector's southernmost force, the 600th Brigade and reconnaissance battalion.

Sharon's orders to vacate the positions without taking steps to safeguard the 162nd's flanks and cover the vital areas that were certain to be grabbed by the Egyptians dumbfounded the division's deputy, the brigade and battalion commanders, senior staff officers, and the division CoS, Colonel Gideon Altshuler. Some of them, including Colonels Even and Altshuler, the chief operations officer, and a number of battalion commanders tried speaking with Sharon, pointing to the Egyptian force that was advancing toward Akavish Road, and even broaching a few ideas for securing this vital area. These officers and others later testified to the verbal confrontations with Sharon over the manner in which the division was evacuating its positions. Sharon had only one rebuttal to all their cogent arguments: "You don't understand the situation. The 162nd is indeed not succeeding, but the Southern Command has issued us an unequivocal order, and this is my order to you. There's nothing more to discuss. We have to obey the order immediately and take the entire division south."

Testifying before the Agranat Commission, Sharon recalled that, despite his "unequivocal" orders, he left the 87th Reconnaissance Battalion holding Akavish Road and Kishuf. At first, he claimed that he did this according to the Southern Command's instructions or with its approval after the division explained the critical importance of the Akavish Road area and its trenchant concern that the Egyptians would seize it. Then he changed his account and "confessed" that he ordered the reconnaissance battalion to remain at Akavish Road and Kishuf without informing the Southern Command but that he now knew from recent debriefings that in a conversation between the Southern Command and the division CoS this move was brought to the command's attention.

In a postwar conference, Sharon again altered his version of the events and stated that, following his deputy's reports on Egyptian movement in the direction of Akavish Road and Makhshir and Kishuf, "we [i.e., Colonel Even and he] decided, or I approved Even's proposal, to keep the reconnaissance battalion in its place [Akavish Road and Kishuf]." A few years later, he attributed this insubordinate yet correct decision to himself. In his autobiography, *Warrior* (Sharon 1989), he states that he deviated from Gonen's final decision to take the division south, and (on his own initiative) left the reconnaissance battalion at Akavish Road and Kishuf. The truth is that neither the Southern Command nor Sharon, but his deputy, Colonel Even, decided to leave the battalion at Akavish Road and Kishuf despite his superiors' orders for the 600th Brigade and reconnaissance battalion to go south.

When Sharon's order came, Even asked the chief operations officer, Lieutenant Colonel Aharon Tal, to double-check the forces remaining in the rear. Tal knew of Sharon's sweeping decision not to leave any troops behind but nevertheless agreed to carry out Even's request. Sharon, who was listening to radio communications, intervened and made it perfectly clear to Tal that there was nothing to check since he (Sharon) had already checked it and Even was to take the whole kit and caboodle and move it south. As Colonel Even remembered:

> I realized that this was too important an issue for such an answer; I wasn't going to shirk responsibility and keep mum. I decided, on my own, to leave the reconnaissance battalion at the critical Akavish Road and Kishuf area, and, if as a result I was crucified, then so be it. The degree to which I made the right as well as absolutely necessary decision is proved not only by Sharon's propensity to attribute it to himself but also by his testimony before the Agranat Commission [July 29, 1974]: "If there's one thing I often regret, it's that I obeyed that order [to pull the entire 143rd Division out of its positions and gallop south]."

At approximately 1045, Gonen, believing in Adan's so-called accomplishments, ordered Sharon to take his division south, attack the Third Army, capture an Egyptian bridge in the vicinity of Suez, and cross the canal. Sharon knew that the 162nd had been unable to roll back the Second Army's bridgehead and, excluding the flawed attack of one of its battalions, had not launched any attacks and avoided contact with the enemy beyond its assigned area. He was fully aware that exploiting the 162nd's success was wishful thinking. He also must have recognized the 162nd's waning ability to withstand Egyptian pressure, which meant that, if the 143rd abandoned the area, the 162nd's problems would metastasize. From these insights, Sharon understood that the 162nd Division's efforts until now had been pointless. To make matters worse, if the 143rd Division vacated the dominating areas, it would be overrun by the Egyptians in no time, in which case ousting the Egyptians—if possible—would exact a heavy price in IDF lives and equipment. At any rate, the enemy's possession of the area would make a canal crossing difficult, perhaps even compromise and neutralize the basic conditions for such an action. In this light, Sharon reckoned that the idea of securing Egyptian bridges and crossing them in the Third Army sector was nothing more than a pipe dream.

Sharon later offered a number of versions of his response to Gonen's order. He told the Agranat Commission, for example, that his division had emphasized to the Southern Command the crucial importance of the Akavish Road area, which had been under attack the whole day, and the division's aversion to abandoning this pivotal terrain. According to his account, which he later altered, Gonen ordered or allowed the reconnaissance battalion to remain at Akavish Road and Kishuf.

According to another version, put forward during the same testimony, Sharon asked himself: "If I thought it was forbidden to take the division [out of its positions before noon], why didn't I challenge this [decision] with the Southern Command?" And his answer to his own rhetorical question was: "When I tried to convince [them], I received a coarse and categorical answer. They said: 'It's a fact, and that's that.' They broke off radio contact, which signified that the matter was closed. . . . They switched off my radio and shut my mouth. In short, I was silenced."

During Sharon's testimony, Lieutenant General Yigael Yadin (Ret.) asked: "When you received the order to move south, you saw that [Adan's] situation was bad, that he wasn't accomplishing his mission. . . . You're a person who asks for clarifications before carrying out an order if you're uncertain about it. [Here] you detached yourself without trying to tell Gonen: 'Look, why are you sending me south? This [division, the 162nd,] isn't doing its job. They're in a bad way. They're being mauled. If I head south now, the situation will worsen.'" And Sharon answered: "I can't remember the conversations [between me and Gonen] or if any took place, but in the prevailing atmosphere there was no one to talk to. . . . I don't know if we spoke about what was happening. . . . The atmosphere [did not allow] you to describe what was happening. . . . This was an order, and there was nothing to say and no one to talk to."

Yadin persisted: "Why do you think you didn't speak with the general of the command about [folding up and moving south]?" Sharon gave a third version of his response to the order to fold up: "Twenty-four hours after we reached [the front] I still didn't question [the Southern Command's] instructions . . . and executed every order that was issued. But the atmosphere was definitely not conducive." In other words, Sharon did not find a justifiable reason to question the Southern Command's orders [i.e., not to obey them] until October 8, but, after that date, his trust—also Adan's—in the Southern Command and its orders ended, and his willingness to obey it plummeted to the lowest level. In his autobiography, Sharon recalls that, when he received the order to take the division out of its positions and move south, he immediately contacted Gonen and argued compellingly that this step would bring about a catastrophe since Adan's division had not even attacked the bridgehead and had not made any gains yet. In effect, there was no success to exploit, and the likelihood of seizing an Egyptian bridgehead in the Third Army's area was remote. Moreover, the 143rd was engaged in a series of firefights attempting to block the Egyptians' crawling advance and doing so successfully. Gonen should make every effort and come to the field and see for himself what was happening. According to Sharon, Gonen's answer was laconic and blunt: he threatened to relieve Sharon of command immediately for insubordination. Sharon said that he thought briefly about this exchange of words and came to the conclusion that he had no choice but to obey. He ordered his forces to pull out of their positions and assemble at Tassa in preparation for the move south. Nevertheless, contrary to Gonen's order, he decided to leave the reconnaissance battalion at Akavish Road.

Sharon had obviously read the situation in the fighting zone correctly and realized the implications of carrying out Gonen's order to break off contact and move south: the 162nd's forces would be at grave risk; vital areas in the sector would be lost; and the 143rd would be used in a debatable move from the point of view of time and space and operational benefit and in the absence of a crossing option. The Agranat Commission's astonishment at the fact that Sharon—so inconsistently with his personality, status, and ability—did not insist that Gonen's plan would most likely contribute to the "darkest day" in IDF history and did not take steps to torpedo the move remains unanswered.

Unfortunately, since both Sharon and Gonen are no longer alive to clarify this conundrum, any attempt to explain it is mere speculation. While we are aware of the limitations of this path, we will try, nevertheless, to determine—first of all for ourselves—the reasons for Sharon's self-restraint and avoidance of going head-to-head with Gonen.

First, it must be remembered that, at the beginning of the war, Sharon was still not the famous and overwhelmingly popular general—the "king of Israel"—that he came to be at the end of the war, when his prestige and fame stood out in glaring contrast to the sullied reputations of Gonen, Elazar, and Adan, which they had rightfully earned at the start of and during the war. In the first days of the fighting, Sharon was surrounded by commanders and fellow officers, led by the CoGS and Gonen and many others of his rank and caliber from the right side of the tracks in the military establishment, who despised him with a passion and were eager to get rid of him quickly and humiliatingly.

The defense minister, whose position in Golda Meir's government was weak, had still not intuited that it was in his interest to ally himself with Sharon against his rivals. Sharon realized from Dayan's actions that he could not rely on his protection and support. In short, at this stage, Sharon found himself alone, vulnerable, and without reliable allies. His sharp instincts sensed that he was dependent on the grace of his enemies in the system and that they would not hesitate to ditch him on the flimsiest pretext. He perceived that in this period he must do everything possible not to give his detractors an excuse.

Until October 8, Sharon was too busy to formulate a substantiated opinion of his superiors' and colleagues' competence (or lack thereof) in their roles, and by default, he assumed that they were all more or less suited for them and thus that there was no reason to disobey orders.

Sharon's autobiographical account and his testimony before the Agranat

Commission regarding his uncharacteristic obedience to Gonen's order to break off contact with the enemy and take his division south do not seem incongruous.

There is room to believe that Gonen did indeed threaten Sharon with dismissal if he refused to obey immediately or tried to sabotage the move that Gonen planned. At this stage of the war, Sharon seems to have had strong reasons to assume that such a threat from someone under as much pressure as Gonen was not an empty one. Under these circumstances, he probably realized that he had no alternative but to keep silent and comply with his superior's orders.

The events of October 8 instantly changed this reality. Both Sharon and Adan lost faith in Gonen. The defense minister, whom the October 8 debacle filled with anger and disgust and whose prestige and status in the government received a devastating broadside, undoubtedly reached a number of unflattering conclusions regarding the CoGS and Gonen. Recognizing Sharon's generalship, he drew closer and cast his lot with him. Sharon now felt protected and to a great degree free of the fear of being sacked, free to devise independent, audacious moves, and free to refuse to execute orders that he judged dangerous and asinine.

There is no testimony regarding Adan's response when he learned of Gonen's disastrous plan to pull out the 143rd Division and send it on a wild goose chase to the Third Army sector while the 162nd Division was struggling to implement its mission and taking heavy casualties. According to Oren (2004), Brigadier General Dov Tamari, Adan's deputy, who arrived by helicopter at the 162nd's FCP at approximately 1000, told Adan that while in flight he heard that Gonen was about to move the 143rd from its positions and send it to the Third Army sector. Thus, Adan knew of Gonen's intention and may have inferred its implications for his division. Nevertheless, it is not known whether he attempted to explain to Gonen that dispatching the 143rd to the south would have negative repercussions and that he was firmly opposed to this hasty move. In his book *On Both Banks of Suez* (1979), he states enigmatically: "When Gonen ordered Sharon to leave the sector, there was still hope that the formation in the field would not make the mistake of breaking off contact and abandoning the area before the relief force arrived" (101). It is well nigh impossible to determine which "relief force" he was referring to and what he expected Sharon to do other than disobey an order. Even less can be learned about whether he thought about taking (or actually took) the steps required of an IDF major general to modify Gonen's orders—for himself and Sharon—to fit the ground situation and the CoGS's orders.

By 1200, the last units of the 143rd, excluding the reconnaissance battalion, left their positions in the Second Army sector, assembled at Tassa, and continued south on Lateral Road. It will be remembered that the division was sent south because Gonen thought that everything was going according to plan on the Second Army front. Also at this time, the Southern Command received reports from the Third Army sector that the Egyptians were withdrawing. Therefore, he decided to exploit the would-be withdrawal and strike while the iron was hot. Somehow, 143rd's staff and brigade and battalion commanders had the impression that a catastrophe was brewing in the 252nd Division's sector, which would explain the hasty manner in which the 143rd had been pulled out and sent south at breakneck speed.

The 143rd was on its way south before it received instructions from the Southern Command regarding its destination and assignments. At noon, it learned that it would proceed on Lateral Road to the Mitla entry area, attack westward in the direction of the city of Suez, establish a small bridgehead, and roll down the Third Army's flank on the western bank from south to north (unlike the original plan). While one part of the division was assembling and refueling at Tassa and another part was dashing south with Sharon in the lead, the reconnaissance battalion maneuvered into position in Akavish Road and Kishuf. About half an hour later, Akavish Road came under relentless shelling. Egyptian infantry and armor were seen moving north of Missouri and Televizia in the direction of Makhshir. The battalion prepared to meet an attack from Makhshir in the direction of Akavish Road. The battalion commander, Lieutenant Colonel Bentzi Carmeli, was killed in the shelling.

Soon after the Southern Command issued Sharon his marching orders, the atmosphere at Um Hashiba changed. The command believed that a major Egyptian armor breakthrough was about to take place in the Third Army sector—at least that was what Gonen told Sharon in order to spur him on. This was also his explanation to the defense minister for the 143rd's movement south.

In the early afternoon, the truth of the 162nd's perilous situation and negligible gains finally began to penetrate the Southern Command. At 1400, Gonen deliberated over whether to continue the 143rd's move or have it return north and attack the Second Army sector. The mauling of the 113th Battalion/217th Brigade under the command of Lieutenant Colonel Assaf Yaguri, which had attacked west like the Charge of the Light Brigade at 1430, finally forced the truth on Gonen. Just before 1500, the Southern Command's CoS, Brigadier General Sasson Yitzhaki, arrived by helicopter at Sharon's FCP to hand him Gonen's order to reverse direction and hasten to the Second Army sector to capture Missouri and the Chinese Farm.

While this was happening, it turned out that, after the 143rd abandoned its positions, the Egyptians captured the areas dominating the Artillery Road–Tassa–Ismailia Axis Junction area (code name Talisman), including

Nozel, Hamutal, and Makhshir. Counterattacks by the 162nd and the 143rd, especially at Hamutal, ended in failure mainly because of the Israeli forces' numerical weakness, the lack of armored infantry, artillery, and air support, and the lack of coordination between the attacking forces. The 421st and the 14th Brigades' attacks on Missouri, which were planned for the evening of October 8, were canceled. The 600th Brigade and the reconnaissance battalion reentered their positions at Akavish Road and Kishuf in the afternoon. Before evening, an Egyptian armored and infantry force with the strength of a reinforced battalion left the Makhshir area and advanced to Akavish Road and the hills east of Makhshir. During the battle, which was fought at ranges of fifteen hundred to two thousand meters, the 600th repelled the Egyptian attack and inflicted severe losses on the attacking force at a very minimum cost to its own units.

"But who can discern their own errors?" (Ps. 19:13)

When darkness fell, October 8's attacks, counterattacks, and counter-counterattacks finally abated. From the IDF's point of view, it had been a wasted, frustrating, humiliating day: two divisions had been thrown into battle and accomplished nothing. On the contrary, the day ended with the enemy finalizing an important part of its mission. It had seized the dominating areas on Artillery Road and inflicted heavy losses on the IDF: sixty Southern Command tanks were disabled, fifty of them in the 162nd Division; nearly 120 men and officers from the division had been killed, hundreds had been wounded, and scores, including a battalion commander, had been taken prisoner or were missing; the 143rd had also suffered casualties and the loss of equipment, although much less so than had the 162nd. Be that as it may, the division was exhausted from the long and needless joyride; its vehicles had suffered wear and tear; and the troops were exhausted and demoralized, especially because of the division's helter-skelter evacuation of its positions on the Second Army front, which had left the 162nd to its fate.

These were the direct results of October 8; the indirect results were more pernicious. The defeat had weakened the IDF, enervated its will to end the war decisively, diminished the political level's trust in it, and pejoratively affected Israel's position in dealing with the Nixon administration. It also decided the fate of the survivors in the strongholds and added scores of names to the list of dead, wounded, and captured.

As a result of the October 8 drubbing, the war dragged on. The complications and difficulties in managing it multiplied, the IDF casualty rate mounted, and the time needed to gain a decisive victory was drastically reduced. If the

Egyptians continue to celebrate October 8 as their victory day in the war, then the debacle played a major part in their ability to construct this myth and cling to it.

Paradoxically, the IDF's defeat on October 8 may have had positive results because it happened so early in the war: the shortcomings in the high command staffs were revealed, first and foremost at the General Staff and the Southern Command levels in everything related to planning the war and its campaigns, in obtaining and relaying MI to the units in real time, in providing commanders with reliable data on the Israeli forces' situation, in making the most of commanders' valuable time for absolutely necessary matters, in interpreting the orders issued from the upper echelons and correctly translating them into detailed orders while remaining bound to their central ideas, in supervising the subordinate levels, and in every instance where decisive generalship and professional staff work was needed.

The real surprise of the war was the disturbing lack of professionalism on the part of certain members of the IDF high command, and heading the list was the CoGS. Worse, the unavoidable steps needed to amend this critical liability were not taken in real time, and the few that were only aggravated the situation. The bankruptcy of professional thinking in the high command became egregiously apparent. At the beginning of the hostilities, the IDF's fighting objectives were shown to be an agglomeration of empty slogans and wishful thinking, and, within a few hours, the ground forces' combat doctrines, whose designers had assumed that the current war would be a genetic clone of the last one, blew up in their faces.

One lieutenant general and three major generals (the CoGS, Gonen, and the commanders of the 162nd and the 143rd Divisions) were the main authors, directors, and actors in the tragedy that the Southern Command engineered on October 8 under the rubric of *counterattack*. The first three shared the responsibility for the debacle. There is no getting away from a discussion of the role that each one played in this sorry drama. Naturally, the charge will be made that today none of them are able to respond to our version of events. All three had innumerable opportunities to tell their story. All three had (and still have) legions of allies and partisans to assist them and hundreds of platforms to recount their side of the story, and, in their day, they made prodigious use of this apologetic capital. If they were alive and able to respond, nothing new would be told that has not been heard before on repeated occasions. Furthermore, our version of their role in the events is intended not to judge or criticize but to analyze errors and shortcomings and derive universal, enduring lessons that may shed light on the path of present and future members of the IDF high command.

The CoGS, Lieutenant General David Elazar

The Agranat Commission recommended relieving the CoGS of command mainly because of his failure to prepare the army for war and mobilize the reserves. But his part in the October 8 collapse was no less damaging.

When on October 7 Elazar realized that a counterattack had to be mounted on the Suez front, he should have told the Southern Command: "Attack the Second Army's bridgehead tomorrow, with the aim of destroying it or disrupting its activity, and bring your plan for my approval by such and such an hour." Instead, he chose to draw up the plan by himself and by doing so assumed direct and unnecessary responsibility for its failure. His operational concept was harebrained and devoid of military value, based on a mistaken situation assessment. He erred in his estimate of the enemy's intentions, and, as a result, he allocated insufficient forces for the attack. He chose an unacceptable method for executing the attack (a graded attack), yet he kept too many forces in reserve, which essentially amounted to self-preservation. Because of his faulty appraisal of the enemy's situation, intentions, and abilities, he failed to judge properly its massive reinforcement during the night of October 7–8 and the egress of this huge force from the bridgehead in order to expand it to the Artillery Road ridges at dawn. Had he correctly evaluated the intelligence reports, he might not have attacked that day and, instead, deployed two armored brigades for defense, left the enemy to attack the defense lines, and then really "broken his bones." Then he could have exploited the success to counterattack and liquidate the bridgehead or damage it irreparably. To illustrate this, we note the activity of Force Tiger under the command of Brigadier General Kalman Magen. On the same day, Kalman's two mechanized brigades had ninety tanks between them, mostly Centurions and Pattons, and approximately twenty Sherman M-51s, all of them equipped with 105-millimeter guns. The force deployed defensively and was shelled and attacked by Egyptian armor and infantry throughout the day. Employing a classic defensive tactic, Force Tiger repelled the enemy and destroyed thirty-five of its tanks and a similar number of APCs while suffering light losses.

The CoGS's plan was evidently derived from the mistaken assessment of the armies' relative strengths. He never imagined that Adan's division would counterattack with only 150 tanks and without armored infantry and artillery, and he miscalculated the Egyptian army's strength, its objectives, and the nature of its fighting east of the canal on the morning of October 8.

The CoGS also erred in failing to assign the attack to the Southern Command's choice unit—the 143rd Division with its 250 Pattons—whose soldiers and commanders were equal to those of the 162nd Division and whose commander, Sharon, was equal in experience, leadership, and military ability to

Adan. This mistake was even more deleterious if we accept, even if partially, the claim that the CoGS's decision was influenced by personal rancor and rivalry. Had Sharon been ordered to lead the counterattack—and we can say this with a high degree of probability—the results would have been far more beneficial than what actually happened.

For reasons that we will not go into, the CoGS did not institute personnel changes in the Southern Command as the circumstances dictated and failed to appoint an experienced general, even from the reserve forces, to take charge of the command. On the same issue, the CoGS's willingness to relinquish the participation of the most dominant, experienced, skilled commander on the front—Sharon—in the orders group that he issued on October 7, according to which the 143rd Division had an important role in the counterattack, also illustrates his predilection to allow personal considerations eclipse his better judgment. This blunder produced disastrous results in the following days' fighting. It will be noted that the CoGS's decision of a few months earlier to appoint Gonen commanding general of the Southern Command also demonstrates his problematic judgment.

The CoGS failed to maintain control—let alone effective control in real time—of the counterattack in the field and Gonen's decisions. In effect, he granted Gonen permission to completely revise the plan that had already been agreed on; that is, Gonen had a free hand to squander the command's main forces in reckless, irrational moves whose inevitable outcome was abysmal failure and heavy losses. This failure alone should have been enough to tarnish the CoGS with the opprobrium of ultimate command failure. Then as now, graduates of squad leader and platoon leader courses are instilled with the golden rule that every commander is personally responsible for making sure that his orders are carried out. This rule is binding at the senior level for commanders and generals, including the CoGS, just as it is at the company and squad levels. Lieutenant General Elazar completely ignored his elementary duty and is, therefore, answerable for the defeat on October 8 and the IDF's heavy losses.

Major General Avraham Adan

As regards Adan's performance as commander of the attacking division on October 8, there is not much to add to what has already been said on numerous occasions. Setting aside his attempts to explain the reasons that led to the debacle of October 8 and cast aspersions in every direction except his own, Adan seems to have displayed a degree of intellectual honesty in relating in his book his own shortcomings that contributed to the division's losses. But even there he denies his part in the failure. "My biggest mistake," he wrote, "was that I attacked in the direction of the canal" (Adan 1979, 119). He blames himself for not making it clear to Gonen, when the latter withheld support and reinforcements from him, that he had no intention of attacking to the west. Adan believes that this was his error (to be discussed later), and in a few noncommittal words, he alludes to the more serious blunders that he made as the commander of the attacking division.

The most serious omission was his lack of control over his forces, which resulted in his brigades failing to move on their designated routes and the division failing to execute even one coordinated, concentrated attack. On that day, not a single IDF division moved in the field other than three reduced brigades that operated independently and, when encountering the enemy, responded as best they could—not always successfully—under fierce pressure. Two telling examples of this mismanagement are the battalion-level attacks. In one case, the 19th Battalion/460th Brigade was demolished by the enemy before noon, and, in the second case, the 113th Battalion/217th Brigade was flung into battle that afternoon without any connection to the 19th's effort except that it ended up shattered after a futile attack. Both attacks were made in the same place, more or less, and in the same direction, and at least one of the battalions (the division commander claims both) initiated the attack without the approval of the division commander and without even his knowledge! In addition to Adan's lack of control over his division's forces, his tendency to set up his FCP far from the fighting area was a point that one of his brigade commanders discreetly mentioned at an orders group, calling it "rather distant from the action" (Nir 2010, 140).

The 162nd launched the counterattack with less than half the table of organization number of tanks for an IDF tank division, with no armored infantry, with hardly any artillery, and with minimal air support. Adan may have felt that, despite the division's weakness, he could accomplish his mission. But, as every military student knows, given the balance of forces on the battlefield, the 162nd's odds of carrying out its mission or at least emerging in one piece fluctuated between zero and obliteration. If Adan really believed that his division could succeed in its assignments or avoid coming out mangled and bloodied, then one can only wonder at his level of competence, acumen, and perception of events on the battlefield. We may assume that he was aware of his division's inability to fulfill its mission, given its relative strength, even if it followed the CoGS's plan to a tee. In this case, the most likely reason for his launching the attack was to stage a kind of shadow boxing show and thus come out intact.

Like all IDF generals, Adan had, or should have had, dual loyalty: first and foremost to the mission he was entrusted with, and second, to the lives and safety of his men and officers and the preservation of the vast amount of material resources under his care. Officers of Adan's rank, role, and stature must assume this dual responsibility as well as take a prudent, proactive, even aggressive approach in fulfilling and mitigating the antitheses inherent in these dichotomous loyalties. A general in his position who realizes that he lacks the means to achieve his mission and that, because of this, his division's gains on the battlefield will stand in inverse proportion to their losses must—for the sake of the mission and his men—turn heaven and earth upside down to remedy the imbalance even it means explicit and uncompromising opposition to carrying out orders until the initial conditions are redressed. This is not only his right—it is his duty. As the war proved on a number of occasions, the rank and role of an officer at Adan's level ensures that his opinions and misgivings will be taken into serious consideration. This is a crucial point in understanding what is demanded of a general in command of forces on the battlefield, and on this point Adan did not distinguish himself.

In his book, Adan (1979) admitted that his biggest blunder was attacking from east to west and not, as in the original plan, from north to south. Without delving into the gravity of this error (relative to his others), a study of generalship requires that we analyze a number of questions stemming from Adan's claims. As is known, Adan carried out the "the biggest mistake" (his words) not on his own initiative but in accordance with the orders he received from Gonen. The question is, When did it dawn on Major General Adan that obeying Gonen's orders was itself a great mistake. Did he realize this immediately on receiving them or later, after his mission went awry and hundreds of men and officers had been killed, wounded, or captured and one-third of his fighting force lost?

Whatever the case, Adan's conduct on this point stands in blatant contradiction to what is demanded of an IDF general and even more so of a general of Adan's rank and experience. Also, his explanations for obeying Gonen's ill-fated orders illustrate, by way of negative example, the traits that an IDF general, let alone a division commander, must avoid. "I've always set certain standards for myself," he said. "When it comes to performance, I always obeyed instantly the orders that I received. . . . With all my experience, I never imagined that orders would be issued without due consideration" (Adan 1979, 119). However, the principle of doing what you're told means doing the minimum required, and Major General Adan's astonishment when he discovered, after twenty-five years of service in command roles up to his present and most senior one, that there are also orders *that do not* spring out of due consideration can be termed, with the utmost benevolence, *pathetic.*

A glaring omission in his book is a reference to his judgment in giving the orders. Naturally, doing the minimum and naïveté or gullibility are not traits worthy of an IDF general.

Adan was present at the October 7 meeting at Um Hashiba when the CoGS issued orders to Gonen and the division commanders. A commander at Adan's level who received orders from Gonen that not only ran counter to those of the CoGS but also compromised the mission and the lives of his men must reach the CoGS as quickly as humanly possible and ask whether he was aware of the discrepancy between his instructions and Gonen's and whether the implications of this inconsistency are clear to him. Only then can he decide whether to obey the orders of his immediate superior. As stated, Adan did not choose this path but preferred to do what he was told.

Major General Shmuel Gonen

Much has been said and written about the frenetic, hysterical conduct of the Southern Command's general on October 8 and its marked contribution to the IDF fiasco. Instead of rehashing the subject, we will sum up Gonen's personal failure: he was the wrong man in the wrong place at the wrong time. On the other hand, as the intermediary between the CoGS and the commander of the 162nd Division, his responsibility for the botch-up was the least of the three generals since it originated to a great degree in his unsuitability for the role and perhaps in the pressure he was under. Alone among those responsible for the botched counterattack, he was sacked almost at once, that is, as soon as its dimensions became apparent. Had the CoGS fulfilled his role as expected, he would have removed Gonen or at least neutralized him before noon. But, as stated, he did not function as he should have that day. Replacing Gonen immediately after the defeat would have been entirely justified, not so much because of his responsibility for what happened as because of the ineptitude that he displayed—a result of his personality and inexperience—in commanding the southern front in a war as complex and challenging as the Yom Kippur War. But the fact that the two other commanders who bore the lion's share of the blame for the debacle—Elazar and Adan—remained in place makes it clear that Gonen played the role of the scapegoat with singular success, as Major General Rehavam Zeevi (Ret.) noted in his eulogy on the ninth anniversary of Gonen's death in September 2000.

Major General Ariel Sharon

The most serious event of October 8 was the 143rd's trek south and back again—exactly at the time when its presence and action in the Second Army area could have thwarted the IDF fiasco and perhaps even snatched something resembling a victory from the jaws of disgrace. Regarding this superfluous and damaging journey, Sharon testified before the Agranat Commission: "If there's anything I often regret, it's that I executed this order [to remove his division from its positions and rush south]."

No explanation has been found, not even the flimsiest one, let alone an acceptable one, for Sharon's willingness to obey Gonen's hapless order. Every explanation imaginable for his obedience boils down to personal considerations and concerns. The only charge against Sharon's conduct that day was that his troops were prepared to sacrifice their lives in executing their task. One would expect their commanders, regardless of rank, to be willing to forgo their egos and reputations for the sake of mission and country—and their men.

"Thou hast run with the footmen, and they have wearied thee" (Jer. 12:5)

Lieutenant General Shazly, the Egyptian CoGS in the war, summarized the IDF attacks on October 8 in the Second Army sector in just one terse and precise sentence: "We were anticipating something altogether more serious and concentrated" (Shazly 1980, 238). From the IDF's point of view, October 8 should have witnessed the delivery of the decisive blow to, if not the total destruction of, the two bridgeheads that would have ended the war in a few days. Instead, the IDF found itself humiliated and licking its wounds on the southern front, with hundreds of soldiers and officers killed, wounded, captured, and missing and its morale shot to hell.

The Egyptian army moved out that morning to complete its missions in the Second Army sector but failed to accomplish all its plans. At any rate, it broke off for night rest with the great satisfaction of having inflicted heavy losses on the IDF and captured Zangavil, Halutz, and Nozel to the north of the 143rd's sector and Makhshir, Televizia, and Hamutal in the 143rd's sector. As mentioned, Force Tiger had beaten off Egyptian attacks in the northern sector, causing the enemy heavy casualties. In the southern sector, the 87th Reconnaissance Battalion, which, it will be remembered, had been left to defend Akavish Road and Kishuf when the rest of the 143rd was galloping south, blocked the Egyptians' attempts to gain control of these critical areas and thus prevented the capture of the Tassa area and Yukon disposition, where the crossing equipment was stored. Above all, the reconnaissance battalion's action left Akavish Road open and accessible for the crossing operation.

According to Shazly's account, the Egyptian high command seems to have been reasonably satisfied with the Second Army's accomplishments. As October 9 approached, the Egyptian army was ordered to complete the takeover of the areas dominating Artillery Road and organize them for defense.

"Nor the battle to the strong" (Eccles. 9:11)

As the bitter truth of the failed counterattack in the south began trickling in to the General Staff in the evening, the CoGS became increasingly aware that Adan's movements had deviated from the original plan, that the division had been mismanaged, had not attacked the designated area, and, instead, had carried out two unplanned battalion-sized attacks that culminated in the forces' destruction. He also realized, to his utter astonishment and outrage, that, after having been uprooted from its sector around noon, the 143rd had not remained assembled in Tassa but instead had been sent south posthaste, where its vanguard had already gone beyond the Gidi opening before the Southern Command stopped it and ordered an about-face on the spot in the hope of returning the division to the same areas it had vacated. In other words, the CoGS finally realized that the Southern Command's attack had accomplished nothing, had cost an intolerable price in lives and equipment in vital areas, and had frittered away the chance to end the war quickly and decisively. When he became fully cognizant of the web of inane reports that had induced him to approve moves that went against not only common sense but also his explicit instructions, he seems to have felt anger, remorse, and shame. We may assume that he made his own reckoning and blamed himself for much of the October 8 fiasco, which only added to his fury and frustration and influenced his decisions the following days.

After weighing the reasons for the counterattack's failure, the CoGS drew the following conclusions: from the estimate of the relative strength, and taking strategic priorities into account, the General Staff was unable to allocate enough forces to two fronts to enable the Northern Command to defeat the Syrians and the Southern Command to attack the Egyptian bridgeheads successfully (whatever that meant), let alone decimate the Egyptian army. Thus, the military strategy would be aggressive and decisive on the less difficult and more critical of the two fronts, that is, the Syrian. After victory was attained in the north, the forces could be concentrated in the south for a decisive victory on the Egyptian front.

In the meantime, the Southern Command would organize where it was and check the erosion of its equipment, mainly by halting initiated attacks. At the same time, a second line would be prepared to which the command could withdraw if necessary. Parallel to this, the Southern Command had to plan the IDF's offensive across the canal.

The phenomenon of false reports, obfuscation, and futility that characterized October 8 must never repeat itself. By the same token, the volatile relationship between Gonen and the division commanders, which reached its nadir after Gonen's performance on October 8, could not continue.

These conclusions were not based on a cold analysis of the relevant intelligence and a correct, if sketchy, understanding of the events on the southern front. The most critical factor in the October defeat is missing from the CoGS's analysis: impartial judgment (as far as it is possible) of the conduct of all those involved in these events, first and foremost Gonen, next the commander of the 162nd Division, and finally the CoGS himself. The impact of the debacle on Elazar is detectable in his analysis and evaluation and brought him to biased and unsubstantiated conclusions regarding the IDF's capabilities, the objectives of the fighting in the south, and the policy for applying the command's forces.

The defense minister's thinking and conclusions also appear to have been influenced by the October 8 events. Dayan seems to have lost confidence in the IDF's ability to roll back the situation in the canal area, especially after his trust in the General Staff's and the CoGS's competence and credibility had been undermined, if not completely blighted. Given his conduct after October 8, Dayan seems to have decided that Sharon was the only reliable general on the southern front.

The defense minister agreed with the CoGS that there was no room for an aggressive approach on the Egyptian front immediately. In fact, Dayan openly professed abandoning the battle on the canal and withdrawing to defense lines in the depth of Sinai. Indeed, he had good reasons for such a stratagem from a military point of view and for political, social, and diplomatic reasons as well. Be that as it may, as for Israel's long-term goals, if Dayan's opinion had been taken into account, it would have been revealed as a misstep of catastrophic proportions.

The CoGS's plan for the counterattack and the organization of the Southern Command for implementing it exposed many shortcomings, each of which was sufficient in itself to increase the likelihood of failure: for example, the lack of air and artillery support, deficiencies in organizing the attacking force and its structure, a fighting doctrine whose ineffectiveness and inherent pitfalls were apparent the moment hostilities commenced, the absence of a command- or General Staff–level FCP, the omission of a General Staff monitor to oversee the command's and division's battle management, and so forth. But the plan also contained positive features that could have reduced the chance of failure. First, it was strikingly simple. The only thing needed to execute it was the ability to identify where north and south are. The plan, which apparently had no need of intelligence preparations, elaborate staff work, and complex stages of maneuvering, guaranteed that commanders who were not among the best and the brightest could carry out the mission. But the three generals who concocted the counterattack or directed its implementation—the CoGS, Gonen, and the commander of the 162nd—failed to rise above the level needed to ensure the execution of so primitive, uninspired, easy-to-implement an operation on October 8. This was the reason for its foul-up.

Thus, the accuracy of the CoGS's conclusions, which were shared by the defense minister and others in the defense establishment, regarding the unprecedented October 8 defeat and to what degree it really was the IDF's day of infamy leaves room for doubt. The blow that the IDF incurred in the south naturally had extremely negative results, but the heart of the problem lay in the fighting forces' feelings, morale, and trust in the high command and the high command's belief in itself. The classic remedy for overcoming this angst is known: return immediately—mutatis mutandis—to the move that failed and succeed this time. Fortunately, the medication still existed in the Southern Command in the required dosage.

Numerically, the Southern Command's losses cannot be considered incapacitating. Oren (2004) describes how, just prior to the counterattack, the General Staff and the Southern Command tried to calculate the tank inventory. The General Staff determined optimistically that the attack would require 650–700 operable tanks; the general of the command estimated that he had 550 tanks on the morning of the attack; and Oren (2004) claims that 500 or so tanks were operating in the fighting zone.

The command had lost about 60 tanks on October 8, most of them in Adan's division. These were serious losses, especially in light of the fact that nothing whatsoever had been gained in exchange. The losses amounted to approximately 12 percent of the command's initial tank inventory. By itself, this number was far from being catastrophic, and, at the end of the day's fighting, the command's actual combat strength had hardly been scratched. Furthermore, two fresh tank brigades arrived: the 164th under the command of Colonel Avraham Baram and the 274th Brigade (code name "Tiran") under the command of Colonel Yoel Gonen. (The Tiran was a Russian T-54 or T-55 tank, war booty from the Six-Day War that the IDF had retrofitted with an American 105-millimeter gun, more reliable, efficient, and so forth.)

On the morning of October 9, the Southern Command was able to muster 675 operable tanks: 143rd Division, 230; 162nd Division, 120; 252nd Division, 150; Force Tiger, 100; and 274th ("Tiran") Brigade, 75. The Egyptian T-62 was qualitatively equal to Israel's tanks, but there were no more than 200 of them on the eastern bank. Also, until the morning of October 9, two Egyptian armored divisions, the 4th and the 21st, were still being kept in reserve on the western bank. Throughout October 8, IDF reserve artillery groups and armored infantry units reached the front. The Southern Command's loss of officers and crews, painful as it was, did not significantly detract from the divisions' combat readiness, in light of the parallel losses in fighting equipment and the influx of reinforcements to the Southern Command. Thus, almost paradoxically, the convergence of the strengthening effort, the addition of armored infantry and artillery units to Adan's and Sharon's divisions, and the reinforcement of the command with two tank brigades provided the Southern Command with a more balanced force on the morning of October 9 than it possessed on the previous morning when it launched the counterattack on the bridgeheads and even more so than at the end of the day when its units, battered, frustrated, shocked, and angry, had withdrawn to their tank parks.

The Southern Command was ready and able to renew the attack on the bridgeheads. It was the right thing to do operationally and psychologically, given the effect of the previous day on the troops' fighting spirit. The CoGS's decision, with the defense minister's blessing, to leave the initiative to the enemy and avoid seeking contact, aptly reflects the General Staff's trauma from the previous day and the impact of the Egyptian success in undercutting the mettle of the CoGS and his staff in all aspects of war management on the southern front.

After midnight on October 8–9, the division commanders and Gonen convened in Um Hashiba for a discussion with the CoGS and the defense minister. Sharon and Mandler argued that an attack in concentrated force had to be made against the bridgeheads, followed by a canal crossing—not on illusory captured Egyptian bridges but on IDF crossing equipment. The two champions of the previous day—Gonen and Adan—sensed or already knew in which direction the wind was blowing in the CoGS's mind and recommended not attacking the canal front a second time. The CoGS adjourned the meeting saying that in the present stage the IDF could not attack on two fronts. Therefore, the attack on the northern front would press on until the Syrian army was unconditionally beaten, and, in the meantime, the Southern Command would go on the defensive in order to preserve the fighting strength of its men and equipment, block the enemy's advance, and prevent it from making any gains and amassing forces for a possible decisive move. It will not initiate battles but, rather, carry out long-range sniping with tank cannons, get some rest, reorganize, and prepare for the crossing.

Given the weakened condition of Adan's and Mandler's forces, the CoGS assigned the crossing to Sharon's division because it had suffered relatively light losses. The 143rd would prepare for the canal crossing in a day or two and avoid exhausting its forces in initiated battles. In view of the conduct of the CoGS and the government in the following days, the CoGS does not seem to have taken seriously the prospect of a massive crossing on October 11 or 12. It is more likely that Sharon was given the crossing mission in order to incentivize him sufficiently strongly to obey the CoGS's order and refrain from an offensive action that would debilitate his forces in the coming days and at the same time provide his superiors with a clear and straightforward explanation when they forbade him from taking offensive steps.

The defense minister also spoke in this spirit when he emphasized the severity of the losses. The meeting lasted one hour. The CoGS and Dayan flew back to Tel Aviv, Gonen remained at Um Hashiba, and the division commanders returned to their respective headquarters.

3

The Twice-Blessed Day

The Events of Tuesday, October 9

> People that delight in war. (Ps. 68:30)

With minor changes, the Southern Command's force deployment remained as it had been up until now: the 143rd Division, the command's reserve force, fanned out between the Tassa-Ismailia Road in the north and the Hurva fortification about twenty kilometers south of Tassa; to the north, the 162nd was in position up to the Kantara line; further north, Magen's Force Tiger deployed up to the end of the front; and the 252nd Division was spread out from the Hurva area south of the command's northern border of the newly established independent Southern Sinai Command. In the 143rd's sector, the 600th Brigade secured the Hamadia and Kishuf localities and the dominating areas east of Makhshir (that had been under its control the day before and overtaken by the Egyptians when the division charged south); the 421st Brigade was fanned out east of Hamutal (which had been seized by the Egyptians on the previous day); the 14th Brigade was positioned in night parks behind the 600th in the Yukon area on Akavish Road; and the 87th Reconnaissance Battalion took up battle stations south of Yukon as far as the Hurva stronghold.

Sharon's deputy had responsibility for overseeing the 600th's operations—the defense of Hamadia—in the most important area of the entire sector. In his autobiography, *Warrior*, Sharon recalls the order he gave to the brigade commanders on October 9: "Commence blocking action against the enemy's advance in our sector. I expect you to demonstrate initiative" (Sharon 1989). In military jargon, *initiative* is a euphemism for *aggression*, while a fine line separates *aggression* from *attack*, meaning that the brigade commanders had to vie with an oxymoron rather than a clear-cut order. These instructions reflect Sharon's mood following the previous day's display of generalship by Gonen, the CoGS, and the commander of the 162nd Division. Sharon also states that, after the October 8 debacle, he lost his faith in Gonen's and the CoGS's judgment, ability, and determination to lead the IDF on the southern front, not to mention achieve a decisive victory. Thus, he drew the conclusion that he was not obligated to accept uncritically their opinions and carry out their decisions to the letter. His finely tuned political instincts sensed that, after October 8, they had lost their authority to sack him or hurt him in any way so long as he played his cards wisely. In practical terms, he ignored the policy of the use of the command's forces that the CoGS had dictated for Gonen, and, instead, he initiated offensive moves as he saw fit. In this light, he decided that his forces' two main tasks for October 9 were the following:

1. Rescuing the men in the Purkan stronghold, in accordance with an agreement with them that they would evacuate the stronghold on the night of October 8–9 and go on foot to a rendezvous point near the Talisman–Artillery Road Junction.
2. Retaking the areas that the 143rd had forfeited as a result of the mad dash south and back, especially the Hamutal and Makhshir localities, which Sharon recognized as crucial for the canal crossing (on Talisman Road) and whose successful recapture he would be responsible for when the time came.

Sharon's plan to develop a major offensive effort in the division's sector confronted him with a dilemma similar to that of a sailor who wants to steer his sailboat into the wind. His intentions ran directly against the CoGS's order to the Southern Command to refrain from offensive action in the coming days. In order for him to translate his plans into action and avoid the serious consequences that could result from blatantly disobeying his superiors' orders, he masked his intentions in three layers of virtual legitimacy.

As there was no argument over his plan to rescue the soldiers in Purkan, Sharon gave the mission top priority but decided to capture those areas that would guarantee the operation's success, in particular the Hamutal compound (as the area north of it was designated as the meeting point with the evacuees). All his statements and reports that day left the impression that the division was concentrating only on a defensive mission. Naturally, to carry out the defensive, the defense line would have to be stabilized—and here the laundered term *stabilizing* was only one step away from *straightening* the line, while the transition from one to the other seemed to remain within the category of a defensive mission. The Egyptians' capture of the Makhshir, Hamutal, Televizia, and Nozel localities on October 8 created a convex bulge east of the IDF line whose stabilization (i.e., straightening) required its removal or destruction, albeit still within the defensive effort. This could be achieved by attacking and seizing the areas that created the bulge. This is how a sailor steers his sailboat into the wind.

The division commander does not use his staff for planning and issuing orders for division moves. Directing a division is done by conveying instructions individually and orally, sometimes compartmentalized, to the brigade commanders. The instructions are rather general, and, while they emphasize the critical importance of the rescue or the need to "straighten the line," they also express the division commander's expectation of the brigade commander to display the initiative that by implication he has been given. The division forces' operating procedure stresses the independent activity of each brigade, each in its respective sector, with as minimal as possible recourse to division headquarters. Furthermore, most of the time, the division commander plays a silent and invisible role in the brigades' moves, although he keeps close tabs on them and sometimes intervenes from behind the scenes. The immediate supervision of the brigades' activity and the operational coordination between them are the job of the deputy division commander, who acts according to his superior's broad instructions.

Before daybreak, October 9, the 143rd's brigades were assigned the following tasks:

> *The 421st Brigade.* The 421st commander, Colonel Haim Erez, received orders orally as soon as Sharon returned from his nighttime meeting in Um Hashiba with the defense minister, the CoGS, Gonen, and the division commanders. The brigade would rescue the men from Purkan but only after first capturing Hamutal.
>
> *The 600th Brigade.* In accordance with Sharon's instructions, at approximately 0600, Colonel Even ordered the 600th's commander, Colonel Tuvia Raviv, to gain control of the Makhshir compound in order to stabilize (straighten) the line in the brigade's sector. Owing to the geographic proximity and closeness in time of the 421st's and the 600th's attacks, the two brigade commanders were instructed to coordinate their activity. Although the emphasis was on avoiding friendly fire and allowing the attacking brigade freedom of maneuver, such coordination necessarily created an integrated, two-brigade (i.e., division) tactical plan.
>
> *The 14th Brigade.* The 14th had deployed in the night parks east of Hamadia on the night of October 8–9. Sharon ordered it to be ready to take part in the rescue of the troops in Purkan (and, it seems, to serve as a kind of reserve for the 421st and as a force that could exploit a potential). The 14th was ordered to enter Talisman east of the 421st.

The two attacking brigades, the 421st and the 600th, approached their objectives at approximately 0700. The 421st's commander allocated one battalion for the attack on Hamutal, and the other two battalions provided fire support. In the end, the 599th Battalion, under the command of Ami Morag, attacked Hamutal, advanced on the objective's spine—from the northeast—to the high area in the southwest, and secured it in a matter of minutes. Then the fighting really began. On its arrival on the high ground, the battalion came under concentrated and effective close-range, antitank fire from Egyptian infantry. The battalion was hit from the west and the north and also, apparently, from Makhshir. It soon had to beat a frantic retreat. Out of twenty-six tanks that took part in the attack, nearly twenty were hit, some of which had to be abandoned during the withdrawal. All told, the battalion incurred fifty-five casualties, including fifteen killed. The 599th was badly hurt and unable to accomplish its mission.

As stated, at approximately the same time, the 600th also attacked Makhshir. The capture of the objective was assigned to the 410th Battalion, under the command of Amnon Marton. The plan called for the battalion to launch the assault from its dominating positions on the ridges east of Makhshir on the elongated side of the objective while the 409th Battalion covered it from its positions at Hamadia. The 407th Battalion, which was spread out on the ridges south of Hamadia, stayed out of the battle. A look at the topographic map of the sector's terrain shows that the eastern slope of Makhshir was marked as untraversable along almost its entire length. This fact became clear to the battalion as it was pushing south to a point from which it could attack the objective. It eventually found itself on the southeast edge of Makhshir and continued moving under heavy artillery fire. When it neared the objective, it too came under antitank fire. At this stage, the battalion commander was wounded and self-evacuated to the rear after delegating command to his deputy, Haim Elkan. Since the companies were dispersed, the battalion's deployment was in a state of chaos. The brigade commander called off the attack and ordered the battalion to assemble the companies, withdraw south to Akavish 55, and replenish. Within a short time, the deputy brigade commander, Lieutenant Colonel Yehuda Bachar, arrived and assumed command of the battalion. As soon as the Egyptians commenced their attack on Hamadia, the replenishment of the battalion was cut short, and it was ordered to return to the morning's positions, east of Makhshir. While the battalion was in transit, the new commander was wounded by artillery fire, and the deputy battalion commander, Elkan, resumed command. The 410th Battalion—like the 599th/421st Brigade, which was attacking Hamutal at approximately the same time—failed to accomplish its mission. But, unlike Morag's battalion, the 410th made no attack on its objective and thus incurred no losses to speak of. In both events, the main cause of the failure was not the enemy's armor but its artillery and antitank infantry that fought well.

The attack failed for two reasons. The 407th Battalion, which was deployed south of Hamadia, did not take part in it, with the result that the brigade commander was left with only two battalions to carry out a two-fold mission—capture Makhshir and prevent the enemy's seizure of Hamadia. With so limited a force, the attack was a tactical error. Also, once the order was given, the attacking battalion failed to prove its mettle and devotion to mission accomplishment.

The Rescue of the Men at Purkan

When the 14th Brigade arrived on Talisman Road east of Tziona, the brigade commander, Amnon Reshef, requested permission from Sharon for his brigade to rescue the troops in Purkan. Permission was granted. The 14th's responsibility for the evacuation did not affect the 421st's mission to capture Hamutal.

On Reshef's orders, Lieutenant Colonel Shaul Shalev of the 184th Battalion organized a rescue force consisting of two tanks and four APCs manned with armored infantry. While the 421st was engaged at Hamutal and providing cover fire, the rescue force reached the designated rendezvous with Purkan's troops between Talisman 23 and 22, south of the road. The brigade commander's tank escorted the force. The evacuees were soon located. While battling with Egyptian infantry in the area, Reshef's force extricated the Purkan survivors on the hull of the battalion commander's tank. The armored infantry contingent in the rescue force suffered five killed and twenty wounded. Three of the four APCs were destroyed. With its mission completed, the brigade returned to Yukon, where it was joined by the 106th Battalion/164th Brigade/252nd Division under the command of Lieutenant Colonel Moshe Gal.

Meanwhile, the Egyptian armor mounted an attack on Hamadia, which the Second Army had also identified as the sector's critical area. At about 0930, an Egyptian armored brigade with approximately sixty tanks and an armored infantry force attacked Hamadia from the direction of Missouri. Defending the compound was the 409th Battalion under the command of Uzi Ben Yitzhak. The battle commenced at approximately 1040. The brigade commander directed the battle, and the battalion fought well. The enemy attack was routed, and the Egyptians abandoned nearly thirty-five tanks on the battlefield, compared to the 600th Brigade's loss of one tank.

This success served as an omen for the events that followed. There is nothing more legitimate than exploiting success, a concept that can be justifiably applied—or, if you wish, a pretext that can be employed, especially if the success was gained in a defensive battle—for offensive moves in many directions, despite orders that expressly forbade it. Toward noon, Sharon gave the brigade commanders warning orders to attack objectives in their sectors. Parallel to this, he began pressuring the Southern Command to permit him to exploit the success in this sector by attacking the rear of the enemy, whose forces, according to reports, were retreating from Missouri and Amir.

Under these circumstances, Gonen found himself between a rock and a hard place. On the one hand, he was duty bound to obey the CoGS's order to avoid offensive initiatives and the erosion of his forces; on the other hand, he was still struggling to pull off the major victory that was snatched from him the day before and that could rehabilitate his reputation after all that had happened. He also hoped that, unlike Adan the day before, Sharon would gain the victory. He was intent on finding a formula that would not land him in hot water with the CoGS while enabling Sharon to justify his initiatives. This explains his orders to Sharon's division not to make any offensive moves but to maintain contact with the enemy, snipe at his stragglers, and so forth. It also explains Sharon's ensuing orders to his subordinates. As Colonel Even recalls:

> On the basis of his interpretation of Gonen's orders, Sharon decided in the early afternoon to capture the Televizia compound and, if possible, attack west in the direction of Missouri and Amir and reach the waterline in the Matzmed and Lakekan area. His FCP remained at Akavish 53 throughout the morning, and, for reasons already described, he preferred not to take direct charge of the attack and, instead, assigned it to me. As I understood his order, my job was to assault Televizia and Missouri with the 600th and 14th Brigades and, if the results proved propitious, advance as far west as possible, without the objectives being explicitly defined. The 600th was to attack with its three battalions; two of them [the 407th and the 409th] were deployed in front, and the third, the 410th, left its positions east of Makhshir to join the other two, follow in their tracks, and attack Makhshir from the south. The 14th Brigade, including the reconnaissance battalion, was to move south on Akavish Road and attack in the direction of Missouri and the Chinese Farm and, if possible, proceed west to the waterline in the Matzmed and Lakekan area.

The attack began at 1330. Even as it approached the objective, it had already gone utterly haywire. Precise and dense antitank missile fire targeted the attacking battalions, especially the 409th, which was moving closer to Televizia. In no time, the battalion lost twelve tanks and almost twenty men. Owing to a misunderstanding or a communications breakdown, the 410th moved north to the area north of Makhshir—intending to attack the target from north to south. Here, it encountered antitank fire from both the target and, apparently, Hamutal. Thirteen tanks were hit. The 407th, under the command of Oved Maoz, was moving on the southern flank of the attack and also received long-range antitank fire from Televizia that stopped it about three kilometers from the target. The battalion exchanged fire with Televizia. With Sharon's permission, the attack was halted, and the brigades assembled and reorganized east of Hamadia. All told, the brigade had about twenty-five tanks hit with over half of them abandoned in the field. Nearly twenty-five men were killed, twenty wounded, a few missing, and a number taken prisoner, including a company commander.

Contrary to what had been agreed, the 14th Brigade mounted the attack not in conjunction with the 600th but, as far as it seems, according to Sharon's direct order to the brigade commander and without updating Even. (The commander, Amnon Reshef, claims that he never received the order.) It may have been that, at the last minute before launching the attack, Sharon did not want to create the impression that a division attack was developing and perhaps be held responsible, at this point, for disobeying orders. Instead, the 14th took up positions on Hamadia and the adjacent terrain, securing the area in the direction of Makhshir, Missouri, and Televizia, the 106th Battalion and the 87th Reconnaissance Battalion deployed south of Hamadia, and a company-sized force, originally from the 600th Brigade but now attached to the 14th, deployed in the Hurva fortification, the southern end of the division's sector.

The 14th's lookouts who were posted south of Akavish Road observed that the areas between the road and Graphite compound were, for all practical purposes, empty of the enemy. In line with Sharon's offensive spirit, the 14th's commander tried to seize the footholds that appeared empty. When he received the green light from Sharon, he ordered the 106th Battalion to pull out of its positions in the Kishuf area and advance southwest toward Lakekan. After moving about a kilometer and a half, the battalion came under Egyptian fire, two tanks were hit, and the crewmembers—including the battalion commander—were wounded. The battalion turned back. At the same time, the brigade learned that the Egyptians too were retreating from Televizia (probably because of the 600th's attack there in the afternoon and the Egyptian command's assessment that it could not hang on to it against a more organized and determined Israeli attack). The 14th's commander, who also wanted to advance along Akavish Road and capture Televizia, requested permission from Sharon, explaining that a 600th Brigade tank had been abandoned at the foot of Televizia and the crew had to be rescued. Also, since the fate of the Matzmed fortification was not clear, it was incumbent on the brigade commander to verify the situation.

While this discussion was taking place, Gonen got on the radio and personally ordered Reshef to avoid offensive action unless it could be done without incurring casualties. Reshef reported this to Sharon, and Sharon emphasized the order to Reshef a second time. Reshef interpreted Gonen's order, in the spirit of Sharon, as permission to attack but without casualties (an order that can be described only as asinine). Thus, Sharon permitted Reshef to advance his left flank (the reconnaissance battalion) to the west. The battalion moved out and traveled south of Kishuf in a deep flanking maneuver to the left in the direction of Graphite and reached the Lexicon-Nakhala Junction north of Lakekan without encountering the enemy. Reshef's request to investigate Matzmed was denied. In any case, the stronghold had already fallen that morning.

At approximately 1600, Reshef was granted permission to advance in the direction of Televizia, after coordinating his move with the 600th. Two battalions participated in the attack. The 79th provided covering fire from Hamadia, while the 184th attacked east of its position at Segol 202. The Televizia compound, which was empty of enemy troops after the 600th attacked it, was taken with almost no problems, but, under relentless artillery fire, the commander of the attacking battalion, Lieutenant Colonel Shaul Shalev, was killed. One of the company commanders and then the deputy battalion commander led the attack until the objective was secured.

Since noon, Sharon had been trying to convince Gonen, and the deputy CoGS who arrived at Um Hashiba in the afternoon, and through them, the CoGS, to grant him permission to capture enemy objectives, such as Missouri and Amir, on the way to the waterline in the Matzmed area. Once there, he could make all the arrangements for crossing the canal on as early a date possible, perhaps even the next day.

Gonen and the deputy CoGS, Major General Israel Tal, were inclined to agree with him. But, every time Sharon's proposals were brought to the CoGS, they were summarily rejected, the CoGS's swelling anger finally exploding when he learned, to his utter stupefaction and outrage, that the 87th Reconnaissance Battalion was already at the waterline. Arguments and pressures were of no avail: on instructions from a fuming CoGS, the Southern Command gave Sharon orders that left not the slightest wiggle room for semantic maneuvering. He was to bring the reconnaissance battalion back to its natural home in the 14th Brigade and cease unconditionally, without any shenanigans or ambiguity, all offensive initiatives.

Gonen, the deputy CoGS, and the CoGS himself all felt that Sharon had displayed disrespect and insubordination toward his commanders and had knowingly violated explicit operational orders. The defense minister, however, was not particularly upset by the disciplinary aspect of Sharon's behavior that day and probably shared Sharon's opinion of Gonen and Elazar. But Dayan also felt that Sharon had acted irresponsibly and out of inappropriate motives, causing the loss of lives and equipment, and undermining the Southern Command's control of its forces. On the evening of October 9, Sharon was probably on the brink of dismissal and undoubtedly aware of it.

Because darkness had fallen, the reconnaissance battalion remained in its place until morning (October 10), when it began its move east. The 184th Battalion, which had captured Televizia, stayed at the fortification and vicinity until morning, when it returned to Hamadia. The 600th Brigade replaced the 14th on the line in the morning and deployed at Hamadia, Kishuf, and, briefly, Makhshir. The 14th Brigade entered Yukon and later Tassa. And, since the 600th had not secured Televizia after the 184th evacuated it, the Egyptians reoccupied it a short time later.

"Woe to you Ariel, Ariel" (Isa. 29:1)

Assessing the balance of damage and gain from the 143rd's actions on October 9 is a difficult task. On the negative side can be listed the following:

- The division failed to capture Hamutal and Makhshir, with the result that sections of Artillery and Talisman Roads remained in enemy hands. The IDF could still travel on Talisman at Hamutal's northeastern end, but Egyptian control of this and other localities in the area precluded the possibility of Talisman serving as an axis for the canal crossing unless breakthroughs were carried out at least twelve kilometers from the waterline. The Egyptian foothold on the Makhshir ridge created a chronic threat to the division's rear since it granted the Egyptian command vital operational options, such as disrupting an IDF crossing based on Akavish Road.
- Nearly 50 of the division's tanks had been damaged and 20 destroyed, and indeed the deputy division command reported the number of operable tanks as 170 on the morning of October 10, although in the course of the day most of the tanks that had been brought to the maintenance battalion returned to the division. The division suffered 160 casualties, including 50 killed, 5 captured, and the same number is missing.

On the positive side are the following:

- The 143rd's greatest achievement on October 9 was routing the Egyptian armor and infantry attack on Hamadia at a heavy cost to the enemy. This can be attributed to the 600th Brigade and its commander, Tuvia Raviv, who wisely deployed the 409th Battalion at Hamadia in a precisely timed "lunging ambush" that forced the enemy to retreat. The battalion fought effectively, courageously, and methodically, producing rapid and accurate fire that decided the battle. The IDF's hold on Hamadia was invaluable for blocking the enemy's access to Yukon and Tassa on Akavish Road, for posing a threat to the Egyptians in Makhshir and Missouri, for obstructing a possible sally from Makhshir in the division's rear, and mainly as the sine qua non for retaining Akavish Road as the main axis in the crossing operation. Furthermore, smashing the Egyptian armored attack on Hamadia provided the division with an opportunity and justification for pursuing its advance or—if you wish—its breakthrough attack to the southwest, to Televizia, Missouri, and the Akavish, Tirtur, and Lexicon Roads almost up to the waterline.

- The reconnaissance battalion's drive to the southwest on October 9 should be seen as a stunning success even though it was not leveraged to achieve decisive objectives. "Success," according to the maxim, "has many fathers." Thus, many claim that they were the first to discover the (supposed) gap between the Egyptian armies, and perhaps there is some truth to their claims. Before noon, it was clear that the whole area south and southeast of Akavish Road was entirely, or almost entirely, void of the enemy (according to the reports of the 14th Brigade's lookouts in its southern flank). In a daring move on the evening of October 9, the reconnaissance battalion proved conclusively that this area—at least up to Graphite and most likely even south of it—was clean of the enemy. But the battalion's unique contribution in its northbound movement from Graphite on Lexicon Road was to identify the northern boundary of the gap between the Egyptian Second and Third Armies and to confirm that Lexicon Road was, in effect, empty of enemy forces in the Lakekan and Matzmed areas. This was the watershed in transforming the IDF crossing from a desultory, faltering idea into a coherent operational possibility. The danger remained that the Egyptians might still spot the reconnaissance battalion as it approached the Deversoir area, thus possibly changing the Egyptian high command's ideas about leaving the area unprotected. This may have been what caused Elazar's blood to boil when he learned that the reconnaissance battalion had reached the waterline.

When the division's gains and losses on October 9 are weighed, the scale unmistakably indicates that this was the day the division began the crossing battle. This was the first stage in the battle for access to the water, whose main objective was to secure the division's use of Akavish Road and clear the way to the water in the Matzmed area. The objective was gained, as stated, and this was the division's outstanding achievement on October 9.

The series of battles that the division fought on October 9, whether on its own initiative or the enemy's, and whether it gained a specific goal in one of the battles produced another pivotal, overarching result. Although the Second Army succeeded in thwarting the 143rd's initiatives and inflicting heavy losses, it too was bruised and battered from defending and attacking the 143rd, no less so than the division. At least fifty of the army's tanks were hit, and armored combat vehicles and lives were lost. These painful losses and the recognition of the 143rd's strength, aggressiveness, and combat capability—and the awareness that its commander was Ariel Sharon—convinced the Second Army to cease its offensive moves in the division's sector and focus its effort on other IDF forces. Thus, the 143rd received a few days of quiet to reorganize, replenish its weapons and crews, and plan the canal crossing.

Two phenomena stand out on October 9:

1. The Second Army initiated one attack with an armored brigade and armored infantry brigade and engaged in four defensive battles of varying degrees of intensity. The attack failed, but the defensive battles were from the Egyptians' point of view successful. A mirror image of this action is the sole defensive battle the 143rd waged and the four attacks it initiated that day. The defensive battle ended successfully from its point of view, but the attacks failed. To summarize: all the attacks failed, or, vice versa, all the defensive battles ended with the defender's victory. It is interesting to note that the Egyptian attack that was repulsed with heavy losses to the enemy side was made by an Egyptian armored force (including armored infantry) and was repulsed by IDF armor, whereas the IDF attacks were blocked by Egyptian infantry. Egyptian armor that tried to intervene in the battle of the 599th Battalion at Hamutal was practically wiped out. On October 9, the light dawned on the IDF when it became clear beyond question that the IDF's tank-based ground forces had run headlong into a vast, densely packed, determined, well-trained, rather mobile antitank infantry disposition under generally skillful command. Antitank infantry was the Egyptian army's backbone in the war and bore the main burden of the fighting. Israel's armor found itself in the same situation as the air force, which was coping with a vast, hermetic antiaircraft layout.
2. It is obvious why Sharon initiated a series of attacks on the Egyptian foothold running the length of Artillery Road on the border of and even beyond the division's sector. The CoGS, his deputy, Gonen, and his deputy felt that Sharon had repeatedly flouted their orders (to avoid all offensive initiatives and attrition of forces). But, where fighting is raging, there is no room for a bureaucratic approach to orders like those Elazar and Gonen had issued. War has to be fought offensively. Commanders at all levels are duty bound to exploit every opportunity to score operational gains and never relent so long as the additional price exacted for their gains (in terms of losses, time, future options, etc.) is less than the operational

> value. This had doubtlessly been Sharon's approach in every war, including the Yom Kippur War on October 9. Gonen and the CoGS should have leveled all their carping at themselves. Sharon's management of the division leads us to conclude that he did not explicitly contravene a single order and that at no time did he dare to violate a clear and unequivocal command. Most likely, he did not carry out this or that order exactly in the spirit of the commander, but a knowledgeable, intelligent commander has to take into account that the spirit of an order is a vague concept whose meaning depends entirely on the interpretation and judgment of the person receiving the order. Therefore, the spirit of the order must be inherent in the order itself; that is, the order cannot leave any room for interpretation by an experienced, assertive, creative subordinate. If the CoGS was dead set against an offensive initiative, he should have made absolutely certain that his orders were scrupulously and unambiguously worded so that they would reach the lower levels exactly as he intended, and he or his representative should have ascertained that the orders reached the lower levels without exception. On October 9, Sharon received a series of oxymoronic orders from the Southern Command that he translated, without a breach of discipline, as approval for initiating offensive action.

An order is one of the most important tools of a commander. A fundamental skill in the art of leading—especially at the generalship level—is the ability to issue a clear and precise order that is incapable of being misunderstood, does not meander, is not overly poetic or semantically ambiguous, and is independent of the spirit of the commander (or the spirit of the order) as a factor that completes it. Every commander—not to mention a general officer—should remember that a subordinate does not always see eye to eye with him.

4

On the Defensive, October 10–14

The six days beginning on October 9 that the Southern Command was on the defensive can be divided into three periods:

October 9. A pseudodefensive; exceptionally violent defense in the 143rd Division's sector.
October 10–13. Restive dormancy.
October 14. Role change and reversal of fortune.

On the surface, this stage of the war was characterized by low-intensity combat interspersed with sporadic bursts of furious fire at key points. But, far from the war zone and under the surface, the drama roiled. In war cabinet meetings with the General Staff, the lights burned long into the night as military and political leaders wracked their brains to figure out the gloomy reports from the recent hostilities, derive the appropriate lessons, and formulate strategies for the fighting to come.

Naturally we were not privy to or even spectators sitting on the sidelines of most of the events in this chapter, but, because of their relevance in completing the picture, we believe that they should be described and analyzed. The facts have been gleaned from what we judge are the most credible sources available. This being said, secondhand sources, no matter how authentic, how diverse, and how meticulously cross-checked, cannot create a perfectly unbiased mosaic of the events. In the thousands of conversations that took place sub rosa, in the corridors of power, in random encounters by drinking fountains, outdoors in godforsaken areas—without witnesses or documentation—crucial issues were decided and future moves planned. No one has a clue what transpired in these discussions.

"And after the fire—a still, small voice" (1 Kings 19:12)

What follows is a summary of the October 9 fighting in the 143rd's sector.

The division failed to regain the dominating areas that it vacated on Artillery Road on October 8. The Egyptians seized Makhshir, Televizia, and Hamutal without firing a single shot and thus achieved a major part of the goal in the first stage of the fighting: the domination of Artillery Road.

Although the Egyptians held Halutz and Nozel, which had also been an objective in the first stage in the southern part of Hazizit Road (Artillery Road's name in the front's northern section), the Ismailia-Tassa Road remained tightly packed and well defended by the 421st Brigade at Tsiona, east of Hamutal.

In the southern part of the division's sector, especially in the Hamadia area, the Egyptians failed to capture their first stage's objectives and incurred heavy losses. They apparently decided to give up on Hamadia and be satisfied with their gains in the 143rd's sector. All of Akavish Road remained in IDF hands.

Given these results, the Egyptians passed through the 143rd's sector on October 10 to the operational halt stage in order to reorganize for defense in the captured areas and draw the IDF's blood when it attacked as was its custom, sloppily, hastily, without accurate intelligence, and still blind to the Egyptians' new style of fighting.

The 143rd's losses on October 9 in its failed attempts to straighten the line and Elazar's and Dayan's responses chilled Sharon's desire to continue the attack. Silence prevailed in the division's sector. The brigades reorganized in the rear and prepared the defense line. The quiet was interrupted by scattered weak attempts by the Egyptians to infiltrate our lines with small forces and overtake empty areas and by artillery fire on our forces on the line or in the rear tank parks. To sum up: the 143rd exploited the imposed calm—as Sharon felt it—to reorganize the brigades, absorb reinforcements, repair equipment, and draw up operational plans for the canal crossing that it might be ordered to execute.

Large sections of Artillery Road remained in IDF hands in the 162nd's sector, especially in the Havraga and Zarkor areas. These were the Second Army's objectives for completing the first stage. Between the morning and the evening of October 10, the 162nd furiously fought off repeated armor and infantry attacks, sometimes at ranges of a few dozen meters. Over the next two days, the division continued fending off Egyptian attacks against Havraga and the areas north of it. Quiet reigned in Force Tiger's sector too. On the morning of October 10, the force renewed its attempt to break through the blockade of the Budapest stronghold after the previous day's failure. This time it found the road to the stronghold open (the Egyptian blocking force had abandoned its positions during the night). For the next few days, Force Tiger operated against Egyptian commando forces that were harassing IDF units and logistic depots in the rear. In the front's southern section, the Egyptians repeatedly attacked the 252nd Division and were repulsed, sometimes at a heavy cost to their forces. Nevertheless, here and there they could claim considerable gains in the sector.

"There is no wisdom nor understanding nor counsel" (Prov. 21:30)

After three days of intense fighting during which the Egyptians completed the first stage of the greater mission—the capture of the canal and the establishment of bridgeheads on the eastern bank—the two sides decided to lower the pace, lick their wounds, and reorganize for the next round. Although the Egyptians did not accomplish all their operational goals, their gains were impressive, and they managed to seriously hurt the IDF.

During this period, the first casualty reports—killed, wounded, missing, and captured—began reaching the defense minister and the IDF chiefs. Although the numbers were skewed toward the bottom, they were outrageously high—and their military, political, and human significance did not escape the eyes of the decision makers. The military leaders, including the defense minister, the CoGS, and the commanding general of the Southern Command, realized that they had to reexamine Israel's goals and the way in which the war was being managed. The questions topping the leadership's agenda were, What, when, why, and at what price? At the end of the process, the security heads, with the government's approval, revised the handling of the war and recalibrated what the IDF hoped to achieve.

The security chiefs focused on the following:

- Implementing a long-range overhaul of the structure, composition, and work style of the General Staff on the southern front.
- Revising the war aims.
- Formulating a position on a cease-fire.
- Determining the goals and allocation of resources for the fighting on the northern and southern fronts.
- Revamping strategic and operational considerations in managing the war in the south.

Change of Personnel in the Division and the Southern Command

> And bring forth the old because of the new. (Lev. 26:10)

On October 10, Major Yehuda Geller, who had been serving in the FCP of the 143rd Division's deputy commander, was appointed commander of the 410th Battalion/600th Brigade. He was an outstanding combat officer whose qualities came to full expression during the crossing.

Major General Mandler, the commander of the 252nd Division, was killed by a tank shell that hit the deck of his APC near the Mitzva fortification on

October 13. In a wise, swift, and honest (for a change) move, all the blabbermouths who had congregated in the war room aching for an appointment were flung aside, and Brigadier General Magen, the commander of Force Tiger, was promoted to major general and immediately put in command of the 252nd—a role that had been designated for him before the war. Magen was the right person in the right place—smart, brave, experienced, amiable, and modest—the natural and correct replacement for Mandler, who was also blessed with these qualities.

Brigadier General Sasson Yitzhaki, the Southern Command's CoS, replaced Magen as commander of Force Tiger, and Brigadier General Asher Levy returned to his previous role as the command's CoS. These were successful appointments.

Lieutenant General Haim Bar-Lev—the New Commanding General of the Southern Command

Of all the appointments in the Southern Command in this period, the most significant was undoubtedly that of Lieutenant General (Res.) Haim Bar-Lev, the minister of trade and industry (Labor Party), who became commander of the southern front. Bar-Lev's appointment meant that Gonen, the commanding general of the Southern Command, was Bar-Lev's de facto subordinate.

When the dimensions of the failure of the command's counterattack were revealed on the evening of October 8, Dayan, and apparently the CoGS too, came to the conclusion that Gonen was incapable of fulfilling his role. Unlike with other matters on the agenda in this period, there were no objections to removing Gonen as supreme commander on the southern front. If Elazar still harbored doubts on the subject, they were blown away the next day when Sharon rode roughshod over Gonen's orders and did whatever he felt necessary in his sector. It may be assumed that the dissatisfaction with Gonen that the commander of the 162nd Division felt also contributed to the realization that he had to be sacked immediately. Both the CoGS and Adan had strong personal reasons for wanting to see Gonen go. Since it was already being claimed that the October 8 debacle was mainly their fault, it was natural that they had an urgent interest in finding a scapegoat that would enable them to continue serving in their roles. Gonen seems to have been chosen as the perfect fall guy: sufficiently senior, responsible to a great (if not decisive) degree for the fiasco, and vulnerable. From the CoGS's point of view, the need to oust Gonen encountered a few personal obstacles at the outset.

Elazar himself had appointed Gonen commanding general of the Southern Command. Many senior officers had opposed the move, arguing that he was unsuited for the role and that at any rate this promotion was coming too early in his career. Thus, if he was unceremoniously sacked, his appointment would be attributed to the CoGS, whose judgment and capabilities were also in doubt given the recent failures. Gonen's dismissal would have to be masked with a justifiable pretext, such as the need to maintain national morale.

Sacking Gonen would serve as a dangerous precedent for the CoGS. If the commanding general of the Southern Command was ousted in the middle of the war and the world continued spinning on its axis, then the removal of a lieutenant general under similar circumstances could also be considered.

Would not Sharon's fame rise in the public's eyes if Gonen's axing were known? Could he, Elazar, avoid Sharon's appointment to commanding general if Gonen was immediately removed?

Gonen's dismissal would also create a problem for Dayan. After all, he had approved the promotion of the rookie, controversial, inexperienced major general to command Israel's most important front. How would the public react? What would his many enemies in the Labor Party say about the haphazard and irresponsible way in which he was fulfilling his role? Be that as it may, he was willing to take the drastic but necessary step and replace Gonen straightaway with someone more suited to command, if only because of the more urgent need to find a scapegoat. Dayan also spoke with the CoGS about the possibility of Sharon's appointment to commanding general of the front but did not press the issue because of the following reasons.

From the legal point of view, ordering or exerting pressure on the CoGS to make certain military appointments went beyond the defense minister's authority. His only privilege in this matter was the right to veto an appointment, a right based on the precedent that Ben-Gurion had set.

Dayan probably feared that Sharon's appointment would raise the level of Sharon's blustery conduct toward and disparagement of his superior officer (Elazar) to the point of open conflict, and this would impede the running of the war.

Recognizing Sharon's political position, Dayan may have wished to avoid working with a commanding general who was widely popular and radiated a personal charisma at least as great, if not greater than, his own.

Dayan most likely figured that in any case the prime minister and some of her colleagues (Allon, Galili, Sapir, and few others) would not agree to transforming Sharon—the head of the election staff of the Likud Party (Labor's rival)—into the superhero of the Jewish people.

On the evening of October 9, after becoming fully aware of the scope and results of Sharon's offensive, the CoGS was finally convinced that Gonen could not continue any longer in his current role. As happens in the IDF, the defense minister and the CoGS appointed as commander of the front not the person who was most suited for the task, Ariel Sharon, but an officer who was less proficient in generalship. The choice was the minister of trade and commerce, one of the leading figures in the Labor Party, Lieutenant General Haim Bar-Lev. The CoGS still had to contend with the conundrum of how to square the circle: how to appoint Bar-Lev as commander of the southern front without Gonen making waves. In the midst of war, he had to devote a great deal of October 9 to planning how to persuade Gonen to accept the decision. He even recruited his deputy, General Tal, to help with the task.

The CoGS came up with a creative solution: inform Gonen that Lieutenant General Haim Bar-Lev was now the CoGS's special envoy on the southern front, without revoking Gonen's position as commanding general. This solution raised Dayan's hackles because he viewed it as a typical maneuver on Elazar's part to evade responsibility by gimmickry (Baron 1992, 143). Bar-Lev agreed to the arrangement, and the decision was conveyed to Gonen, who, as expected, reacted furiously and threatened to quit but eventually calmed down and even accepted the decision—it must be noted to his credit—with humor. Bar-Lev landed at Um Hashiba on the morning of October 10 and without ceremony immediately took matters into his hands. In a few slow and measured sentences, he made it clear that a new sheriff had arrived in town and that it was in everyone's best interest to internalize this fact. It was especially important that Sharon should understand that Bar-Lev's appointment came with the authority to sack him if he did not instantly comply with the new commander's orders. Bar-Lev came to the command with a balance of positive and negative attributes.

On the positive side are the following attributes.

Unlike Gonen—a relatively green major general compared to his subordinates, the division commanders—Bar-Lev was a lieutenant general whose rank put him above all the commanders in the Southern Command, including Sharon.

Unlike Gonen, Bar-Lev had a great deal of military experience and was still fresh from command and control of the highest military levels. As a former CoGS, he was able to deal with the General Staff, the CoGS, and, if necessary, the defense minister in every detail related to the front.

Although with his appointment to commanding general of the front Bar-Lev had to resign from his ministerial post, he was still tied to the highest echelons of political power and enjoyed the trust of the prime minister and her cronies as an equal among equals. This status served as a counterweight to the fact that he was less popular and charismatic than Dayan and Sharon and that Sharon's burgeoning strength in the political arena was undoubtedly greater than his.

As commanding general and a human being, Bar-Lev was intelligent, calm, levelheaded, utterly restrained, and admirably composed and, at the same time, assertive, resolute, and authoritative.

On the negative side are the following attributes.

As opposed to Bar-Lev's background in managing the entire military system, his direct experience in commanding large formations in wartime was, at best, outdated and irrelevant. His last wartime role was as commander of the 27th Armored Brigade in the 1956 Sinai Campaign, and he had never served as the commanding general of a territorial command. He had little, if any, experience in making crucial decisions at the operational level and weighing the operational risks. As the war progressed, these shortcomings would prove critical.

Bar-Lev's tenure as CoGS was characterized by the War of Attrition in the south, IDF preparations, and many daily security events. To the CoGS's credit, the IDF was very successful in these areas. But, by the same token, the Battle of Karameh (March 21, 1968) had been a costly failure, a harbinger of the flaws in the political and military performance in the Yom Kippur War, and was attributed, first and foremost, to the CoGS at the time, Haim Bar-Lev. Furthermore, several of his decisions and actions eventually proved to be mistaken and catastrophic:

- He determined the defense principles on the southern front, which included the construction of the Bar-Lev Line.
- During his tenure, a ground forces' doctrine developed that was based on irrelevant lessons from the past, inane principles, and wishful thinking. The land branches, especially armor, trained according to this doctrine, which proved fatal in the Yom Kippur War.
- Under Bar-Lev's leadership as CoGS, the ground forces' combat and support echelons were structurally imbalanced. The IDF and the IAF failed to absorb correctly the lessons and manner in which the War of Attrition had ended. As a result, the IAF was blocked from operating as it should have in the ground battles in the south (and to a large degree in the north) during most of the war.
- Although Bar-Lev repeatedly stated that as CoGS he was unaffiliated with any political party, on occasion he subordinated the management of the IDF to the ruling Labor Party's bidding. The most famous case concerned the forced retirement of Ariel Sharon. The matter was leaked to the finance minister, Pinchas Sapir, the all-powerful boss of the Labor Party, who rang up Bar-Lev from the United States, chewed him out on his irresponsibility toward the party, and ordered him to retain Sharon in the IDF. Sapir explained that his involvement in the affair was due to the up-and-coming elections. Also, Major General Tal, the commander of the armored forces and Sharon's ally in the struggle for the defense concept in Sinai, was transferred from the IDF to the defense ministry.

- On assuming command of the southern front, Bar-Lev brought to the new role all the resentment and bitterness that he felt toward Sharon. Unfortunately, but not surprisingly, he was incapable of rising above these sentiments, to which was added the political rivalry between Bar-Lev and Sharon. This combination of antagonism gave rise to Bar-Lev's hostile expressions toward Sharon to his face and behind his back, to his repeated attempts to oust him from command, and to several important decisions that he forced, or tried to force, on Sharon (see below).

On the surface, Sharon reacted to Bar-Lev's appointment with mixed feelings. On the one hand, he remembered his bitter struggles with him over the defense concept for Sinai, and he certainly had not forgotten that he was the progenitor of the Bar-Lev Line. Also, Bar-Lev's attempt to get rid of him undoubtedly left Sharon with an open wound. Nevertheless, his conduct suggests that Sharon also harbored a certain degree of respect for Bar-Lev—the man and his rank. Despite his qualms about Bar-Lev's personality, abilities, and generalship, he may have hoped that this appointment would prove a blessing to the forces. These moments of grace, if indeed there were any, did not last long. The sabers were quickly unsheathed as old differences and animosities surfaced and new ones were soon added. All this affected the management of the war in the south pejoratively and sometimes destructively. Twenty years later, Sharon recalled his feelings at the time: "[Bar-Lev's appointment] was the last thing I needed to hear. The single person missing from the stew of intrigue and internal politicking was Bar-Lev. And now I had him on my plate too" (Sharon 1989, 305).

It is interesting to note what Elazar said to Dayan when they discussed Bar-Lev's appointment: "Haim is thoughtful . . . and has authority, not brilliant . . . operationally, but he is not frozen" (Ronen and Meltzer 2003, 156). Incidentally, Bar-Lev was not a great fan of Elazar's. Dayan's adjutant, Aryeh Baron, related that on one occasion Bar-Lev told Dayan confidentially after the military situation in the south improved: "[Elazar] is driving us crazy. He's constantly interfering with the work" (Baron 1992, 221). Dayan thought that Bar-Lev "suffer[ed] from conservatism and rigidity" (Carmit Guy 2002, 268). All these opinions seem to be right on target.

"Why should ye be stricken anymore?" (Isa. 1:5)

The IDF went to war on October 6 to supposedly achieve an explicit goal that the political level had approved a few months earlier: to deny the enemy any territorial gains and to inflict a military defeat based on maximum destruction of military force and infrastructure. Achieving this goal should provide Israel with a significant advantage in relative power as well as on the armistice lines.

The first two days of fighting in the south and the 162nd Division's counterattack on the third day were designed to realize this goal by putting the Second Army's bridgeheads out of commission, if not totally destroying them, in order to create the conditions for defeating the enemy. As stated, the IDF's failures on the third day, and especially the fiasco of the October 8 counterattack, stemmed mainly from the following reasons:

For starters, there was faulty command and control from the CoGS down to the general of the Southern Command and the commander of the attacking division. Intelligence failures and conceptual shortcomings in the General Staff, the IAF, and the armored corps headquarters from before the war contributed to the flawed, catastrophic fighting doctrines. The value and advantages of the infantry, artillery, and combat engineers were underestimated. The IAF was thwarted from participating in the ground battles in the south. And the highest political and security levels failed to comprehend the concept, goals, and stages of the Egyptian offensive plan. The counterattack was not designed, planned, or instructed to achieve a specific decisive goal. It was a kind of division-sized fishing expedition.

Owing to the CoGS's misplaced fear of horrific catastrophes and his irrelevant considerations, the counterattacking force was too small, poorly composed, and commanded by generals who were far from what was needed.

The October 8 debacle brought the IDF's fighting in the south to a low point because of its total failure to accomplish its mission and the enormous number of casualties and loss of fighting equipment it incurred. As soon as the dimensions of the drubbing became known, the highest security-military level began searching for the reasons for the shameful performance, formulating excuses, and identifying scapegoats.

The CoGS's Estimate of the Situation—Its Development and Results

The CoGS had initiated the October 8 counterattack, concocted the attack plan, and been in direct command (theoretically at least) of its execution and was now the first to demand immediate conclusions after the results of the attack became clear. In the evening of October 8, he seems to have already realized that the way to cover up his responsibility for the setbacks in the south was to assess that the IDF was incapable—given its geographic deployment, the relative strength of its enemies, and other constraints—of carrying out its mission (preventing the enemy from making any military gains). Indeed, in the Um Hashiba meeting on the night of October 8–9 that was attended by Dayan, Elazar, Gonen, and the division commanders, the CoGS announced: "We have to think of a way of ending the war in terms different from those we were accustomed to before the war" (Baron 1992, 127–28). This declaration contained two subclauses:

- The war aims have to change. This means abandoning the idea of victory as the IDF's goal and replacing it with something that the CoGS did not clarify at this stage.
- The management of the war must be completely revised.

The CoGS's estimate of the situation was influenced by the collapse of the southern front and the following two factors:

The IAF's estimate of the situation. In the first days of the war, the IAF accomplished very little on the canal front other than sustaining heavy losses. Major General Benny Peled, the IAF commander, drew the conclusion that the only way in which the air force could contribute to the ground fighting and reclaim its status as a key element in defeating the Egyptian army was if the ground forces launched a large-scale canal crossing and took out the Egyptian SAM layout. On October 9, he began to sing a different tune: at the present rate of erosion, in a few days the number of IAF aircraft would reach the redline; any lower, and the IAF would not be able to assist the ground forces. After the war, Peled admitted that he had fabricated this assessment in order to convince the government and the CoGS of the urgent need to cross the canal (and annihilate the antiaircraft disposition). The CoGS, whether he accepted Peled's estimate as the word of God or considered it merely a bureaucratic bluff, quickly adopted it—to Peled's sorrow—as one of the reasons for an immediate cease-fire (Baron 1992, 141; Wald 1987, 109–10).

The transfer of the Egyptian 4th and 21st Armored Divisions. One of the IDF's most serious blunders was the failure to build and maintain a strategic reserve in place of the one that had been flung into battle at the outbreak of the war. Equally damaging was the intelligence branch's continuous failure to interpret correctly the Egyptian war plan and its extent and stages. As a result, when it became clear that no Egyptian armored divisions had crossed into Sinai until October 9 (and even later)—in accordance with the Soviet military doctrine—the pessimists at Israel's highest security level, first and foremost the CoGS, saw this as a sign of a double danger: if these divisions did not cross when the IDF crossed, they would pose a lethal threat to the IDF forces on the western bank; and, if they crossed to the eastern bank, the IDF forces would be situated on the western side of the canal or in transit there, in which case the question became, Who would stop the Egyptian armor from barreling ahead to Tel Aviv, heaven forbid? Here, the CoGS vacillated between trepidation that his scenario might materialize and the awareness that the likelihood that it would be infinitesimal. He may have realized that the Egyptians were not charging north from the Nile to the Yarkon, but he raised these alarming possibilities whenever anxiety overcame him and especially when he explained his operational decisions, which were characterized by inertia and lethargy.

In light of this, we can reconstruct the so-called estimate of the situation that the CoGS devised for himself between October 9 and 11:

- The IDF is too weak to destroy the Egyptian armies' bridgeheads and is incapable of achieving a decisive victory.
- Every attempt to nibble away at and inflict damage on the Egyptian army and antitank defenses east of the canal is destined to fail or at the least exact a heavy toll in lives and equipment that the IDF—and the nation—would not brook.
- The IDF is too weak to wage offensive battles on the two fronts, let alone decisively defeat the enemy on both simultaneously. The Egyptians might succeed in pushing the IDF back to the mountain passes or even further to the east.
- Until now, the IDF has been successful in fighting defensive battles to ward off the Egyptian armor and infantry attacks. For this reason, and because of the fear that the Egyptians might use their armored reserve, the IDF has to remain in static positions until the Egyptian armored divisions cross the canal and launch an attack, at which point it can decimate them in tank battles.
- To sum up, the absolutely necessary condition for IDF action against the Egyptians, when the time comes, is to cross the canal and fight in areas west of Suez. The main question is, What is the aim of the IDF campaign?

The CoGS's estimate of the situation was not the product of an organized, rationally calculated, comprehensive analysis. On the contrary, it expressed his visceral, defective perception of the actual military situation on the southern front and was probably also influenced by personal considerations and defeatism.

The first golden rule in dealing with an estimate of the situation is that it cannot be an individual undertaking based on emotional biases and raw feelings. It must be the major product of staff work that is void of trauma, personal survival instincts, and a jumping-to-conclusions culture, a joint effort that employs analysis, objectivity, information, and military professionalism.

The second golden rule is that an estimate of the situation cannot be based on a faulty operational reality. Identifying and correcting the flaws and defects in the fighting must precede any attempt to assess an operational situation. Before the CoGS could accurately assess the situation on the southern front after the October 8 events, he had to harness all his intellectual resources and moral integrity to get to the source of the weaknesses and shortcomings in the functioning of the General Staff (including himself), the Southern Command, and the divisions. Only after this clarification was made could he undertake an honest assessment of the military situation on the front.

The third golden rule is that every estimate of the situation must be derived according to a clear and meaningful definition of the goal, regardless of the data, time, and analysis of the problems related to its production. Without this guideline, the estimate of the situation is merely deception and claptrap.

The CoGS took none of these rules into account in his estimate of the situation and, as a result, arrived at a totally misleading conclusion on the use of the IDF on the southern front.

The CoGS Poses Possible Methods of Operation, October 10–12

The Northern Command also launched a counterattack on October 8 to push the Syrians back across the "purple line" (the 1967 cease-fire line). While the counterattack in the south ended disastrously, the northern front did a superb job. Major General Yitzhak Hofi expressed this in his memo to the CoGS on October 10: "The cease-fire lines on the Golan are in our hands [excluding the Mount Hermon stronghold]." The CoGS wanted to pursue the attack and knock the Syrians out of the war, but Dayan preferred to push them off the "purple line," then have the IDF advance east, capture more territory on the Golan Heights, and confront Damascus with a tangible threat.

After the failed counterattack in the south, Elazar saw no sense in attacking a second time. The IDF had to prepare a defense, wait until the two Egyptian armored divisions crossed the canal into Sinai as expected, and allow them to attack and incur losses. This would create the conditions to enable the IDF to take the initiative. It should be noted that the idea of waiting for enemy divisions was not in the IDF's combat doctrine and did not necessarily solve an operational situation. The CoGS may have judged that the military effort at this stage had to be focused in the north and thus used this as a reason—perhaps a pretext—to postpone IDF activity on the southern front for an undetermined time.

The CoGS was also concerned that the Egyptians might force the IDF back to the mountain passes and perhaps even further, to Bir Gafgafa; therefore, the Southern Command had to plan and prepare for such a contingency. On October 10, the cat was let out of the bag. The CoGS realized at last—as the upshot of his estimate of the situation—that from this point on the goal was to obtain a cease-fire as quickly as possible. That evening, he disclosed to Dayan the spirit in which he wanted the war to continue: "In the north the Syrians are not broken yet. They're still fighting. Progress is slow and painful; our forces are exhausted. [Therefore, I have] decided to break off contact with the enemy in order to allow the troops to reorganize." Moreover, in his opinion, the Syrian disposition would not collapse if the IDF continued the attack in the direction of Damascus, which meant that significant gains, greater than what had been achieved until then, would not be possible. As for the southern front, the CoGS confessed to the defense minister that he was in a "dark mood" that would grow even darker (as may be inferred from Elazar's words) "if we don't reach a cease-fire": "Everything that we do [must be directed] toward a cease-fire" (Baron 1992, 149).

During this fascinating conversation, the CoGS revealed his ideas for the conduct of the war. Because they reflect with amazing clarity his firmness and determination, we set them out here at length:

> For four days now [since the beginning of the war] I've been living with the assumption that war aim is to return to the 1967 cease-fire lines with [border] corrections. [This was the goal of the war as he understood it when it was set forth a few months earlier.] . . . Today I can say that there will not be any [border] corrections in Syria. This is only a cease-fire. [As for] Egypt I ask: is returning to the cease-fire line a realistic goal? The answer is—no. [Currently] we lack the strength to drive [the Egyptians] back to the cease-fire line.

The defense minister believed that the war could be ended after the IDF gained control of areas west of the canal even though the Egyptians were still clinging to their bridgeheads on the eastern bank. The CoGS, however, felt that this was unrealistic because Egypt would not agree to a cease-fire if the IDF was in possession of areas west of the canal. He summed up his unfounded assessments thus:

> It's realistic to reach a cease-fire when we're [on the purple line] in Syria. . . . and here [in the south] we still haven't returned to the status

> quo ante bellum. . . . I'm speaking what I feel right now: the goal is to obtain a cease-fire on the present line on the [Egyptian] front. This is the best we can ask for. . . . Therefore we [by *we* does he mean the IDF?] want a cease-fire as things are now . . . something that will let us immediately rebuild the army. (Baron 1992, 149–51)

This passage raises a number of questions. In whose name is the CoGS speaking? It is hard to imagine that his opinion reflects that of most of the generals on the General Staff or the commanders of the arms, fronts, and divisions. By the same token, it is extremely doubtful that IDF combat troops and field officers would greet such a cease-fire favorably since it essentially signified surrender.

The two passages express Elazar's belief that the IDF's capability had been strained to the limit in expelling the Syrians from the Golan Heights and that beyond that the IDF was incapable of achieving a victory on the northern front. However, as he saw it, a cease-fire could be reached on one condition. The original war aim, as he interpreted it, had been gained. However, his conception of the original war aim related only to one of its mechanical aspects—"preventing the enemy from any military gain"—which meant obliterating the Syrian army's ground achievements. The CoGS ignored the other dimensions of the war aims that had not been attained: "the maximum destruction of the enemy's forces and military infrastructure[, which] would provide Israel with significant military advantages in relative power as well as on the armistice lines for many years." He certainly disregarded the army's "oral doctrine," which stated that the IDF had to achieve gains that improved Israel's bargaining position in the political arena (Wald 1987, 97–98).

In the Egyptian arena, Elazar's obsession with the cease-fire kept him from seeing the potential for a decisive victory inherent in the canal crossing, in the destruction of the Egyptian SAM layout, in attacking the Egyptian bridgeheads from the rear, and in posing a threat to the Egyptian regime. All this could be achieved in a classic, multidimensional move via the indirect approach. Later in the war, the CoGS would still be unaware that the Clausewitzian center of gravity in the Egyptian war machine was its antiaircraft layout deployed on the western bank.

The CoGS seems to have pretended not to see that an agreement for an in situ cease-fire, while the IDF was still without any gains on the front, was tantamount to unconditional surrender, with all the toxic ramifications of such a deal. If he was aware of the implications and even advocated the cease-fire, then it testified, more than anything else, to the depth of his despair and unwillingness to fight. As he saw it, a cease-fire would enable the army to be rehabilitated. This was a hollow statement with nothing behind it. Did the army have to be rebuilt? Could it not lick its wounds and replenish its units in the course of the fighting? Furthermore, after a humiliating surrender was imposed, as the CoGS proposed, what would the army have to rehabilitate? And, of course, who would be in charge of carrying out the task?

The Defense Minister's Estimate of the Situation—the Territorial Balance

Throughout the war, Dayan's perception of the military situation was much subtler than was the CoGS's. Contributing to this were Dayan's cognitive skills, courage, breadth of vision, intellectual honesty, and leadership ability, all of which surpassed those of Elazar and most of the other generals.

Dayan always believed that the only way to get the best understanding of the happenings in wartime was to be present where the fighting was. Thus, as CoGS and defense minister, he always preferred to be close to the front rather than in the General Staff compound in Tel Aviv in order to obtain an up-front picture of the events and the mood of the general in the command and the division commanders and their headquarters and then draw his own conclusions. Elazar spent most of the first eight days in discussions in the "Pit" (the heavily protected underground headquarters in the Kirya) and the prime minister's office. Between October 9 and 14, Dayan visited the northern and southern fronts six times, whereas the CoGS made only three visits and his deputy a mere two.

As minister of defense, Dayan naturally focused more on the political and strategic aspects of the fighting and its results than on the operational management at the command and division level, though he had no qualms about expressing his opinion on this area too when military events had (real or apparent) political and public implications.

Dayan was disappointed in the IDF generals and particularly infuriated by the IDF's desultory fighting and heavy casualties between October 6 and 8 and the collapse of the counterattack. Like the CoGS, he too concluded that the IDF might be incapable of brushing off the Egyptians from the bridgeheads. Therefore, the war aims that he approved in April might not be relevant under the present conditions, at least as long as the current generals were in the Southern Command.

Unlike the CoGS after the October 8 debacle, Dayan believed that the IDF would eventually find the way to win the war. But the mounting losses and the absence of a strategic reserve began to worry him. At this stage, he still felt that an all-out effort should be made to knock Syria out of the war. Afterward, the forces from the north could be transferred to the southern front for a concentrated effort. The difficulties that the IDF faced in the north, the sluggishness and lack of energy that characterized its operations, Dayan attributed—mistakenly in our opinion—to the lack of fighting spirit on the part of some of the commanders there. Time and space constraints, as well as reports that reached the government regarding the superpowers' intention to enforce a quick cease-fire, brought him to renounce, for all practical purposes, the war aims that had been in effect until that point. In their place, he formulated the concept that from thenceforth the IDF's role would be to improve the negative "territorial balance" on the Egyptian front. In other words, the IDF had to capture territory and achieve geographic gains that would amend the negative impression of Israel that the Egyptian army had created by crossing the canal, overrunning the Bar-Lev Line, and seizing territory in Sinai. According to Dayan's estimate, the territorial balance could be improved in the following ways:

- Crossing the canal and capturing areas west of the canal, thus counterbalancing the areas held by the Egyptians on the eastern bank.
- Capturing strategic sites with sexy media appeal in the northern part of the canal, such as Port Said and Shadwan Island at the entrance to the Gulf of Suez.
- Achieving dramatic gains in Syria that would serve as a counterweight to the defeat in Sinai. As Dayan told the CoGS: "[The IDF's entry into Damascus] has enormous advantages: it would compensate for the IDF's retreat from the canal." And to General Dan Laner he avowed: "Reach the gates of Damascus and our loss of the canal will be redressed. . . . We can't throw off the Egyptians, but this will be balanced out if we reach the gates of Damascus" (Braun 1992).

Dayan's statements clearly show that an improvement in the territorial balance was designed to serve Israel politically toward the end of the war and afterward, but the real message was directed at the Israeli public and intended to soften its criticism of and rage at Golda Meir's government and at Dayan personally. Dayan intuited that the public outcry would be unprecedented after the war. Improving the territorial balance was only internal politics in the guise of statesmanship or, to paraphrase Clausewitz's rule, the continuation of internal politics by military means.

Like the CoGS, Dayan failed to identify the potential of a decisive victory contained in the canal crossing and in an offensive by two or three armored divisions on the western bank. While in moments of euphoria the CoGS dreamed that the capture of areas west of the canal would spur the Egyptians to sue for a cease-fire, Dayan had no illusions. In general, he viewed the idea of the crossing apathetically and only within the context of rectifying the territorial balance; victory over the Egyptian army he regarded as a pipe dream.

Bar-Lev's and Sharon's Estimate of the Situation

The estimate of the situation of the two dominant figures on the southern front—the front commander, Bar-Lev, and the commander of the 143rd Division, Sharon, were the antithesis of the CoGS's and Dayan's. Bar-Lev and Sharon thought identically on this matter. Except for a few minor details, they both believed in the need for and the possibility of defeating the Egyptian army. This was the only way to force the Egyptians to stop the war. The main goal—the destruction of the enemy forces or the creation of a credible threat—remained unchanged. Rectifying the territorial balance was a by-product. The necessary conditions for a victory were the following:

- Enabling the Israeli army to wage campaigns based primarily on armored maneuvering and tank battles.
- Enabling the IAF to take a vigorous proactive part in the ground fighting.

Bar-Lev presumed that, when these conditions were met, there would be no need to stipulate these or other moves on the Egyptian armored reserve. On the contrary, it was preferable for it to remain on the western bank. This would make it easy for the Israeli armor to destroy it. As stated, the necessary conditions could be created only on the western side of the canal. Bar-Lev preferred to wait for the conditions to ripen for the crossing, but he stressed the need for speed in carrying it out. In his opinion, the conditions were already ripe, and the Southern Command could launch the attack on the night of October 13–14. Sharon thought that every minute of the day was the right time to execute the crossing and transfer the powerful armor forces west.

Bar-Lev's and Sharon's assessments clearly express the qualities of generalship: determination, audacity, aggressiveness, striving to take the initiative and maintain its momentum, wisdom, perspicuity, farsightedness, and a professional approach devoid of posturing.

October 12—the CoGS Demands an in Situ Cease-Fire

Beginning at midnight October 11–12, and lasting for the next twenty-four hours, the IDF and Golda Meir's war cabinet frenetically checked, rechecked, and deliberated on the continuation of the fighting. A penetration was made in the north on the evening of October 11, and from the south Bar-Lev informed the CoGS that conditions were ripe for the canal crossing. In the background, two limiting processes were at play: the two superpowers were seeking ways to call a cease-fire "within hours," and the IAF commander, Benny Peled, was manipulatively warning that the air force was almost out of oxygen and in a day or two would no longer be able to support the ground forces.

Two main questions stood on the agenda:

1. Had the time come to recalibrate the effort on the southern front, and, if so, would it be a canal crossing or something else?
2. If a crossing was decided, should it begin at once or wait until the Egyptian armored divisions had crossed the canal and attacked the IDF defense line (admittedly, a difficult plan), with the offensive on the western bank being launched only after they were decimated?

Discussion of these matters was held in four phases.

The Preliminary Discussion on the Night of October 11–12

At midnight October 11–12, Elazar assembled his closest assistants—Generals Tal, Zeira, Peled, and Gandhi. The CoGS's conclusion expressed the dichotomy that dominated his thinking and vacillation. He realized the need for the crossing as a means of attaining a cease-fire within twenty-four hours from the time of the crossing. After stating this wishful thinking, he expressed his doubt that the Egyptians would accept a cease-fire. But his willingness for a crossing was a case of putting the cart before the horse. "OK," he told the generals, "we crossed. But what do we do next to implement the cease-fire?" The simple and only answer—to fight until the enemy's will to fight was broken—eluded him.

The General Staff Discussion at Noon October 12

After the night discussion, Bar-Lev was called to Tel Aviv at noon the next day for a second talk on the same matter. Dayan, who had been inspecting the northern front, was also requested to join the meeting. The CoGS summed up his thoughts: "The military action [the canal crossing]—whether we do or not—has to be examined in the light of where we have a better chance of obtaining a cease-fire: with this move or without it." Bar-Lev presented the Southern Command's plan: two divisions would cross the canal at Deversoir (the Matzmed stronghold area); their objective would be the Egyptian armor on the western bank. According to Bar-Lev, the primary aim of the attack was to win the war and not necessarily achieving a cease-fire.

The defense minister disagreed with the CoGS's linking the canal crossing to quickly obtaining a cease-fire. On the contrary, in his opinion, the chances that the Egyptians would agree to a cease-fire would be greater if the IDF remained in Sinai and did not capture areas west of the canal. The CoGS agreed with Dayan. However, he realized that the Egyptians would reject a cease-fire as long as their military situation was in good shape, but for some reason he believed that, even if the crossing did not force the Egyptians to accept a cease-fire, it would increase the chances that they would. In other words, the difference between the CoGS's and the defense minister's views was this: If the IDF held areas west of the canal, would it either increase or diminish the likelihood of the Egyptians agreeing to a cease-fire? By itself, this argument today sounds surreal, as it probably did then. But even more extraordinary was the CoGS's demand, as a condition for his part in carrying out the crossing, that the political level validate his assumption as correct. The defense minister again made it clear to the CoGS that he supported the crossing—without even bothering to examine its rationale—if the IDF decided that the crossing would improve the military situation on the front, but not as a means of attaining a cease-fire. "Elazar doesn't have a clue what the cease-fire means," he told Bar-Lev later, which may have implied his opinion of Elazar's comprehension of other matters as well.

The Security Cabinet Meeting during the Afternoon of October 12

Elazar demanded a meeting with his deputies and the security cabinet (Meir, Galili, Allon, and Dayan) to discuss the dispute. After presenting his assessments and expectations, he said: "I think that we've reached the stage where we need the cease-fire. . . . One of the criteria for tomorrow's attack is whether it increases the chances of a cease-fire or not. As I see it, this is practically the only criterion for implementing such an attack." The other officers repeated what they said earlier. Before the ministers had time to state their opinions, the issue was solved by a deus ex machina–like event: the head of the Mossad, Zvi Zamir, reported that he had just received reliable information that the Egyptians would be launching an all-out attack that day or the next with their armored division crossing the canal into Sinai. In light of this surprising development, Israel's forces would wait until the Egyptian army crossed the canal and attacked the IDF's positions. The CoGS and his officers immediately left the meeting—each to his assigned task.

Afternoon, Evening, and Night, October 12

The Israeli ambassador to the United States, Simcha Dinitz, and the Israeli foreign minister, Abba Eban, worked overtime to convince Kissinger to do everything possible to postpone the UN decision on the cease-fire that the Soviet Union was aggressively demanding. Their need to convince Kissinger was like elbowing the way into an open room. Perhaps even more than the Israelis, Kissinger wanted to give the IDF additional time, regardless of Soviet pressure, to clobber the Syrians and the Egyptians. He went to great lengths to spell out to the Israeli war cabinet that he wanted the IDF to continue fighting.

After the military men left the meeting, Dayan spoke to his colleagues in the war cabinet: "Now that we've heard the CoGS say that he wants a cease-fire, how can we justify ordering the fighting to continue? And what if something bad happens to us politically or militarily? Why does Kissinger have to prevent a cease-fire if the CoGS wants it?" In Dayan's opinion, the government had to remove its opposition to the superpowers' effort to end the fighting. Lest he be labeled a defeatist, he made it clear that he did not believe that the Syrians, let alone the Egyptians, would agree to a cease-fire, and without their agreement the United Nations would not make such a decision. Thus, his proposal should be seen as a political ruse and nothing more, a ploy that was designed to help Israel's relations with the United States. Israel must be perceived not as the party asking for a cease-fire but as the party not opposed to one.

From the CoGS's statements on the canal crossing the next day, the prime minister and the war cabinet realized that their message was that a cease-fire was critical and urgent. Also, since no substantial gains could be expected on the two fronts, Meir also came to the conclusion that Israel no longer had to block the diplomatic activity to bring about a cease-fire.

When the report came in of the Egyptian armored division's imminent crossing, the CoGS decided not to inform the cabinet of its full implication and its potential as a springboard for creating the conditions for a decisive IDF gain. Dayan and the generals who were present also kept silent on this point. It may have been difficult to demand of Dayan to relate to the military aspect of the Egyptian crossing. But the generals who were in active service were obliged to make the military significance of the Egyptian move absolutely clear to the war cabinet. By not doing so, the CoGS and his officers failed in their duty to the political level.

Without an authoritative military assessment of the impending Egyptian move, Meir and her war cabinet were left with the bleak impression that the CoGS had created in his presentation of the events. This impression grew even more ominous as ground developments progressed. By evening, the situation on the northern front became more complicated with Iraq's entry into the war. At 1730, Dinitz received a telegram from the government stating its agreement to a cease-fire. The recipients of the telegram (Abba Eban, Dinitz, and Kissinger) were flabbergasted. Kissinger, who wanted the IDF to continue thrashing the Syrians, even demanded an explanation from Meir, as did Dinitz.

The war cabinet reconvened at midnight and decided to accept a separate cease-fire with the Syrians if it was proposed (Bartov 1978, 195). Now all the masks were removed: Meir phoned Dinitz and described the IDF's appalling situation (especially on the northern front), which required an immediate cease-fire. She instructed him to entreat Kissinger to submit a proposal to the UN Security Council that very night. From later accounts by Dinitz, Eban, and Kissinger, we learn that neither Dinitz nor Kissinger had the impression that this was merely a tactical move—as Dayan and other Israeli cognoscenti later claimed. Kissinger explicitly stated that the Israeli government appeared desperate to obtain an in situ cease-fire as quickly as possible. The person who saved the day was Sadat. Kissinger asked the British to bring the proposal for a cease-fire to the Security Council on the morning of October 13. However, before doing so, the British foolishly asked Sadat whether he was interested in a cease-fire. Naturally, he refused flat out. This was how the cease-fire was nipped in the bud. In the north, the IDF had to prepare for continuing the offensive to Damascus—with or without Iraqi involvement—with the aim of bringing the city into artillery range (which would goad the Syrians into demanding a cease-fire). In the south, preparations for the canal crossing finally went into high gear.

Two Comments to Sum Up the Affair

First, in all of these maneuverings, the key question was, Who will sue for a cease-fire? For obvious reasons, this was a cardinal political question for Meir and Dayan, and it also explains the decision to strike Syria first. A swift and successful attack was considered feasible and as possibly leading to two possible cease-fire scenarios: either the Syrians would beseech the Soviets for a cease-fire (and Israel could say, "We're not asking; they're asking"), or the Soviets and Americans would, on their own initiative, force a cease-fire on Israel (and Israel could claim, "We were railroaded into it. What could we do?"). For some reason, no one in Israel thought of a third possibility: the Soviets might intervene militarily on Syria's side.

Second, it is well nigh impossible to determine the exact point of contention between the CoGS and Dayan regarding the crossing's impact on the chances for a cease-fire. The only explanation that comes close is that each wanted the other to be blamed if the crossing ended catastrophically. But even this explanation seems too simplistic and full of holes. Thus, the question remains unanswered. The CoGS may have created all this blather as a way to quickly convene the war cabinet and force it to realize the seriousness (in his opinion) of the IDF's situation and the pressing need to obtain a cease-fire at any price so that he would not have to dirty his hands with an explicit request to save the IDF.

Epilogue

On the night of October 12–13, a large contingent of the Egyptian armored reserve crossed into Sinai. One thousand tanks amassed at the bridgeheads, and, on October 14, the Egyptians attacked the entire length of the front. In a series of tank battles, they were forced back to the bridgeheads without having achieved anything and at the cost of 250 of their tanks. This crescendo ended the IDF's protracted defensive stage on the southern front that had been ongoing since October 9 and may be seen as signaling the onset of the crossing campaign that would decide the war and bring the Egyptians—after Syria was smitten and drowning in its blood—to their knees. Because of October 14's significance and its link between the defensive stage on the southern front and the transition to the offensive, a separate chapter will be devoted to it.

5

The Egyptian Attack, October 14

A time to rend. (Eccles. 3:7)

Deployment

On the evening of October 12, reports started coming in on the Egyptians' intention to dispatch commando units against various targets—irrefutable proof that they were rapidly preparing to attack the canal front and transfer armored reserves into Sinai. By sunrise, October 14, most of the Egyptian 21st Armored Division, the 3rd Tank Brigade/4th Armored Division, artillery, armored infantry and infantry units, antitank forces, services, and fifteen SAM batteries, some of them mobile, had assembled at the bridgeheads in Sinai. Nearly one thousand Egyptian tanks were now amassed on the eastern bank.

Since the previous day, when the first reports arrived of Egyptian preparations, until the attack at daybreak October 14, the General Staff, the Southern Command, and the forces in the field had been taking what they believed to be the necessary steps to meet the onslaught. Notably, the command succeeded in creating a very large reserve force. The command's forces were deployed on the line from north to south in the following manner.

Force Tiger consisted of two mechanized brigades, the 11th and 204th, and tank units that together came to about sixty tanks.

The 162nd Division had two tank brigades and the division headquarters taken off the line and concentrated south of Tassa to reorganize for the canal crossing. The division (less the 500th Brigade) also served as the Southern Command's reserve. The 500th Brigade's sector was held by the 274th Tank ("Tiran") Brigade under the command of Colonel Yoel Gonen. The 500th Brigade deployed at the Talisman–Lateral Road Junction as a reserve to the 274th. The 162nd division's deputy commander, Brigadier General Dov Tamari, was in charge of the sector's forces.

The 143rd Division was deployed on the line with the 421st Brigade on Talisman Road, the 14th Brigade was deployed on Akavish Road at Hamadia, Kishuf, and Hurva and in the area east of Makhshir, and the 600th Brigade was left as the command's reserve on Lateral Road south of Tassa. The 407th Battalion was temporarily attached to the 252nd Division. The 143rd's FCP positioned itself on Akavish Road between Tassa and Yukon. The division had 140 tanks deployed on the line.

The 252nd Division was spread out defensively on the Gidi and Mitla Passes and the approaches to Southern Sinai (an independent command known as the Shlomo District). The 164th Brigade blocked the Gidi Road, the 401st Brigade was deployed defensively on the Gidi and Mitla Roads, the 875th Brigade was located in the eastern egresses of the mountain passes, and the 202nd Battalion/35th Parachute Brigade and a reduced tank company secured the division's southern flank. The infantry and armored infantry forces were spread out on the passes and secured them. The division deployed a total of 145 tanks.

The Southern Command had mustered approximately 750 operable tanks by October 14: 450 on the line and the rest in reserve or reorganizing and replenishing for the crossing.

The Egyptian Attack—Objectives, Forces, and Missions

To this day, the final operational objectives and strategic goals of the Egyptian offensive are unclear. It can be said only that the offensive was the brainchild of President Sadat, who died without ever explaining his rationale. Dealing with this question is an exercise in futility. Nevertheless, the attack may have been designed to chalk up another impressive success before Sadat agreed to a cease-fire and prevent the IDF from crossing the canal in a single tactical move. With this reservation, and in retrospect, the attack seems to have been carried out on the following axes.

In the Egyptian Second Army's northern sector (opposite Force Tiger), the 18th Infantry Division and the 15th Autonomous Tank Brigade were tasked with breaking through to Baluza on the Ma'adim Road.

In the Second Army's central sector (mainly opposite the 143rd Division), the 21st Armored Division would gain control of the Tassa area while attacking the Akavish and Talisman Roads; the 24th Tank Brigade would attack the 274th Brigade on Spontani Road.

The Third Army planned two efforts: the 25th Autonomous Tank Brigade was moved to the Gidi Road; the 3rd Tank Brigade and an infantry battalion would outflank the entrance to the Mitla Pass from the south through Wadi Mabrook, reach Lateral Road, and break through from the south to Wadi Mabrook on Yura Road and south of it, opposite the 202nd Parachute Battalion.

Seven Egyptian tank brigades and infantry, armored infantry, artillery, and antitank units took part in the attack. Some of them lacked their allotted number of tanks so that, when the Egyptians attacked, they had less, perhaps much less, than the upper estimation bound of 750 tanks. In any case, they were up against a well-organized, well-prepared defensive layout of four armored divisions with the force ratio and tactical plan that guaranteed their failure.

"And I will . . . smite Egypt" (Exod. 3:20)

In Tiger's sector, the Egyptian attack commenced at 0630 October 14 with an air attack and artillery barrage. After clashes in the northern area, the Egyptian 15th Brigade attacked at approximately 0845 and was driven off with the loss of about forty tanks (the IDF lost no tanks). At 0800, the Egyptian 24th Tank Brigade and infantry and armored infantry forces attacked the 274th Brigade, which was fanned out on Havraga and Zrakor. The fighting was intense, and, although the 274th came under stiff pressure, it managed to repulse the attack with the assistance of the 500th Brigade. Toward evening, the Egyptians attacked a second time and were again pushed back. Their estimated losses in this sector were thirty-five tanks and other armored combat vehicles. The IDF lost fourteen tanks (including two from the 500th Brigade).

In the 143rd Division's sector, the Egyptian 21st Armored Division launched the attack at 0600 with two brigade-sized efforts from the Missouri area; the Egyptian 14th Tank Brigade attacked the 421st Brigade in the Tziona area, and the Egyptian 1st Armored Brigade moved directly east in the direction of the Israeli 14th Brigade, which was deployed at Hamadia and Kishuf and the surrounding areas. The 421st fought off the attack, knocking out approximately thirty enemy tanks to the loss of one of its own, and the 14th Brigade routed the Egyptian 1st Tank Brigade, destroying about forty tanks to the loss of four of its own. In the afternoon, the Egyptians attacked the 421st Brigade a second time. The 599th Battalion fended off an attack and destroyed around ten Egyptian tanks. Thus, the Egyptian 21st Armored Division lost approximately eighty tanks on October 14. Its morning attack was made in echelon: the Egyptian 14th Tank Brigade attacked after the 1st Brigade had been shattered by Israel's 14th Tank Brigade and retreated, battered, to Missouri.

In the 252nd Division's sector, all the Egyptians' offensive actions ended in failure: the 164th Brigade easily blocked two attacks by the Egyptian 25th Tank Brigade, one beginning in the morning and the other at noon, hitting around twenty T-62s. The Egyptian 3rd Tank Brigade, east of Wadi Mabrook, attacked the 252nd's southern flank in the morning, but, before it reached Lateral Road, it was blocked by the 46th Tank Battalion, armored infantry forces, and elements of the 202nd Infantry Battalion. The 3rd Brigade stumbled into an ambush in Wadi Mabrook at a point beyond the range of the Third Army's antiaircraft defense—and halted when it began to incur casualties. The IAF joined the battle and struck the enemy's armor. Two hours later, the Egyptian 22nd Diminished Tank Brigade with infantry forces attacked in a deep flanking maneuver to the south of the 202nd Battalion. This attack too was driven off by tanks, artillery, and support weapons (medium machineguns, eighty-one-millimeter mortars, and recoilless guns) attached to the battalion. Again, the IAF provided effective assistance in the defensive battle. To sum up: the 252nd knocked out sixty Egyptian tanks and the IAF another twenty.

Estimated Egyptian tank losses on October 14 in all the sectors were 200–250, where the upper bound came ironically from the Egyptian side (see, e.g., Shazly 1980, 248). According to all estimates, the IDF hit approximately 230 Egyptian tanks.

Reflections and Assessments

October 14 can be summarized briefly. A day or two after receiving a valid warning, the Southern Command deployed approximately 750 of its tanks defensively—roughly 60 percent on the line and the rest in reserve. The preparations for meeting the enemy proved effective. Seven Egyptian tank brigades, most of whose tanks were of poorer quality than ours, attacked the IDF's defense layouts. All the attacks failed. The Egyptians made no gains whatsoever, not on the ground, and not in causing the IDF heavy casualties. In return, they lost close to one-quarter of their tank order of battle in Sinai. The day's events were relatively simple, expected, and implicit. Nevertheless, a number of points connected with them should be discussed because of the lessons they hold.

Did the IDF, in its supreme wisdom and foresight, really wait for the Egyptian armored divisions to cross to eastern bank and their defeat before crossing to the western bank? At first glance, the answer is yes. The CoGS stated on various occasions that it was prudent to wait until the Egyptian armored divisions crossed the canal and attacked since, as he understood it, the Egyptian defeat on October 14 signaled the turning point in the war. On the morning of October 15, he elaborated on this point to his staff officers:

> We assumed that this attack would benefit us, that we would probably be able to block it and cause them losses, which would enable us to shift to the offensive. This is what happened yesterday. . . . If I have to sum up [the events of] today: We did the right thing not to launch a crossing two evenings ago and instead wait for the opportunity for them to attack and now go on the offensive. I think that yesterday's results prove themselves, and I am happy that we postponed the crossing.

(The reader will remember that "two evenings ago" the CoGS made it clear to everyone, including the government, how much he desired a cease-fire.)

In effect, Elazar tried to attribute a situation over which he had no control to his shrewd tactics and create the myth that he had ordered the IDF to wait until the Egyptians were kind enough to transfer their armored divisions into Sinai and attack the IDF's defense line and that only after the Egyptians were pulverized had the IDF planned to execute a large-scale counterattack whose main goal was the canal crossing. The myth seems to have been accepted far and wide, though the facts belie its truth:

- No such decision was made by the General Staff or the Southern Command. Orders and instructions to wait for the Egyptian armored crossing were not issued and did not go down the chain of command.
- The two dominant commanders in the Southern Command—Lieutenant General Bar-Lev and Major General Sharon—agreed that an Israeli canal crossing had to be given top priority and that there was no connection between the timing of the crossing and the transfer of Egyptian armored divisions into Sinai. On the contrary, Bar-Lev preferred that the Egyptians remain on the western bank, where they could be decimated most efficiently.
- The main difference between Bar-Lev's and Sharon's approach to the crossing had to do with its timing. Sharon felt that every minute was the right time, while Bar-Lev, as was his wont, thought it better to wait until conditions ripened. From his point of view, these conditions depended mainly on reorganization and strength buildup, certainly not on the movement of Egyptian divisions into Sinai.
- Only on October 12, when Bar-Lev told the CoGS that the conditions were ripe for a crossing, did the CoGS discuss it with his staff (and Bar-Lev), the main question being whether to cross and, if yes, then why. As stated, on his own initiative, the CoGS brought the matter to the war cabinet. And there, for some absurd reason, all that he wanted as a stipulation for his agreement to cross was that the political level approve that the crossing had the potential to increase the likelihood of a cease-fire. Lest any doubt remain, Elazar's dream in these hours was for an immediate cease-fire, whether or not the Egyptian divisions crossed the Suez Canal.
- It will be remembered that, while the government was in the midst of discussing this issue, a report came in that the Egyptians were planning to attack the IDF line on October 13 or 14, the meeting was cut short, and the officers rushed back to their posts to meet the challenge. Even then, the decision to cross was not made. On the contrary, the war cabinet acted as though it had been brainwashed by the CoGS into believing that the IDF's situation was desperate and that a cease-fire had to be obtained in all urgency and at any price.
- Only when it became clear on the morning of October 13 that the cease-

fire, regardless of how degrading and damaging it might be, was nothing more than a fata morgana did the CoGS finally realize that he had no choice but to fight. The contention that, when the intelligence report arrived, a decision was made to delay the crossing until the Egyptians amassed their forces on the eastern bank and attacked is pure hogwash. Could anyone imagine—in all honesty—that, while two Egyptian armored divisions were crossing the canal into Sinai and planning an immediate attack on the IDF defenses, the IDF would carry out its own crossing operation? The CoGS had to wait, willy-nilly, until the enemy's armor forded the canal and commenced the attack.

Was the Egyptian Defeat on October 14 of Major Significance for the Continuation of the War?

The upshot of the Egyptian defeat on October 14 lies mainly on the psychological-morale plain for both the IDF and the Egyptians. Regarding the IDF, the results of the battle unquestionably contributed to exorcising the despondency and defeatism that had enveloped the CoGS since October 8 and injecting a new-found euphoria in him. The men and officers on the front were also reinvigorated by the victory and found their backbone restored. The Egyptian staffs and headquarters—from the General Staff down—may have begun to feel resentment toward the highest political and military levels, and the Egyptian fighting spirit may have been punctured, but in the best case (from the Egyptian point of view) the setback was temporary, if it was a setback at all, and the men and officers of the army continued to prove their mettle. On the professional level, the defeat's impact on the army's ability was negligible. At the most, it was a slight dent in the fender. The following simplified model of the Egyptians' overall strength assesses the effect of the October 14 defeat on the Egyptian war machine:

- The Clausewitzian center of gravity, the central pivot that enabled the Egyptian army to apply its full power, was its SAM layout, which contributed to over half the army's strength.
- The second element that was its infantry antitank layout, which is estimated as one-quarter of its total strength.
- The air force, artillery, combat engineers, and armor, taken together, contributed, according to these simple assumptions, the remaining quarter of the army's strength (with the assumption that all the parts are equal).

Given these assumptions, Egyptian armor contributed approximately 5 percent of the army's total strength. On October 14, the Egyptians lost around 25 percent of their armor at the bridgeheads (or about 18 percent of their total strength on both sides of the canal).

With these simplistic and schematic assumptions, it would not be exaggerating to say that 1 percent of the overall strength of the Egyptian army was taken out of action on October 14. In any imaginable scenario, this is a negligible amount. These sizes can, of course, be changed but only in rather limited areas, and, as primitive as the model may be (it is doubtful that the calculation can be improved unless one adopts an intuition-based method), no acceptable change in its assumptions will essentially alter the conclusion.

Furthermore, on October 8, after Israel's failed counterattack and the related events, the IDF lost the vital area in the 143rd's sector. On the other hand, after the attack failed, the Egyptians forfeited nothing in terms of war gains except for losing manpower and equipment (which amounted to very minimal damage and may have been more of a nuisance than anything else). The Egyptians' failure to accomplish their offensive goals was (apparently) nugatory for them, which may explain why the real reason for the attack defies understanding.

The Fighting of the 252nd Division

The IAF played a considerable, albeit not decisive, role in holding back Egyptian activity in the southern part of the 252nd's sector. This development should have induced the General Staff and the Southern Command to think outside the box and assign priority to the use of IDF armor west of the canal as part of a bona fide joint battle. The IAF commander, Major General Benny Peled, raised this point and repeatedly pressed for a canal crossing. Sharon too was acutely aware of this, and the first thing he did on the western bank was to send the 421st Brigade's commander at the head of a battalion-sized task force to attack the SAM batteries. But this mood seems to have dissipated in the following days, and we will return to it later.

The battle in Wadi Mabrook was important for the lessons that can be derived from it. The 46th Tank Battalion/401st Brigade, with infantry and armored infantry support (and partial IAF assistance), caught the Egyptian 3rd Tank Brigade and its auxiliary forces in a three-sided ambush in the wadi, blocked its advance, routed it, and inflicted extremely heavy casualties on it.

Another surprise is that the Southern Command and the 252nd Division erred in their estimate of the enemy's course of action by assuming that it would avoid a flanking maneuver and direct its main effort frontally toward the Mitla and Gidi Passes. As a result, the division mistakenly deployed its forces and left the southern flank—where the main Egyptian effort fell—held by insufficient and especially ill-suited forces on the wadi's ascent: the 202nd Parachute Battalion with a few tanks and an armored infantry battalion. The Egyptian attacks in this secondary sector were broken by the 46th Tank Battalion, which was summoned into action, the support weapons and a handful of tanks of the parachute battalion, and the air force. Very few of the division's battalions took part in fighting that day. These events strengthen the view that MI cannot be solely responsible for estimating the enemy's likely courses of action. The senior commander has to make an independent assessment and act on it. The time has come to realize that MI is only an opinion: intelligent in the best of circumstances, of dubious accuracy in general, and always deserving of deep suspicion.

Can an Old Dog Be Taught New Tricks?

The Southern Command's orders to the division regarding the defensive were categorical: initiating offensive moves is forbidden; only a strictly defensive battle will be fought from static and defended positions situated at as great a distance as possible from enemy tank and antitank fire. On October 14, immediately after the 14th Brigade routed the Egyptian 21st Brigade, Sharon was keen to exploit the dust and flurry on the ground and capture territory west of Hamadia—Makhshir, Televizia, and other areas—because, as he explained, counterattacks and the exploitation of successes were integral factors in defensive combat. But he was specifically ordered not to make any offensive move and to remain in situ. And, despite his griping and disgruntlement, he obeyed the orders.

The truth is, in this situation, there was little justification for a counterattack on Makhshir, Televizia, and other areas. From the IDF's point of view, every battle was superfluous, and, when the IDF engaged the enemy, it was for lack of another option. The Southern Command's explicit and categorical orders led to a change to tolerable Israeli losses during the Egyptian attack—twenty to twenty-five tanks—and, unlike for the Egyptians, for the Israelis every tank was of supreme importance. Had the 143rd incurred heavy casualties in aggressively initiated attempts, the crossing would have been delayed for an indefinite period. Strange to say, Sharon seems to have been unaware of this since he would not have knowingly taken even the slightest risk if it meant delaying the crossing or increasing the uncertainty of its success.

6

The Crossing Battle, Part 1

Preliminaries

Hearken unto me, ye stouthearted. (Isa. 46:12)

Prologue

Operation Stouthearted Men was forced on Israel just as the hand that, owing to the CoGS's pressure, the IDF extended in surrender (a cease-fire in situ) was rejected by Egyptian president Sadat with a blend of arrogance and folly. As the saying goes, "He who Jupiter wishes to destroy, he first makes mad." Sadat's response left Israel with no choice but to continue fighting. It also illustrates the degree of error of those who saw an immediate cease-fire in situ as the quintessence of Israel's security and how propitious Sadat's grace was that saved us from ourselves.

The defense minister, the CoGS, and the commanding general of the Southern Command envisioned (or at least expressed) the goal of the operation as decisively defeating the Egyptian army, knocking Egypt out of the war, and ending the war. On the basis of military and political considerations, Israel's strategists concluded that the IDF could best achieve this by crossing the Suez Canal and waging decisive battles. The campaign to attain this objective, Operation Stouthearted Men (also known as Operation Crossing and Operation Crossing Campaign), began on October 15 and lasted until the implementation of a cease-fire ten days later.

The first battle was the crossing battle. Large, protracted, dramatic, unique, and significant, it had all the features of a classic battle: a unity of time, place, and action and simplicity, inasmuch it was only one phase of a complex military operation, the defeat of the Egyptian army. The simple, powerful *crossing battle* suits it best.

Despite the many early failures in the war, the IDF proved its absolute superiority over the Egyptian army in the crossing battle. Perhaps even more than its encirclement of the Third Army and the implied threat to the Second Army, the crossing battle was Sadat's wake-up call letting him know that under no circumstances would he ever have the slightest chance of defeating the IDF; in other words, the Egyptian army's fate was to be defeated by the IDF always. Over forty years have passed since the events described in this book, and this awareness still rings true among the Egyptian leadership.

The IDF was not the first army to cross the Suez Canal in the war. The Egyptians had successfully done so nine days earlier. But, in order to accomplish this, they spent years in political and military planning, invested enormous resources in rearmament and replenishment, and, above all, carried out endless drills. The IDF, on the other hand, had only two or three days to shift from the babbling stage to the beginning of the battle, a triumph that any army would be proud of, from the Roman legions that forded the wide rivers of Europe to the massive tank formations that crossed the same bodies of water in World War II two thousand years later.

The burden of the crossing battle fell on the 143rd Division, whose strength had been doubled by the arrival of reinforcements. The 162nd Division remained in the background, playing an active role that was at times important and at others of disputed significance.

The battle commenced on the evening of October 15 with the division's movement to contact and ended on the night of October 18–19 with the onset of the massive flow of Israeli armor west on the bridge that the 143rd had established.

The crossing battle had an electrifying effect on the IDF troops and most of the field commanders in the Southern Command. It was, and still is, the largest and most complex decisive battle in the IDF's history. Nearly twenty tank battalions fought in different stages of the battle: three paratrooper brigades, two reinforced artillery groups, bridging forces, a reinforced combat engineer brigade group, a vast logistic formation, and two mobile antiaircraft artillery battalions. The 143rd and 162nd Divisions participated in the battle, but the 143rd bore the brunt of the fighting. It was a land battle in which IDF armor fought without air support and, uncharacteristically, at night. Only one man could have successfully commanded such an enterprise and led it confidently to victory. Miraculously, despite all the obstacles and pitfalls, fate wedded the man with the battle.

The books on the crossing battle alone can fill the shelves of a medium-sized library. It has been the subject of countless investigations, studies, and symposiums, hundreds of articles have been written about it, a few films have even been made, and the list goes on. It is not our intention to repeat what has already been described and analyzed in detail from every angle and agenda. This chapter and the following three deal with various processes and events that are still relevant at the highest level of generalship. As background to the discussion, we explain in depth the assumptions, orders, briefings, and preparations prior to the battle as well as those events that influenced the battle's direction, pace, intensity, and results.

The Political Directive

The prime minister and the defense minister called a government meeting for 2100 on October 14 to discuss and approve the crossing operation. Three hours earlier, in a talk with newspaper editors, Dayan had said: "I know how [the war] will end in victory. . . . A major decisive battle will be fought in Egypt" (Baron 1992, 180).

The defense minister and the CoGS presented their estimates and recommendations for the continuation of the fighting in the south. This time, the CoGS's advice was befitting an IDF commander. Its two main points were as follows:

- A recommendation to cross the canal in a move "unrelated to any other aspects." That is, the crossing was no longer linked to its impact on the likelihood of a cease-fire, as Elazar had insisted only two days earlier.
- A conviction that this was the only operation move "that has the possibility of reaching a decisive battle." That is, the objective is nothing less than Egypt's defeat.

The defense minister, who heretofore had argued against the crossing, followed suit and stated: "[Given] the best assessments of all those who studied the matter, including General Tal, the crossing had the likelihood of succeeding and ending the war in victory." The CoGS and the defense minister now phrased their views with utmost caution (e.g., "the likelihood"), but the message was clear: the IDF would open an offensive in the south that was designed to win the war. After the government discussion, Minister without Portfolio Israel Galili, the "master of semantics," produced the following statement: "[The government] approves an option for the IDF to cross the canal in the coming days with the aim of destroying the Egyptian army's main force." The government decision also noted "the prime minister's announcement that the operation is designed for a military goal."

Excluding such administrative matters as the delegation of authority to the prime minister and the defense minister and subjects for further discussion, the decision dealt with two main issues: an approval (in effect, a directive for the IDF to act in a specific way in order to achieve a specific goal, i.e., cross the Suez Canal and destroy the Egyptian army) and a quasi-definition of the operation that it was only a military matter. A close examination reveals the decision to be a jumble of message-challenged words. In phrasing it, the government sinned twice against its responsibility:

- The sin of failing to define its intentions precisely. That is, it failed to state the ultimate political goal that the Egyptian army's destruction was supposed to produce. The circumscriptive wording "the operation is designed for a military goal" was no doubt intended to cover up the missing political definition (and thus silence the ministers who started asking irksome questions, such as the operation's real goal).

- The sin of superfluous definition. That is, "destroying the main strength of the Egyptian army" is not the final political goal but a method, one of many that the army had to weigh for obtaining the political metagoal that the government had avoided defining.

The conclusion that can be derived from these omissions is that the government had no idea what it wanted to achieve for the tremendous price in blood that it had just approved.

Orders and Perceptions at the General Staff Level

Following the government's decision, the General Staff Operations Branch issued the following order to the IDF on the Egyptian front on the morning of October 15: "Shift to the offensive, cross the canal, and destroy the Egyptian army on both sides of the canal. The IDF will continue to attack and destroy the Syrian army. 'H' hour and 'D' day are set for 1900, October 15. This order countermands the Southern Command's previous orders."

To its credit, the order was terse. Its shortcoming was that it assigned multiple tasks to both fronts—some of them possible, others impossible. And it illustrates the IDF's tendency in this period to bog itself down in unachievable tasks (e.g., "denying the enemy any gain"). Furthermore, to the order's detriment (though its authors are not to be blamed), it made no mention of the ultimate strategic objective. Could the cliché "destroying the army [this one and that one]" really be taken as a national strategic goal?

Further evidence of the semantically foggy blubbering at the highest military level can be seen in the CoGS's address to his officers on the morning of October 15. The purpose of the IDF's offensive in the south, Elazar stated, was "to be a decisive move that finally alters the deployment, the relative strength, and our situation in Sinai": "The enemy's collapse may be a welcome by-product, to a certain [degree], of the Egyptian army's disintegration" (Ezov 2011, 1).

The Southern Command—the Order for Operation Stouthearted Men

While the government discussed the crossing operation, the Southern Command's orders group met at Um Hashiba at 2240 October 14. Present were all the senior commanders, first and foremost Bar-Lev, Gonen, and the division commanders. The following are the main points.

The Intention

The Southern Command was to cross the Suez Canal at Deversoir with two divisions and gain control of the area between the Suez Canal in the east, the freshwater canal in the north up to Jebel Iweibid in the west, and Jebel Ataka in the south; it was then to destroy the enemy forces and capture the city of Suez. The Southern Command's forces were to be on standby to pursue the breakthrough west to Cairo, block any further Egyptian advance into Sinai, and engineer the surrender and destruction of the Egyptian forces east of the canal.

The Method

General

The Southern Command was to establish a bridgehead at Matzmed on both sides of the canal, assemble at least two bridges, cross the canal with two armored divisions while two divisions hold the eastern bank, secure the bridgehead area with armor, infantry, antiaircraft, combat engineer forces, and the 88th ("White Bear") Amphibious Reconnaissance Battalion, destroy the enemy in the sector, and remain on standby to proceed west. The Southern Command's forces were to exert pressure on the enemy and block all attempts to advance. The Southern Command was to raid the antiaircraft missile bases north of the freshwater canal.

Stages and Timetable (D-Day, October 15, and H-Hour, 1700)

By H-hour plus ten (within ten hours!), the bridgehead was to be captured and secured, construction of the bridges was to be completed, and the Southern Command forces were to have crossed the canal and secured the passages on the freshwater canal while destroying the enemy's forces and advancing west and south.

By H-hour plus twenty-four, the enemy's forces in the combat sector were to have been destroyed.

By H-hour plus forty-eight, the city of Suez was to have been captured, additional bridges captured, and the two banks cleared of the enemy. Forces were to be on standby for movement west.

Forces and Missions (Summary)

The 252nd Division and Force Tiger were to hold their sectors (east of the canal) with Force Tiger securing the 162nd's sector.

The 143rd Division—consisting of three tank brigades (the 14th, the 421st, and the 600th), the 247th Paratrooper Brigade, the 605th and the 630th Bridging Battalions, and the 643rd "Crocodile" (the IDF code name for the Gillois amphibious tank carrier) Battalion, two artillery groups (the organic 214th and the 215th/162nd Division), two mobile antiaircraft battalions (the 206th and the 207th), the 424th ("Shaked") Reconnaissance Battalion, a two-company paratrooper force ("Force Shmulik"), the 582nd Reconnaissance/Antitank Battalion/317th Paratrooper Brigade, and the White Bear Amphibious Reconnaissance Battalion—was assigned the following:

- Capture the Amir and Missouri localities, hold to the west and north, and secure the bridgehead.
- Capture and secure the bridgehead on both sides of the canal.
- Establish at least two bridges, and bring the Southern Command's forces westward across the canal on them.
- Capture Jebel Iweibid or the city of Suez.

The 162nd Division (less the 500th Brigade) was to remain on Lateral Road without a mission during the breakthrough to the bridgehead in order to conserve its forces for the next stages in the operation. The division was to cross on command and move northwest according to its position in the order of the crossing (first or second).

The 500th Brigade was to deploy in the Lateral Road area as the Southern Command's reserve.

Comments on the Operations Order

The order did not state which division would cross first. It determined only the directions of the breakthrough of the first and second divisions to cross (northwest and southwest, respectively). The Southern Command's graphic battle overlay clearly showed that the 143rd would cross and turn northwest and that the 162nd would cross and turn southwest. One could conclude that it had been decided at this stage that the 143rd would cross first, but, according to a later decision (that the 162nd would cross first), one could also conclude—in retrospect—that there was no significant connection between the order and the graphic overlay.

The order itself raises serious questions. One could say that, as an instruction to the command's formations, it lost its value immediately on being issued, collapsing under the weight of its technical flaws:

- The section on "intention" is rife with impressive verbs: *will cross, will gain control of, will destroy, will be ready to, will prevent,* and so forth. These are merely sentence fragments that have nothing whatsoever to do with intention. A hint of the true intention of the operation lies at the end of this verbal outpour: "The Southern Command . . . will bring about the surrender of the Egyptian forces east of the canal." The defense minister and CoGS defined the goal of the Southern Command's crossing operation as the "defeat of the Egyptian army," that is, the "destruction of the Egyptian army on both sides of the canal." This and only this definition had to constitute the intention section of the order. And, although this definition still suffered from overgeneralization, it was the only one that bound the Southern Command. The rest of this verbosity belongs to the section on the "method." The last paragraph in the "intention" section—"will lead to the surrender and destruction of the Egyptian forces east of the canal"—can be interpreted as a call to kill the surrendering enemy, which, of course, was not the meaning. This was simply clumsy phraseology.
- The order's "method—general" section was supposed to express the selected course of action. This section, however, is only a summary of the analytic process whose aim was to formulate the tactics and maneuvers that were to guide the operation and the main and secondary efforts. It is a kind of laundry list of assignments, some important and others superfluous or trivial, devoid of a common denominator. It leaves the recipient baffled as to what the Southern Command, as a goal-oriented military system, wanted to do and how it intended to do it.

It is also surprising that the General Staff order instructed the Southern Command to "raid" the Egyptian SAM batteries instead of insisting on their destruction as a top priority; no less surprising is this item's absence from the list of tasks that the Southern Command gave to the divisions. These omissions point to the General Staff's and the Southern Command's disregard, if not lack of understanding, of the pivotal importance of Egypt's antiaircraft layout to the overall war effort. Destroying the Egyptian SAM system was tantamount to overpowering the Egyptian army in the fastest and most economical way possible. It should also be noted that the Southern Command instructed the 143rd to wage the crossing battle at night.

As the implementation of a military operation approaches, the conceptualization stage should be characterized by continuous information gathering, examination, skepticism, deliberation, brainstorming, and analysis. Just as a butterfly is completely different from the pupa from which it emerges, so must an operational order be different from the intellectual processes that created it. The order cannot contain unresolved issues or suggest options or create obfuscation and ambiguity. The Stouthearted Men order addressed only one section of the campaign, albeit an important one—the crossing battle. Other than that, it contained no information or clear instructions for its recipients, only silence, stuttering, and options. It will be noted that the order's inherent shortcomings were far more serious than its technical flaws and doomed it even before it had time to emerge from its chrysalis (see below).

The godsend was that, despite the semantic deficiencies of the order, most of the commanders in the Southern Command realized the order's true intention, the main points of the campaign plan, and what they had to do to implement them. This understanding, however, was initially only partial, and, until it was complete, the forces that crossed the canal wasted several difficult days of fighting on half-baked moves (see below).

Briefings and Clarifications in the Southern Command

In a briefing at Tassa before noon October 15, Gonen outlined the main idea of the campaign and the division's missions, and the division commanders presented their plans. Gonen emphasized the following:

- The crossing would be made at only one bridgehead (Matzmed).
- The 143rd Division would break through and open a corridor at least four kilometers wide that included Akavish and Tirtur Roads.
- The 143rd would cross first, expand the bridgehead, secure it in a northwest direction so that artillery fire could target the SAM bases north of the freshwater canal, and thus enable the IAF to support the ground forces. The 162nd Division would follow the 143rd, turn south, and capture the Jebel Ataka area, the Gulf of Suez (including the city of Suez), and Adabiya salient. At this point, the forces would be ready to advance toward Cairo or the oil fields.

The operational concept was to encircle the Egyptian Third Army. IDF armor on the western bank would attack it from the north and west and smash it like a hammer, while the 252nd Division in Sinai served as the anvil. Implicit in this plan was the awareness (perhaps hope) that the Third Army's destruction would force the Second Army to withdraw across the canal immediately, incurring heavy losses, if not suffering total annihilation. This would be a classic indirect approach to bringing about the Egyptian army's collapse and Egypt's complete surrender. But the sine qua non of its realization was a tenacious blitzkrieg, and this style of fighting requires air superiority in the fighting zone, experienced, skilled, intrepid, but not impulsive formation commanders, and the presence at the front of commanders in at all levels, including front commanders. Unfortunately, this type of generalship was scarce on the southern front. The front commander at Um Hashiba directed the two divisions on the western bank, and the attempts to gain air superiority were made offhandedly rather than being assigned top priority. The intellectual process behind the order to capture the city of Suez is unclear.

Risk Factors in the Southern Command's Order and Briefing

Medical scholars can for any person identify a specific bundle of risk factors inherent in his constitution that, if they materialize, are liable to induce various disorders and even cause death. Inherent in the Stouthearted Men order and its briefings were several risk factors, the most serious being the following.

The Road System

The transportation networks in the theaters of operation on Israel's desert and mountainous borders are a strategic weapon always in critically short supply and with a low flow rate. Therefore, their use must be planned down to the minutest detail, and their control must be in the hands of the supreme commander in the theater. The Stouthearted Men order not only failed to deal with the Southern Command's control of this strategic resource; it ignored it and completely abandoned it.

How the front commander and his officers failed to recognize the disastrous implications of this omission defies understanding. The only explanation is that most of them were professionally deficient and conceptually challenged as a result of their inexperience in commanding large armor formations in combat where the roads were choked with armored combat and other vehicles. This oversight threatened to compromise the entire operation and even foil the Southern Command's plan to wage a lightning armored war to destroy the Egyptian army. By abandoning the roads in the immediate rear and close to the fighting theater to whomever happened by, the Southern Command squandered one of its most critical resources, perhaps the most critical resource, for carrying out the operation—prioritizing traffic.

Optimism in Planning

The late Paul Fussell observed: "Optimism is an attitude inappropriate to such creatures as human beings" (Fussell 1975). This may or may not be true, but the attitude is inappropriate for the military planner, who cannot assume unqualified optimism as a starting point and expect it to come to full realization on the battlefield. The Stouthearted Men order is rife with unbridled optimism, as expressed in the failure of the timetable to take into account the risk factors inherent in both the plan and the operational situation. The inevitable result of this approach was a meaningless plan that was more like a draft for a simplistic tactical exercise without troops than a solid, realistic, effectual operational plan. The unreserved optimism reached its apogee in the planner's failure to correctly evaluate the time and space factors and the enormous impact that friction in battle has on these assessments. The necessary conditions to a realistic approach to these matters are recent experience in a senior command position in combat, frequent exercises of the senior command levels in peacetime, professionalism, and honesty. A healthy sense of skepticism is an asset. Emphasizing the skeptical approach in planning is not a sign of defeatism; it is an attempt to estimate the worst possible developments that could sabotage the plan and to offset their realization by preparing for them through planning and resource allocation.

Relying on Unfamiliar and Unreliable Crossing Equipment

The Untested Roller Bridge

Much of the excessive optimism in the Stouthearted Men plan seems to lie with the knowledge- and technically challenged commanders who believed that the IDF had the equipment to rapidly bridge the canal while simultaneously advancing and engaging the enemy. The magic bullet was the roller bridge, the brainchild of Brigadier General David Laskov and Major General Israel Tal. We will not elaborate on the technical specifications and operational advantages and disadvantages of the roller bridge or the unique history of its gestation, birth, and development. We will only note a few facts that rendered it a risk factor of the first order:

- The bridge weighed four hundred tons, was almost two hundred meters long, and had a turning radius that was practically zero. To tow it and secure it, a specially trained tank battalion and several bulldozer tanks were needed as well other heavy engineering equipment, ordnance and maintenance elements, close antiaircraft support, and air cover. Its rigidity in swinging or turning meant that its travel path had to be a straight line almost from the point of departure to the launching, and the route that it rolled on had to be flat and free of obstacles.

- Unfortunately, Operation Stouthearted Men put the bridge to the ultimate test—its contribution to the battlefield—before it was fully tested according to the IDF's R&D procedures. In effect, the IDF began procuring this type of bridge even before its development was complete and its advantages and limitations discovered.
- All the controlled presentations and partial trials that the bridge underwent had taught that it had to be dismantled into four fifty-meter sections before it could traverse a great distance. Only when the sections came within, at most, four kilometers of the waterline would there be sufficient room to reassemble it with quickly applied joints and tow it as a single unit to its destination. The problem was that the war broke out before the joints were ready, which meant that the bridge was assembled as a single, two-hundred-meter-long unit that had to be towed the entire distance to the launching point.
- The bridge was assembled in the Yukon compound on Akavish Road about twenty kilometers as the crow flies from the canal. It was supposed to be towed first on Akavish and then on Tirtur, which had been specially prepared to receive it. It could not be towed the entire length of Akavish Road because it was unable to negotiate the turns; therefore, its designated launching spot on the canal north of the Great Bitter Lake was out of reach. Moreover, closer to the canal, Tirtur Road crossed marshlands that the tanks and heavy mechanical equipment could not traverse. Before the war, the Southern Command's chief engineering officer, Lieutenant Colonel Aharon Teneh, had reconnoitered the route and marked a path through it. But he alone was privy to this information. During previous battles, sections of the road had been held by the Egyptians, and the fate of Teneh's markers was unknown.
- The units of the 7th Armored Brigade that had practiced towing the roller bridge were sent to the Golan Heights at the outbreak of war with the rest of the brigade and ordered to remain there. The Southern Command had to provide other tank units a crash course in roller bridge towing.

The Unifloat Rafts

The Unifloat rafts' long service in the IDF and the combat engineers' and armored forces' familiarity with them guaranteed them as a reliable means of crossing the canal. Their mobility on the back of special wagons enhanced their maneuverability and speed and economy in towing them. Nevertheless, their serious drawbacks had not been ironed out by the time the war erupted. The first problem was their monstrous size: each raft was seventeen meters long and eleven meters wide. This was a critical limitation in sandy terrain and swampy areas where the few narrow roads were jammed with thousands of other vehicles. The Stouthearted Men plan had failed to assign top priority to the rafts' passage through dozens of kilometers from Yukon and Romani to the launch site on the canal. This omission could have torpedoed the timetables and put the operation in question.

After the rafts entered the water, hours were needed to assemble them into a bridge. This was a known limitation. The IDF had begun developing quickly applied joints that would enable a raft bridge to be constructed in a matter of minutes. For sundry reasons, the primary one being, as usual, the absence of a sense of urgency combined with a surfeit of military bureaucracy, the replenishment of the joints had not even begun when the war came. Construction of the Unifloat raft bridge was a primitive, strenuous, time-consuming, bloody ordeal.

The Crocodiles

Unlike the roller bridges and the Unifloat rafts, the French-made "Crocodile" (Gillois amphibious tank carriers) crossing apparatus had many of the features of a modern assault-crossing vehicle: independent movement, the ability to travel long distances, traversability in difficult terrain, rapid launching, performance in multiple configurations, and convertibility into a bridge. Biased parties claimed that the Crocodile's main drawback was its vulnerability to artillery fire, but this was largely a false allegation that was overly emphasized as part of the bureaucratic infighting that accompanied the whole process of developing and building a crossing layout and that also served as an excuse, generally retrospectively, for rejecting the Crocodile's use when a pressing operational need arose for it during the crossing battle. The Crocodile raft was indeed vulnerable to artillery fire, but the risk could be minimized by exploiting its speed and maneuverability and shuttling it between different embarkation and disembarkation areas. During the first two days, the Crocodiles were hit soon after entering the water mainly because of their use at fixed loading-unloading points on the canal. This played into the hands of the Egyptian forward artillery observers, who were swarming in the area, and left the rafts easy prey.

In this sense, the Crocodiles were not a risk factor. On the contrary, the risk factor linked to them was related to their shortage. At the time of their acquisition, thirty-two were envisioned by cannibalizing sixty vehicles that had been purchased in a scrap yard in Europe. As the idea of a roller bridge gained traction and the head of the General Staff Operations Branch became the backer, financier, partner, and technical director of its development, the ax fell on the Crocodile-replenishment plan. A lot of the money was diverted to the accelerated development and replenishment of the roller bridge. In the end, less than twenty Crocodiles were built and transferred to the combat engineers, a number that enabled a few rafts to be constructed but not enough for a bridge to span the Suez Canal. Their vulnerability, too, precluded a protracted floating effort.

Ego and Personal Factors

The personal and political motives of the senior commanders in the General Staff and on the southern front and their muddled relationships with their fellow officers were risk factors of the first degree, even as they had been kept in the background in the Stouthearted Men order and the Southern Command briefing. Despite the expectation that the operation would be launched with all units joined in the common cause, personal animosity and conflicting political affiliations among the senior officers were so acute that the smallest spark could have set off an explosion. Some of Sharon's bitter rivals were champing at the bit even before the battles started, as the following story illustrates.

On the eve of the crossing (October 15), a number of senior officers, including Elazar, Dayan, and Yigal Allon (a former general and a minister in Golda Meir's government), arrived at the southern front forward headquarters at Um Hashiba. At 1812, just as the battle was about to commence and the 143rd's forces were moving to the attack and crossing objectives, Dayan spoke with Sharon over the phone. The defense minister's aide-de-camp reported: "When Dayan laid the receiver down, the CoGS told him of his thorny relationship with General Sharon, such as the latter's habit of gathering journalists around him and refusing to obey orders. Elazar complained to the defense minister and Allon. . . . Dayan said nothing, but later he told me that it pained him to hear this talk at the start of the battle and he was annoyed that journalists and newspaper editors had been invited to the command's FCP to hear senior officers disparage Sharon" (Baron 1992, 185).

The 143rd Division—Plans, Orders, Preparations

The Missions

The Stouthearted Men order tasked the 143rd with the following missions:

- Break through to the crossing area via the Missouri and Amir localities and clean out the enemy from Akavish and Tirtur Roads.

- Secure a bridgehead on the western side of the canal and secure it to the north and west.
- Raid and shell the SAM bases.
- Erect bridges on the Suez Canal for the two divisions to cross on.
- Open and secure at least a four-kilometer-wide corridor to the bridgehead.

Derivative Tasks

Additional tasks were derived from these missions. At first glance, they appear logistic, but they were actually of critical significance to the operation. They included:

- Collecting and concentrating crossing and bridging equipment: half-tracks and rubber boats for the 247th Paratrooper Brigade, Unifloat rafts of the 630th Bridging Battalion from Refidim and the 605th Bridging Battalion from Baluza, and the 634th Crocodile Battalion from Refidim.
- Training tank units in towing the roller bridge.
- Controlling and supervising traffic on Akavish Road.
- Securing the division's rear and cleaning out Egyptian commandos and forward artillery observers.

The Division's Strength

In preparation for the crossing battle, the 143rd Division was reinforced with the following formations and units:

- The reduced 247th Paratrooper Brigade under the command of Colonel Danny Matt consisted of two paratrooper battalions (the 565th commanded by Lieutenant Colonel Dan Ziv and the 416th under the command of Lieutenant Colonel Zviki Nur), a third battalion, the 564th, under the command of Lieutenant Colonel Yossi Yaffe, was still attached to Force Tiger, and another infantry company had been sent to the 217th Tank Brigade in Adan's division.
- The 582nd Reconnaissance/Antitank Battalion (from the 317th Reserve Paratrooper Brigade), under the command of Major Natan Shunari, reached Tassa on the evening of October 15.
- The White Bear Amphibious Reconnaissance Battalion, under the command of Major Yosef Yudovitch, joined the division on October 15.

- The Shaked Reconnaissance Battalion, commanded by Lieutenant Colonel Moshe Spector, consisted of three infantry companies, one of which was made up of officer cadets.
- Force Shmulik was a (reduced) battalion-size force of paratrooper companies commanded by Major Shmuel Arad.
- Two medium battalions of the 215th Artillery Group/162nd Division were under the command of Lieutenant Colonel Haim Granit.
- A General Staff battalion of 240-millimeter rocket launchers was under the command of Lieutenant Colonel Uriel Kedar.
- Two mobile antiaircraft battalion, the 107th and the 208th, were under the command of Major Nisan Elad.
- Finally, there were two 175-millimeter ("Long Tom") battalions, one from the General Staff and the other from the Southern Command.

In the first stage of the crossing battle, the division had twelve artillery battalions composed of different-sized guns. The crossing equipment was as follows:

- There were twenty-four Unifloat rafts, each raft divided into nine sections, with half of the rafts at Refidim and the other half at Romani. The division went to battle with only fifteen rafts. The Unifloat rafts were organized in two bridging battalions, the 605th, under the command of Lieutenant Colonel Moshe Edelstein, and the 630th, under the command of Lieutenant Colonel Avi Zohar. The sections of the 605th's rafts were stored in Romani, and the 630th's at Refidim. Twelve rafts were assembled in each of the concentrations and loaded onto specially designed trailers.
- When the war broke out, the 634th Bridging Battalion, under the command of Lieutenant Colonel Yigal Yaniv, brought sixteen Crocodiles from their base at the Sea of Galilee to staging areas west of Refidim.
- Parts of one of the roller bridges were stored in the northern sector and parts of the second in the Yukon compound on Akavish Road southwest of Tassa. The bridges were assembled as the crossing time approached. According to the Stouthearted Men order, the bridge at Yukon would span the canal a little north of Matzmed. On October 13, the bridge was completed and ready for use.
- Approximately sixty of the 630th Bridging Battalion's rubber boats were available to the 247th Brigade at noon October 15. The boats were concentrated at Akavish 64, about two kilometers east of Yukon.

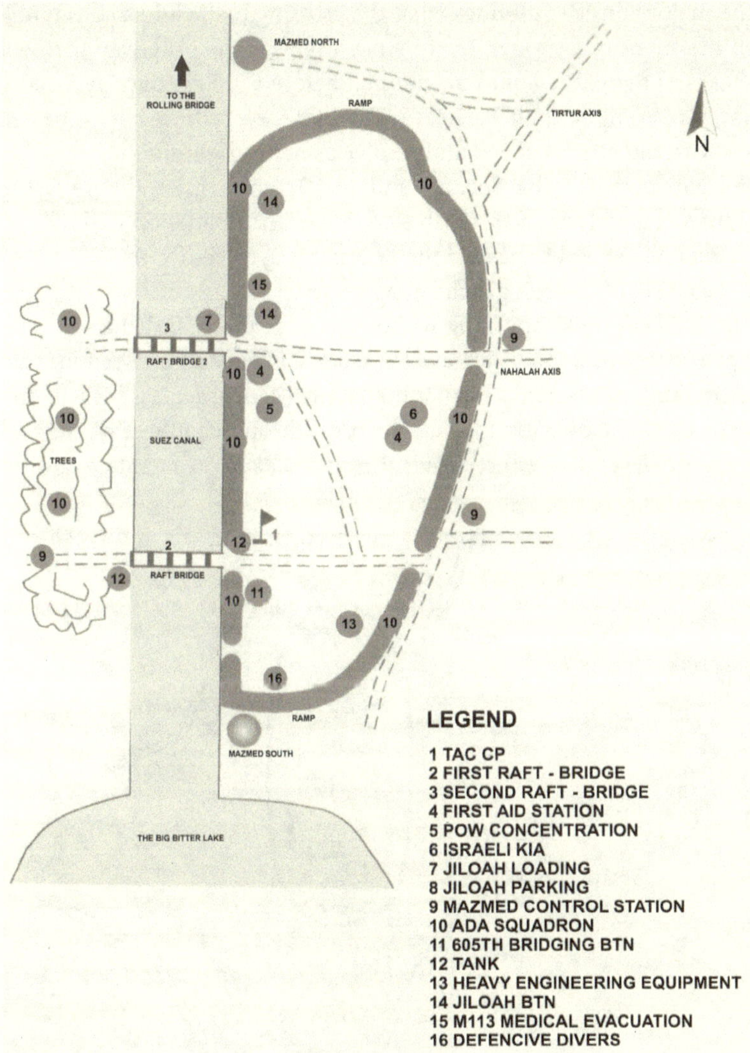

Map of Matzmed Yard. Based on a sketch by Jacob Even.

The Division's Plan

Considerations and Guidelines

In the holding stage, a few days before the Southern Command issued its order, the division had already begun to prepare for the crossing battle. Its plan was based on the following objectives and assumptions:

- The major consideration was that the crossing battle had to be completed on the night of October 15–16 since this was the only way the decisive phases of the battle could be attained before the Egyptians realized what was happening in their backyard. Therefore, everything had to be carried out with the utmost speed and resolve as befit a lightning war.
- The gap between the Second and the Third Armies in the Lakekan-Matzmed area (which the 87th Reconnaissance Battalion had discovered on October 9) had to be exploited for moving forces for the breakthrough and capture of the bridgehead at Matzmed.
- The division must not bang its head against the wall. It had to take the indirect approach and increase the chance of success and reduce the loss of life and equipment. The Stouthearted Men order assisted in this by instructing the division to wage the breakthrough battle at night.
- A major deception effort would be undertaken to facilitate the break-

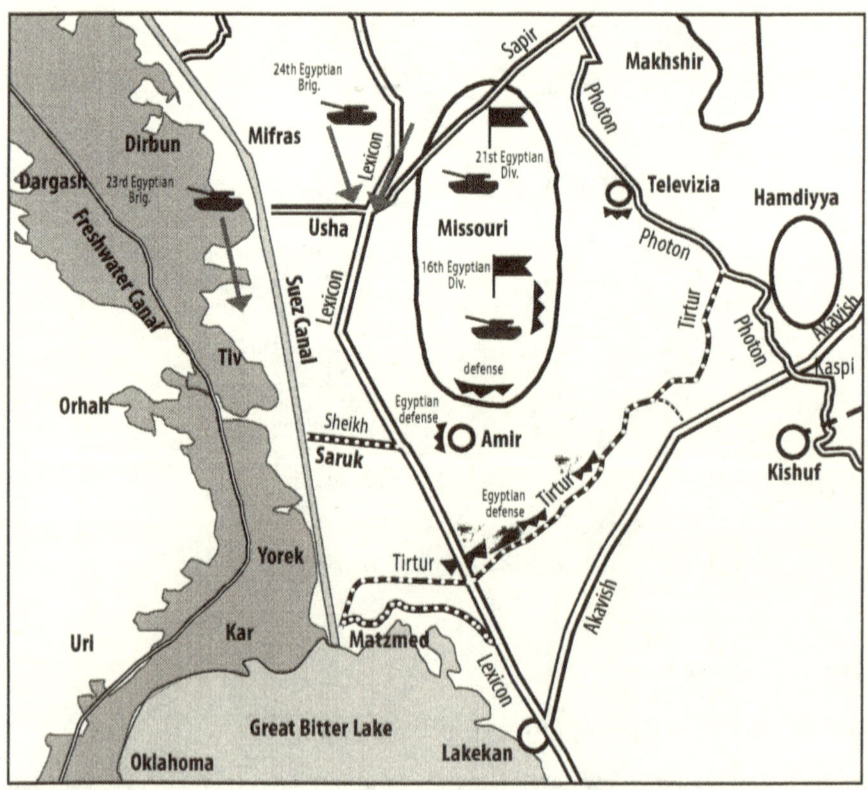

Egyptian positions in the crossing military theater on the night of October 15–16. Courtesy of Amiram Ezov.

through and enable the brigade to capture the bridgehead by sneaking into the water.

- A large number of forces would be allocated to towing and escorting the bridging equipment to the water; all the crossing gear would be put on standby in case of mishaps in the transportation of the main bridging equipment.
- Small armored forces had to cross the canal quickly in order to protect the bridgehead, capture the key passages on the freshwater canal, and raid the SAM bases.
- Crucial intelligence discovered that the Lexicon-Tirtur Junction was free of Egyptians and could be relied on, though this eventually proved wrong.

The Plan

The plan called for the division to execute four almost simultaneous missions beginning on the evening of October 15:

- The 600th Brigade (less the 407th Battalion), under the command of Tuvia Raviv, would leave a detachment at the Hamadia compound to secure it and launch a diversionary attack, from east to west, with the rest of its force in the Televizia-Missouri sector at 1700.
- Reshef's 14th Brigade would be reinforced with the 407th Tank Battalion/600th Brigade, under the command of Yishiyahu Beitel, and the above-mentioned infantry units (mostly half-tracks). At 1600, the brigade would cross from Yukon to Caspi 56 (about eight kilometers south of the Akavish-Caspi Junction) and, at nightfall (1800), move west to Lexicon 263 (about two kilometers south of the Lakekan stronghold). From there, it would head north to Lexicon Road, assume control of the Matzmed stronghold, advance in the Second Army's rear on both sides of Lexicon to Usha Road (about twelve kilometers north of Matzmed), open Akavish and Tirtur Roads from west to east, and clean out the buildings at the Chinese Farm. After accomplishing its missions, it would prepare to cross the canal.
- The Reduced 247th Paratrooper Brigade under the command of Danny Matt would move out of its staging area at Pundak 76 (about thirty kilometers east of Tassa) on half-tracks. On the way, it would receive rubber boats from the 630th Bridging Battalion. A tank company from the 599th Battalion would join it, and it would proceed to the Caspi-Akavish Junction and from there follow in the tracks of the 14th Brigade. After the 14th turned north on Lexicon and cleaned out Matzmed, the 247th Brigade

would keep moving west on Nakhala Road, occupy Matzmed, cross the canal on rubber boats, and establish and secure a bridgehead.

- The 421st Brigade, under the command of Haim Erez, would begin towing the bridging apparatus. One part of the brigade would continue in the tracks of the 247th, and another would travel on Tirtur Road when it was opened. The movement on Tirtur would proceed as follows. At the head of the column, a mechanized reconnaissance unit from Lieutenant Colonel Amatzia Chen's "Force Patzi" would lead and protect the roller bridge convoy; following Force Patzi, the 257th Battalion and its auxiliaries would tow a roller bridge; the 599th Battalion would follow in the rear, behind the roller bridge convoy.
- At 2300, the convoy would reach kilometer 95.5 on the canal. Here, the towing battalion would launch the bridge in the water, the 599th would cross on it to the western bank, and the towing battalion would follow suit.
- Part of the 264th Battalion, under the command of its deputy commander, Ilan Maoz, would harness itself to the 630th Battalion's Unifloat rafts at their concentration point on Padui Road, tow them to the Tassa Junction, and convey them to the battalion commander and the rest of the battalion at Yukon. The 605th Battalion would arrive with its rafts from Romani. From this staging area, the whole battalion would follow the 247th Brigade as it escorted the Crocodile battalion and towed the Unifloat rafts to Matzmed.

The division's timetable was derived from the Stouthearted Men order. Its critical points focused on launching the boats, seizing a bridgehead on the western bank, launching the roller bridge and the Crocodiles, building the Unifloat bridges, and crossing into Egypt. The plan envisioned boats in the water by 2000. The roller bridge would be launched at 2300 and ready for use soon after.

Battle Preparations

On October 13, Sharon ordered his deputy to organize a team and draw up a detailed crossing plan. He personally chose the locations for the bridges on the canal, while the team planned the crossing operation in detail. This included identifying, locating, and collecting the crossing equipment, transporting it to the staging areas, training the units in towing a roller bridge, determining the timing and sequence of movement for the bridging apparatus, and organizing traffic control on the roads in the division's sector. Sharon worked on planning the breakthrough, opening Akavish and Tirtur Roads near Missouri and the Chinese Farm, and capturing the bridgehead.

The planning team consisted of the division's engineering officer, Lieutenant Colonel Baruch Dileon, the chief operations officer; Lieutenant Colonel Aharon Tal, the division's logistics officer; Lieutenant Colonel Zion Masuri, the assistant bridging officer to the chief of engineers; Colonel Menashe Gur, the commander of the 630th Bridging Battalion; Avi Zohar, the commander of the division logistics group; Lieutenant Colonel Moshe Tzapler, the deputy commander of the 421st Tank Brigade; Lieutenant Colonel Israel Sa'ar; and other officers in the deputy division commander's FCP. The work proceeded under a thick cloud of uncertainty, without information on the rafts at Refidim or Romani or the location of the 630th Battalion's rubber boats. The Crocodiles were somewhere at Refidim, and their journey west had only just begun. Only the roller bridge was under control. Furthermore, the assessment of the division's ability to transport the Unifloat rafts on the roads was quite pessimistic, although at this point no one could imagine the immensity of problems they would face. These uncertainties threatened to undermine the division's stringent timetable for the crossing battle and, essentially, the entire operation. Added to this was the units' inexperience in towing a roller bridge. At dawn October 15, it also became clear that the information regarding Tirtur Road had not been updated and that Teneh's markers may have been removed by the Egyptians on at least part of the road. In the midst of the planning, these problems too required solutions.

A major drawback in the engineering effort from the planning stage to its implementation was that the corps of engineers was unprepared, organizationally and doctrinally, to carry out the engineering part of a joint operation of this size. Taking everything into consideration, this was the critical element in the crossing operation, owing to its importance in the operation and professional demands. At one point, Sharon tried to create an engineering group headquarters, to be manned by those Engineering Corps officers who were attached to his division, but this effort ended in failure. It was impossible to organize a crossing group, formulate its doctrine, and train and drill it in one or two days, even if the required manpower was found. The result was that the division had to deal with the engineering aspect of the operation through its chain of command—from the deputy division commander to the 421st Brigade commander and his battalion commanders, who worked directly with the commanders of the three bridging battalions now under the division's command. The engineering officers served as assistants and professional advisers to the division's chain of command.

The 421st Brigade was assigned the role of crossing brigade. Its tanks had to tow all the crossing equipment (the roller bridge and the Unifloat rafts) to the water and escort and protect them on their drive to the bridgehead, as in the case of the Crocodiles.

The Unifloat Rafts

On October 13, the 599th Battalion sent twelve of its tanks to the Mavdil-Padui Junction, southeast of Tassa, to meet the 630th Bridging Battalion's rafts, coming west from Refidim. The rafts remained at the junction until October 15. The 164th Battalion, under the command of Giora Lev, was ordered to tow the rafts and escort the 634th Bridging Battalion's Crocodiles to Matzmed. Before noon October 15th, the 164th Battalion's deputy commander, Ilan Maoz, took twelve tanks to the 630th's staging area to bring the rafts to Tassa and from there on Akavish Road in the direction of Matzmed, in accordance with orders. The raft convoy ran into many problems on Mavdil Road south of Tassa. It became stuck in a massive traffic jam on Akavish Road on leaving Tassa, and breakdowns occurred when the relatively weak tow lines on the IDF's newest model Patton tanks snapped or tanks got stuck in deep sand. The raft convoy stood on Akavish Road near Tassa for hours hardly budging.

On the morning of the fifteenth, the commander of the 605th Bridging Battalion was ordered to move his twelve rafts to Tassa. With superhuman effort, he managed to muster eleven tanks from Force Tiger, but already in this initial stage one of the rafts had to be left at Romani. As the rafts moved south on Lateral Road, they became enmeshed in the 162nd Division's endless logistics convoys that had forced their way onto the road and were trying to work their way south. The traffic on Lateral Road ground to a halt in a massive gridlock. There was no central control since no one had prioritized the movement with the overall operation in mind and no one had organized a supervisory force to direct the traffic and clear the road. The law of the jungle ruled supreme: the strongest had the right of way. As a result, only three of the rafts arrived in Tassa and were sent to the 630th Battalion. The rest either got stuck or were shoved into the sand along Lateral Road as mute witnesses to the imbecility and lack of leadership at the highest levels.

The Crocodiles

The 634th Crocodile Battalion moved from its assembly area west of Refidim to Tassa and Yukon on October 15 without any major breakdowns despite the serious obstacles it encountered. The Crocodiles bypassed the huge traffic jams. Toward evening, they linked up with the half of the 264th Battalion that had remained at Yukon with the deputy battalion commander.

The Roller Bridge

On October 13, the roller bridge was fully assembled at Yukon, ready for action. The 257th Battalion/421st Brigade, under the command of Lieutenant Colonel

Shimon Ben Shoshan, was ordered to tow the bridge and protect it on its journey. Except for the battalion commander, who had seen one or two demonstrations before the war, none of the officers or men in the battalion had ever laid their eyes on the bridge. The next day, the battalion harnessed itself to the roller bridge and practiced towing it under the supervision of the deputy division commander, Colonel Even, and his assistants, Colonel Menashe Gur of the Chief Engineering Headquarters, Lieutenant Colonel Fredo Raz and his aides from the Engineering R&D Unit, and the Southern Command's chief engineering officer, Lieutenant Colonel Aharon Teneh. The deputy commander of the 421st Brigade, Lieutenant Colonel Israel Sa'ar, supervised the drill. The training lasted until early morning the next day and was carried out even as the forces received an alert that Egyptian commando units had landed by helicopter in the vicinity. Colonel Even ordered the tanks to ignore these interferences and continue drilling. Meanwhile, in conjunction with Force Patzi, Rafi Bar-Lev organized a force to deal with the situation.

After innumerable training setbacks, mainly owing to the towing forces' exhaustion and unfamiliarity with the gear, the bridge finally arrived at a stretch of level ground. The battalion managed to tow it another two and a half kilometers west along Akavish Road. The drill was halted toward morning, the bridge camouflaged, the battalion reorganized, and maintenance performed. In the afternoon, the battalion resumed towing practice, pulled the bridge two more kilometers, stopped, and waited for orders.

Summary of the Deployment of the Crossing Equipment as the Battle Approached

On the evening of October 15, the crossing equipment stood as follows:

- The 630th Battalion's rubber boats were concentrated at Akavish 64 between Tassa and Yukon, waiting futilely for the 247th Brigade to complete its replenishment.
- The roller bridge was about four kilometers west of Yukon, waiting on the side of Akavish Road, ready to move. The 257th Battalion was harnessed to it. Accompanying the towing unit were Patzi's force, two platoons of bulldozer tanks, tractors, antiaircraft batteries from the 207th and 208th Battalions under the command of Major Nisan Gilad, and armored infantry units to protect the force.
- The Unifloat rafts were stuck in a mammoth traffic snarl near Tassa, on Akavish and Kartisan Roads. Most of the 605th Bridging Battalion's rafts had been pushed into the sand and were thus lost to the crossing operation.
- The Crocodiles were parked in the Yukon area, ready to move to the water.

Had there been a small measure of foresight and creative thinking in the General Staff and the Southern Command headquarters and more assertive involvement on the part of the Chief Engineering Headquarters in the thinking process in the General Staff and the Southern Command as the crossing approached, then one of the most serious mishaps in the Yom Kippur War could have been averted: the floundering (inertia, to be precise) of the journey of the Unifloat rafts from their staging area to the canal on October 15. This failure reflected, perhaps more than anything else, the inexperience, unprofessionalism, ineptitude, and, to a certain degree, negligence and irresponsibility of certain IDF generals and senior staff officers on the General Staff and on the southern front.

The Deployment of the 143rd Division and Its Units Before the Battle

The 600th Brigade deployed at Hamadia with the 409th and 410th Battalions and about forty-five tanks and was ready to attack in the direction of Televizia and Missouri as a deception at 1700.

The 14th Brigade with its three battalions (the 87th Reconnaissance Battalion and the 79th and 184th Tank Battalions) was parked in the Yukon area along with Force Shmulik and the 424th Reconnaissance Battalion. The 407th Tank Battalion was in transit from its short stay with the 252nd Division and had not linked up with the brigade yet. Shunari's 582nd Antitank/Reconnaissance Battalion had also not arrived yet.

As for the 421st Brigade, the 257th Battalion was harnessed to the roller bridge near Akavish Road, about four kilometers southwest of Yukon. The 599th Tank Battalion, without a defined assignment, was in the Yukon area together with half the 264th Tank Battalion. The other half was harnessed to the Unifloat rafts of the 630th Bridging Battalion and was trying in vain to forge a way through Akavish Road near Tassa.

The 274th Paratrooper Brigade, concentrated in the Pundak 76 area, searched desperately for half-tracks. It somehow managed to round up about sixty of them (not always by kosher methods), a number sufficient to transport only one battalion. Its attempt to find rubber boats came to naught—the boats seemed to have vanished into thin air.

The Southern Command Shirks Responsibility

The 143rd Division was assigned several missions—perhaps too many—in the crossing battle before it began moving to the assembly areas and objectives. Some of these missions far exceeded what the division had to or could accomplish. For all practical purposes, it became the Southern Command's replacement and to some degree the CoGS's surrogate. The CoGS had assigned Operation Stouthearted Men and the crossing battle to the Southern Command. By any standard of military logic, the officer in charge, the commander of the southern front at the very least, should have assumed tactical control of the operation. Had the commander of the front not been a former CoGS, then a rather convincing argument could be made that the CoGS should have overseen the crossing battle and Operation Stouthearted Men. After all, this was IDF's main effort, the action that would decide the war. Today, more than ever, no one can deny that the operation's results had inestimable significance for Israel's future. But, instead of assuming command, Bar-Lev and Gonen cobbled together an operational order that fizzled like a dud. They announced on this and other occasions that the 143rd had been given the full onus of planning and preparation, thus washing their hands of the responsibility for any part of the operation. Not only did the Southern Command relinquish its duty and exhibit passivity in the management of the operation; it even avoided lending minimal assistance to the division, such as supplying half-tracks to the 247th Brigade, planning and assuming control of the roads, and curbing their wanton and unjustified use by forces that had no part in the crossing effort.

It defies understanding what stood behind the Southern Command's decision to divest itself so bluntly and categorically of the responsibility to perform its duty and instead assign it to a subordinate level—the 143rd Division and its commander, Ariel Sharon. The only logical explanation is that there were no senior officers with Sharon's status and experience in command—from the commander of the front down—who could lead so challenging and complex an operation as the crossing battle confidently, intrepidly, and professionally. Despite the animosity that the senior officers in the Southern Command felt toward Sharon, they had to admit his consummate capability, not openly or publicly heaven forbid, but unequivocally nevertheless, as testified by their decision to place on his shoulders what they were supposed to do. In other words, on October 15–16, Sharon, from his headquarters in Tassa and his FCP in the field, performed the duties of the commander of the southern front and perhaps those of the CoGS as well.

Sharon Wins the War

By noon October 15, Colonel Even and Haim Erez realized that the Unifloat rafts had no chance of overcoming the logjam to and from Tassa southwest on Akavish Road. Erez suggested that Sharon postpone the operation by a day, but, from bitter experience gained over many years, Sharon made it clear that he was deeply concerned not only by what the enemy might do but also by the machinations of some of the Israeli forces; therefore, the operation had to move forward as planned. He spoke with his deputy about the means available to the division for crossing the canal that night. Even informed him that at this stage the Unifloat rafts were out of the game and that only the roller bridge and Crocodiles could be relied on, having just forced their way through the massive gridlock on Akavish and reached Yukon. At around 1500, Sharon reported to Bar-Lev about the quagmire on the roads and the news that the Unifloat rafts would probably not make it to the water on time.

The senior officers in the Southern Command wanted the operation to be executed that evening, but they left the decision to Sharon. After his deputy informed him a second time that the Crocodiles were ready for action and perhaps the roller bridge too (whose tie-up on Tirtur Road was still not imagined). At 1600, Sharon called Bar-Lev again and told him that he had decided not to put off the operation but to commence the crossing battle that evening as planned.

This development, more than anything else, proves that on the afternoon of October 15, when the southern front faced the moment of truth, it was Sharon, the commander of the 143rd Division, whom the commander of the front asked to assume formal and actual responsibility for the management of the front in the coming days. Sharon's decision, which was conveyed to Bar-Lev at 1545, was the decisive moment of the war. Thus, he declared, not only on his or his division's behalf, but also on behalf of the entire IDF, that the battle to win the war was being launched. Not tomorrow, not in two days, but that very night! This act alone would have been more than enough to earn Sharon his nation's lasting esteem.

7

The Crossing Battle, Part 2

The Night of October 15–16

> As for that night, let darkness seize upon it. (Job 3:6)

Prologue

The 143rd Division had to carry out two main tasks in the crossing battle on the night of October 15–16:

1. Open and secure Akavish and Tirtur Roads for the division's forces, heavy bridging equipment, logistics units, and other forces' access to and from the bridgehead.
2. Bring the division, followed by the 162nd Division and other forces, to the western side of the canal in order to carry out Operation Stouthearted Men.

Sharon assigned the first mission to the 14th Brigade, the 600th Brigade, and most of the 143rd's infantry units, which were put under the command of the 14th Brigade. The 600th transferred one of its tank battalions to the 14th Brigade and began implementing deception maneuvers from Hamadia in the direction of Televizia and Missouri mainly to support the 14th. Given its position and the nature of its mission, the 600th seems to have been tasked with an even more important assignment than this: securing the division's area of action from enemy activity in the direction of the key areas of Tassa and Hamadia.

Sharon assigned the second mission to the 247th Brigade: seizing a bridgehead across the canal. The 421st Brigade would protect and tow the crossing equipment to the water, and the bridging battalions would operate the various rafts and rubber boats and construct and maintain bridges on the canal.

The 247th's assignment was the linchpin of the division's entire mission. While the rest of the forces were fulfilling critical tasks (some more, some less so), the success of the crossing battle and Operation Stouthearted Men depended on the 247th's capture, securing, and defense of a bridgehead. Sharon based his plan on this and concentrated most his energy on its realization.

From the Assembly Areas to the Objectives

The 600th Brigade's Deception Maneuver

A deceptive maneuver has to be carried out in a carefully selected place, in sufficient force, and with determination while maneuvering and producing sufficient fire that the enemy identifies the effort as being operationally logical. Only if these conditions are met can the enemy be convinced that the deception is the real thing, which is the goal of the maneuver. The worst situation is when the enemy quickly identifies the maneuver as nothing more than a deceptive effort.

The 600th Brigade's two remaining battalions (the 409th and the 410th), with the direct support of two heavy mortar battalions, were supposed to execute a brigade-like deceptive maneuver on the eastern extremity of the Missouri locale at 1700. The brigade commander assigned the task to the 410th Battalion, under the command of Yehuda Geller. The battalion left its assembly area at the Tirtur-Futon Junction and drove due west, firing on various targets in order to spook the Egyptian command in the sector. However the battalion did not attack Missouri or advance to attack, even if not to actually capture, Televizia.

At 2015, the 600th's commander, Tuvia Raviv, informed Sharon that the 410th had advanced to Missouri and hit many enemy vehicles on the route but that he was not interested in attacking Televizia (at this stage the 409th remained at Hamadia, far from the fighting). Sharon ordered Raviv to turn north as soon as the battalion reached the edge of Missouri and exert pressure on it from that direction. Raviv had reservations about the plan. He requested permission to withdraw the battalion to the rear as he feared that, the more the battalion advanced northwest, the greater the danger of friendly fire from Reshef's brigade. Sharon reassured him that this fear was unjustified.

Later, when it seemed to Raviv that the 410th might enter the area between Televizia and Missouri, he ordered it to return east while it was moving south to Televizia to reach Futon (also known as Artillery) Road. When it reached the southern extremity of Televizia at 2140, it ran into a minefield, and, in the extrication attempt, six tanks were damaged and had to be abandoned until morning as there was no possibility of pulling them out.

At 2150, Raviv informed Sharon of this event and asked to withdraw the battalion to Hamadia. At approximately the same time, the 14th Brigade encountered an antitank defensive that suddenly came to life at the Tirtur-Lexicon Junction and began to take casualties. While this was happening, the 79th Battalion, which had reached Usha Road west of Missouri almost without incident, came under increased enemy pressure. Thus, in these critical moments, the 600th Brigade's deception effort was aborted with the removal of the 410th Battalion from Missouri to the east.

Sharon ordered Raviv to immediately replace the 410th, which appeared to be completely out of action with Ben Yitzhak's 409th Battalion. Raviv replied that his first priority was to extricate the 410th from the minefield and that this could take twenty minutes. The 409th remained at Hamadia and west of it for at least another hour following this conversation.

At 2240, Sharon explained the 14th Brigade's critical situation to Raviv and ordered him to immediately instruct the 409th Battalion to exert pressure on the southeast part of the Missouri compound in order to alleviate the pressure on the 14th. At this point, Sharon wanted the 600th Brigade not just to implement a loud distraction but to attack Missouri and Amir in full brigade strength, even if six of its tanks had been hit. For some reason, he did not communicate this wish as an explicit order, and twenty minutes passed until Raviv issued this order to the 409th, but he still did not order it to attack. According to Ben Yitzhak, the battalion commander, the brigade commander ordered him "to assemble" at Segol 104 (a point on the coded map), at the southeast edge of Missouri, and remain there in a night park. This is what Ben Yitzhak understood. The battalion moved out at 2300.

At 2315, Sharon again asked Raviv if the 409th Battalion had moved out, and Raviv answered that it had and was heading to Missouri. Sharon was under the impression that the battalion was moving to attack and made it absolutely clear to Raviv the importance of this move for the 14th. At 0005, Sharon again inquired whether the 409th Battalion was mounting an attack, and Raviv answered that the battalion was at Segol 104 and moving northwest (i.e., it was at the target's perimeter and about to enter).

In the meantime, the 409th assembled at map point 104 and was being sporadically shelled. An hour after his conversation with Sharon, Raviv requested permission to withdraw the 409th because of artillery pressure. As for Sharon's demand that the attack continue on Missouri, Raviv explained that he was deeply concerned over a possible clash with the 14th Brigade. Sharon insisted that Raviv coordinate his movement with Reshef. Another hour passed, and, at 0200, Raviv contacted Sharon and explained that the 409th was not attacking because Reshef had asked it not to, fearing an accidental firefight between the brigades.

After the war, the 409th's commander claimed that he had understood the reason for assembling at Segol 104 was to prepare there for a night park. When the battalion reached Segol 104 after midnight, the battalion commander judged the area unsuitable for a night park. After a long wait, the battalion pulled back, with the brigade commander's permission, to a night park at Segol 194, two kilometers east of Missouri.

The losses of the two battalions that took part in the deception effort were

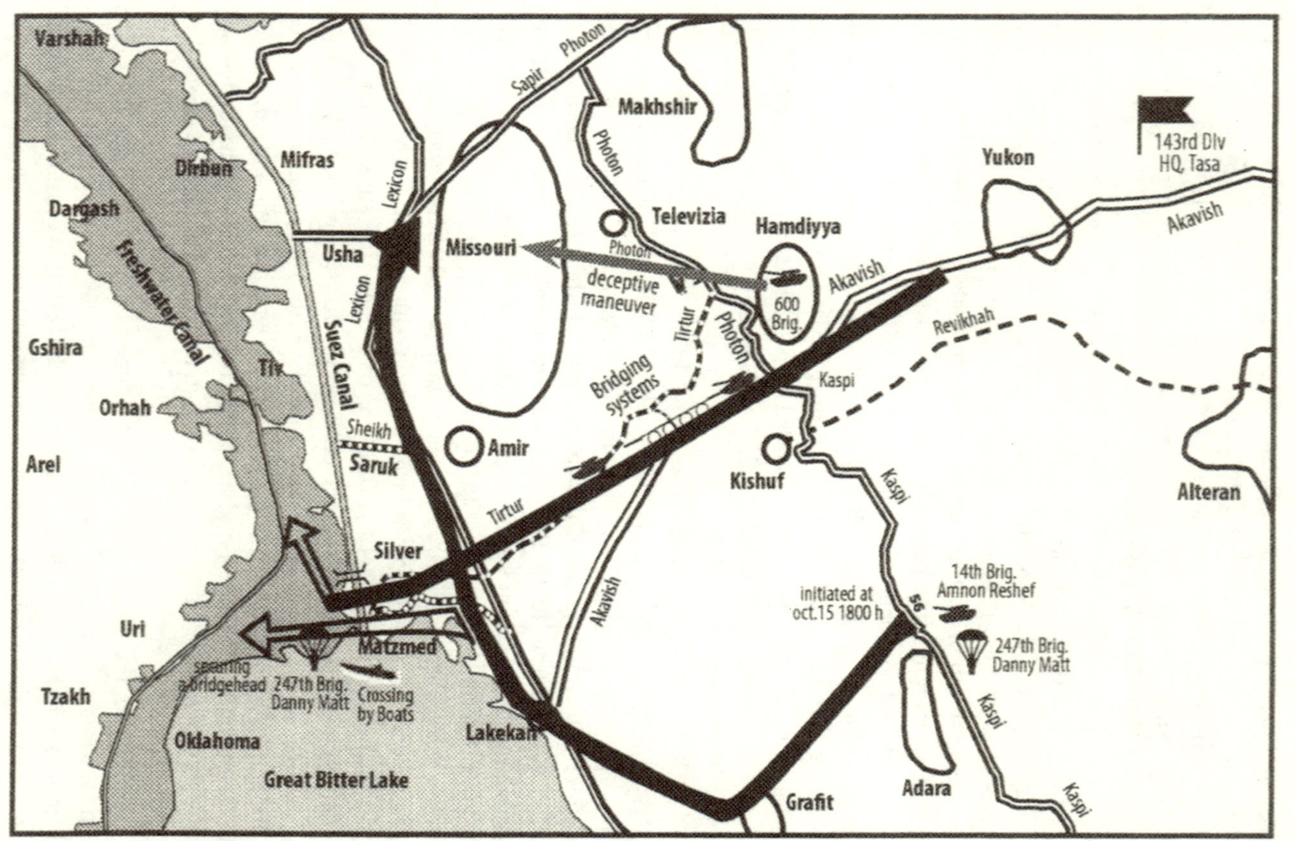

Planned crossing of the Suez by the 143rd Division. Courtesy of Amiram Ezov.

one crewman killed and six tanks damaged by mines. The brigade's third battalion, the 407th, which was attached to the 14th Brigade, also suffered casualties that night.

The 600th Brigade was assigned two missions on the night of October 15–16:

- Prior to the battle, the reduced brigade (minus the 407th Battalion) had to execute a deceptive attack east of Missouri and Televizia. Only one battalion, the 410th, was sent on this mission, but it was not carried out as effectively as expected. The battalion commander, Yehuda Geller, testified: "The assignment wasn't clear. . . . [If it had been,] I would have accomplished much more. We didn't carry out a classic deceptive action" (Ezov 2011, 171).
- After the 14th found itself in furious engagements west of Amir and Missouri, deception was no longer necessary. What was needed was an actual attack on Missouri from east to west as a secondary effort to lighten the pressure on the 14th Brigade and perhaps even enable the division to complete its missions. Such an attack could have been assigned to the 409th and to Geller's crippled 410th. Although the 410th had lost six of its tanks, its combat fitness was not been fatally impaired, and its nearly forty-five tanks available to the brigade commander were enough to play a major role in the battle.

This intention may simply not have been understood.

The upshot was that, on the first night of the crossing battle, each of the division's three brigades carried out its mission, but the 600th's contribution (excluding its 407th Battalion, which fought heroically with the 14th) was negligible. It seems that, between 1700 October 15 and 0700 October 16, only 10–20 percent of the potential of the brigade's forty-five tanks operating east of Missouri was exploited. The reason for this lies in the lackluster performance of Sharon and Raviv. Sharon sinned against Raviv by saddling him with a purely independent mission without making any arrangement for overseeing its execution. To add insult to injury, Sharon failed to give him explicit orders that left no room for judgment or interpretation and instead called for vigorous implementation. Raviv was given a degree of latitude that exceeded what was desirable under the circumstances. Furthermore, since Raviv was far from the center of activity, he was apparently unable to read accurately the battle at the division level and fully understand what was expected of him in light of the critical and unplanned development in the fighting during the night. We may also assume that his orders to the battalion commanders were incompatible with the missions that Sharon had assigned him or that, under the circumstances, he should have understood that.

Acapulco (the Western Shore Reached)—the 247th Brigade on the Night of October 15–16

On October 13, the 247th Brigade (excluding Yossi Yaffe's 564th Battalion, which had been transferred) deployed in the Mitla area as the Southern Command's reserve. The next day, it received a warning order regarding its role in the crossing and its transfer to the 143rd Division. On the night of October 14–15, the brigade came under the 143rd's command and moved into the staging area at Pundak 76. While the deputy brigade commander, Lieutenant Colonel Yehuda Bar, and the deputy battalion commanders were moving the brigade, the brigade commander, staff officers, and battalion commanders gathered at Tassa to plan their assignments in the crossing battle. It was decided that an ad hoc battalion, under the command of Arik Achmon, would cross in the first wave and gain control of the bridgehead on both sides of the canal at Matzmed. Following Achmon would be the 565th Battalion, under the command of Dan Ziv, and the

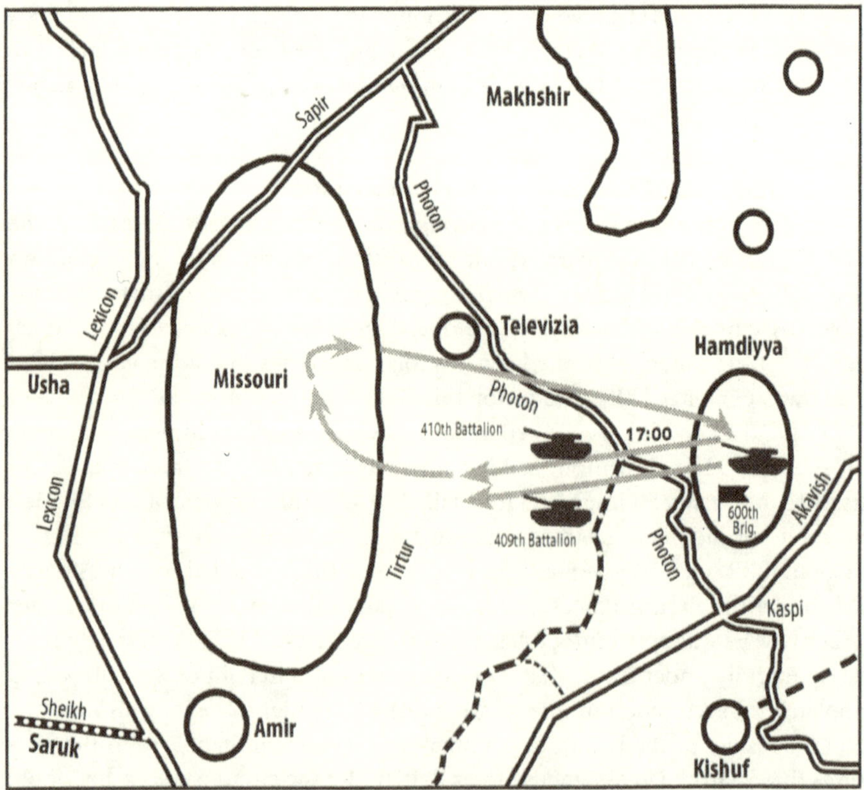

The deception, 600th Brigade, the night of October 15–16. Courtesy of Amiram Ezov.

416th Battalion, under the command of Zviki Nur, both of which would mop up the bridgehead and expand it west to the freshwater canal and up to four kilometers north of the Great Bitter Lake.

The brigade would be supplied at Pundak 76 with about ninety half-tracks, courtesy of the Southern Command, at 1000 October 15. The brigade understood that it would also be receiving one hundred rubber boats from the 630th Bridging Battalion at noon. The half-tracks failed to arrive, and the commander of the 565th Battalion had to appropriate about thirty half-tracks that were intended for another unit. These were added to the brigade's thirty, with the result that sixty half-tracks would have to carry one battalion across—about six hundred men. In reality, over a thousand men crammed into them in the first wave.

After a long delay, and thanks to a good deal of luck, the rubber boats were found. They had been mistakenly sent to Mavdil 76 instead of Pundak 76. Since the blunder was discovered too late, they were transported to Akavish 66, where the brigade was supposed to pick them up while in transit west. The egress from Pundak 76 was scheduled for 1630 October 15 and boats in the water for 2000.

Changes, Adaptations, and Readjustment

Because of the half-tracks' delay and their limited number, Sharon and Matt had to rework the brigade's movement and battle plans. The original plan called for the 247th Brigade following the 14th Brigade on the dune route that bypassed Akavish Road from the south. But, at 1500, Sharon decided, for navigational reasons, to move the brigade—followed by the 421st Brigade's rafts and Crocodile convoys—on Akavish after the 14th opened it. This change caused a major setback in the tight timetable of the original plan and created an additional stipulation for the stages in the battle. Boats in the water would be later than 2000. Matt decided to move the 565th Battalion on half-tracks to the head of the brigade convoy and have the deputy brigade commander's force seize Matzmed, clean it out, and transfer the 565th west in rubber boats to capture the bridgehead. Achmon's ad hoc battalion would be dismantled: the engineering company was attached to the first wave, and the reconnaissance company joined Nur's 416th Battalion, which would be transported in buses right behind the brigade's convoy on Akavish. The idea was to return the empty half-tracks, under Major Shmuel Shaked's command, from Matzmed via Tirtur Road, which was supposed to be opened by then, to Akavish 55 or 52, load them with the 416th Battalion, and bring them across in the second wave.

The Paratroopers Go to Battle

The 247th Brigade left Pundak 76 at 1630 and moved west. The closer it approached Tassa, the greater the road congestion became, and, when it reached the junction, all hell broke loose. Movement practically ground to a halt in a massive traffic snarl. There was no way to keep to the timetable. The plan called for boats in the water at 2000, but the brigade began to wrench itself free of the gridlock only at 1930, about thirty kilometers from the waterline.

The massive traffic jam at the junction resulted from, among other things, the 630th's giant rafts, which were being towed by the 264th Battalion's tanks, which had arrived in the Tassa area on Mavdil Road. Aware of the priorities of the battle and the urgency of the situation, Colonel David Maimon, acting on behalf of the 143rd Division, was struggling to control traffic on Akavish by getting the rafts off the road so that the 247th Brigade could pass. What use would there be for the rafts if a bridgehead was not established?

It took the brigade over an hour to travel the four kilometers from the Tassa Junction to Akavish 66. When it arrived, it found the rubber boats waiting for it there and uploaded thirty-four of them on the half-tracks. Inflating the boats and organizing them on the half-tracks took valuable time, and the brigade resumed its drive to the water only at 2230.

The 247th Brigade's Timetable to Matzmed on the Night of October 15–16

The 247th Brigade's timetable (according to Ezov [2011] and the brigade log) was as follows:

- 1630: The brigade moved out from Pundak 76.
- 1830: It reached the Tassa traffic circle.
- 2100: It linked up with the boats at Akavish 66 (spending an hour inflating the boats and loading them on the half-tracks).
- 2220: Reshef reported to Sharon a second time that Akavish Road was open.
- 2230: Sharon ordered Even to intercept Matt at Akavish 55 and told him to begin moving to Matzmed on Akavish.
- 2250: The 247th Brigade (which included the 565th Battalion, the brigade FCP, an engineering company, and a company from the 416th Battalion) arrived at Akavish 53, linked up with the H Company/599th Tank Battalion, under the command of Yochi Gilad, and proceeded to Matzmed.
- Midnight: The brigade reached Lakekan and ordered its artillery to soften up the western half of the bridgehead. The brigade commander dispatched

the attached tank company to the Akavish-Tirtur Junction according to the plan that was drawn up with the 599th's commander.

- 0030 (October 16): The brigade commander reached the entrance to Matzmed and waited half an hour for the softening-up barrage to end.
- 0115: Artillery fire ended; the brigade entered Matzmed; boats were launched in the water.
- 0125, "Acapulco": The first boat, under the command of Lieutenant Eli Cohen of the brigade's combat engineers company, touched the far shore.

The 565th Battalion and the brigade's combat engineers company swiftly and stealthily crossed the canal. Within an hour, the entire first wave, including the brigade commander's FCP, was on the western bank and had captured a bridgehead as planned. Tirtur Road remained blocked, and the commander of the 14th Brigade warned Matt not to send Shaked's half-tracks on it to bring Zviki Nur's 416th Battalion to Matzmed. The battalion had to wait several hours on Akavish until a route was found for it to reach the brigade. The battalion eventually set out on a nighttime, rutted Akavish bypass route (which had been reconnoitered by Lieutenant Colonel Amatzia Chen) and arrived at the bridgehead at dawn October 17.

The 247th Brigade completed its mission, though it failed to keep to the timetable, which had become a dead letter even before the wax of the grease pencils hardened on the planning maps. The brigade's success can be attributed first of all to the determination of its troops, from the brigade commander to the most recently arrived private, to carry out the missions in a manner to be expected of a superb, combat-tested brigade. The men exhibited tenacity in deliberately seeking contact with the enemy. Scattered individuals strove ceaselessly to rejoin the brigade and take part in the initial breakthrough. The brigade's success also stemmed from the flexibility and efficiency of the division plan and its translation into the brigade plan, the last-minute changes made in the original plan that increased its feasibility, the fighting proficiency and sacrifice of the 14th Brigade, Colonel Matt's outstanding leadership, and the division commander's proximity to the brigade throughout all the stages of its movement and operations.

This being said, the decisive part that luck played in the brigade's success cannot be denied: the discovery of the rubber boats at the last minute; the lucky headquarters company commander of the 565th Battalion, Major Hanan Erez, who discovered a convoy of thirty empty half-tracks at Refidim that the Southern Command had allocated to another unit; the quick-wittedness that Erez exhibited in appropriating these vehicles and their drivers and forcibly and doggedly delivering them to the brigade; the absence of lethal enemy fire on Akavish Road when the brigade's half-tracks, each one carrying twenty to twenty-five troops with rubber boats balanced on their heads, traveled on it. These are examples of the unimaginable luck that enabled the brigade to go to battle and that faithfully accompanied it as it fought its way to glory. This brings to mind Napoléon's question about each officer who was recommended to him for a senior command position: Is he also lucky? Matt was a superb combat officer from every point of view: experienced, daring, composed, clever, and admired by his men but also lucky.

Luck also shined on the brigade afterward when it had to wait at the bridgehead for five hours without any support from IDF tanks—from the moment it completed the crossing at 0230 October 16 until 0700, when the Crocodiles arrived at Matzmed escorted by the 264th Battalion's tanks and the tanks began rolling across to the western bank.

Incidentally, the 14th Brigade's night action provided an additional stroke of luck for the 247th. The 14th's clashes with the Egyptians at the Akavish-Tirtur Junction, Amir, and west of Missouri throughout the night of October 15–16 and the following morning undoubtedly diverted the Second Army's attention from the real or imagined danger threatening its own bridgehead and thus prevented Egyptian intervention against the 247th's moves. In this sense, the 14th Brigade executed the most effective deceptive maneuver in this stage of the battle, and that may have been the 14th Brigade's most important achievement that night. Also, the absence of enemy tanks from the west bank that could have thwarted the 247th Brigade was the result of the 14th Brigade's fighting on the eastern bank in the rear of the Egyptian bridgehead.

The 421st Brigade's Action on the Night of October 15–16

Draw me: we will run after thee. (Song of Sol. 1:4)

The Brigade's Missions

The 421st Brigade (the "Crossing Brigade"), under the command of Colonel Haim Erez, was tasked with the following:

- Tow the roller bridge from Yukon on Akavish and Tirtur Roads and launch it in the water at kilometer 95.5.
- Tow the Unifloat rafts from Refidim to the bridgehead.
- Escort the Crocodiles to the bridgehead.
- As soon as the roller bridge is launched, cross the canal with two battalions, secure the bridgehead, capture the passageways on the freshwater canal, and raid the SAM batteries up to ranges of twenty kilometers from the bridgehead.

The Brigade's Plan and the Battalions' Missions

To recall, the 257th Battalion, under the command of Ben Shushan, was tasked with towing the roller bridge. The battalion practiced bridge towing on the night of October 14–15 and towed the bridge two kilometers west on Akavish Road. The following morning it continued the training exercises and managed to tow it another two to three kilometers. By the afternoon, the bridge was at Akavish 59, while the whole armada of towing tanks, escort tanks, tractors, and bulldozer tanks stood in front and back of it waiting for the green light to commence towing.

The 264th Battalion, under the command of Giora Lev, was assigned the towing of the Unifloat rafts from their concentration on Mavdil-Padui Road, where they had been dragged the day before by the 599th Battalion's tanks, to the bridgehead and escorting the Crocodiles there. As stated, half the battalion, under the command of the deputy battalion commander, Ilan Maoz, was tasked with the mission and encountered difficulties on its way north to Tassa. At the head of the brigade column, the battalion commander with the other half of the battalion was supposed to lead the 630th Bridging Battalion's rafts as well as the 605th Bridging Battalion's three rafts to the bridgehead and launch them in the water.

Thanks to the Crocodiles' superb mobility, they were able to circumvent the bottlenecks at the Tassa-Akavish Junction, advance, and spread out along the road, to Akavish 55.

The 599th Battalion (minus H Company) under the command of Ami Morag had not been assigned any role in the approach to the water. Its task was to follow in the tracks of the roller bridge and, immediately after the bridge's launching, cross west on it. The towing battalion would follow.

At 1830, the brigade commander, in the presence of the deputy division commander, convened an orders group and briefing for the brigade commanders and the commanders of the bridging and crossing battalions. It was decided that, during transit, the bridging battalions' commanders would be under the command of the tank battalion commanders. At this point, Colonels Even, Erez, and Lev realized that the 630th Battalion's rafts, which were bogged down in the vicinity of Tassa, would not make it on time, but they still believed that the roller bridge and the Crocodiles were viable options that could be exploited.

The Movement of the Unifloat Rafts

At 2000 October 15, the 264th Battalion was still divided into two groups. At Tassa, the deputy battalion commander, Ilan Maoz, at the head of the 630th Battalion's eleven Unifloats, was determined to press forward despite the immense difficulties. With the rafts' arrival at Tassa, which was inextricably congested, he received a series of contradictory orders from the division that further impeded the snail's pace of the Patton tanks. The battalion also encountered a series of technical breakdowns—such as the tanks' towing hooks' shackles being ripped apart—with the result that Maoz's raft convoy had to be extricated from the Tassa traffic circle tie-up. It then reorganized on Akavish Road and began inching toward the bridgehead only at 2300.

From this point on, things started improving. Nevertheless, this route too was jammed with hundreds of vehicles, most of which were of limited in terms of the terrain they could traverse: logistic groups, medical units, ambulances, artillery ammunition trucks, and troop-carrying buses. Although the giant rafts could be moved, the job demanded a continuous, often brutal effort to clear every meter of the road. The rafts' journey on Akavish was anguishing and time-consuming, and there was little hope that they would reach the bridgehead during the night. By midnight, the only means of getting the forces across in time seemed to be the roller bridge and the Crocodiles.

Thus, the Unifloat convoy reached Akavish 55 at 0630 October 16. Colonel Even met the rafts' battalion commander, Lieutenant Colonel Avi Zohar. After Zohar updated him, Even ordered him to present himself to the division commander at Matzmed. The convoy proceeded as a separate column in the 421st Brigade's drive to the water. When the convoy (which included the 257th Battalion and the brigade commander's FCP) reached the area between Akavish 52 and 51, it began to take antitank fire from the north. As soon as a bulldozer tank was hit, the other three immediately ran for cover. Akavish Road was under fire and too perilous for the rafts and tank movement. The raft convoy halted at Akavish 55 with the head of the column close to Akavish 53. Thus, the plan for a swift erection of a raft bridge across the canal was indefinitely postponed, and the battle situation had to be reassessed at once.

The Roller Bridge's Movement on the Night of October 15–16

After the 421st Brigade orders group broke up, the commander of the 257th Battalion returned to the roller bridge at Akavish 59 and organized a phalanx of tanks and heavy engineering equipment to tow the bridge. For many reasons, mainly the battalion's inexperience and only partial training in bridge towing, the operation got off the ground only at 2300.

At first, the effort went smoothly, but, the longer the journey took, the greater became the road problems that the battalion encountered, such as potholes that had to be filled in and damaged or parked vehicles that had to be negotiated. The roller bridge finally arrived at Akavish 55, six kilometers northwest of the Tirtur-Akavish Junction, on the morning of October 16. At 0600, the bridge ripped apart because of an incorrect move by the towing tanks that was the result of ground obstacles. Repair would take at least six hours.

Even without this mishap, the towing problems, and the slow pace (walking speed), the deputy division commander realized that the roller bridge would reach the launching point, sixteen kilometers from Akavish 55, at noon at the earliest. To compound the problems, it turned out that the 14th Brigade had failed to open the Tirtur-Akavish Junction despite its costly efforts, and, as a result, the bridge towing would be held up for an undetermined time. The rupture of the roller bridge dashed the hope of its launching in the water that morning or at least before noon. Already at midnight, Sharon and Even had begun to doubt that the bridge would arrive on time, especially when it was discovered that, notwithstanding its sacrifice and prodigious attempts, the 14th Brigade had been unable to open Tirtur Road.

"The stone which the builders refused becomes the head stone of the corner" (Ps. 118:22)

At midnight October 15–16, Sharon and his deputy weighed the availability of the crossing equipment. The prognosis was dismal in the extreme: the Unifloat rafts were stuck near Tassa, and, although the roller bridge could move, it proceeded only at a snail's pace, and its access to the water was still blocked by the enemy positions along Tirtur Road. In other words, the main crossing equipment was unavailable for an indefinite period of time, and, in the meantime, a thousand paratroopers were occupying the western bank holding on to the bridgehead without attached armor support. At 0100, Sharon drew the conclusion that the only attainable bridging equipment at this stage was the Crocodiles—the equipment that ranked last in priority for the crossing in both prewar-period calculations and the Stouthearted Men planning. Colonel Even describes this wake-up call:

> Sharon asked me where the Crocodiles were, and I answered: "At Akavish 55." He then made one of the most important decisions of the war: he ordered me to bring them, together with Lieutenant Colonel Lev's 264th Battalion's ten tanks, to him at Akavish 52 as quickly as possible. "We'll cross with what we have!" I ordered the Crocodile Battalion commander to organize for movement. Under my command, the convoy moved to Akavish 52. I delivered the goods to Sharon and returned to my place at the roller bridge.

Sharon ordered Lev to lead the convoy to Matzmed while he himself traveled in its rear. The head of the convoy reached Matzmed at 0400. Sharon ordered the bulldozer tanks to break through the dirt embankment and personally supervised the work. An hour later, the embankment was breached by a gaping hole. The Crocodiles entered the Yard (see chapter 9 below), refueled, organized as rafts, and entered the water. At 0700, Lev's ten tanks crossed the canal to the western bank.

The moment the first tank touched the canal's western bank was one of the climaxes of the crossing battle. Preceding this had been Sharon's decision on the evening of October 15 to continue the operation despite the ominous clouds threatening his entire plan and Matt's report of Acapulco after midnight. And now came the third high point: Israeli tanks on the western bank in the rear of the Egyptian bridgeheads and opposite the SAM batteries. All three of these great moments can be attributed, first and foremost, to Sharon's generalship and unflagging determination to accomplish the mission, no matter what, and overthrow the Egyptian army. This moment, like the two others and those that would follow, had one and only one meaning: nothing would stop the IDF from defeating the Egyptian army.

The 14th Brigade's Operations on the Night of October 15–16

The Brigade's Assignments

The 14th Brigade's assignments were as follows:

- Clean up the Matzmed compound and surrounding area.
- Secure the bridgehead from the north.
- Open Nakhala and Akavish Roads for the 14th, 247th, and 421st Brigades and crossing equipment to and from the bridgehead.
- After completing these assignments, prepare to cross the canal and engage the enemy on the western bank.

The Brigade's Forces

The brigade's forces consisted of four tank battalions, three of its own (the 79th, under the command of Amram Mitzna, the 184th, under the command of Avraham Almog, and the 87th Division Reconnaissance Battalion, under the command of Yoav Brom) and the 407th Battalion/600th Brigade, under the command of Shaia Beitel. This amounted to almost one hundred tanks. In addition, the brigade had three crack infantry battalions (the 582nd Reconnaissance/Antitank Battalion/317th Reservist Paratrooper Brigade, under the command of Major Natan Shunari, the 424th Shaked Reconnaissance Battalion, under the command of Moshe Spector, and Force Shmulik, consisting of battalion headquarters and two paratrooper companies under the command of Shmuel Arad). The brigade received direct support from two medium artillery battalions, one self-propelled M109 (155-millimeter) artillery battalion, one battalion of self-propelled 160-millimeter mortars, a General Staff battalion of 240-millimeter multiple rocket launchers, and two batteries of 175-millimeter Long Tom guns. Additional artillery was available for general support.

The Brigade Plan

The brigade plan was based on intelligence that the entire area between Lakekan and the Lexicon-Tirtur Junction, including the junction, was clean of the enemy. The plan was simple and at the same time sophisticated:

- A nighttime operation would be conducted.
- The brigade column would move and infiltrate on a sand route south of Akavish that the reconnaissance battalion had reconnoitered.
- It would move on Lexicon Road south of Lakekan, turn north, and continue on Lexicon on Missouri's flank.
- It would leave the reconnaissance battalion's companies at the Lexicon-Nakhala and Lexicon-Shik Junctions. The reconnaissance battalion would capture Nakhala Road, clean it out, and seize and clean out Matzmed and the area north bordering Shik Road, Lexicon Road, and the canal.
- The 79th Battalion, followed by the 184th Battalion, would continue north to Usha Road and deploy to secure the bridgehead.
- The 407th Battalion would follow the 184th Battalion, leaving A Company on the Lexicon-Akavish Junction; the company would open Akavish Road and travel on it from southwest to northeast. As the battalion advanced north, it would leave B Company at the Lexicon-Tirtur Junction and assign it the task of opening Tirtur Road, one similar to the opening that A Company executed on Akavish Road.
- The paratrooper battalions would come on the second wave, clean up and seize the dominating areas and the newly opened roads.

Movement to Contact—from the Assembly Area to the Objectives

1600 October 15

The 14th Brigade moved from its staging areas to the assembly area at Caspi 56. It entered the sand route south of Akavish at 1800 and traveled in the direction of Lexicon 263. The 87th Reconnaissance Battalion led the brigade column and was followed by the 79th, 184th, and 407th Battalions, with the 424th Battalion and Force Shmulik closing the column. The 582nd Reconnaissance/Antitank Battalion joined the brigade in the vicinity of Lexicon Road and served as the brigade's reserve.

2020

The 87th Reconnaissance Battalion passed the Lakekan stronghold. B Company moved through the Lexicon-Tirtur Junction, and, as it approached the Lexicon-Shik Junction at 2100, it encountered enemy vehicle concentrations, opened fire, turned west on Shik Road, and, while still engaging the enemy, reached the canal and deployed at Saruk (five kilometers north of Matzmed). C Company and the FCP arrived at the Lexicon-Tirtur Junction, turned west on Tirtur Road, and deployed at Tirtur 50. A Company turned west on Nakhala Road, encountered the enemy at Matzmed, returned fire, and linked up with C Company and the battalion's FCP at Tirtur 50.

2106

The 79th Battalion followed the reconnaissance battalion and also passed the Lexicon-Tirtur Junction without injury and reached the Lexicon-Shik Junction a few minutes after the reconnaissance battalion's B Company passed through it. The brigade commander's FCP, moving behind the 79th, deployed slightly north of the Lexicon-Shik Junction. The report that the junctions were empty of the enemy appeared correct at first.

As the 79th continued north on Lexicon, Egyptian resistance increased. Tanks were hit, commanders and men killed and wounded. At 2130, the battalion reached Usha Road and deployed defensively. On its arrival, enemy pressure intensified, and the battalion came under a withering attack by infantry, antitank missiles, and company-sized (and greater) tank forces. Over half the battalion's tanks were hit.

2153

The 79th's commander described his forces' situation to the brigade commander and requested permission to withdraw to the Lexicon-Shik Junction. Permission was granted. While moving south, the battalion commander, Mitzna, was wounded and evacuated. The deputy battalion commander, Natan Ben-Ari, took over.

2115

Avraham Almog's 184th Battalion reached the Lexicon-Tirtur Junction, and the gates of hell opened. The junction that was thought to be empty suddenly came ferociously to life. It turned out to be a fortified antitank position bristling with dug-in tanks, antitank missiles, and personal antitank weapons that concentrated accurate fire on the battalion, causing it heavy losses within minutes. The battalion commander withdrew north after leaving over half his tanks inoperable on the battlefield. The rest of the tanks scattered far and wide, and the remnants of the battalion retreated on foot south to Lakekan. The battalion commander and two other tanks headed north, reached the Lexicon-Shik Junction, and were soon joined by six more tanks from the battalion. At 2130, the battalion commander reported the results of the ambush to the brigade commander, and, after ten minutes, he reported that he was left with only seven or eight tanks northeast of the Lexicon-Shik Junction and experiencing difficulty in advancing.

The 407th Battalion/600th Brigade, under the command of Shaia Beitel, had been following the 184th Battalion in the brigade column. With the 407th were A Company, under the command of Ehud Gros, and B Company, under the command of Gideon Giladi. C Company, under the command of Gabi Vardi, had been divided between the Shaked Battalion and Force Shmulik and remained with them at the Lexicon-Nakhala Junction.

While the 184th Battalion was heading north to the Lexicon-Tirtur Junction, the 407th Battalion arrived at the Lexicon-Akavish Junction. The battalion commander left A Company (nine tanks) there, ordering it to enter the road and scour it in a northeast direction to Akavish 52. The company traveled on the road, reached Akavish 52, and reported that the road was open, approximately at the same time as the 184th Battalion at the Tirtur-Lexicon Junction encountered the enemy. Sharon's FCP received the report at 2130. This was the signal for Sharon to move the 247th Brigade, which was waiting at Akavish 55, to its objective at Matzmed. A Company lost five tanks (not from enemy fire). With its mission completed, the company returned west and, at 0300 October 16, parked at Lakekan for a few hours until daybreak.

As soon as the 184th fought its way north from the fire-riddled Tirtur-Lexicon Junction, B Company/407th Battalion, under the command of Gideon Giladi, and the battalion commander arrived at the junction. This force had not been updated on the ordeal that the 184th Battalion had gone through at the same junction. B Company and the battalion commander did not identify the entrance to the Tirtur road, continued north through the junction, discovered their mistake, returned to the junction, and came under intense antitank fire. Three tanks were hit. The battalion commander tried to organize the rest of the company, but he too was hit (at 2140) and had to be evacuated. The company commander assembled the remaining four tanks and, on orders from the brigade commander, waited near the junction. Tirtur Road remained blocked.

2200

Reshef ordered Force Shmulik to move on Lexicon, gain control of the situation at the Lexicon-Tirtur Junction, and evacuate the wounded. At the same time, he sent the 424th Reconnaissance Battalion to clean out Nakahla and Tirtur Roads (west of Lexicon) in the direction of Matzmed so that the 247th Brigade could enter the stronghold. A kilometer west of Lexicon, the company that was moving on Nakhala Road came under antitank and tank fire, probably from the Chinese Farm. One of the half-tracks exploded and blocked the road (nine soldiers were killed in the half-track). The company began taking heavy casualties. The second company, which was moving on the western section of Tirtur Road, also came under withering fire. Nakhala appeared blocked.

2322

However, this was not the case. The commander of the reconnaissance battalion informed the brigade commander that, in his opinion, Nakhala was relatively clean of the enemy, and he suggested that his battalion clean it and Matzmed of all enemy forces. This was very good news since it would enable the 247th Brigade to capture the bridgehead and commence crossing.

2200–2330

The brigade commander ordered his deputy, Eitan Ariel, to organize the evacuation of the wounded and collect the troops who were widely dispersed in the vicinity of the Lexicon-Tirtur Junction. He assigned the task to the 424th Battalion and Force Shmulik.

2230

The 582nd Reconnaissance/Antitank Battalion finally reached Lexicon 263, left its recoilless guns to block access from the south, and immediately turned north to assist in the evacuation of the wounded from the antitank positions at the Lexicon-Tirtur Junction.

Midnight October 15–16

The 14th Brigade commander ordered the 582nd Battalion commander, Natan Shunari, to take the four tanks of B Company/407th Battalion under his wing and open Tirtur Road, but Shunari had more than he could handle in evacuating the wounded from Tirtur, and the order remained dangling in the air.

In the meantime, the 79th Battalion and its six tanks under the command of the battalion deputy commander, Natan Ben-Ari, were desperately in need of reinforcements. At midnight, the brigade commander ordered the 87th Reconnaissance Battalion to send B Company, under the command of Rafi Bar-Lev, to the 79th as a reinforcement. Because of a navigational error, the company traveled northeast and came under antitank fire from the south—apparently from Amir. Two tanks and an APC were hit and the company commander killed. The rest of the company, under the command of the deputy commander, joined the 184th Battalion, which was deployed in the same area. Eight of the company's wounded were evacuated south on an APC. The APC was hit and all aboard killed.

"Until the breaking of the day" (Gen. 32:25)

It will be recalled that the 247th Brigade, with H Company/599th Battalion leading, reached Lakekan at midnight. On its arrival, the brigade commander sent H Company north to the Lexicon-Tirtur Junction. The company's movement was made without informing the 14th Brigade, and the company commander was not updated on the continuous clashes taking place at the junction. Eventually, the 14th Brigade spotted H Company and instructed B Company/407th Battalion, which was in the area to pick up H Company on its radio frequency, to link up with it and attack the junction's antitank defensive. Contact was not made.

0100 October 16

H Company came under heavy fire from unidentified sources. Seven or eight of its men, including the company commander, were killed and four of its seven tanks knocked out.

0200

The 582nd Battalion and the four remaining tanks of B Company/407th Battalion attacked the fortified antitank position at the Lexicon-Tirtur Junction from the west. Half an hour later, Shunari reported to the brigade commander that the tanks had driven over mines and he was busy evacuating the wounded. The attack was aborted. It was now the 87th Reconnaissance Battalion's turn.

0300

The battalion also attacked the antitank defensive from west to east. It took fire from Amir and the canals north of the junction.

0400

The battalion commander, Yoav Brom, was killed, and the commanders of A and C Companies were wounded. Several officers and men were killed. The B Company commander, Rafi Bar-Lev, was dead, and the deputy battalion commander, who was not a tank officer, would not assume command. The battalion's command skeleton was wiped out, and the 87th Battalion ceased to exist as a fighting unit.

Reshef planned another attack on the junction. He ordered his deputy, Eitan Arieli, to take Ehud Gross's A Company/407th Battalion, which was parked in the Lakekan area all night, and capture the junction, bring Shunari's battalion and B Company/407th Battalion through it on Tirtur Road so that they could clear the road of enemy for the roller bridge to pass through.

0430

This plan fell apart before it began. For sundry reasons, the deputy brigade commander's force was delayed and did not make it on time for the battle. Instead, Shunari's battalion, which numbered six half-tracks, and the tanks of B Company, under the command of Gideon Giladi, launched the battle. The tanks led the force, but, of all the tanks under Gialdi's command, only two continued at the head of the column; the rest either detonated antitank mines, or were lying on their sides in ditches, or had lost their way. The battalion began to take heavy antitank fire from Adom 256 (a point on the code map), one kilometer north of the junction. B Company's tanks received hits, the crewmen killed and wounded, and the company commander killed.

In effect, B Company was wiped out. The half-track column scattered in every direction. Its lead section, with the battalion commander, managed to disengage and move forward, but the rest were caught in the killing zone or remained in the rear. The battle now became an individual effort on the part of each half-track to fight its way out of the trap. Most of these efforts failed, and the survivors abandoned the half-tracks and dug in where they were. Only a few escaped under the cover of the morning fog.

0515

The brigade commander ordered his deputy to move with A Company from the 407th Battalion to the junction and rescue Shunari's men. The force reached the junction in half an hour. Ehud Gross, A Company's commander, describes what happened next:

> [The brigade commander ordered his deputy to take the company and break through to the junction.] . . . The deputy brigade commander did not respond. . . . I exchanged tanks with him because my radio was still working [and I thought that his wasn't]. Afterward I learned that there was nothing wrong with his tank's radio. We moved toward Tirtur with the deputy brigade commander leading. When we reached the junction, we saw tanks smoldering. The deputy brigade commander halted. I passed by him and saw that he was signaling me to pass. . . . I ordered my tanks to move quickly while firing. Just as I reached the junction, my tank was hit. . . . I ordered the driver to move back. . . . I decided to abandon the tank as it began belching smoke. . . . The rest of the tanks moved hastily to the rear when my tank was hit. I went on foot to the junction to organize the damaged tanks. The deputy brigade commander's tank received a direct hit in the engine. He jumped out and ran south without leaving instructions to his crew. . . . I sized up the situation and decided it was not critical and collected over twenty men and began evacuating them . . . to Lakekan. I stayed at the junction with three tanks. (Gross 2013, 406)

The 14th Brigade's Accomplishments and Failures toward Dawn of October 16

> And the evening and the morning were the third day. (Gen. 1:13)

To sum up the 14th Brigade's situation after the fighting through the night of October 15–16, two tank battalions, the 79th and the 184th, were damaged and depleted. Each was left with six to eight tanks and deployed north of Shik Road on both sides of Lexicon, and, with the last ounce of strength, was holding off repeated tank attacks. Fortunately, these attacks were made by company-size forces, but the battalions' endurance was ebbing. Starting at midnight, the enemies' attacks tapered off. Although the bridgehead to the north was not completely secured, it seemed, at first glance, to be so. The goal of securing a four-kilometer-wide corridor to the bridgehead also had not been achieved.

The eastern part of Tirtur Road and the Lexicon-Tirtur Junction were still gridlocked. The attempts to remove the obstructions and open the road to the bridgehead had come to naught. The bridge was bogged down near Hamadia. The point was that, even if the junction were captured, Tirtur Road would still be blocked for the passage of the roller bridge westward.

The brigade had already lost about half its manpower and weapons. Two of its four tank battalion commanders were wounded, and one was dead. The brigade's senior command had been severely impaired, as had the junior command level, and many of the tank crews were depleted (though their absence was not felt because of the loss of so many tanks). Battalions and companies had been erased from the brigade's strength. The brigade seemed to have suddenly lost its ability to initiate decisive moves.

Nevertheless, the brigade had accomplished its primary mission with great success and contributed decisively to the 143rd Division's crossing battle. Thanks

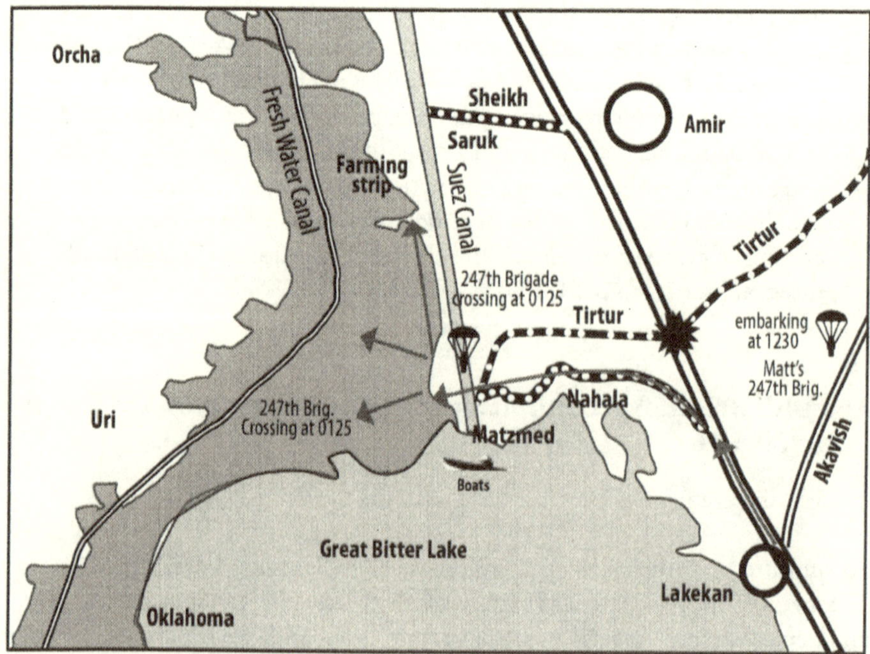

The forming of the 247th Brigade's bridgehead, October 16, from 1300 to 0600 hours, and the 14th Brigade's drive, the night of October 15–16. Courtesy of Amiram Ezov.

to its stubborn fighters, who strove for contact with the enemy, Akavish and Nakhala Roads had been opened and the Matzmed stronghold at least partially cleaned out. The Second Army's forces in Amir and Missouri were pinned down and devoting all their energy to self-preservation and defending their positions, incurring heavy losses. Their will to continue fighting for every kilometer was receding. These achievements enabled the crossing forces—the 247th Brigade and units of the 421st—to reach their objective with relative security, capture a bridgehead, convey the Crocodiles, and bring Israel's armor forces to the western bank.

Major General Israel Tal summed up the brigade commander's efforts thus: "Amnon Reshef underwent an incredible test. I have not heard of an armor commander who experienced such an ordeal as he did that night" (Reshef 2013, 259). Under inconceivably difficult circumstances, Reshef kept his nerve, remained levelheaded, and displayed an inexhaustible drive for contact with the enemy, absolute devotion to his mission, and outstanding leadership in combat.

The quantity, complexity, urgency, and severity of Reshef's problems on the battlefield appear unbearable, far exceeding what seems possible to assign to an IDF brigade commander. At first glance, his span of control appears unacceptable for a brigade commander, whose headquarters and staff were not built for such a test, let alone a nighttime operation in the chaotic, blood-soaked battles that were fought simultaneously across a large area. In these circumstances, he had to command seven battalions and dozens of individual companies and company fragments, replenish ad hoc forces for unforeseen missions such as the evacuation of catastrophic numbers of casualties, and reinforce units that had been severely reduced while in the immediate background stood the unrelenting need to absorb, process, and verify a vast amount of information and patch together a continuously changing estimate of the situation. Added to this was the remorseless pressure, sometimes bordering on moral blackmail from Sharon, to open Tirtur Road. Sharon, with all his experience and sensitivity, was perfectly aware of Reshef's intolerable situation even without this pressure and seems to have been trying to alleviate it, but he was under inexorable pressure because of the delay in carrying out the division's mission and waging the crossing battle and also because of the grating noise emanating from the kibitzers who had congregated in the war room at Um Hashiba.

Many authors and military scholars accept this version. But, from another, less emotional perspective, Reshef's brigade strength on the night of October 15–16 was probably no more than a regular tank brigade, slightly reinforced with infantry, some of it armored, not organic to the brigade, but crack troops nevertheless, if compared to regular armored infantry. At its maximum strength, the brigade numbered one hundred tanks that night, slightly less than an IDF

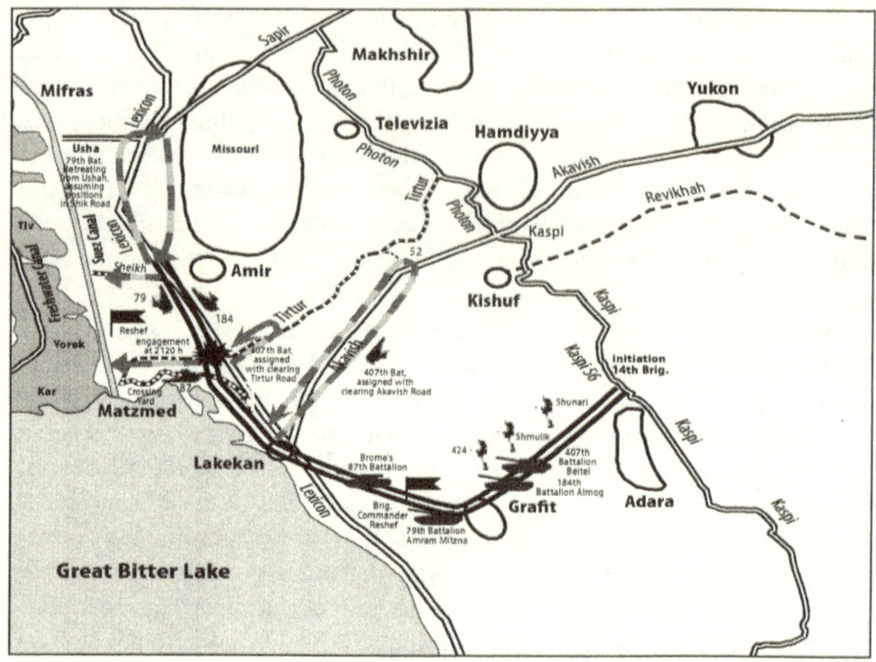

The crossing means voyage. Courtesy of Amiram Ezov.

tank brigade table of organization and equipment. Reshef organized these tanks in four reduced tank battalions instead of three stronger impromptu assembled ones. Had he opted for three battalions, he might have created a more efficient span of control and diminished his battalions' rate of attrition, but his decision to maintain four battalions was correct. The offensive capacity of every unit and formation stands in direct relation to the proportion of commanders in it. The framework of a four-battalion brigade is preferable, from the point of view of maximizing its combat strength, to a brigade with the same number of weapons and manpower in a three-battalion framework.

Reshef's infantry was formally made up of three reduced battalion frameworks that, from the point of view of their numerical strength, were a far cry from the IDF's standard infantry battalions. With all due respect to the courage and sacrifice of the soldiers and officers in these battalions, their contribution to the brigade's performance and achievements during the night battle was minimal. The battlefield on the night of October 15–16—like that of the following night—was no place for such vulnerable and poorly protected infantry; surely it could not be employed as a major fighting element, at least not in the way it was used.

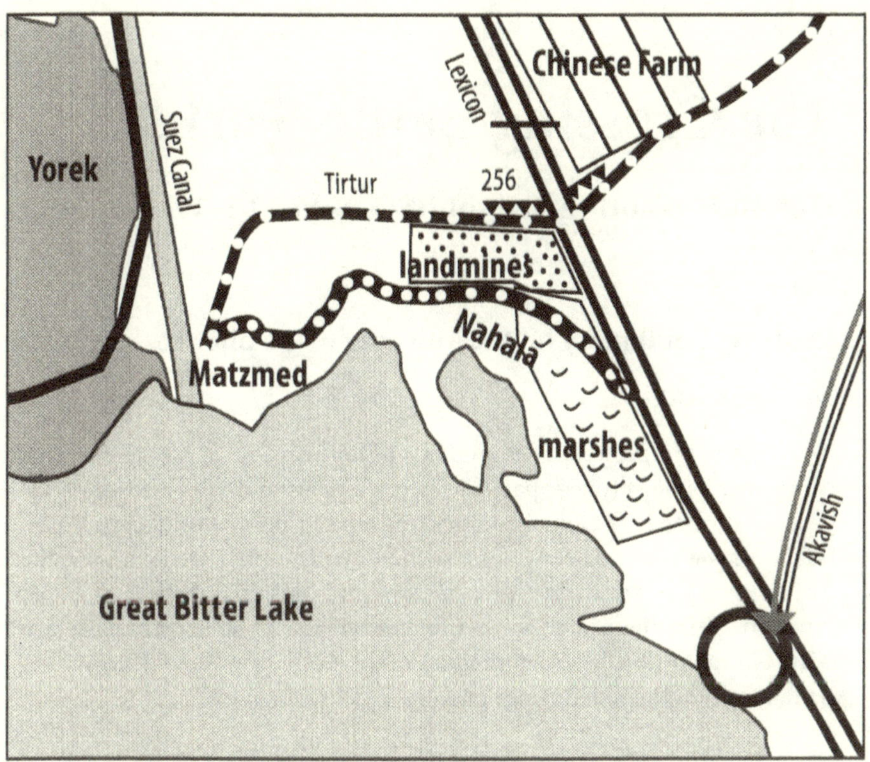

The Lexicon-Tirtur Junction. Courtesy of Amiram Ezov.

Reshef's infantry units were probably not a serious issue in terms of command attention and span of control. His main concern with them was rescuing them from their deplorable situation on the battlefield and evacuating their casualties.

8

The Crossing Battle, Part 3

October 16 and the Night of October 16–17

Crossing Equipment on the Morning of October 16

The Roller Bridge

At 0600, the bridge, weighing hundreds of tons, lay idle in the sand near Akavish 55 after having broken apart during towing by the 257th Battalion/421st Brigade. According to the initial estimate, the repair would be time-consuming. But this news was meaningless as long as the Egyptian infantry and armor blocked Tirtur Road and thus the way to the antitank position at the Tirtur-Lexicon Junction. Thus, the bridge was no longer seen as a viable crossing means. At 0610, Sharon ordered the commander of the 421st Brigade to detach the 257th Battalion from the roller bridge and proceed to Matzmed.

The Unifloat Rafts

The Unifloat convoy numbered ten rafts from the 630th Bridging Battalion and two from the 605th Battalion. The commander of the 630th, Lieutenant Colonel Avi Zohar, was in charge of the force. Major Ilan Maoz, the deputy commander of the 264th Battalion, was in charge of the tanks towing the 630th's rafts. Force Tiger's tanks towed the 605th's two rafts (later, another raft was added). At 0630, the convoy reached Akavish 55, and Colonel Even ordered Zohar to take the rafts to Matzmed and receive further instructions from Sharon. The convoy proceeded as ordered, while the 257th Battalion and other units joined it, with the raft battalion's bulldozer tanks between them. Between Akavish 51 and 52 the force came under antitank fire from the north, and one bulldozer tank was set ablaze. The others raced for cover. Some of the battalion's tanks were also hit, and the battalion commander, Ben Shushan, was wounded and evacuated. The raft column halted, with its lead at Akavish 53. Akavish Road appeared blocked. At this point, the Unifloat rafts too appeared unavailable for bridging operations in the coming hours.

The Crocodiles

At 0400, the Crocodile convoy arrived at Matzmed escorted by ten tanks from the 164th Battalion under the command of Giora Lev. The Crocodiles refueled and, after the dirt embankment was breached and the roads in the Yard cleared, were launched in the water and connected to the rafts. At 0700, Lev's tanks commenced the crossing to the western bank.

The Crocodiles saved Operation Stouthearted Men from stillbirth, the IDF from an ignominious defeat, and Israel from a fatal blow with unimaginably catastrophic immediate and long-term results.

The 143rd Division—Its Strength and the Results of Its Action on the Morning of October 16

The 14th Brigade

The four-kilometer-wide corridor to the bridgehead had not been achieved yet, and Egyptian fortified antitank positions still dominated Tirtur Road from point 40 to the Tirtur-Lexicon Junction and the junction itself. All attempts to oust the enemy and open the road and the junction had failed. The Egyptian antitank emplacement at the Tirtur-Lexicon Junction endangered the brigade since it blocked operational and logistic movement on Lexicon Road. Sharon correctly perceived the destruction of the fortified antitank position at the junction as the 14th Brigade's primary mission that morning.

The brigade had incurred heavy casualties: half its tanks were inoperable, two of its four tank battalion commanders were wounded (Mitzna and Beitel) and one (Yoav Brom) killed, and many company, deputy company, platoon, and tank commanders and tank crews were dead, wounded, or missing. The 87th Reconnaissance Battalion and the 407th Battalion were erased from the brigade's order of battle and their remnants distributed among the remaining battalions. Nearly all the brigade's operable tanks were low on fuel and ammunition. The brigade's armor and infantry forces, commanders, and soldiers were exhausted, but their fighting spirit remained stiff, as they proved later that day. The infantry battalions had also been severely damaged in the night fighting—the 582nd Antitank/Reconnaissance Battalion in particular, as well as the 424th Battalion and Force Shmulik.

Nevertheless, the brigade's accomplishment of its primary mission proved a major contribution to the 143rd Division's success in the crossing battle. The 14th had doggedly struggled to open Akavish Road and the western part of Tirtur and Nakhala Roads and had partially cleaned out the Matzmed stronghold. The Second Army's forces at Amir and Missouri were boxed in, concentrating on self-defense and the defense of their positions while they incurred heavy losses. The 184th and 79th Battalions posed a palpable threat to Amir and southern Missouri. The Egyptians' will to fight for every square meter was waning fast. Their higher headquarters, from the division level to the General Staff in Cairo, had totally misconstrued the real intentions of the IDF's determined all-night offensive. As the Second Army strove to prevent the capture of the Egyptian bridgeheads, it failed to see the catastrophe looming on the canal banks at Matzmed. The 14th Brigade's feint, in addition to its other achievements, had made it possible for the 247th Brigade to fulfill its assignments and the Crocodile rafts and Lev's ten tanks to reach the bridgehead. Equally important, the deception maneuver provided the IDF with a relatively effective and lasting cover-up for its failure to bring the bridges to the water and for the faulty decisions that the Southern Command and the General Staff would later make because of this failure.

The 421st Brigade

The activity of two of the 421st Brigade's three battalions depended on the roller bridge being launched. The 257th Battalion, under the command of Lieutenant Colonel Shimon Ben Shushan, was assigned the bridge towing. The 599th Battalion, under the command of Major Ami Morag, would follow in the 257th's tracks, protect it during the towing, and after the bridge was launched, cross it into Egypt proper.

The breaking apart of the roller bridge at sunrise October 16, in addition to the closure of Tirtur Road for the bridge's movement and the lack of any estimate of when the road would be opened, brought the 421st commander, Haim Erez, Sharon, and Even to the realization of the need to break off the dependence of the 257th and 599th Battalions on the fate this bridge.

Therefore, Sharon ordered the 257th to unhitch itself from the bridge. The brigade's third battalion, the 264th, under the command of Major Lev, split into two groups: half of the battalion, with Lev, accompanied the Crocodile convoy early in the morning and crossed on the Crocodiles to the western bank, while the other half of the battalion, parked on Akavish and harnessed to the Unifloat rafts at Akavish 55, waited until the way to Matzmed, which was blocked by long-range antitank fire from the north, was cleared.

The 600th Brigade

Two of the brigade's battalions, the 410th, under the command of Yehuda Geller, and the 409th, under the command of Uzi Ben Yitzhak, were deployed at Hama-

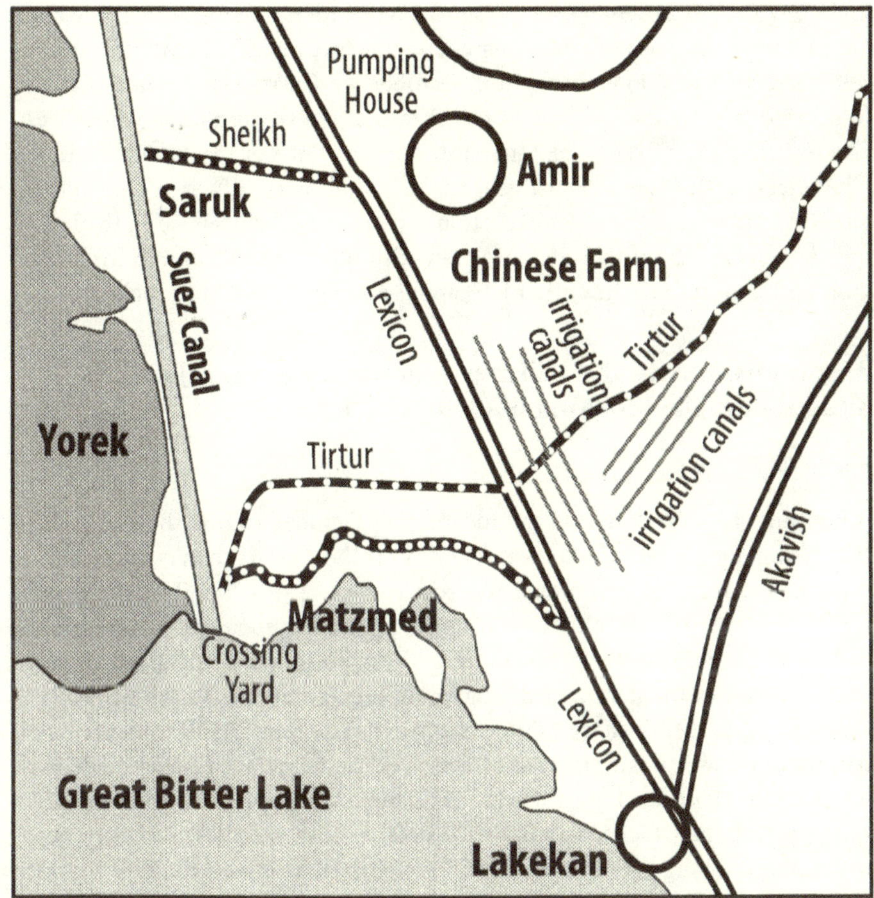

The Chinese Farm. Courtesy of Amiram Ezov.

dia and the dominating area to the west. After six of the 410th's tanks detonated mines during the night and lay in the field, the brigade (minus the 407th Battalion, which was operating with the 14th Brigade) numbered about forty tanks.

The 247th Brigade

The brigade's 565th Battalion, under the command of Lieutenant Colonel Dan Ziv, reinforced with elements from the 416th Battalion and other brigade units, was deployed with the FCP of the brigade commander, Danny Matt, at the bridgehead on the western bank of the canal, defending the Matzmed perimeter. Most of the 416th, under the command of Zviki Nur, had joined the 257th Battalion's convoy but was sent back to Akavish 55 by order of the 421st Brigade commander after the brigade's morning encounter (see below). Thus, the battalion remained in its positions throughout October 16. The morning found the reinforced 565th Battalion holding a bridgehead on the western bank whose western border was the freshwater canal, three kilometers west of Matzmed and five kilometers north of the IDF bridgehead, for a total area of fifteen square kilometers. Ten tanks from the 264th Battalion arrived at the bridgehead in the morning. Added to the antitank defense were also fifteen recoilless 106-millimeter guns and hundreds of the antitank weapons and lighter antitank rockets.

Accomplishments and Failures—Summary of the Division's Situation on the Morning of October 16

Accomplishments

It was clear beyond doubt on the morning of October 16 that the 143rd Division had gained a rather wide bridgehead on the western bank, succeeded in bringing infantry and armor forces across to protect it—although only temporarily—and carried out other operational assignments such as destroying SAM batteries. The magnitude of the success in establishing a bridgehead stood in stark contrast to the failure of the Egyptian high command in the field and in Cairo to comprehend what was happening in its backyard. As a result, the Egyptian response was passive instead of massive. The Egyptians proved inadequate on October 16 in dealing decisively with the imminent threat to their initial gains. Instead, they focused on the static defense of their forces and bridgeheads without developing a determined counteroffensive. This gave the IDF a golden opportunity to cover up its blunders in conducting the crossing battle and its failure to exploit the initial success that morning.

The following results can also be seen as the division's accomplishments.

Of the four brigades that set out to battle, only the 14th, with its seven battalions, had suffered heavy losses. One of the 600th Brigade's battalions, the 407th, which was attached to the 14th, lost a company and a half during the night. But, from a broader perspective, on the morning of October 17 the division could still marshal five tank battalions in good condition (the 409th and the 410th/600th Brigade and three battalions of the 421st, of which only the 264th had been actively engaged in combat). And, although the 14th Brigade was exhausted from the nighttime battles, it was still a viable fighting force and able to muster forty to forty-five tanks in two battalion frameworks (the 79th and the 184th) that included remnants of the 407th Battalion and the 87th Reconnaissance Battalion. Its three armored infantry battalions had been hit in the nighttime fighting but were still relatively combat capable, and the 247th (reduced) Paratrooper Brigade was operating vigorously, although with only half its strength because the 416th Battalion was still cut off from the brigade.

Morning October 16 found the 143rd Division with seven tank battalions, five of them in satisfactory condition, and four, in effect, idle (one battalion was designated to tow the roller bridge after its repairs were completed and Tirtur Road was opened). During the bitter night of October 15–16, the division had lost 60–65 tanks, a little more than a quarter of its original strength. But in the morning it was able to muster 160–70 combat-ready tanks and five paratrooper battalions (some had been hurt in the fighting, and others had not seen action yet).

Although the 14th Brigade had been hit hard on the night of October 15–16, the Egyptian Second Army apparently suffered twice as much. The tenacious fighting of the 14th, combined with the Egyptian Second Army's heavy loss of its armored units and armored reserves, undoubtedly filled the Egyptian command levels with concern that their forces at Amir and the easternmost defensive positions on Tirtur Road might be encircled and forced to relinquish ground. In other words, the Egyptians probably considered abandoning the forward areas at the southern entranceway to the army's sector.

Failures

Despite the timetable, there were still no bridges across the canal on the morning of October 16. The only operational and logistic link between the two parts of the bridgehead was by means of the Crocodiles, whose long-term reliability and survivability were questionable. This was the division's major failure, at least as Elazar, Bar-Lev, and Gonen understood it. Contributing to the failure was the total chaos on Akavish Road and the gross impracticality of the crossing equipment—the Unifloat rafts and the roller bridge—that had been considered the keys to the operation for assault bridging under fire. Added to this was the ignorance of southern front's top brass, Sharon included, regarding the specifications and limitations of the bridging apparatus. The equipment's unsuitability for the task came to expression in its need to travel on rigidly defined routes and specially prepared terrain and the strain and anguish involved in its transportation. The generals' unawareness of these factors was translated in the planning stage into overly optimistic timetables and estimates and the lack of alternative answers in the event that the exaggeratedly confident scenarios went awry. Therefore, when the division's efforts failed to open the two main roads in the action sector, Akavish and Tirtur, for the roller bridge and the Unifloat rafts at the appointed time (at least as the commander of the front wished), the operation's timetables and the ordering of phases regarding the allocation of forces for missions collapsed like a deck of cards, and the entire campaign stood in danger of crashing.

The 162nd Division on the Morning of October 16

Orders and Plans

In the Southern Command's orders group just before Operation Stouthearted Men, the 162nd Division received two alternative missions depending on its place in the order of battle crossing the canal. If the 162nd crossed first, it would advance west and northwest (toward the freshwater canal); if it crossed second, it would pivot west and south, opposite the Third Army. While the order left open the question of which division would cross first, from the briefing it can be understood that it intended the 162nd Division to receive the place of honor.

In the Southern Command's orders and briefings to the divisions, the 162nd Division was not assigned any role in the fighting for the bridgehead, in assisting the 143rd, or in serving as a reserve in the 143rd's battle for a bridgehead. Likewise, it had no part in protecting the 143rd's rear and flanks when it was capturing the bridgehead and clearing the roads. Adan's 162nd Division was also left out of the picture in the deception maneuvers that the 143rd had tasked a reduced tank brigade (the 600th) to carry out. The Southern Command created a sharp, artificial separation between the missions of the two divisions in the initial stages of the operation: the 143rd would open the road for passage to the bridgehead, its armor forces securing the western side of the bridgehead and raiding the SAM bases; the 162nd would cross the canal on the bridges that would be erected on the night of October 15–16 (to be more precise, on the roller bridge) and open the decisive stage in the war on the soil of Egypt proper. But, until this stage was reached, the 162nd was removed from the events taking place on the eastern bank. It spent its time resting, organizing, planning, and attending briefings on future stages on the western bank, and it waited anxiously for the order to cross (first!) so it could reap the accolades. This recalls Napoléon's view on the exploitation of military resources: "A general who retains fresh troops for the next day is almost always beaten."

The impression given by Adan's own admissions as well as by his conduct later in the day is that he felt no remorse over this state of affairs. He passionately wanted to be the first to cross the canal at the head of an armored division that would lead the IDF to victory in Egypt. His goal was to realize this desire, and nothing else mattered. He seemed oblivious to the powerful link between the results of the 143rd's fighting and his mission in crossing the canal.

Neither the Southern Command nor the 162nd Division planned a response to the difficulties that befell the 143rd Division and pushed back the timetable for the breakthrough. Unrestrained optimism reigned supreme. All the experienced generals had forgotten that the Stouthearted Men operational plan, like all operational plans since time immemorial, would shatter as soon as it slammed into the wall of reality.

The 162nd's Forces and Deployment

At noon October 15, the Southern Command appropriated the 162nd's 500th Brigade and held it in reserve. Adan now had 155 tanks in two brigades: Gabi Amir's 460th Brigade with 77 tanks in four battalions, and Natan Nir's 217th Brigade with 78 tanks in three battalions.

On the night of October 15–16, the 162nd's brigades advanced west on Revicha Road—a sand track south of Akavish. In the morning, the 460th Brigade reached the spot where Revicha and Artillery Roads intersected. At 0600, the 217th Brigade arrived at Revicha 59, a few kilometers east of the 460th. Adan set up his FCP near the Kishuf fortification. The 500th Brigade was deployed on Mavdil Road ten kilometers southwest of Tassa.

October 16, the 143rd Division, the Fighting Continues

The 14th Brigade

During the morning discussion between Sharon and Reshef, Sharon realized that the 14th Brigade was in bad shape in terms of its casualties, the disruption of its combat forces, and its logistics and that it urgently needed to reorganize, replenish, evacuate the dead and wounded, and obtain reinforcements. Reshef's immediate task was to open the Lexicon-Tirtur Junction and strengthen his deployment on Shik Road, where the remnants of the 184th and 79th Battalions were holding out. To assist him, Sharon transferred to the 14th Ami Morag's 599th Battalion/421st Brigade (which was idle that morning after the failure to bridge the canal on the night of October 15–16) and Ben Yitzhak's 409th Battalion/600th Brigade (combat ready and without an assignment).

Reshef himself moved to Tirtur 50, a kilometer and a half west of the junction, where he located the remnants of the 87th Reconnaissance Battalion. Near the Lexicon-Nakhala Junction, he found C Company/407th Battalion, which had lost four tanks during the night. He appended the two reduced companies to his brigade and drew up plans for a three-directional attack on the Tirtur-Lexicon Junction and the Amir fortified defense position. The 599th would attack from east to west on Tirtur Road, the brigade commander's tank with the remaining tanks of the reconnaissance battalion would attack from west to east on Tirtur Road, and C Company/407th Battalion would attack along Lexicon Road from south to north. The 409th Battalion would attack the antitank position at point 185, one kilometer north of Tirtur Road (on the old railway track, two kilometers east of Amir).

Morag's 599th Battalion moved out at 0700 and, immediately on entering Tirtur Road, came under antitank missile fire and retreated. Reshef insisted that it renew the attack, and Morag took six tanks, each commanded by an officer, and reattempted to break through the road from east to west. Morag spotted the source of fire at Segol 185, and the 409th Battalion was sent to deal with it. During its maneuvering to attack, the 409th was hit with antitank fire from Missouri and the fortified positions on Tirtur. The commander of the 600th Brigade observed the events from Hamadia and reported that his men were being killed. Reshef ordered the battalion out of the inferno. Morag continued west on his via dolorosa, arriving at a point (Tirtur 43) two kilometers east of the junction at 1000. His force, which had lost two of its six tanks owing to obstacles on the road that could not be pushed aside or bypassed, encountered the enemy. Morag's tanks fought their way out to Akavish 51 and continued toward Kishuf. In this action, four of the battalion's soldiers were wounded and three tanks hit.

At 0800, the 14th Brigade commander's improvised force, which included his own tank, remnants of the reconnaissance battalion, and remnants of C Company/407th Battalion, attacked the junction from the west and the south. After a ferocious hour-long battle, C Company captured the junction and continued north until its ammunition ran out and it had to withdraw. The brigade commander's FCP and the reduced company of the reconnaissance battalion took C Company's place at the junction. Although the immediate benefit was limited to movement on Lexicon Road, the advantage of this route was immediately used to evacuate the brigade's causalities (assembled north of the junction) to the battalion aid stations at Lakekan. Tirtur Road remained blocked by two Egyptian fortified antitank positions east of the junction. The gain from the junction's capture indirectly increased the Second Army's sense that the pressure on it and the threat to its survival were increasing.

Two hours after Morag's attempt to open Tirtur Road, the commander of the 14th Brigade ordered Uzi Ben Yitzhak's 409th Battalion/600th Brigade to move out of Segol 194 and attack Segol 185. Considering the enemy's deployment (at Televizia, Missouri, and Segol 185), this immediate attack was doomed from the start, and, unsurprisingly, the battalion took antitank fire as soon as it set out. Tanks were hit, and the attack was aborted before it began. The 409th Battalion was ordered back to the safety of its parent brigade.

At the conclusion of these battles, the 14th was in critical condition, especially regarding logistics. Its battle fitness was severely impaired, and reinforcement was imperative. Thus, at noon October 16, it received Amir Yaffe's 198th Battalion/162nd Division, under circumstances that will be described shortly. The 198th replaced the 184th, which had fought the whole night and was now down to five or six tanks, its company command spine depleted, and the still operable tanks out of fuel and ammunition.

The 421st Brigade

As stated, at approximately 0610, Sharon ordered the 421st Brigade commander to decouple the 257th Battalion from the roller bridge that had broken apart a few minutes earlier at Akavish 55 and reach him at Matzmed with the battalion. After a quarter of an hour, the Unifloat raft convoy arrived in the same area, which was blanketed with heavy fog. It had taken the 257th Battalion's tanks considerable time to disengage from the roller bridge and organize for convoy movement on Akavish. The battalion was joined by the brigade commander's FCP and that part of the 416th Battalion/247th Brigade, under the command of Lieutenant Colonel Nur, which had managed to rustle up some half-tracks. The 421st Brigade commander also seems to have ordered the raft convoy (which in the meantime had also reached the area) to move to Matzmed, in a separate column a short distance behind the tank and half-track convoy. The brigade commander appropriated the raft battalion's four bulldozer tanks and reassigned them to the 257th's convoy, with the intention of using them to clear the road of obstacles in preparation for the rafts' passage.

As the fog lifted, the convoy set out on Akavish Road at 0700. Later, the brigade commander would realize that he had been told that the road was clear. It should be remembered that both the 257th Battalion's movement and the rafts' movement were the responsibility of the 421st Brigade commander. The tanks towing the rafts were from the 264th Battalion and under the command of the deputy battalion commander.

When the head of the convoy reached Akavish 52 (the brigade commander reported it as Akavish 50 to the division commander), it came under antitank missile fire from the north. Four tanks were hit, one of them a bulldozer tank. Ben Shushan, the battalion commander, and one of the company commanders were wounded and had to be evacuated. Erez ordered the 416th Battalion to return to Akavish 55. The raft battalion's three remaining bulldozer tanks sought cover and withdrew, and the rafts halted with the head of the convoy at Akavish 53. At 0843, Erez reported to Sharon from Lakekan what had happened. After abandoning Akavish Road, the brigade commander led the battalion on the sand track south to Akavish and Lakekan and from there via Nakhala to Matzmed. At 0930, Erez reached Sharon in the Matzmed Yard. Sharon ordered Erez to hitch part of the 257th Battalion onto the Crocodiles, cross the canal, and link up with the 264th Battalion's ten tanks and its commander, Giora Lev, from his brigade.

It is interesting to note the disconcerting discrepancies between the descriptions regarding when and where the 257th Battalion encountered the enemy.

A History of the Yom Kippur War by the historian Elhanan Oren (2004) describes what happened to the 257th after it disengaged from the roller bridge and began moving, with the brigade commander in the lead, in the direction of Matzmed. Oren notes that the encounter took place between Akavish 52 and Akavish 50. He then states that the battalion's tanks and APCs arrived at Matzmed with the brigade commander at 0700. Thus, the battalion was apparently hit by enemy antitank fire at 0630. Oren seems to confuse two different events. The first is the arrival of Lev with the Crocodiles at the head of part of his battalion at Matzmed and the start of the canal crossing by his ten tanks on the Crocodiles at 0700, an hour-long journey. The second event is the movement with Erez of the 257th Battalion, which arrived at Lakekan at 0840 (according to Erez's radio report to Sharon). Erez reached Sharon at the Yard only at 0930.

Adan (1979, 198) claims that the 257th Battalion's encounter took place at 0900 (without citing the place). Two pages later, he mentions the encounter again and states that the battalion's convoy came under missile fire two or three kilometers northwest of his observation post, which was located on a hill south of Kishuf. The hill that best fits Adan's excellent panoramic observation, as he describes it, was at elevation point 95, a kilometer and a half southwest of Kishuf. About three kilometers northwest of this observation post is Akavish 52. This, according to Adan, was more or less where the encounter occurred.

The crossing report, written in March 1974 by Colonel Maoz, who served in Colonel Even's FCP, places the encounter between Akavish 52 and Akavish 51.

According to a detailed study carried out by the historian Amiram Ezov (see Ezov 2011), the 421st Brigade commander reported from Lakekan the 257th's encounter to Sharon at 0843. If we take into account the time and space data and the amount of time needed to reorganize the convoy, then the encounter had to have occurred at 0825 at the latest. Elsewhere, Erez stated (according to Ezov) that the 257th Battalion came under a missile barrage when it reached Akavish 50—six kilometers southwest of Adan's observation point (and not three kilometers northwest of it, as Adan claims).

As usual, the truth lies somewhere in the middle. The encounter probably took place between Akavish 52 and Akavish 51 at 0830, maybe a few minutes earlier. Either way, the upshot of the event was the 421st Brigade commander's report to Sharon that Akavish Road was blocked and dangerous for movement.

As stated, acting on Sharon's order, Erez, together with the 257th Battalion, crossed to the western shore, where he met Lev, the commander of the 264th Battalion. After the brigade commander organized the force, he left a reduced tank company at the bridgehead and set out at noon with a twenty-tank task force and APC company under Lev's command to raid the area beyond the bridgehead. The main purpose of the raiding force was to destroy SAM bases west and north of the bridgehead and thereby punch a hole in the Egyptian SAM umbrella. The task force traveled many kilometers in the area and destroyed two missile bases that afternoon. The brigade commander felt that the entire area was clean of significant enemy forces and that "the Nile" could have been reached easily.

The 247th Brigade

On orders from Sharon, the 247th Brigade concentrated on expanding the bridgehead west of the canal. At 1000, one of the companies gained control of the Deversoir airfield without a fight. Here and there, the brigade encountered small pockets of bewildered enemy forces, but, by and large, October 16 passed without any dramatic events at the bridgehead.

The 162nd Division Joins the War Effort

The Estimate of the Situation in the Southern Command on the Morning of October 16

By dawn on October 16, Bar-Lev, Gonen, and Ben-Ari realized that the timetable for Operation Stouthearted Men had collapsed beyond repair. Indeed, the bridgehead was captured, and a reinforced paratrooper battalion and ten tanks were operating on the western bank, but the two bridges, whose completion the plan envisioned, were still far from the waterline, and the only link between the two halves of bridgehead was by Crocodiles. As for the roller bridge, no one doubted that, until the Egyptians' fortified antitank positions on Tirtur Road were eliminated, Tirtur could not be used.

By 0900, the commanders in Um Hashiba understood that Akavish Road, too, was dominated by long-range antitank fire between Akavish 52 and Lakekan. This meant that the Unifloat rafts would be unavailable for bridge building at Matzmed until the threat was removed. During the night, however, A Company/407th Battalion/600th Brigade had passed on the road without

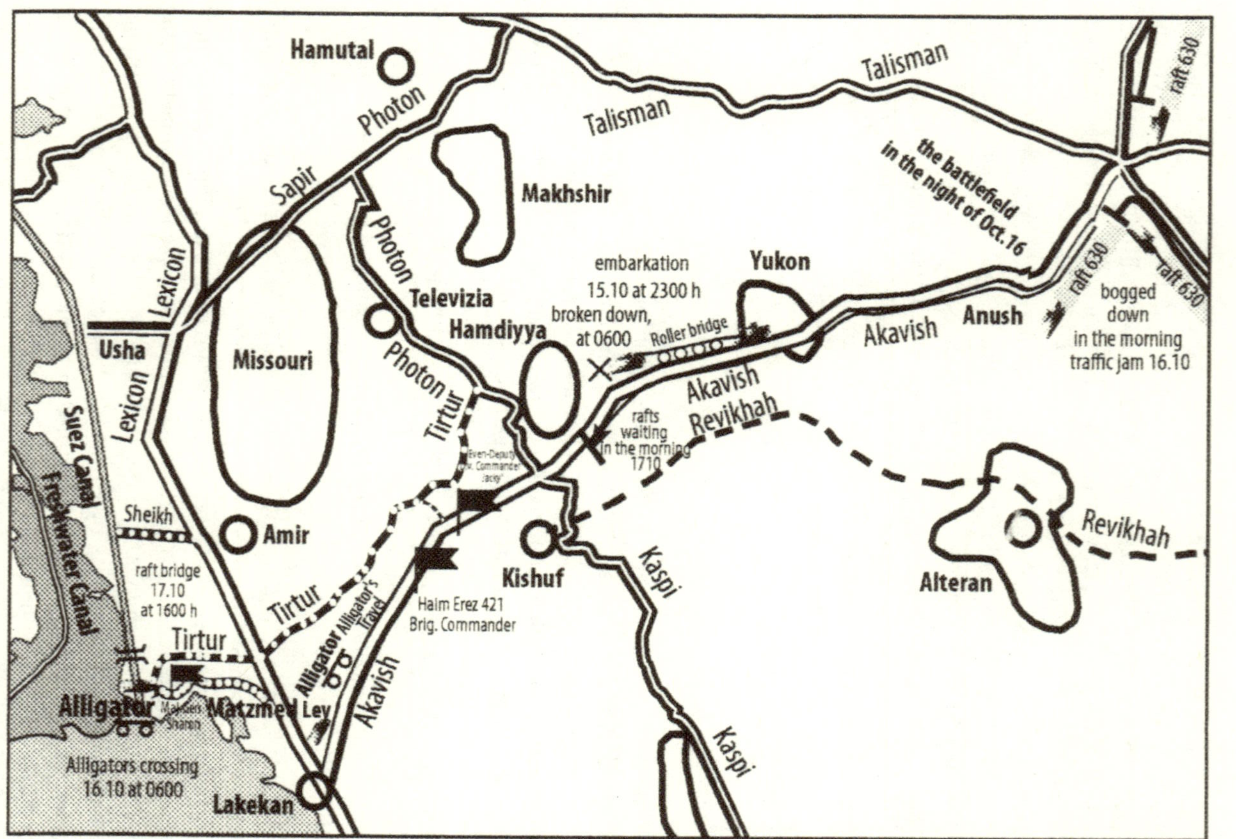

The fording equipment delivery on the night of October 16–17. Courtesy of Amiram Ezov.

being fired on and apparently opened it. But the passage of a small force on a foggy night was no assurance that at daybreak, when the fog dissipated, the road would remain protected from antitank fire from the north. Later, this event would be seen as extremely instructive.

This matter worried the front's headquarters. It had to quickly reassess the situation's immediate implications and exploit the remaining course of action.

These considerations went to the heart of the campaign and, by implication, the results of the entire war. The generalship challenge that the Southern Command faced can be summed up as its need to weigh the risks and potential gains from the events of the night of October 15–16 in order to determine the level of risk that it would be prepared to take in the pursuit of the operation.

The possible risks, as the Southern Command perceived them, were the result of the 143rd Division's failure to establish permanent bridges across the canal because of the delays in getting the bridging equipment to the water. The main reasons for the delays were that Tirtur Road was blocked, Akavish Road was dominated by enemy antitank fire (at least during daylight), and, to a large degree, bedlam abounded on Akavish and Kartisan Roads, a situation that to a lesser degree was the result of technical breakdowns. At the core of these failures towers the unrealistic optimism that characterized the Southern Command's plan and its failure to prepare solutions to setbacks in its implementation.

The potential gains depended on the 143rd Division's success in establishing a viable bridgehead, its ability to get infantry, armor forces, and supplies across the banks, the possibility, which became increasingly realistic, of punching holes in the Egyptian antiaircraft defense system, and the lack of information and the resultant misconception at the highest levels of the Egyptian command regarding what was happening on the ground, which provided the IDF forces on the western bank with near total freedom of action. Added to these was the fact that the Southern Command had another tank division (albeit reduced) parked in orderly rows, fueled and loaded with ammunition, ten to fifteen kilometers east of the canal.

Not just operational considerations riveted the attention of the CoGS, the front commander, and the commanding general of the Southern Command and his deputy. The 143rd's failure to complete its mission on the night of October 15–16 exactly as the written order dictated gave these commanders a golden opportunity to close accounts with General Sharon. What happened later in the day can be more easily understood if attention is paid to this point. That is, they expressed their bitter disappointment in the 143rd's accomplishments while ignoring—except for lip service—the furious fighting, the gallantry and sacrifice of the men and officers, and the division's high casualty rate and achievements. This is a strange and fascinating phenomenon: the CoGS and the generals in the Southern Command, all of them intelligent, experienced combat veterans, were disappointed in Sharon, yet they should have known that the fate of an operational plan is to go awry—if not be altogether shattered—the moment it is implemented. At first glance, the adage "the greater the expectation, the greater the disappointment," comes to mind, and the expectations of Sharon seem to illustrate the extraordinary respect the IDF generals and the Southern Command had for the man and their faith in his abilities. But we may question whether this disappointment was genuine or disingenuous, honest or dissimulated—as a point of departure for slandering Sharon in the following hours and days. As stated, some of the key events of October 16 and the following days will be discussed with the personal-political factor lurking in the background.

Brigadier General Dov Tamari Leads the Unifloat Rafts

To recall, at 0630 October 16, the Unifloat raft convoy arrived at Akavish 55 and continued, under Colonel Even's command, to Matzmed. After the 421st Brigade convoy came under fire on its way to Matzmed, the Unifloat convoy halted between Akavish 55 and Akavish 53 at 0830. It remained there the whole day until after midnight (October 16–17), when travel to Matzmed was renewed. These facts were affirmed by the raft commander, Avi Zohar, in the already-mentioned crossing conference in May 1974.

The repair of the roller bridge was completed at 1200. Instead of the 257th Battalion/421st Brigade, which had disengaged from the bridge, the 410th Battalion/600th Brigade, under the command of Major Yehuda Geller, was assigned to tow it. As soon as the preparations were completed, the battalion commenced bridge-towing practice. The bridge was towed two or three kilometers and halted next to Akavish near the Unifloat rafts. Tirtur Road was still closed to traffic. According to Adan: "Uri [Ben-Ari] arrived from Southern Command by helicopter and told me to assume responsibility for pushing the rafts to the canal and assign the task to my deputy, [Brigadier General Dov] Tamari. . . . I asked the reason for the change[, and Ben-Ari said]: 'Bren [Adan], for crying out loud, this is a sensitive matter; we'll speak about it after the war.' . . . I kept silent and ordered Tamari to take charge of the task" (1979, 201). Adan failed to note the hour of this conversation. Ben-Ari reached Adan's FCP around 0720 and no later than 0740. In other words, when Ben-Ari ordered Adan to assign Tamari the task of moving the rafts, the raft convoy had already been extricated from the strains of the previous night and reached Akavish 55, and the raft battalion's commander had received orders from Colonel Even (see below). On the other hand, the 257th Battalion had not encountered the enemy yet, and Akavish Road was still considered open. Ben-Ari and his superiors believed, for some inexplicable reason, that Tamari would intercept the raft convoy while it was in movement or preparing to move and bring it to Matzmed.

In accordance with military protocol, the 630th Bridging Battalion, with its rafts, equipment, and men, was under the command of the 143rd Division. The towing tanks and their crewmen and officers were from the 143rd's 264th Battalion. There was only one way the rafts could reach Matzmed: Akavish Road. The distance from Akavish 53 to Matzmed via Akavish and Lexicon Roads was fifteen kilometers. This was a short distance, without navigational problems. The road was clear of other vehicles, and movement on it should have been fast, easy, and safe. The convoy was commanded by the deputy battalion commander and an engineering officer with the rank of lieutenant colonel. The convoy was supposed to move as a separate column but within the framework of a larger administrative movement, led by an armored brigade commander.

In light of all this, we may ask, What was the purpose of the exercise? What motivated the heads of the Southern Command to expropriate the role of leading the rafts to the bridgehead from the 143rd Division and assign it specifically to Adan's deputy, Tamari? At no stage did they trouble to explain the reasons for their decision. When Adan asked Ben-Ari the meaning of it, the latter rebuffed him: "For crying out loud Bren [Adan], it's a sensitive matter; we'll talk about it after the war." (That is, it was a personal-political matter, and a word to the wise was sufficient.) At 1115, Gonen radioed Sharon and informed him that Tamari would be leading the rafts—again without an explanation.

We can suggest a number of reasons why the heads of the Southern Command decided to take the key role of leading the rafts from Sharon's division and assign it to Adan's. The most logical one is that this was an opening shot in the battle of the CoGS and the three heads of the Southern Command (Bar-Lev, Gonen, and Ben-Ari) to truncate Sharon's stature, clipping his wings as it were, and present him as the commander who had failed to accomplish his missions. At the same time, they may have wanted to restore Adan's prestige, which had been sullied in the scandalous counterattack of October 8, and endow him, his deputy, and his division with virtual achievements at the expense of Sharon's division. This is to show that, no matter how tough the battle, enough time and energy will always be found to initiate missions and actions, and even engage in combat, whose conception is personally and politically motivated, as we shall presently see. The point is that the 162nd Division's mission to lead the rafts to Matzmed was a bogus assignment and that the operational value-added that its commander and deputy brought to it was zero. Air reconnaissance photographs from noon October 16 clearly indicate that part of the raft convoy was parked on the road with the roller bridge next to it a few hundred meters northeast of Akavish 53 and that the road was empty and clear for movement.

Time Out: No Bridges and No Games

Israeli air supremacy, whether partial or absent, had a crucial impact on bolstering the IDF on the western bank, prolonging its action there and its ability to withdraw to the eastern bank if necessary. From a broader perspective, the IDF's air situation had a profound influence on its ability to defeat the Egyptian army "quickly, overwhelmingly, and elegantly," as Bar-Lev said on the eve of the Six-Day War.

Even before the ink was dry on the paper that ended the War of Attrition, the Egyptians had already advanced SAM bases to the canal area in blatant violation of the terms of the agreement. Israel's response was nil.

After this display of faintheartedness, the only way in which Israel could achieve air supremacy in the fighting zone was by having its ground forces eliminate the SAM bases on the western bank. This required a large-scale canal crossing with tanks, mobile artillery, and crack armored infantry. One need not be a professional strategist to realize the far-reaching possibilities for the IDF if such air supremacy was swiftly attained. Many of the commanders who were conducting the war in the south may have been aware of this. The IAF commander, Major General Benny Peled, certainly was, as his relentless pressure to cross the canal as soon as possible showed. The first armored force that passed over the canal had orders from the Southern Command to take out the SAM bases in the area north of the bridgehead.

The bridgehead itself was spared massive attack by Egyptian armor and infantry reserves. Egyptian artillery paid almost no attention to it, and the little it did was nugatory and failed to obstruct the 143rd's maneuvering on the two banks. Although Akavish, the main access road, was targeted by long-range antitank fire from the north, it was not the only route to the canal. Tanks and APCs could easily move to and from the bridgehead on alternative, albeit less convenient, roads.

Sharon felt that the Southern Command should be exploiting the crossing's success and pushing more forces—armor, infantry, and artillery—on Crocodiles to the western bank. He knew that the rapid concentration of a large force in Egypt proper—much more than the current thirty tanks—would immediately enable the IAF to play an effective role in the ground battle, in terms of both fighting and logistic support. A strong IDF presence on the western side would also provide the new forces arriving after the bridge was erected with favorable conditions for launching their attack. In other words, Sharon understood that bringing large-scale ground forces across the canal on October 16 and the increased involvement of the IAF in the ground battle would defeat the Egyptian army "decisively, quickly, and elegantly" at the cost of relatively few IDF casualties.

The front commander saw things differently. In his view, the sine qua non for the flow of more forces to the western bank was at least one bridge spanning the canal, an open road to and from the bridgehead, and the road's protection from enemy intervention. At 1100 October 16, Bar-Lev explicitly forbade Sharon from transporting additional tanks to the western shore, beyond the thirty already there, until a permanent bridge was standing (which implied that a main access road would be open). In his 1115 conversation with Sharon, Gonen reiterated this order.

During this altercation, the key element of generalship came to expression: the ability to assess risks, that is, the inherent conflicts in the principles of war.

One of the outstanding features of generalship is the ability to correctly size up the circumstances in which one should choose one principle of war over another. Along with the personal attributes that lie at the heart of this ability, such as high intelligence, self-control, moral stamina, intellectual courage, and the skill to effectively employ centers of information and thinking, the commander's own battle experience at the highest leadership level holds a crucial place. This ability and the indispensable combat experience on which it is based are not always compatible with rank and position in the military hierarchy. In the final tally, the decision maker's propensity and attitude toward risk are the decisive factors that determine the choice of modus operandi. Personal and political agendas, often latent, often have a powerful impact on the selection of the course of action.

Bar-Lev and Sharon based the choice of course of action on their assessment of risk and gain in each alternative. Each general had a different and ostensibly objective estimate of the risk level and expected benefit of each alternative. Here, their different approaches to risk taking came to expression, which is to imply not that Sharon was a risk seeker but that his rich and relatively recent operational experience as a high-level commander, which only he and General Tal possessed, enabled him to weigh the expected risks and potential gains more accurately than Bar-Lev could. The lack of a sufficient amount of recent experience at the senior command level in wartime can often restrain a rational, levelheaded person to an exaggerated degree when it comes to risk taking. Bar-Lev was not a risk seeker. Those who knew him were aware of this. For example, his biographer, Carmit Guy, relates a conversation between Dayan and Elazar in which the former "speculated that Bar-Lev suffered from conservatism and rigidity" (Guy 1988, 268). What are conservatism and rigidity if not risk aversion? On another occasion, Elazar described Bar-Lev as authoritarian and not "operatively" brilliant (Bergman and Meltzer 2003, 158), characteristics that can easily be translated into risk aversion.

A few years after the war, Bar-Lev and Sharon tried to explain their reasons for and against the flow of additional forces on the Crocodiles. Presumably, a significant gap existed between what they thought at the time of the events and what they said years later. Be this as it may, the reader can still draw his own conclusions from their approaches and their explanations for them. The following are some of the insights that Bar-Lev presented at Israel's National Defense College in 1976.

Describing Sharon's proposal (without specifically mentioning his name), Bar-Lev said: "The second possibility [Sharon's] was to continue crossing with the Crocodiles before the roads were opened and the bridges built so that two to three hundred tanks could be concentrated on the western bank and carry out the planned moves." He admitted that he rejected this idea because he failed to see how so large a force could receive logistic support without a bridge and roads. In order to strengthen his argument, he resorted to semantics: "The concentration of two to three hundred tanks on the western bank before a bridge was established and the roads cleared of the enemy would have turned the crossing into a kind of raid, whereas divisions designated for the crossing . . . were needed not only to foray the western bank but to win the war." The course of action that Bar-Lev chose was "to continue executing the original plan with other forces and a different timetable," but a plan that would "guarantee us a *stable* bridgehead and the development of a three-division offensive" (emphasis added).

The logic behind Bar-Lev's choice is extremely instructive: as he perceived the situation, the timing for the cease-fire was linked to the military situation on the ground, that is, the Egyptians would not press for a cease-fire unless they were convinced that they faced imminent defeat. Therefore, "on October 16 there was no political pressure . . . The possibility of coming with three divisions with a twenty-four-hour delay" was decided on because, in Bar-Lev's words, "What was the hurry?"

Sharon, too, spoke at the National Defense College that year. His ideas for continuing the operation on October 16 were the exact opposite of Bar-Lev's. His main argument was that, although a permanent bridge was not in place yet, the IDF had to continue flowing west and crossing the canal on the Crocodile rafts while the permanent bridging equipment approached Matzmed. This would enable the forces to commence the decisive battles as early as possible or create a wide and mighty (greater than brigade size) bridgehead on the western bank that would eliminate the need to wage breakthrough battles into Egypt proper (as indeed Adan's Division had to do on October 18). Sharon felt that the Southern Command had failed to exploit his division's success in capturing a bridgehead by not strengthening it with a substantial armored force. All the operational factors were in the IDF's favor on the morning of October 16:

the enemy had been completely caught by surprise, the Egyptian command was unaware of the IDF's plans and what had happened, and the IDF's freedom of action on the western bank was practically absolute.

Bar-Lev's presentation of Sharon's positions seems misleading. Even if Sharon was pleased with the Crocodiles' capabilities, he did not suggest bringing three divisions across on them or leaving the approach to the bridgehead unprotected or abandoning the effort to construct permanent bridges. Sharon's statements imply that he believed that no more than one division should cross the canal before the bridges were erected. His assessment of the risk on October 17, when the bridge building began, was that, as time passed and the construction neared completion, there would be less risk in having additional tanks cross to the western bank. Bar-Lev, it will be remembered, forbade the passage of tanks west before a permanent bridge was standing. Thus, while Sharon stressed the dynamic essence of the risk, Bar-Lev was fixated on its initial level.

Like his antagonist in the dispute, Sharon too employed semantics to bolster his argument. From his point of view, at no time had Akavish Road been "clogged" or "blocked." Although it was sometimes subject to long-range Egyptian antitank fire, significant administrative movement had traveled on it on October 16, and vehicles with good traversability could bypass it to the south. Sharon lamented that the prohibition on conveying forces on the backs of the Crocodiles had "missed the greatest opportunity of the war." Considering the Southern Command's forces' fighting in the following days, Sharon's opinion sounds exaggerated.

It is not our intention to judge who was right in this debate, but there is room to raise several points regarding generalship in this case.

Bar-Lev's main reason for objecting to force buildup on the western bank before a permanent bridge was completed and the roads were opened was that political pressure for a cease-fire had not been exerted yet and that therefore he could delay a massive reinforcement of the forces that had crossed in the last twenty-four hours. As far as this reasoning goes, Bar-Lev seems to have forgotten that, the more time that passed, the greater the likelihood that the Egyptian high command would have caught on to the IDF's intentions, discovered the IDF forces on the western bank, and taken vigorous steps to counter them.

Bar-Lev's position can be argued to be justified because, the moment the Egyptians had identified major IDF activity west of the canal, they would have ordered a massive artillery barrage on the bridgehead that would preclude completion of the construction. This argument will have to remain in the realm of speculation since its validity cannot be corroborated. The events on the ground, however, do not support it.

Egypt had been closely following progress on the bridge. Forward artillery observers were swarming around Matzmed, and Soviet reconnaissance planes and Egyptian surveillance equipment were operating round the clock. The Egyptians intensified their shelling as soon as they realized that the construction was nearing completion, and the climax came when they spotted large-scale IDF forces heading to and across the bridge. But, until the bridge was standing, they had no way of gauging correctly whether the IDF armor on the western bank numbered forty tanks (as it did) or a hundred. Bar-Lev himself did not raise this point since he was focused on more concrete and immediate matters related to the bridge building.

Furthermore, the chain of events at the bridgehead after the bridge was standing also invalidates this hypothesis. From the moment it was constructed until the cease-fire went into effect, the bridgehead came under air attack and the heaviest artillery bombardment in IDF history until that point. Nevertheless, the Southern Command forces crossed back and forth on it day and night, and the bridgehead functioned as a vital facility without a break. In addition, in the midst of the murderous artillery shelling, another bridge was put up in the Yard, and the Unifloat bridge was restored. These facts are incompatible with the horrific scenario of deadly barrages that would have deterred bridge building.

As a rule, every hypothetical claim contains two basic flaws. By its very nature, until it is tested and found to be, with a certain degree of confidence, contrary to reality, it is merely an assertion without validity or value. And, as a merely hypothetical, unverified claim is the subject of our discussion, then several hypothetical answers, no less impressive, can be produced to refute it, and the whole issue is mere claptrap.

The 162nd Division Steps in to Open the Roads

Prepare ye the way of the people; cast up, cast up the highway. (Isa. 62:10)

The Division Tries to Do the Job Alone

On the morning of October 16, the generals of the Southern Command intimated to Adan that his halcyon days were over: the 143rd Division had been unable to open Tirtur and Akavish Roads and was close to exhaustion, and the 162nd Division would enter the fighting that day. Gonen was the first to mention this to Adan, much to the latter's remorse that his forces' might be bloodied even before they crossed the canal.

After Gonen and Tamari's foot patrol on Akavish and Gonen's visit to Akavish 53, where the roller bridge and a few Unifloat rafts had been forced to park, the likelihood increased that the 162nd would be called into action. Gonen issued Adan a warning order to capture the area east of the bridgehead. He also cajoled him with the strongest of inducements: "Sharon disappointed us." At 1200, Gonen radioed Adan: "Open Akavish and Tirtur and bring the [rafts]." The 162nd would capture of the Chinese Farm (code name Amir) and lead the roller bridge to the water.

At this stage, the 162nd had two tank brigades: the 460th, under the command of Gabi Amir, and the 217th, under the command of Natan Nir. The Southern Command was holding the 162nd's third brigade (the 500th) in reserve. Adan had sent the 460th's 198th Battalion, under the command of Amir Yaffe, to Matzmed as a foot in the door, but the Southern Command had transferred it to the 143rd Division. When Adan's order came through, the two brigades deployed at Kishuf south of Akavish. Adan left the 460th Brigade as a reserve and covering force and ordered the 217th to move to the hills north of the Akavish-Tirtur Junction and open the roads.

The attack appears to have been one large, drawn-out ruse on the part of the brigade and division commander. According to Adan's account, the 217th was indeed deployed north of Akavish, where the brigade commander deployed one battalion and kept the second in the rear on standby. Thus, of the division's five or six battalions, only one was designated to execute the attack, and the rest remained in reserve or on standby. The brigade's action turned into a veritable fiasco later as it bumbled through a series of halfhearted attempts to sally forth from its positions but withdrew at the first show of resistance, carried out bogus maneuvers on reverse slopes, engaged in radio or face-to-face consultations, and so forth in order to create the impression of combat activity, wasting maximum time and minimum energy instead of accomplishing the mission.

The bizarre element in the story is Adan's admission: "The only area where our action proved fruitful was with Tamari, who assembled the rafts and brought them forward. Tamari reported by radio that he was advancing with the rafts on Akavish (from where? to where?) and asked whether the roads were open." (This was a strange question from a senior and very experienced commander who was on Akavish Road and listening in on the division's operations wireless network.) Adan elaborates further on Tamari's efforts to muster the rafts and prepare them for movement: "[Tamari] left for the mission with two jeep platoons . . . and added two more offices to his FCP: Lieutenant Colonels Guy and Saul [Nagar]. The rafts were discovered stuck at different points along Akavish Road leading to Tassa. They used bulldozers to drag the vehicles off the road, [then] 'freed the traffic snarls' and cleared the way for the rafts. The effort required ingenuity and resourcefulness, and, finally, after hours of backbreaking work, they were on the move with twelve rafts" (Adan 1979, 203).

It is not our intention to downplay the efforts of Tamari, Guy, and Nagar.

From personal experience, we know that this type of task is excruciating, grueling, heartbreaking. But on one detail Adan seems to have erred. This Sisyphean effort was apparently made not on Akavish but on Kartisan Road on the way to Tassa, a description whose geography makes sense and also correlates with the truth—all the more so, it should be noted, since the entire event took place on October 15. The rafts that are being spoken of are the rafts of the 605th Bridging Battalion. As we have seen (and the commander of the 630th Battalion testified to this), the 630th's rafts had been in movement together with the 605th's the whole time, and at no point had they been pushed off the road into the sand. In fact, they had been parked on Akavish Road between Meteg 53 and Meteg 55 since morning. Tamari and his two assistants managed to round up three of the 605th's rafts being led by its excellent deputy battalion commander, Yehuda Hudeda, and join the 630th's convoy. The rest of the 605th's rafts remained helplessly stuck in the sand of Kartisan Road (some of them until the end of the war).

A direct line links this pseudocombat event with the October 8 debacle. Adan's book offers a somewhat surprising explanation for the ineffective implementation of his forces: "The difficulty stemmed from the battlefield being dynamic and fluid—with repeated threats of enemy armor movement" (1979, 203).

A credible, honest description of the 162nd Division's conduct in the afternoon of October 16 is supplied by the brigade commander himself, Natan Nir, one of the true heroes of the IDF who confessed to the historian Amiram Ezov: "I didn't receive clear assignments. I preserved my tanks. I didn't want to move down to low ground" (2011, 181).

The concise and perhaps most accurate assessment of the manner in which the 162nd performed its mission was made by Brigadier General Uri Ben-Ari in a Southern Command conference in July 1974: "In light of what we heard today, [Adan's] entire division was concentrated south of Akavish and made no attack of any kind on those two roads [Akavish and Tirtur]."

The amazing part of Ben-Ari's summary is that Nir [the 217th commander] did not cross Akavish to the hills north of Akavish 52 and in any case did not try to sally forth south from the line of hills as in Adan's description. This being the case, what really happened there is not clear, but one thing is certain—that nothing positive did.

The 890th Airborne Battalion Replaces the 162nd Armored Division

On the morning of October 16, the possibility arose in the Southern Command of putting Colonel Uzi Yairi's 35th Airborne Brigade under the command of the 162nd Division to aid in securing the roads or fighting to open them. The brigade had been operating in the Ras Sudar area with its brigade units and only available battalion, the 890th, under the command of Lieutenant Colonel Yitzhak Mordechai. The other battalions were detached from it on other missions.

The 162nd received orders from the Southern Command at 1325. Yairi issued a warning order to the 890th's commander to prepare to move to Refidim and from there to the staging area at Tassa. The battalion saddled up and was flown to Refidim, arriving there at 1600. Yairi had to reach Adan's FCP for further instructions.

Yairi flew to Tassa and arrived there at 1600. From Tassa he tried to get to Adan's FCP at Kishuf, twenty kilometers away, by vehicle. After six frustrating hours on Akavish, he returned to Tassa and was brought by helicopter to Adan's FCP. Already at this stage, serious questions must be asked. Why did Yairi not fly directly to Adan's FCP from Ras Sudar as Ben-Ari had done that morning and as Gonen and Dayan had also done? Instead, he wasted precious command time (not through any fault of his own) in a vehicle unsuited for a jammed road in a futile attempt to reach the 162nd Division commander's FCP. And, if he had flown to Tassa, why was he not provided with an APC that could have negotiated the sand route south of Akavish and reached Kishuf?

The 890th Battalion assembled at Refidim at 1600 and was bussed to Tassa, a distance of seventy-five kilometers, arriving there at 1930. From Tassa it was supposed to be helicoptered to the assembly area at Akavish 55. At 2200, six hours after the battalion had reached Refidim, it assembled at Akavish 55 and prepared for a six-hour march to the deployment area in the Akavish 52 area.

These prebattle details are conveyed not merely for the sake of pedantry but to emphasize the incredible degree of nincompoopery, laxity, and just plain apathy at all levels, both in the planning of the transportation and in the staff work involved in implementing it, especially at the command and division levels and to a certain degree at the brigade and battalion levels too. It is inconceivable that the transfer of an infantry battalion without its heavy weapons from point A to point B, with no more than two hundred kilometers between them and in administrative movement on roads in broad daylight and without the threat of enemy interference, was stretched out for eight hours, that is, that it proceeded at the pace of twenty-five kilometers an hour. Even less tolerable is the incredible story of Yairi squandering over six valuable hours trying to reach Kishuf (a distance of twenty kilometers from Tassa) in order to receive an order for an attack that was planned for that night.

The battle—if it can be called that—on the night of October 16–17 that the 890th Battalion fought between Tirtur 42 and Akavish 51 has been studied down to minutest detail from every possible angle. Put bluntly, there is no added value in regurgitating the results. Nevertheless, a number of points related to generalship in this event have to be raised.

Yairi reached Tassa at 1600 and received a phone call from Bar-Lev, his former immediate superior officer (Yairi had been Bar-Lev's bureau director when the latter was CoGS). The gist of Bar-Lev's rather long pep talk was this:

> The situation is difficult.
>
> The purpose of the operation is not just an offensive. We're heading to a victory that will decide the war.
>
> Although Sharon was assigned the capture of the roads, the "gentleman" [Sharon] screwed up, and it's now your responsibility to pull the irons out of the fire [a lieutenant general belittling a major general in front of a colonel!].
>
> Sharon tried to [clear the roads] this morning and got burned [if the truth is being told, why not tell all of it? Adan too had tried and failed]. . . . Bar-Lev now conveys some choice information: two divisions couldn't accomplish the task, but you, Yairi, take your force [four infantry companies] and save Israel [as Yairi heard this, a red light should have flashed in front of his eyes].
>
> The mission isn't so bad. The enemy in your sector consists of a few tanks and some infantry with antitank weapons . . . and regular infantry [not paratroopers like you guys] who crawled in during daylight because Sharon didn't secure the road. . . . Right now and until nightfall the IAF is in action so that the enemy [who crawled in during the day] will have a rough go of it as night approaches. [You see, there's nothing to worry about, buddy.] (Ezov 2011, 184–85)

And finally comes the whammy, the emotional-patriotic-moral blackmail:

> If we clean the road of the enemy, we can execute a move of decisive importance. If not, then sooner or later we'll have to bring back [to Sinai] the guys who crossed [to the western bank]. (Segel 2007, 98)

Here, in one throw, Bar-Lev tosses on to the paratrooper brigade commander's shoulders the full burden of responsibility not only for the fate of the operation but also for the fate of the entire war and the state of Israel.

This speech should not have been delivered by a commander to his subordinate and certainly not by a senior commander. A commander at Bar-Lev's level must give a subordinate at Yairi's level an order rather than play on his personality and values and certainly not vilify a division commander who is fighting on the front.

At one level below that of a lieutenant general—at the level of a division commander—Yairi received alongside his orders fragments of information and flawed estimates about the enemy. This is not to imply that mistaken information was purposely passed on to him, but at least one critical point of which the commanders of the 162nd Division were aware was not made sufficiently clear and its implications not brought to his attention as they should have: the fact that two armored divisions had tried to open these roads and failed and that one of them had fought with the greatest tenacity and had been hit hard in repeated attempts to open the roads to Matzmed.

It would be more reasonable to assume that, of all the considerations facing the Southern Command and the 162nd, an important place was reserved for the wish to keep Adan's division out of harm's way and the burning desire to have it cross the canal fresh and ready for action and see it crowned with the laurels of victory.

The experience of the previous few days should have taught that traditional infantry, such as the 890th Battalion, had no place on the battlefield in the canal front—in either daytime nor nighttime—without meticulous planning and close coordination with armor, air, and artillery. The Southern Command and the division should have learned this lesson in real time, internalized it, and brought it to Yairi's attention immediately. This was their duty.

At 2300, the 890th left the assembly area at Akavish 55 on foot to Akavish 52 for forming up. After an hour and a half march, it was ready and moved out in a screening formation (as the division ordered) from Akavish 40 between the two roads. When the vanguard reached Akavish 42 at 0245 October 17, it came under fire, and the battalion's mission was over. All its efforts, like those of the division's armored units that came to its assistance, were directed toward one goal: getting out of the killing field, reducing the mounting pile of casualties and evacuating them, and hightailing it out of there as fast as possible.

After midnight, at the start of the 890th's screening, which began later than scheduled, Adan became concerned that the paratrooper force was too weak to clean out the roads in time for Tamari to bring the rafts through to the bridgehead. By 0200, the uncertainty gave him no rest, and he suddenly had the idea to send a reconnaissance platoon on Akavish Road to Lexicon to check whether the road was safe for movement. "There was a risk involved," he said, "but we had no choice. It was a calculated risk I had to take."

He ordered an APC reconnaissance platoon of the 460th Brigade's B Company, under the command of Captain Shlomo Goren, to reconnoiter the road. The platoon moved out at 0230, fifteen minutes before the 890th encountered the enemy. At 0315, half an hour after the battalion came under fire, the patrol reported from the Akavish-Tirtur Junction that all of Akavish was open from where the rafts were parked to Lexicon Road. When the patrol reached the junction, Adan ordered it to return the way it came. At about the same time, he instructed Tamari to bring the rafts to the bridgehead. The reconnaissance platoon returned to Akavish 53 at 0345 and joined the raft convoy, which had begun its journey to the bridgehead with Tamari in the lead jeep. The convoy advanced on Akavish without encountering the enemy; just before 0600 Tamari reached Sharon at Lakekan, and Sharon took the rafts to Matzmed.

So Who Opened Akavish Road and How?

The reconnaissance patrol that Adan sent to check Akavish Road at 0230 reached Akavish 51 twenty-five minutes later. North of this point was where the 890th Battalion had been hit ten minutes earlier. At 0400, the raft convoy left Akavish 53 on its push to the waterline. The ten kilometers to Lakekan took two hours to traverse. According to our calculation, the convoy arrived at Akavish 51, where the 890th had encountered the enemy, somewhere between 0430 and 0500, when, according to Adan, "a ferocious battle was still raging between the paratroopers and Egyptian infantry, and under its cover the raft column continued on Akavish Road" (1979, 198).

This description gives the impression that the paratroopers were engaged in a stubborn battle for several hours that threatened the Egyptian antitank defensive positions not only in the area of the encounter but also further away, forcing the Egyptians to focus all their strength and attention on this desperate battle and abandon their primary mission of sealing off Akavish and Tirtur Roads. This is a heartwarming tale that serves to justify the shoddy, irresponsible manner in which the 890th Battalion was sent into battle and provides the battalion's men and commanders the feeling that their sacrifice was not in vain.

It also explains why certain commanders enhanced this theory over the years and elevated it to the status of a myth. One of the 890th's deputy battalion commanders at the time, the historian Dr. Zeev Drori, wrote in the Israeli daily *Ma'ariv* on April 30, 2004, "how . . . the battalion accomplished its mission and allowed the passage of the crossing and fighting equipment to reach the other side of the Suez Canal." In the same issue, the former cabinet minister Dr. Efraim Sneh, who was commander of the brigade's medical company at the time, states: "The Chinese Farm Battle . . . enabled the road to the canal to be opened and a large force to cross."

The most imaginative of all was that of the battalion commander, Yitzhak Mordechai: "[In the midst of the fighting,] I turned around and witnessed an amazing sight: the rafts were traveling on Akavish Road just like in an Independence Day parade, without being hit by a single bullet. This was a surreal celebration. And from within the inferno I realized that the mission to open the roads was being accomplished." On another occasion, Mordechai's rhetoric soared to stratospheric heights when he proclaimed: "Without the action at the Chinese Farm, the IDF would not have made it across the canal and would never have defeated the Egyptians in the Yom Kippur War" (http://rotter.net/cgi-bin/forum/dcboard.cgi?az-show_thread&om-5834&forum-gil&omm-0).

Even Yairi, the commander of the 35th Brigade, a conscientious, brave, and intelligent man, sought consolation in the myth. "According to the mission's definition, we failed," he summarized in a brigade briefing, adding: "In retrospect, there's one thing that I can take consolation in: despite all the bickering that went on—things [equipment] were flowing to the bridge." Unfortunately, Yairi was unable to find solace in this myth. The man was too straight and honest.

The historian Amiram Ezov also seems to have accepted the fantasy version of the 890th Battalion's battle and its results. The only source backing his position is the head of the Egyptian General Staff Operations Branch at the time, Major General Muhammad Abdel Ghani el-Gamasy. Ezov quotes from el-Gamasy's book *The October War* (1993): "The paratroopers suffered many casualties. . . . This battle held the Second Army Command's attention, and on its right flank the fighting raged in the 16th Infantry Division's sector. During this time Major General Adan managed to move the floating pontoons forward to the water" (Ezov 2011, 229).

Ezov seems to construe el-Gamasy's noncommittal expression "during this time" as meaning "because of," but this is a patently false reasoning, as old as humanity and known as the cum hoc, ergo propter hoc logical fallacy (according to this fallacious reasoning, if event B took place while event A did, then B was brought about by the occurrence of A). As noted, el-Gamasy did not explicitly utter this fallacy; at most, he led Ezov to it.

The truth, as reflected in the traffic on the radio networks and commanders' reports during the events that night and later, is that, from their positions along Tirtur Road, the Egyptians discerned the battalion approaching them, allowed it to continue west until it entered the killing zone, and then raked it with murderous fire. At no time did the battalion pose a threat to the Egyptian defensive positions. Almost immediately at the start of the encounter, after the two lead companies tried to maneuver in the area and were instantly blocked, the 35th Brigade commander and the commanders and soldiers of the 890th Battalion had to abort their mission and any attempt to attack and capture the defensive positions that were threatening them. They focused all their attention and what little firepower they had left in a desperate attempt to escape the trap.

In the battalion's first encounter and its subsequent attempt to extricate itself, it suffered 160 casualties, including 40 killed. The commanders of the two lead companies were killed almost instantly, and the companies disintegrated. The men in the two rear companies brashly rushed forward to rescue their comrades and were cut to ribbons. In effect, in the late hours of the night, the 890th ceased to exist as an organized fighting military body. The efforts to pull out the battalion with its dead and wounded took until the next morning (October 17) and ended at 1800, when the last group of soldiers, some wounded, was extracted.

If we look carefully at the events of the night of October 16–17 and all aspects of the rafts' passage to the water, then we come to the irrefutable conclusion that their movement was the result of the timing of Adan's decision to send B Company's APC platoon to check Akavish down to Lakekan and the patrol commander's report that he was not fired on. This was not the first time in the crossing battle that a small armored force had traveled back and forth at night on Akavish between Lakekan and Akavish 52 without being hit. On the previous night, A Company/407th Battalion/600th Brigade made the same journey. To recall, the company, under the command of Major Ehud Gross, left Lakekan, traveled on Akavish to Akavish 52, and returned to Lakekan on the same road, completing the round trip at 2245. Furthermore, on the same night, between 2200 and approximately midnight, a 247th Brigade convoy of dozens of half-tracks moved west on Akavish without encountering enemy opposition.

Adan states that, at 0200 October 17, he came up with the brilliant idea ("an idea popped into my mind") to dispatch B Company's reconnaissance APCs on the route that Gross's A Company as well as a battalion of the 247th Brigade had traveled the previous night (although A Company had gone in the opposite direction). The result was same. Therefore, the following question persistently arises: Why did Adan get this idea at 0200 and not earlier? Why did he not send a patrol to check Akavish Road before the 890th left the staging area or even later, when it set out from the deployment area? Solid evidence supports the view that Akavish Road was partially dominated by long-range antitank fire from enemy positions on Tirtur Road and to the north only in daytime and that the road was almost completely safe for movement after dark. This conjecture seems to have been confirmed by A Company on the previous night. The fact that Akavish was the scene of significant, unhampered movement the following night (the B Company reconnaissance patrol and the passage of the raft convoy) only strengthens this hypothesis.

Maybe this is only conjecture and nothing more, and maybe it is even wrong (though it seems not to be), but was it not the duty of the commander of the 162nd Division to check it out as early as possible? Adan describes his decision to send the B Company patrol on Akavish as an unavoidable risk, a *calculated risk* in the language of cliché. If so, what prevented him from taking this calculated risk earlier and thus perhaps saving the 890th Battalion scores of dead and wounded?

The above discussion exceeds the realm of tactics, grand tactics or strategy. It descends to one of the deepest roots of generalship: the ability to estimate risks correctly under pressure and without delay. It is also surprising that an experienced senior combat commander could inform his readers that his decision to send a reconnaissance patrol was a brainstorm, a calculated risk, and not standard operating procedure, a matter of routine.

No less surprising was the belief of the front commanders and the 162nd that Akavish Road was closed to movement. This belief developed after the 421st Brigade convoy's encounter and the report of its commander, Haim Erez, on the morning of October 16 that the road was blocked by enemy fire. From that time until the 890th marched west to its fate, sixteen to seventeen hours passed, and in all this time nothing was done to ascertain whether movement on Akavish drew fire and, if so, to identify its sources and employ a smoke screen, tank fire, and artillery against it.

Operations and Politics

It is hard to ignore the political and interpersonal aspects of the absurd drama starring the deputy commander of the 162nd, Brigadier General Dov Tamari, in which he led a convoy of twelve to thirteen rafts plus a number of other vehicles ten kilometers from Akavish 53 to Lakekan and presented them to Major General Arik Sharon. Sharon, too, was not blind to these aspects, and the results were forthcoming.

At 0600 October 17, Tamari reported to Ben-Ari that he had reached Sharon with the rafts. Ben-Ari told Tamari that he should continue escorting the rafts to their launching in the water and that Adan had given his assent. Half an hour later, Tamari reported that the rafts were being launched and that he intended to return to the division. Ben-Ari ordered him a second time to remain at the bridgehead and make sure that the raft entered the water. Tamari groused that he would merely be the "fifth wheel of the wagon," and Ben-Ari gives him a lesson in cynicism: "Some wagons have five wheels." Adan ordered Tamari to remain at the bridgehead even if he was there "only revving the motor in neutral." In desperation, Tamari went to the 162nd's 198th Battalion, which was located in the Shik Road area under the command of the 143rd Division, to see how the battalion was faring and whether it needed anything.

The details of this story are unimportant, but the story itself illustrates the private, interpersonal, and political drives behind military moves and the assigning of missions to formations and individuals. Another example of this is Adan's sending Amir Yaffe's 189th Battalion/460th Brigade to Matzmed in the late morning of October 17 as a way of getting a foot in the door and ensuring that the first force to cross the canal after the raft bridge was completed would be from the 162nd Division. Unfortunately for Adan, when the battalion arrived at Matzmed before noon, Bar-Lev's veto on the passage of additional armored forces to the western bank was already in effect. Sharon explained the situation, probably with a touch of schadenfreude, to the surprised battalion commander and to Adan, and requested from Adan, and received, the temporary transfer of the 198th to his division for further assignments. The 198th Battalion replaced the 184th Battalion/14th Brigade on the line, deployed for defense to the north on Shik Road, and did a superlative job.

The generals (*right to left*): Ariel Sharon, Haim Bar-Lev, David Elazar, Moshe Dayan. Courtesy of Uri Dan.

Order group for Operation Stouthearted Men at Tassa, October 15, 1973. Courtesy of Uri Dan.

Major General Ariel Sharon with Colonel Amnon Reshef, commander of the 14th Tank Brigade. Courtesy of Amnon Reshef.

Colonel Haim Erez, commander of the 421st Reserves Tank Brigade. Courtesy of Nadav Mann.

Colonel Danny Matt, commander of the 247th Reserves Paratrooper Brigade. Courtesy of Uri Dan.

Colonel Gideon Altshuler, CoS of the 143rd Division. Courtesy of Uri Dan.

Defense Minister Moshe Dayan visiting the bridgehead on the afternoon of October 17 (*right to left*): Brigadier General Avraham Tamir, Lieutenant Colonel Aryeh Baron, Lieutenant General Moshe Dayan, minister of defense, Major General Ariel Sharon (whose head is bandaged), Colonel Jacob Even (standing, facing the camera), engineering officer Shmuel Barrel (with helmet), and Colonel Yehoshua Sagi, divisional intelligence officer (standing in the left corner). In the background, the rafts are nearing completion. Courtesy of Zalman Anav.

FCP of the deputy commander of the 143rd Division (*right to left*): Lieutenant Colonel Amos Na'aman, operations officer Captain Ilan Oko, Colonel Simcha Maoz, Colonel Jacob Even, and communications officer First Lieutenant Moshe Shapira. Photograph by an FCP soldier.

Right to left: Colonel Ya'akov Aknin, artillery group commander, Colonel Tuvia Raviv, commander of the 600th Reserves Tank Brigade, Colonel Jacob Even, and Major General Ariel Sharon.

Ariel Sharon in the midst of the division's soldiers, and to his left, Colonel Haim Erez (with a mustache), commander of the 421st Reserves Tank Brigade. Courtesy of Nadav Mann.

Duel at the Lexicon-Tirtur Junction. Courtesy of Amnon Reshef.

Mazmad Yard on the eastern bank of the Suez Canal, October 16. Courtesy of Shlomo Arad.

Barrage in the crossing area. Courtesy of Amiram Ezov.

Tanks crossing the raft bridge. Courtesy of Nadav Mann.

Tanks of the 421st Reserves Tank Brigade crossing on Gillois. Courtesy of Nadav Mann.

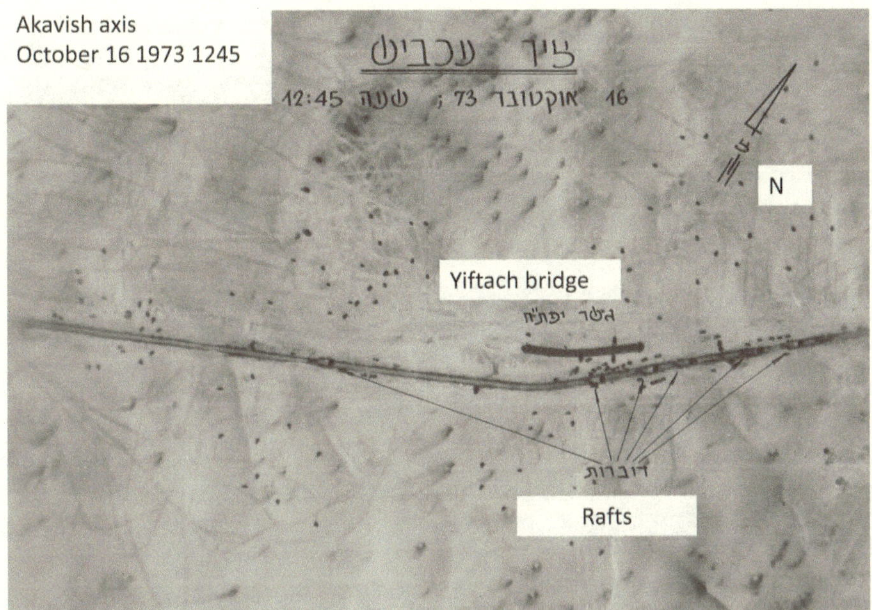

Aerial photo of Akavish Road, October 16. The Unifloat rafts of the 630th Reserves Bridging Battalion are parked on the road next to the roller bridge. Courtesy of Colonel Menashe Gur.

The roller bridge, October 19. Courtesy of Nadav Mann.

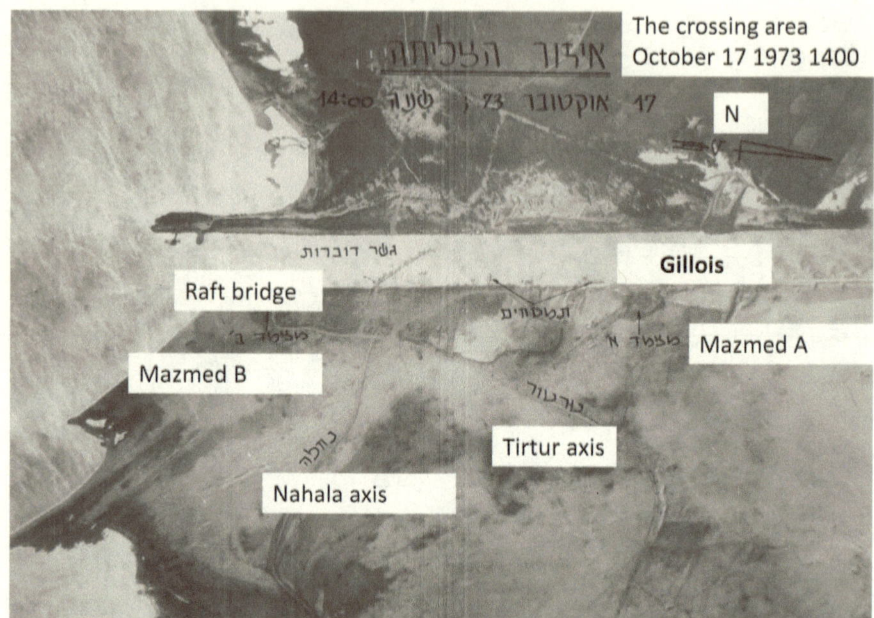

Aerial photo of the rafts bridge two hours after its completion, and anchoring on the western bank of the canal, October 17. Courtesy of Nadav Nann.

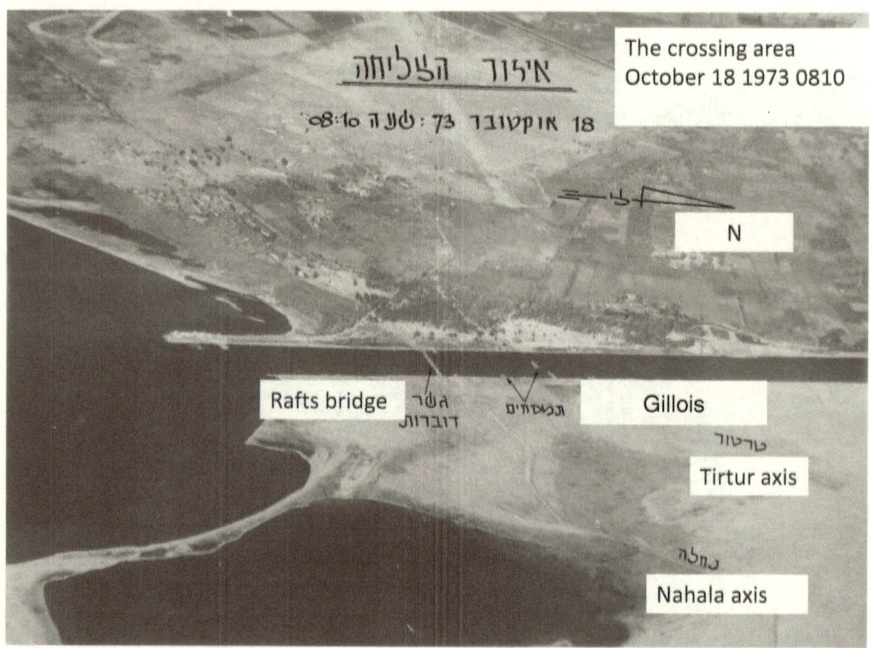

The bridgehead. Diagonal aerial photo looking west, October 18. Courtesy of IAF.

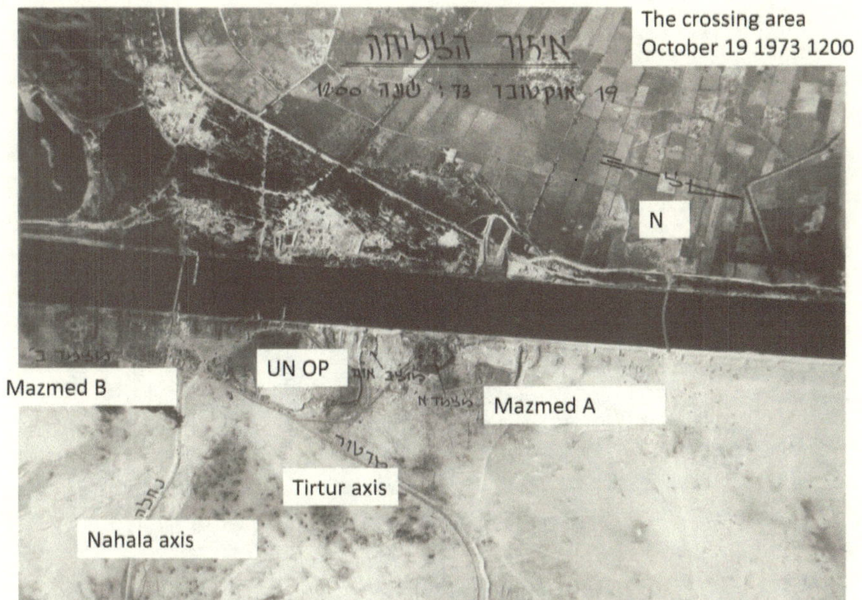

The bridgehead shown in an aerial photo, October 19. Near the Bitter Lake, the rafts bridge is visible, and to the north, the roller bridge.

Diagonal aerial photo of the bridges on the Suez Canal (*looking south to north*), late December 1973. The raft bridge is shown in the foreground, followed by the roller bridge, and in the distance, the land crossing.

The authors at the Port of Adabiya, January 1974. *Right to left:* Colonel Jacob Even and Lieutenant Colonel Simcha Maoz (only his head is showing). *Foreground:* Lieutenant Colonel Zvi Sinai, the former editor of *Maarachot* (the IDF journal).

President Anwar Sadat and Major General Even discussing the canal crossing during a state visit after the war. See page 281 for more information. Courtesy of David Rubinger.

9

The Crossing Battle, Part 4

From the Morning of October 17 to the Night of October 17–18

The Situation of the 143rd Division—Morning October 17

The Crossing Equipment

The roller bridge was still lying north of Akavish Road waiting for Tirtur Road to be opened. The Unifloat raft convoy set out from Matzmed at 0400 and reached Sharon at Lakekan at 0600. Tamari escorted it to Matzmed on the orders of Ben-Ari (Gonen's deputy), and the convoy arrived there at 0630. Three Crocodile rafts were in the water. A number of 421st Brigade tanks crossed on them the day before. At 0730, Egyptian artillery fire sank a one-directional raft.

The 14th Brigade

On the morning of October 17, the 14th Brigade was deployed on Lexicon Road and west of it in the following manner. Lieutenant Colonel Amir Yoffe's 198th Battalion (on loan from the 162nd Division) was spread out along Shik Road from Lexicon to the west, defending to the north. Lieutenant Colonel Abraham Almog's 184th Battalion (with remnants of C Company/407th Battalion/600th Brigade) was reorganizing at Tirtur 50. Securing to the south at Lexicon 263 were the 79th Battalion (with remnants of the 87th Reconnaissance Battalion and A Company/407th Battalion/600th Brigade) and paratrooper units (Shaked Reconnaissance and Force Shmulik, consisting of two paratrooper companies) plus a company of recoilless guns from the 582nd Reconnaissance and Antitank Battalion.

The 421st Brigade

The 264th Battalion (with elements of the 257th Battalion) and the brigade commander's FCP were on the western side of the bridgehead operating against a small number of Egyptian armored forces trying to attack the bridgehead from the west. Part of the 599th Battalion, under the command of the deputy commander, Major

Yehuda Beutel was attached to the 14th Brigade since the morning. Beutel's force linked up with the 198th Battalion, seized positions between point 148 and the Shik-Lexicon Junction, and secured toward Amir. The rest of the battalion, headed by its commander, Ami Morag, crossed the canal on the Crocodiles and joined its mother brigade (the 421st). At this stage, forty of the brigade's tanks organized in two battalions (the 264th and 599th) were operating on the western bank.

The 600th Brigade

The 409th Battalion was deployed between Hamadia and Missouri, and the 410th was harnessed to the roller bridge at Akavish 53. At 0745, the 600th came under the command of the 162nd Division, which was engaged in a number of battles along Akavish Road, in order to open the road and extricate the 890th Paratrooper Battalion. After a brief discussion with the brigade commander, Adan ordered him to return the 409th Battalion to Hamadia and secure toward the southwest slopes of Makhshir. The battalion deployed at point 194, two kilometers south of Televizia.

At 0900, the 410th Battalion disengaged from the roller bridge as Sharon ordered, returned to Hamadia, and deployed toward Makhshir. The reduced brigade now included forty tanks in two battalions, the 409th and the 410th (with remnants of A Company and C Company/407th Battalion still with the 14th Brigade). Deployed thus with long-range tank fire, the 600th Brigade fulfilled its role in the 162nd Division's morning battles.

On October 16, a platoon from L Company/410th Battalion, under the command of Lieutenant Uzi Zelichover, was dispatched to the Hurva fortification (twenty kilometers south of Hamadia) for observation.

The 247th Brigade

Most of the 247th was deployed on the western side of the bridgehead. No significant events occurred during the night of October 16–17 except for the 416th Battalion's linkup with the brigade after it was led to the bridgehead on the Akavish bypass route by Lieutenant Colonel Amatzia Chen's Force Patzi. On October 16, the brigade assembled a small ad hoc task force to secure the eastern part of the Yard and direct the light vehicular movement in it.

The Situation on the Roads to Matzmed

Tirtur Road was still blocked by Egyptian antitank defenses, which included two battalions of infantry, tanks, and antitank missiles. The Tirtur-Lexicon

Junction had been open since the previous day, and movement on Akavish to Lakekan was deemed possible, depending on visibility (day/night, moon phase, fog). Some of Adan's reconnaissance APCs and a convoy of Unifloat rafts had traveled on it the previous night without any problems. South of Akavish was a bypass route that occasionally enabled movement for vehicles with high traversability, such as tanks and APCs.

The 162nd Division

The Chinese Farm Battle

Since 0400, October 17, the 460th Brigade (less the 198th Battalion, which was attached to the 14th Brigade/143rd Division) helped get the 890th Battalion out of the killing zone on Tirtur Road. At first light, the (reduced) 100th Tank Battalion, under the command of Lieutenant Colonel Ehud Barak (the future CoGS and prime minister), attacked the Egyptian defense positions at Tirtur 42 with a tank company. The Egyptian force was attacked, but the attacking force immediately came under devastating antitank fire from several directions simultaneously, and within minutes five tanks were hit and the assault aborted. The battalion retreats to the starting point, leaving several of its wounded and wounded paratroopers in the field. Most of the 890th with its FCP and the brigade found shelter in the network of irrigation canals in the area. As the battalion's ammunition dwindled and the casualties mounted, the battalion was shelled relentlessly and came under light arms fire.

The brigade commander, Colonel Uzi Yairi, then realized that the 890th was of no benefit and that his only option was to request permission from the division commander to evacuate it as quickly as possible. Adan, too, saw no sense in leaving the paratroopers in the field and agreed to pull them out. He reported his intention to the commanding general of the Southern Command. To his surprise, Gonen denied permission. His reason was that the 890th was blocking the Egyptian infantry from approaching Akavish.

At first glance, there is some military logic to this decision, but it illustrates Gonen's misreading of the true situation on the ground. Adan was a division commander, a general; he had missions to carry out and powerful forces that his superiors had entrusted to him; his job was to execute his missions by making maximum use of the forces available to him to the best of his ability. His immediate superior was not supposed to intervene in the way in which he employed his forces as long as he accomplished his missions as expected. Instead, his immediate superior, dozens of kilometers from the area of events, instructed him exactly how to use his forces, and Adan consented.

Dayan arrived at Adan's FCP at 1000, and Bar-Lev landed half an hour later. Adan took advantage of their presence to get them to agree to the paratroopers' evacuation. The orders were given, and, by noon October 17, most of the paratroopers were pulled out. About ten soldiers, some wounded (two from the 100th Battalion), remained in the field because of their proximity to the Egyptians, and their rescue was delayed until the evening. The battalion reached Tassa and reorganized during night.

This event points to the basic flaws in the way in which the front headquarters operated after Bar-Lev's appointment. Ostensibly, there were two commanders on the front: Bar-Lev and Gonen. They were differentiated by their rank, an important but not essential difference, but the real difference was that Bar-Lev had been given sole responsibility for the front. With Bar-Lev's arrival, Gonen felt relieved of all responsibility, yet he still had the right to issue orders to his subordinates, but without the necessity of weighing their results. Only against this background can we understand his refusal to evacuate the 890th Battalion and Bar-Lev's decision to countermand it. Bar-Lev's judgment reflects not only common sense and concern to get the men out of an intolerable situation but also Dayan's demand to withdraw the troops. Thus, the principle of unity of command was dangerously disrupted.

The source of the fatal flaw in the front's command lies in the indecisiveness and lack of resolve that often pervades senior IDF commanders when a subordinate has to be given marching orders. In wartime, the pursuit of maximum success in performance must be the only criterion. If a commander proves eligible for sacking—be he the most accredited or senior commander in the army—he must be removed without counterproductive compromises or extraneous considerations, and the dismissal must be done immediately as necessity dictates, rather than at the end of the war or after a board of inquiry hands down its verdict. The following historical example is instructive.

In mid-February 1943, Rommel attacked the US Second Corps in the Kasserine Pass in Tunisia. The performance of the senior American commanders, headed by Major General Lloyd Fredendall, was deplorable in the extreme. The Second Corps was repeatedly bashed. Eisenhower, the supreme commander of the American forces in North Africa, realized that he had to sack Fredendall, but, because of his own inexperience as a commanding general, he hesitated too long, and the American forces continued to incur casualties and were finally defeated. Eisenhower recouped, dismissed the commander of the Second Corps, and appointed Major General George Patton in his place. Before Patton left for the front, Eisenhower told him: "You must not retain for one instant any man in a responsible position where you have become doubtful of his ability to do the job. This matter frequently calls for more courage than any other thing you will have to do, but I expect you to be perfectly cold-blooded about it" (Ambrose 2010–2011, 91).

In a letter to his friend General Leonard Gerow, Eisenhower wrote: "Officers that fail must be ruthlessly weeded out. Considerations of friendship, family, kindliness, and nice personality have nothing whatsoever to do with the problem. You must be tough" (Ambrose 2010–2011, 91–92).

William Gladstone, the nineteenth-century British prime minister, said: "The first essential for a great Prime Minister is to be a good butcher." We would add: "The same goes for a great general."

Lessons from the Chinese Farm Battle

During the battle (incorrectly termed the "Chinese Farm Battle"), the 162nd Division suffered 190 casualties, including 50 killed. Forty of the fatalities and 120 of the wounded were from the 890th Battalion; the rest were tankers. Seven tanks and two APCs were hit and three of the tanks destroyed. This was the price paid for gaining nothing. The 890th and 100th Battalions fought in vain. Claiming that the paratroopers' sacrifice enabled the transport of the rafts to Akavish to Matzmed is a disingenuous attempt to give the soldiers' effort a positive gloss and whitewash the commanders who carelessly and irresponsibly sent them to their deaths (see the previous chapter).

There is a tendency to forget that the Chinese Farm Battle was not the private affair of the 890th Battalion and the 35th Brigade. It was the 162nd Division's battle. The 162nd initiated it, determined its objectives, planned it, decided which of its forces would take part in it, briefed the commanders who were being sent into battle, allocated support units, and determined when, where, and how the battle would be fought and the tactics that would be applied. Like the battle to open the roads that the division conducted on the afternoon of October 16, the Chinese Farm Battle ended in failure. The mission was not accomplished. But this time, unlike the afternoon event, it exacted a heavy price in the lives of the division's men. The 890th's night battle was undeniably superfluous and its results were foreseen. How was it possible to ignore the 143rd Division's inability, despite its struggle and sacrifice on the night of October 15–16, and the 162nd Division's attempts in the afternoon of the same day to open Tirtur Road? It is difficult to accept that the 162nd's commanders and staff officers were blind to the events on Tirtur Road the previous nights. It is equally difficult to believe that those officers thought in all honesty that four infantry companies—without intelligence, without support weapons, without artillery liaison, and without close armor support—could accomplish what two armored divisions had failed to.

The only conceivable reason is that the commanders of the 162nd expected that the 890th Battalion would somehow enable the Unifloat rafts to pass through on Akavish Road and that, for this reason alone, they were prepared to risk the battalion. But here, too, Adan spoke in more than one voice: "At 0130, October 17, I realized that the timetable put the completion of the mopping up in doubt. I decided to narrow the area in question and ordered Uzi Yairi [the commander of the 35th Brigade] to call in the southern company [which was designated to clean out Akavish Road] to mop up only Tirtur Road" (Adan 1979, 212). But, in the Southern Command conference on July 24, 1974, he testified: "What mainly worried me . . . was that Yairi would open the road because, after all, the fate of the crossing depended on the rafts reaching the canal."

The rafts that Adan was referring to were, of course, the Unifloat rafts, and the road that was supposed to be opened for them was Akavish. It is difficult, then, to understand what exactly Adan expected from the battle, but his actions testify that he wished to open Akavish as a conduit for the Unifloat rafts. In the previous chapter, we noted (and wish to reemphasize) that elementary military logic dictates that a patrol should have been sent to test the movement on Akavish before the paratroopers' and tankers' blood was spilled, not after scores of dead and wounded had been sacrificed for naught. In this light, there is much justification in claiming that the Battle of the Chinese Farm was embarked on before its unavoidability had been demonstrated.

In *Real Time* (1993), Ronen Bergman and Gil Meltzer quote the responses of Brigadier General Tamari, the deputy commander of the 162nd Division, regarding the criticism that several veterans of the paratrooper brigade voiced against the division commander:

> The problem with the 35th's paratroopers was not only that they came unprepared to the Chinese Farm but they came unprepared to the entire war. . . . [The paratroopers and the Golani Infantry Brigade] were not ready for real war. . . . What difference does it make if there's intelligence or not? If you think this is the test then you're very wrong. The question is whether you're ready for different types of battle. They [the paratroopers] only know how to capture a fortified objective when they have maps, air photos, a [planned] attack route, etc. Suddenly they have to deal with something different, and they arrive without an artillery liaison officer, without APCs, without prior preparations, and that's what it looked like. So what's the ruckus all about? (1993)

Tamari might very well be correct regarding the paratroopers. But, if the men of the 35th Brigade were as poorly prepared for the challenges of the Yom Kippur War as he claims, why did the 162nd Division assign them so important a battle? Was it only after the 890th failed to accomplish its mission and suffered such heavy losses that the 162nd's commanders realized that the paratroopers had come to the war lacking sufficient weapons and training and were unqualified for and incapable of waging the type of war that Adan and Tamari were—at least in their own minds—so proficient and experienced at?

Furthermore, although the 890th may have failed to carry out its mission and incurred heavy losses because it was sent into battle without artillery liaison and proper training, as Tamari charged, for the sake of honesty, he should also have mentioned that the 162nd was given faulty, misleading intelligence that convinced it to assign to four paratrooper companies a mission that two armored divisions had been unable to accomplish.

Some still argue that the 35th Brigade commander, Colonel Yairi, erred in going to battle without the minimal resources (reliable intelligence, suitable equipment and support weapons, artillery coordination, battle procedure, etc.). Indeed, under ordinary circumstances, one might expect an officer of Yairi's rank not to agree to go out to battle until the required conditions were met, for the sake of both mission accomplishment and his men's lives, but the circumstances that compelled him to lead his soldiers to the Chinese Farm Battle were extraordinary. The commander of the front, who was a former IDF CoGS and three ranks above him, personally contacted him and placed on his shoulders the yoke of responsibility for the victory or defeat of the IDF in a critical operation that would determine the future and perhaps the fate of the country. This burden of responsibility, which was described in the previous chapter, made it imperative for Yairi to enter the battle unconditionally and as quickly as possible. The point is that, given the military situation on October 16, there was no need to blackmail Yairi with the emotional-patriotic steamroller.

Cairo, First Steps: Blather and Decisions

The reports and memoirs of Israeli commanders frequently lack a rudimentary element: the exact time that a certain event happened. One of the reasons for this is to frustrate the ability of a reader or a scholar to cross-check the information with other independent sources to get to the truth (to the extent that such a thing exists). Information dissembling is not an Israeli invention, as the memoirs of Shazly, the Egyptian CoGS in the war, testify to in his book *The Crossing of the Suez.* In describing the Egyptian response to the IDF's moves in the Deversoir area on the night of October 15–16, he claims that already, in the planning stage, the Egyptian high command assumed that the IDF would react to the crossing with its own crossing and even identified Deversoir (in the Matzmed vicinity) as a possible fording site. He also states: "The 16th Division [Second Army] from the north met the 7th Division [Third Army] from the south [in a seam that] was the classic area for enemy penetration" (1980, 253). This "meeting point" or "seam" (as the IDF called it) between the armies was actually a gap tens of kilometers wide between the Egyptians' two bridgeheads that extended nearly the entire length of the eastern shore of the Great Bitter Lake.

Shazly explains that at first the high command saw no reason to panic at the IDF crossing. The Second Army reported that it was capable of dealing with the situation.

Towards noon October 16 reports reached Cairo from SAM bases fifteen kilometers west of the canal that they were under attack by small Israeli armor units. In the afternoon the Egyptian high command started discussing the course of action to be taken against the Israeli bridgehead. Destruction of the bridgehead would begin the next day. As usual in such cases, two possible courses of action were on the agenda: concentrating forces on the western bank and attacking the Israeli bridgehead on the western side of the canal or using the armies' forces in Sinai for a coordinated pincer attack from both south and north on the eastern bank.

For grand strategic considerations and possibly military ones, the Egyptian commander of the armed forces, General Ahmed Ismail Ali, preferred the pincer attack from the bridgeheads in Sinai rather than attacking on the western bank, the option that Shazly and the bridgehead commanders favored. That evening, the "generalissimo," President Sadat, arrived and scornfully brushed Shazly's ideas aside, which goes to show that at this level political considerations trump all others. At midnight October 16–17, the high command ordered the armies to prepare to counterattack in the morning. The plan envisioned a coordinated pincer attack on the bridgehead at dawn by the Second Army from the north and the Third Army from the south. According to Shazly, the attack was based on three efforts:

- The 116th Infantry Brigade, deployed on the western bank, would attack east, directly toward the bridgehead.
- The 21st Armored Division would attack south with the aim of cutting off the main access road to the bridgehead.
- The 25th Armored Brigade would egress from the Third Army's bridgehead and head north to the Israeli bridgehead in Sinai.

The pincer battle on the eastern bank was scheduled for the morning of October 17 with the forces from the north and the south acting in coordination.

Shazly (1980) notes that an operational order was issued to the armies at midnight October 16–17. Israel apparently intercepted it because, six hours before the attack, Ben-Ari informed Adan, according to the Southern Command's operational diary, that an enemy force was "moving from north to south." Therefore, the 143rd Division was ordered to the Lakekan area to block toward the south. Also, the 162nd Division's CoS radioed the division's chief operations officer, Lieutenant Colonel Gilad Aviram, about the Southern Command's warning that an Egyptian armored brigade had been ordered to move north on Lexicon Road from the Third Army's bridgehead and attack that night and that the 162nd had to block somewhere south of Edara and set up company blocking positions. In *On the Banks of the Suez* (1979), Adan describes the discussions in Cairo and the decisions that were reached, but he makes no mention of the warning that he received of an armored brigade movement from the Third Army's bridgehead and its mission to attack the IDF's bridgehead from the south. On the contrary, he claims that he knew nothing of the Egyptian plan.

The Southern Command's operational log notes that, in the evening of October 16, the 143rd received a warning that the bridgehead might be attacked the following day by a force from the Third Army's bridgehead moving on Lexicon. This explains why Sharon ordered Amnon Reshef, the commander of the 14th Brigade, to secure the division's southern flank in the Lakekan area. Reshef assigned the task to his deputy and allotted him the brigade's infantry forces. As daylight approached, he sent the remnants of the 87th Reconnaissance Battalion (five tanks) of the battalion's former C Company and now H Company/79th Battalion, under the command of Lieutenant Yair Litvitz, to carry out observation at Graphite and put the remnants of another company on standby: A Company/407th Battalion/600th Brigade, under the command of Major Ehud Gross, was now also part of the 79th Battalion.

The Fighting Before Noon October 17

At 0600, Adan's division launched an attack of sorts designed to clean up Akavish finally. Four battalions took part: Nathan Piram's 142nd/217 Brigade operated in the Akavish 51 area toward the north; to its right the 100th Battalion/460th Brigade engaged mainly in the rescue of the 890th Battalion on Photon Road in the Akavish 53 area; and north of it operated the 196th and 19th Battalions of the 460th Brigade. Later, the 600th Brigade came under Adan's command and was sent to exert pressure from Hamadia toward the west.

The 460th's 198th Battalion, now attached to Reshef's brigade, was deployed for the defense on Shik Road. (More about its fighting will be related below.) The 217th Brigade's 126th Battalion, under the command of Giora Kopel, and the

112th, under the command of Zeev Ram, remained at Edara to secure the area of action from the south.

The five battalions that were deployed against the Egyptian defenses on Tirtur Road began to apply pressure to the west and southwest in the form of long-range tank and artillery fire on the Egyptian armor and infantry concentrations while staying clear of the Egyptian line. The historian Amiram Ezov notes: "In this manner, the threat from Tirtur on Akavish gradually lifted" (2011, 230). By 0730, the 162nd granted permission to combat vehicles to travel on Akavish, and, at 1100, it reported that the road was open for movement.

From these descriptions, it is absolutely incomprehensible on what basis the 162nd Division reported opening Akavish for traffic. Apparently, its battalions opened what was already open.

The fact is that, at 0622, Colonel Even radioed Adan, "Is Akavish clear?" and Adan replied, "Akavish has been cleared and [still is] clear." This exchange took place more than an hour before the 162nd granted permission to the combat vehicles to travel on the road and four and a half hours before the division announced that Akavish was open for traffic. This conversation, especially the second part of the message, where Adan describes the "opening in stages" of Akavish on the morning of October 17, leaves us amazed.

The Egyptian Counterattack

Adan Learns That the Third Army's 25th Brigade Has Arrived

At 0805, the commander of the 600th Brigade informed Adan: "My units at Hurva in the far south identified a large force moving north-northwest from Lexicon 283–285." In other words, the enemy was already moving on Lexicon, two to three kilometers southeast of the Lexicon-Caspi Junction. This was Adan's signal. Only now did he become aware that the Egyptian counterattack was unfurling in his sector. He ordered the 217th Brigade commander, Colonel Nir, to immediately take the two battalions securing at Edara and deploy them on Graphite and Yachfan, southwest of Edara. Nir, who had been with the 142nd Battalion in operations at Akavish 53, joined the two battalions in the south and set off to meet the enemy. The battle with the Egyptian 25th Tank Brigade began to unfold.

The Second Army Attacks from the North

At 0800, the Second Army opened the attack. The remnants of the Egyptian 21st Armored Division and units of the 16th Infantry Division moved out of Missouri and the Chinese Farm and attacked Adan's brigade and the 600th Brigade on Akavish and between Akavish and Tirtur. The armored battles in that area were fought with varying degrees of intensity throughout the day, mostly in the form of long-range tank and artillery fire.

The 198th Battalion in Combat

On the night of October 16–17, Egyptian infantry attacked the 198th Battalion (attached to the 14th Brigade/143rd Division), which had deployed defensively on Shik Road. The Egyptians were repulsed as their casualties mounted. The 14th's intelligence officer warned the 198th commander of an armored brigade attack of sixty tanks north to south along Lexicon. Egyptian armor (the 24th Brigade, according to the intelligence officer) made repeated attacks. In the morning, the 198th's fourteen Centurion tanks, which had been deployed along Lexicon facing east to meet an attack from Amir that never materialized, were joined by a tank company from the 599th Battalion led by the deputy battalion commander. In the ensuing battle, which lasted a few hours, the 198th broke several waves of Egyptian armor attacks. From the reports and tallies, the 198th's commander reckoned that his battalion knocked out forty-five tanks in addition to APCs, artillery pieces, and other vehicles without losing a single tank (see below).

The rest of the 599th was smuggled over to the western bank on the back of the Crocodiles in the early morning of October 17 and linked up with its mother brigade, the 421st. This event prompted Ben-Ari and Gonen (each in his turn) to reiterate to Sharon that he was forbidden to bring any more tanks across the canal. Later, Bar-Lev joined the chorus of naysayers.

The Yard Compound Is Born

Initial Construction of the Raft Bridge

As already mentioned, at 0600 October 17, Tamari, the deputy commander of the 162nd Division, handed the Unifloat rafts to the "fatso" (Sharon, as Tamari referred to him in his report to the Southern Command) at Lakekan. Under Sharon's supervision, the convoy reached Matzmed at 0630, and earthworks preparations were immediately begun in order to launch the rafts into the water. At 0700, the first raft was in the canal.

From this moment on, the engineers began assembling the rafts to form the bridge.

Construction was delayed because of technical problems with the couplings.

The fast couplings that the corps of engineers developed had not been produced yet. To make matters worse, shortly after the rafts arrived at the Matzmed bridgehead, Egyptians shells began landing in the Yard. The shelling was continuous with fluctuations in intensity. At first, it was relatively weak, but the Yard was accurately targeted. Despite the relatively restrained fire, a number of combat engineers at the bridge were hit, as were three rafts, and one Crocodile was destroyed. The engineers worked gallantly under fire. At 0815, a third of the bridge seemed to be in place; by 1100, it appeared very likely that it would be completed by 1600. This was reported to the division commander. However, the rafts had already been assembled into a bridge by 1400, and only two hours of work remained to finish the project.

At 0630, when Gonen made it clear to Sharon that no more tanks would cross the canal unless on a bridge, most of the Crocodiles were lying idle on the eastern bank. Even if we concede a sliver of logic to the Southern Command's obstinacy against bringing tanks across until the bridge was standing, then with the start of construction, not to mention its progress, the injunction was transformed from an operational error to a major, whimsy-based blunder. As the counterattack on the western part of the bridgehead intensified, the crossing of additional armored forces became imperative. Precious time should not have been wasted. Enough tank units were sitting idle in the area or engaged in worthless tasks.

The Establishment of the Yard Perimeter

The arrival of the Unifloat rafts ushered in the concentration of forces on the eastern side of the bridgehead. Besides the three bridging battalions (the 630th, the 634th, and the 605th) operating at the bridgehead, other engineering elements were also there, such as the division's 229th Engineering Battalion and the 606th Bulldozer Tank Battalion. Mobile antiaircraft canon batteries (the 207th and the 208th), medical evacuation teams, and other forces soon arrived. The bridgehead area on the eastern bank was bordered by a dirt embankment roughly in the shape of a rectangle 500 meters long and 150–200 meters wide between Matzmed in the south and Matzmed "A" in the north. At first, this area was simply called the Yard, but it was soon dubbed the Death Yard or, for short, the Yard.

Toward the capture of the bridgehead, the commander of the 247th Brigade, Danny Matt, appointed Lieutenant Colonel Yossi Fradkin, the former commander of the brigade's 28th Battalion, as Yard commander. Fradkin and a handful of men began organizing the compound, setting up a control point, marking internal roads, establishing perimeter security, and so forth. This arrangement lasted as long as the Yard was not terribly busy.

But, with the arrival of other forces, the need for a division command and control system became acute. According to IDF doctrine, the deputy division commander was supposed to supervise the bridgehead. But this doctrine was built on the assumption (or wishful thinking) that the crossing would be made without a battle to the waterline and that the crossing equipment would arrive as planned, quickly and without pernicious problems. The reality of October 1973 turned the doctrine upside down: the deputy division commander's responsibility was spread out in areas far from the bridgehead with the result that the initial focus of his activity, the responsibility for getting the crossing equipment into the water, was located ten to fifteen kilometers from the canal and demanded his presence there.

As long as it seemed that the 162nd Division would open Tirtur Road and clean out Akavish of enemy and by doing so enable the Unifloat rafts and roller bridge to reach the canal, Even had to be present where the equipment was. But, when it became clear that Tirtur remained blocked and there was no telling when it would open, and especially after the Unifloat rafts reached the Yard and construction on the bridge began, Even and Sharon came to the conclusion that Even's place was at the bridgehead. Thus, the deputy division commander and his FCP reached the Yard at 1100, and Sharon immediately put him in charge of the bridgehead.

As soon as Even arrived, the enemy shelling escalated. There were three reasons for this. First, the more time that passed, the clearer it became to the Egyptians that the Israeli bridgehead was not just a trick to raise national and army morale but a decisive, intentional effort to alter the direction of the war. Second, the Egyptian Second Army's counterattack failure in the north of the sector, combined with the cloud of disaster hanging over the 25th Brigade and its dithering far from the bridgehead in the south of the sector, created the need to terminate construction of the Israeli bridgehead and disrupt the movement on it. This forced the Second Army to play its last card: massive shelling of the bridgehead. Finally, the Egyptians undoubtedly possessed real-time information on the pace of the bridge's construction. Thus, the closer it came to completion, the more the shelling intensified.

Appendix B details the bridgehead's objectives and structure and the forces that worked on it, defended it, and secured it.

The 25th Brigade's Counterattack, Part 1

Adan states that, at 0805, he first learned from Raviv, the commander of the 600th Brigade, that the 600th's lookouts at the Hurva fortification had identified a large tank force moving on Lexicon, three to four kilometers southeast of the Lexicon-Caspi Junction. In his book, he claims that he ordered the commander of the 217th brigade, Nir, to move two battalions from Edara to Graphite, conceal them in the Edara hills, and destroy the enemy in an ambush on the plain beneath Graphite where the killing zone was designated. The division radio traffic records make no mention of this task or the preparations that had to be undertaken at Edara, nor is there even a hint in Adan's order via radio to the 217th commander of the mission to annihilate the enemy. Learning of the approaching enemy tanks, Adan instructed Nir: "Deploy on Akavish to the left of the division's sector [a reference to the 142nd Battalion]. Bring the rest of the brigade toward Graphite to block the enemy armor that might be coming from south on Lexicon. . . . Take two battalions with you" (Adan 1979, 219). Nir organized his two battalions, and the brigade was ready, a kilometer to a kilometer and a half west of Edara. At this stage, Adan was with his FCP at the Kishuf fortification, from whence he directed the sporadic clashes between the 460th Brigade with its attached units (the 142nd Battalion/217th Brigade and the 600th Brigade's battalions) and the Second Army forces that were attacking from the north. Later, Adan's forces took part in rescuing the 890th Battalion.

On the morning of October 17, unrelated to the 217th Brigade's preparations, the commander of the 14th Brigade of the 143rd Division sent the five tanks (under the command of Lieutenant Yair Litvitz) that remained of C Company (of the 87th Reconnaissance Battalion and attached now as H Company to the 79th Battalion) to Graphite for observation. Since the force was nearly out of fuel and ammunition, it was dispatched to the rear at 1000 to replenish. At noon, Reshef sent A Company's four tanks, under the command of Major Ehud Gross, to Lexicon Road south of Lakekan to block the Egyptian 25th Brigade (this was the same A Company of the 407th Battalion/600th Brigade and attached to the 14th Brigade that on the night of October 15–16 had opened Akavish; it was now part of the 79th Battalion). The company apparently deployed at Lexicon 265. Reshef determined the force's position in the field and its mission (blocking the Egyptian force approach from the south) without any connection to the 217th Brigade's mission and its battalions' location. The commander of A Company did not even know that he was operating within the framework of a division ambush. The only coordination between the 14th Brigade and the 217th was the reciprocal updating of their locations. In other words, tactical coordination was missing; only administrative coordination was maintained for safety purposes.

The table of organization and equipment of an Egyptian tank brigade was ninety-four tanks organized in three battalions as well as an armored infantry battalion, reconnaissance forces, an artillery battery of eighteen 122-millimeter canons, a battery of mobile antiaircraft cannon, a detachment of SAM-7 antiaircraft missiles, antitank missile vehicles, and other units. The 25th Brigade went to battle with its tank strength less than the standard. It is not clear whether the brigade was organized in two tank battalions or three reduced ones, and, in any case, it does not really matter. What is certain from the various reports is that the 25th went to battle with about sixty T-62s, the Egyptian army's most advanced tank.

Without going into the details of the battle, we will discuss the main points and the timing to illustrate the principles that were either underlying the battle or broken during its execution.

The Battle—Morning October 17

On the morning of October 17, the 25th Brigade began its advance to contact on Lexicon from the Polish Camp on the Gidi–Canal Road Junction. Just before 0800, 14th Brigade observers at Graphite radioed the 14th's commander, Amnon Reshef, that a large "cloud of dust" was moving in the Lexicon area from south to north. A few minutes later, the 600th's observers at Hurva reported to the brigade commander, Tuvai Raviv, that a large enemy force was moving north on Lexicon three to four kilometers southeast of the Lexicon-Caspi Junction. The report was relayed to Adan, who ordered the commander of the 217th Brigade to annihilate the force in an ambush. At 0900, the 183rd Battalion of the 164th Brigade (of the 252nd Division), commanded by Lieutenant Colonel Hagai Cohen, moved west from its positions at the Gidi–Artillery Road Junction and opened fire on the tail of the 25th at Lexicon 289. The Egyptian brigade responded with a few tanks and antitank missile launchers. The 164th Brigade reported that the battalion had knocked out sixteen enemy tanks, but this number has been questioned. At the same time, the observers at Hurva reported that a forty-tank force of the 25th was visible at Habakuk, Botzer, and Lexicon 275. At 0937, Gonen checked the 25th's situation with Adan and offered him the Southern Command's reserve force—the 500th Brigade. The offer went unanswered for an hour and a half (according to the Southern Command radio traffic records). At no point did Adan mention Gonen's offer. According to some reports, Adan categorically denied that Gonen offered him Aryeh Keren's 500th Brigade. The 25th sent a force to outflank Nir's 217th Brigade from the south (via Yachfan) at 1005, but the effort was blocked. Twenty minutes later, another attempt was made to outflank or attack Hurva. Zelichover's platoon that was deployed there repulsed the attempt. At 1030, the commander at Hurva reported that his force had scored hits on enemy tanks and that he was "improving his position" to the bend in Caspi Road at point 61. This ended the 25th's attempt to get onto Caspi Road, and, henceforth, it would move only on Lexicon. While this was happening, the commander of the 217th Brigade took under its wing the force from the 600th Brigade at Hurva (in effect, the entire 600th Brigade was now under the command of the 162nd Division). After the 25th's attempts to travel on Caspi Road were thwarted, it was delayed, inexplicably, between Botzer and Lexicon 273.

At 1045, an hour after Gonen offered Adan the 500th Brigade, the division's chief operations officer, Gilad Aviram, asked Colonel Nir whether he thought the 500th could be brought into battle in the south. Nir had reservations: "I don't think so. If [the Egyptians] reach us, I'll deal with them." But, on second thought, he added that the 500th should be brought into the fray. Aviram issued Colonel Aryeh Keren, the commander of the 500th Brigade, a warning order with details on the size of the Egyptian force (brigade size), its location (between Botzer and Lexicon 273), its status (idle), and the location of Israeli forces (the 217th at Yachfan, and informed Keren: "We might be sending you south of Yachfan to destroy the enemy. Keep in radio contact." To recall, at this stage, the lion's share of Keren's brigade was being held in reserve ten kilometers southeast of Tassa (at the Mavdil-Revicha Junction), and one of its battalions was parked on Talisman Road at Tziona.

At 1055, Aviram repeated the warning to Keren, and, two minutes later, the deputy division commander, Dov Tamari, ordered him to move south on Mavdil, turn west to Kronika, and reach the approach to Tzikhtzu'ach (a shallow compound overlooking Lexicon Road from Botzer to Lexicon 271). The mission was defined as "a golden opportunity to knock the bejesus out of the [enemy]." Keren had to execute this mission with two battalions—the 430th, under the command of Lieutenant Colonel Eliashiv Shimshi, and the 433rd, under the command of Lieutenant Colonel Nahum Zaken (the 429th remained at Talisman). Shortly after 1100, the brigade commander began his approach. He had to travel fifty kilometers, mostly on the Pazoom sand track that linked Mavdil with Kronika Road, three kilometers from Kronika-Caspi (the Ikool compound). While advancing slowly on this problematic road, he tried coordinating with the division's chief operations officer his position in the battle. Aviram directed him to Nir, who updated him on his location at Graphite and instructed him to proceed with his entire force to Ikool and from there south between Yachfan and Tzichtzuach, where he deployed opposite the enemy on Lexicon 275, 271, and 269. A few minutes later, Nir corrected his instructions and ordered him to deploy opposite the enemy on Lexicon 269–73.

At this point, we leave the Egyptian 25th Brigade with the storm clouds approaching and move to another event of that afternoon: the top brass meeting at Adan's forward headquarters in the sand dunes south of Kishuf.

"Let's go crazy in the sand" (Shaike Paikov, an Israeli songwriter)

Assembly

At noon October 17, a day and a half after the start of the crossing battle, a faint light finally appeared at the end of the tunnel.

The threat of enemy fire was removed from Akavish, the main access road to the bridgehead, although the road was still plagued by terminal arteriosclerosis owing to the enormous number of limited traversability vehicles parked on it and preventing it from functioning efficiently as an access road. Once the Unifloat rafts reached Matzmed in the morning, the bridge building commenced. Despite the merciless shelling and myriad technical foul-ups, construction was scheduled for completion by 1600.

Throughout each stage of the fighting, no essential changes were made at the senior command level in the definition of the Southern Command's missions with regard to implementing them. But, during the past day and a half, the Southern Command's plan proved impossible to execute for reasons already discussed. The impracticality of the battle plan was expressed in the dangerous collapse of the overall timetable, the disruption in the allocation of the forces for combat missions, and the unavailability of the crossing equipment at the designated time (if at all). The crossing operation was saved from total catastrophe only because the Crocodiles were in the right place at the right time.

These developments naturally required a situation reassessment that would lead to corrective measures and drastic changes in the battle plans. Such a turnabout demands swift and efficient staff work at the General Staff, command, and division levels. But the top brass glossed over this stage and substituted for it an impromptu discussion that took place at noon October 17, enabled by pure chance that brought together Dayan, Elazar, Bar-Lev, Adan, and Sharon at the same time to Adan's FCP at Kishuf. As Adan notes: "No one convened a commanders' meeting at my FCP" (Adan 1979, 218).

Dayan and Bar-Lev reached Kishuf at 1030 October 17. At one point, Dayan asked to see Sharon at the bridgehead, but Bar-Lev and Adan dissuaded him and suggested inviting Sharon to Kishuf. Sharon, with all his acumen and experience, was nonetheless as naive as a newborn lamb in some ways. When he left Matzmed for Kishuf, he expected his colleagues to congratulate him and express their heartfelt admiration for his division's achievements in the crossing battle. Instead, when he arrived at Kishuf at 1230, Bar-Lev rebuked him. His first reaction, he remembered, was to slap Bar-Lev across the face, but he restrained himself, probably to Bar-Lev's chagrin since it was he who apparently initiated the provocation. Thirty minutes later, Elazar and Major General Rechavam Zeevi

("Gandhi"), special assistant to the CoGS, landed at Kishuf to complete the quorum, and the discussion in the sand dunes began.

The Discussion in the Sand Dunes

The meeting of the senior members of the military-security establishment in the Kishuf sand dunes is one of the most tragicomic yet instructive episodes of the Yom Kippur War. What did the meeting hope to achieve? Military scholars as well as the participants themselves present differing answers. The background to the meeting was the report that the first bridge would be ready by 1600.

Adan writes: "The first question on the agenda was: should we bring a large force over the Canal and keep the momentum of the breakthrough into 'Africa,' and if so, who would do the crossing and who would stay behind to secure the bridgehead?" (1979, 218) In his opinion, this was the most important question in the world. But, on second glance, the reader wonders whether anyone at Kishuf considered the possibility that large-scale forces might not cross the canal and would not pursue the momentum of "the breakthrough into 'Africa'"? Adan seems to be gilding the lily more than documenting history, and the reader can only conclude that, as far as Adan was concerned, the sole goal of the meeting was to determine who would cross first.

Lieutenant Colonel Aryeh Baron, Dayan's aide-de-camp, who was present at the meeting, recalled that, while he was in the Southern Command's operations room with Dayan on October 16, he "heard most of the senior officers, including the CoGS, discussing mainly how to prevent Sharon from crossing the canal before the others [i.e., Adan] and usurping all the glory" (Baron 1992, 188), Baron also states that the discussion in the sand dunes on October 17 revolved around two questions: the necessary conditions to bring most of the forces across and who would cross first. As to the answer to the first question, there were two opinions, Bar-Lev's and Sharon's. But the real point of the meeting was answering the second question: would Adan or Sharon cross first. Unlike Adan, who erred in his description, Baron touches a nerve. Given the almost certain assessment that the bridge would be completed by 1600 (in less than three hours), the question was: should the armored forces be ferried across on the Crocodiles or wait until the last bolt in the bridge was tightened and only then commence the large-scale transfer to the western bank. This was apparently the crux of the matter, but, even here, the real issue is missed. The fact is that there was no question at all: Elazar's and Bar-Lev's decision was final, and any attempt to change it fell on deaf ears. The two generals refused to take the smallest risk.

The historian Elhanan Oren attempts to turn the sand dune discussion into an event of historical proportions: "The senior commanders met to reach a joint estimate of the situation as the basis of the orders that would seal the fate of the crossing and the battle [i.e., campaign] in Egypt proper." But something—probably intellectual honesty—apparently drove Oren to note almost immediately: "For all practical purposes the discussion focused on which division would cross first once the bridge was standing and the Egyptian counterattack from the south had been blocked" (Oren 2004, 222). It is fascinating that, given all the theories in play, no one among those who were bickering about the subjects on the agenda imagined that the bridge would be standing idle for ten hours without the IDF's armored brigades crossing on it. The noted historian Ezov (2011) correctly points to another aspect of the sand dune meeting: it was designed to show Sharon in a most decisive manner who was boss (and perhaps make clear to Dayan the limits of his power).

One must unavoidably conclude that the meeting in the dunes was certainly not intended for any operational purposes. It was merely a bureaucratic meeting whose raison d'être was to inform all the parties concerned that the 162nd Division would cross first, followed by the 143rd when and only when Bar-Lev and Elazar chose to loosen the shackles on Sharon. A no less critical, even if rather latent, purpose of the meeting was an aggressive attempt by these two generals to put Sharon in his place in the front's hierarchy.

The 25th Brigade's Counterattack, Part 2

We left Nir's 217th Brigade and Keren's 500th Brigade about to confront the Egyptian 25th Brigade after the latter recovered from the inertia that had seized it after its failed attempts to get on Kaspi (Artillery) Road at Hurva. At the same time, but without any connection to the 162nd Division's deployment or missions, a reduced company of the 14th Brigade had deployed at Lexicon 265 in order to block the 25th's movement north.

At this point, Adan was still in his headquarters at Kishuf. At 1030, Dayan and Bar-Lev arrived first, followed by Sharon and Elazar. The meeting began at 1300. Adan's main interest—preserving his status as the first to cross—obligated his presence at the meeting. Nir, the commander of the 217th Brigade, was in the position of actually directing the battle. He was coordinating the deployment of his battalions as well as the approach and the eventual deployment of Keren's 500th Brigade. Naturally, he was also responsible for deciding when his brigade would open fire (but not when the 14th Brigade's detachment would).

Adan had been lucky up to this point. The 25th Brigade had closed in on itself with the result that Nir was unable to open fire and join the battle to destroy it. But the Egyptian brigade was capable of coming to life at any moment and continuing its drive north, which could have major implications for the person who would be springing the ambush against the 25th Brigade and manage the armor-versus-armor battle.

Bar-Lev, too, was interested in what was happening in this sector. From Kishuf, he contacted Gonen at 1130 and spoke with him briefly about the 25th's inaction. He expressed his concern that the Egyptian brigade might not advance north but dig in at Hurva. He correctly identified the 25th Brigade's potential to pin down the main forces of the 162nd Division without a fight, thus disrupting the Southern Command's plans, or to compel the 162nd to attack prematurely and give up on the ambush idea. At this stage, Bar-Lev seems to have realized that the 25th had the potential of threatening the crossing operation unless meticulous attention was paid to countering it.

Indeed, at 1300, the 25th Brigade's advance guard moved out from Lexicon 273, followed by the rest of the brigade, seven kilometers south of Lexicon 265, toward the bridgehead. Half an hour later, the advance guard came within range of fire from the A Company/14th Brigade's four tanks. A Company opened long-range fire and reported destroying part of the spearhead.

The main body of the 25th continued north, and part of it entered the 217th's killing zone. At the right moment, Nir ordered his forces to open fire. The exact time is uncertain, either in the radio or in the 162nd's operational logs. According to Adan, the battle began at 1445, that is, after he reached the ambush area and took direct command (1979, 220).The problem with this version is that, at 1428, Nir had already reported to him that he had opened fire on the 25th and set a large number of tanks ablaze, and Adan even chided him, saying: "Too bad that you began so early and didn't let the enemy enter fully into the killing zone." In other words, why did you not wait until I got there?

Discussing the 25th Brigade's counterattack (*Maarachot* 247–248), the historian Lieutenant Colonel Dr. Zeev Eitan (Ret.) writes that the 217th opened fire between 1300 and 1400, that is, at least forty-five minutes before Adan reached the area and took direct command of the battle. Ezov states that, during this time, Nir brought his battalions into firing position, but, on the basis of the conversation between Nir and Adan, Nir's brigade opened "effective" fire at 1420. The coupling of the adjective *effective* with *fire* raises the possibility that perhaps ineffective fire had been discharged earlier, and, indeed, according to the battle diagram in Ezov (2011, 168), fire commenced at 1330. In our opinion, Eitan comes closest to the truth. The only interesting conclusion to this elaboration is that the ambush battle began at least forty-five minutes prior to Adan's presence in the area to take control, if not much earlier. Thus, on the basis of this conclusion, we can understand Adan's impatience with the meeting in the dunes and his haste to get away as quickly as possible, directly oversee the action against the 25th Brigade, and take home the prize.

Back to the Discussion in the Dunes

> But where shall wisdom be found? And where is the place of understanding? (Job 28:12)

To recall, Dayan flew to Um Hashiba to speak with Bar-Lev and from there proceeded to Adan's command post at Kishuf at 1000. Bar-Lev arrived at approximately the same time. A three-way conversation ensued. Sharon came to Adan's headquarters at 1235, and, when half an hour later the CoGS and Zeevi arrived, the discussion commenced.

The exchange of opinion took place in stages, according to those present: first, between Adan, Dayan, and Bar-Lev, then with Sharon, and finally with Elazar. The following section describes the content and decisions of the meeting without reference to the particular stage.

In effect, the meeting looked more like a series of monologues than an actual discussion. Each of the participants had a pet issue and a firm opinion that he wished to raise without a genuine desire to listen to the others and weigh their contribution to the success of the war.

Dayan wanted only the swift buildup on the western bank and its immediate use in action. He said so specifically to the deputy CoGS in the Kirya (IDF headquarters in Tel Aviv) before departing for the south. Bar-Lev claimed that Adan's division was unavailable for this mission since it was on standby to block the 25th Brigade, which was coming from the south, and the division's forces were presently engaged with the Second Army, which was attacking from the north. Bar-Lev reminded Dayan that, after the division's current and expected battles, its replenishment and reorganization would take considerable time. In response to Dayan, who had wisely recommended not getting embroiled in unnecessary battles, Bar-Lev stressed, without an explanation, that this fighting was vital for the continuation of operations.

To satisfy Dayan somehow, Bar-Lev mentioned the possibility of elements of Sharon's division immediately crossing the canal once the bridge was assembled. Bar-Lev's reason for this about-face in his position was that, in any case, Sharon was not operating as expected in the corridor on the western bank. "Nothing I assign [him] is carried out," he groused to Dayan (Baron 1992, 195). This bizarre explanation may have been intended to provide Adan with a simple explanation since he was undoubtedly deeply disappointed with Bar-Lev's ideas. Bar-Lev, however, may have broached the idea for much more serious reasons than those he confided to Dayan. First, despite his displeasure with Sharon, he still believed that Sharon, who had crossed first and would soon be leading a considerably large armored force, was the right person in the right place. Second, he must have figured that, following the battle with the 25th Brigade and the valuable time spent in reorganization, Adan's division would be ready to cross the canal much later than Dayan had demanded. Ezov (2011, 142) states that Adan did not "buy" Bar-Lev's curious explanation for granting Sharon the privilege of crossing first and was quick to assure his superior that he would be ready to cross at 1600 since he could block (he no longer said *annihilate*) the 25th Brigade with only one brigade. The point is that, in either case, he did not have a third brigade to cross with as long as the 500th Brigade was the Southern Command's reserve.

Sharon, who yearned to be the first to cross into "Africa," was not satisfied with having won this privilege as his division's 247th and 421st Brigades were already fighting on the western bank. He argued that the success had to be exploited immediately and that additional forces from his division that were sitting idle in the Yard should be ferried over by the Crocodiles, which were also unemployed, anchored to the canal bank.

Bar-Lev firmly opposed bringing a large armored force to the other side before the bridge was completed, and he had Elazar's support on this. He was willing to leave fifty tanks at most in Africa, that is, the armored force (the 421st Brigade and a tank company) already operating there. All Adan's concerns were split between preserving his status as the first to cross and his burning desire to get away from the meeting and take command of the battle against the 25th Brigade that was being fought under Nir's direction. Pulled by these conflicting drives, he supported Bar-Lev's position and even strengthened it with two learned theses of his own: that the bridgehead that Sharon had established was not yet a bridgehead in the strict doctrinal sense and that it had to be expanded and bolstered before large-scale forces could be brought across, implying that, while all this takes place, he was capable of destroying the 25th Brigade, replenishing his units, and leading the Southern Command's forces across the canal.

Adding to his anxiety, Bar-Lev again proposed that both division commanders cross together, each at the head of one of his brigades. There is no need to repeat Bar-Lev's arguments. Suffice it to say that it was a bureaucratic solution to a serious operational problem. The CoGS categorically rejected this idea and determined, also on a purely bureaucratic basis, that Adan would cross first and Sharon would remain on the eastern bank to stabilize the bridgehead. There was no estimate of the situation or practical military consideration at the basis of this decision.

Dayan, who probably despised this bureaucratic fracas, concluded the meeting by saying that, if Bar-Lev's conditions were met (a viable bridge, the end of the battle against the 25th Brigade, and the stabilization of a corridor to the bridgehead), then as large a number of tanks as possible had to be sent across, as Sharon proposed: "Unless something unexpected happens, we have to cross today starting at 1600." In their childhood, we would have said of such an inane summing up: "So he said; so what?" Dayan would soon learn the difficulty in getting sluggish bulls to budge.

Assessment of the Meeting in the Sand Dunes

The only decision that was reached, or, rather, approved, in the sand dune meeting was to leave the bulk of the 143rd in Sinai and only a fraction on the western bank solely to establish and secure the bridgehead and to allow the 162nd Division to cross the canal first after the 25th Brigade was eliminated. Adan calls this "a council in which major decisions were reached on the continuation of the war" (1979, 218). By the same token, it should not come as a surprise that Sharon held the opposite view: "The real meaning [of the decisions made in the meeting] would have caused additional and superfluous delays and disruption in exploiting the success. [It would have been] the ultimate missed opportunity to crush the Egyptian army by advancing rapidly and encircling the [two] armies before the Egyptian defense had time to organize and stiffen on the western bank" (Oren 2004, 222).

The main point in this discussion is that all the participants, excluding Bar-Lev, ignored the time and space factors in the battle with the 25th Brigade as it related to the 162nd Division crossing first. The facts were clear and simple: it was almost 1400, the battle would not be over in a minute but would take much longer, the tanks would have to refuel, and all the division's brigades and units would have to load up with ammo and reorganize; then the division would have to move the brigades to Matzmed and bring them over to the other side. All this complex activity (the battle, the replenishment, and the movement to the bridgehead) was supposed to be accomplished in the two hours between 1400 and 1600.

The participants in the discussions, except perhaps Dayan, were highly versed in the logistics of employing large-scale armored forces. This was true of Elazar, Bar-Lev, and Adan, who had all been commanders of armored formations, and even Sharon, who had converted to armor, commanded an armored brigade and recently an armored division, and conducted large-scale combined-arms battles. Small wonder, then, that Moshe Dayan summed up his understanding of what was to transpire thus: "It seems that until the bridge is completed Adan will have had enough time to finish the battle with the 25th Brigade and be ready to cross." And on Adan's position he noted: "Bren [Adan] wanted very much to cross the canal as soon as possible and promised to quickly destroy the Egyptian brigade, refuel, and cross that evening" (Dayan 1976, 649).

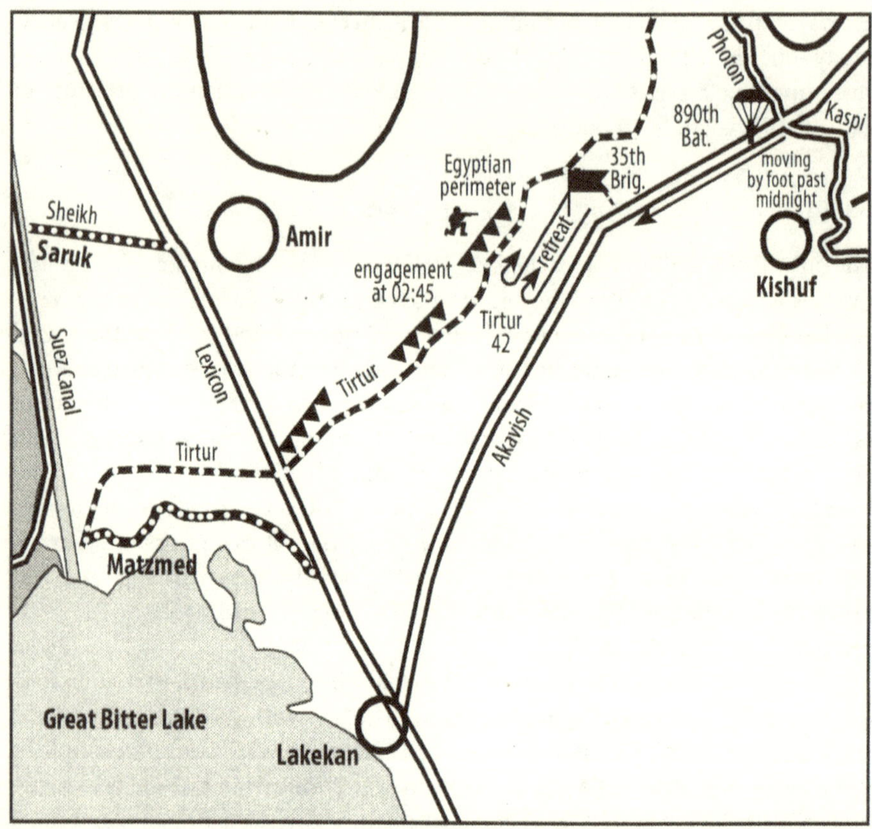

The fighting of the 35th Brigade's 890th Battalion on Tirtur Road on the night of October 16–17. Courtesy of Amiram Ezov.

The others present kept silent, except Bar-Lev, who apparently realized the unreality of the timetable that Dayan had swallowed and the folly of Elazar's decision that Adan's division should be the first to cross but did not even try to convince the others of his opposing view.

Elazar's conduct in the meeting is also of special interest. Bar-Lev, the front commander, thought that for important operational reasons (though he also raises personal matters as a cover) it would be a good idea to send one of Sharon's brigades and one of Adan's to the western bank once the bridge was completed. But Elazar intervened and rejected the proposal, and, by doing so, he erred twice: first, he intervened in a decision regarding the use of forces that the front commander was authorized to make; second, his veto of Bar-Lev's decision had no operational justification and was only a bureaucratic measure stemming from personal motives. Equally interesting is Bar-Lev's response to the CoGS's behavior: "Instead of putting Elazar in his place, as he should have, he bellyaches to Dayan about Elazar's intervention and decision" (Baron 1992, 198).

The CoGS seems to have been well aware of Sharon's opinion that his decisions in the sand dune meeting were the main cause for the delay in exploiting the crossing and achieving far less than was actually possible. According to Bartov, Elazar summed up the affair thus: "In retrospect I don't regret the delay. It was a good thing that Bren [Adan] was there when the 25th Tank Brigade came from the south and [Colonels] Natke [Nir] and Aryeh Keren decimated it beautifully; it was a good thing that Bren [Adan] was in the east when the Second Army attacked from the north. If we had advanced and crossed, we would have achieved a greater gain in the west, but might very well have lost in the east" (Bartov 1978, 261).

The meaning of this assessment is that, with hindsight, the CoGS believed that the Stouthearted Men plan was rotten and dangerous and that it was a stroke of luck that it was not implemented as planned. His words clearly point to a basic misunderstanding of the conduct of operations. Did he believe that the Second Army was going to attack from its bridgehead in the east if the IDF was about to encircle it from the west, destroy its bridges, and neutralize its antiaircraft missile umbrella—or gallop to Cairo? His assessment also reflects his miscomprehension of the tremendous damage that had been caused to the IDF's main effort by the 162nd's so-called annihilation battle against the Egyptian 25th Brigade.

The 25th Brigade's Counterattack, Part 3

We left the 25th Brigade with its vanguard reaching the area between Lexicon 269 and Lexicon 267. On its arrival, the Israeli tank company at Lexicon 265 opened fire. The time was 1300. The Egyptian advance guard ground to a halt, and several tanks were hit. An hour and a half or so later, the company was out of fuel and ammunition and was replaced by Lieutenant Litvitz's H Company. The brigade commander's tank, which had been part of the blocking force, joined H Company's five tanks. Between them and A Company (which returned to the fight after replenishing), the 14th Brigade's tanks destroyed the 25th's advance guard.

It will be noted that, like Zelichover's platoon at Hurva a few hours earlier, A Company opened fire on its own initiative, without connection to Adan's and Nir's plans.

The sand dune meeting ended at 1400, and Adan and his FCP moved on Caspi Road to the Caspi-Kronika Junction (fifteen kilometers from Kishuf), where he planned to set up the FCP. According to our reckoning, he reached the designated spot after 1440 since at this time he reported to the commander of the 500th Brigade that he was "on the way to the sector" and simultaneously asked the commander of the 217th Brigade, "Describe to me how the enemy is deployed," whereas elsewhere he enthusiastically mentions the excellent visibility from his position (after he arrived there). The place that Adan chose for his FCP was at least ten kilometers east of Lexicon Road, and certain sections of this road west of the shallow ridges of Yachfan and Graphite may have been in an area unobservable from Caspi 59.

As stated, Colonel Nir deployed one battalion at Graphite and a second at Yachfan. At 1400, with the arrival of the lead element of the 25th at Lexicon 267, he grew very concerned about the brigade overrunning the blocking forces and reaching the bridgehead, where it could make mincemeat of the units there. Thus, before 1400, he ordered his two battalions to open fire and at one point instructed them to shorten the range in order to increase the number of hits.

Beginning at 1100, two of Keren's battalions (the 430th and the 433rd) were on the sand track trudging toward the west. Once Adan's FCP was set up, he put merciless pressure on Keren to double speed it south to prevent the 25th from escaping south and to "roll up its tail" (his exact words) from Botzer to Matzmed. The hour to an hour and a half delay between the brigade's availability to the division and the division commander's decision to use it turned out to be a serious flaw, and, no matter how much the division commander exhorted and upbraided the brigade commander, nothing can alter this fact.

The 217th's initial tank fire found its mark, and the 25th halted and attempted simultaneously to counterattack and seek safety. At 1445, Nir reported to Adan: "I'm in the middle of battle, setting them on fire. They're running around like chickens with their heads cut off." But, despite this running around, the 25th's efforts to counterattack still caused Nir considerable apprehension, as can be detected in his messages to Adan twenty-five minutes after the above exuberance: "[Reshef, the commander of the 14th Brigade,] has to relieve some of the pressure." And in the same breath he reported: "[The Egyptians] are putting a hell of a lot of pressure on me."

Adan answered: "I'll send you part of [Keren's] force immediately. Calm down and set ablaze what's left [of the 25th] and the pressure will go down." Adan's words may have boosted Nir's confidence and encouraged him to double his effort because, at 1600, he elatedly reported to Adan: "We got our revenge. [The 25th] Brigade can be erased from the map." Adan, who saw his mission as wiping out the 25th, replied: "We've already erased it but keep smashing what's left." That is, pulverize them into dust. It is known that, in such processes, the universal rule is that the additional time needed to destroy more tanks increases inversely. At 1600, Keren's brigade joined the battle. One of his battalions maneuvered to block the 25th's escape, and another maneuvered on the southern flank of Nir's southern battalion. As dusk fell, Nir brought his third battalion (the 142nd) into battle, and it seems to have scored a number of hits.

At 1730, just after sunset, the battle was over. The 25th ceased to exist as a fighting unit, at least for the next day or two. About fifty Egyptian tanks and scores of APCs, artillery pieces, and other combat vehicles were burning or abandoned. The 25th's commander, a few dozen of his men, ten tanks, a couple of APCs, and antitank missile vehicles found refuge in the Botzer stronghold, and some of the tanks may have slipped away to the Third Army's bridgehead. The 162nd lost three tanks, all of them from the 500th Brigade, and a few men had been hit by antitank missiles and air strikes by eight MIGs that had swooped down on them at 1620.

The Results of the Ambush

See, I will tarry in the plain of the wilderness. (2 Sam. 15:28)

The battle with the 25th Brigade, purely as a military event, ended in a stunning IDF victory despite the many flaws in its planning and execution (see below). The 25th not only failed to accomplish its mission but also ceased to exist as a fighting unit for all practical purposes, at least for a few days. The Egyptian army lost fifty first-line tanks and scores of armored combat vehicles, field artillery pieces, and logistic and supply equipment. Dozens of Egyptian commanders and crewmen were dead or wounded.

The battle, however, took place not in a strategic void but in the widest possible framework. And, as such, it was not an especially significant contribution to the Egyptian army's defeat. In this sense, the 162nd Division may be said to have succeeded in hooking the sardine while letting the tuna escape. The ambush battle ended at dark, at 1730. An hour and a half earlier, the Unifloat bridge had been completed and sufficient conditions established, even in the eyes of the wariest generals, to order the forces across on a massive scale into decisive battles.

Because of the battlefield dynamics, the pace of bringing the Southern Command's forces into battle on the western bank was of key importance, especially as time was of the essence. But, instead of moving his forces as soon as the bridge was up, the 162nd's commander, who was so keen on being the first to cross the canal and had even won the privilege, dallied for over six hours from the end of the battle or almost eight hours from the moment the bridge was standing until his brigades started trundling across it. But even this information is misleading since the third tank to cross the bridge, from the 460th Brigade, caused a break in the bridge's western end. The repair took an hour and a half, and, in the meantime, the trusty Crocodiles were again called on to save the situation, but the pace of the crossing was slow.

This delay had, of course, intolerable consequences, which we will discuss shortly. Here, we will deal with the main reasons for the delay as well as the dithering at the highest levels of command in connection with it.

Adherence to the Ultimate Mission

From the start of the crossing battle, the 162nd was assigned to cross the Suez Canal in massive strength as soon as the conditions were ripe. The CoGS reaffirmed this in the sand dune meeting notwithstanding Sharon's and Bar-Lev's reservations. But developing situations in the battle demanded the 162nd's action in the fighting. On October 17, for example, although the division was ordered to prevent the Egyptian 25th from attacking the bridgehead, this did not diminish the overriding importance and urgency of its main mission. The defense minister regarded the main mission as the key to the war in the south and remained uneasy until some of the participants in the meeting, including Adan, convinced him that the 162nd could counterattack the 25th, which Dayan felt was superfluous, without impeding the division's role in the main mission. Thus, those who conceived the battle had to draw up plans that kept the time and space factors of the 162nd's role in the main mission intact. Even the historical sources do not make it clear who determined the principles of the battle's plan and management. In any case, even if the Southern Command did not plan the battle (though it seems that the basic operational concept was Gonen's and Ben-Ari's), the point is that the Southern Command gave its approval (or was supposed to) to the principles on which the plan was based and intended to meticulously oversee the conduct of operations.

The battle with the 25th was meant to achieve one practical goal: preventing that brigade from reaching the bridgehead and taking part in destroying it. But, since this goal did not dictate the battle's operational concept, the principles according to which the battle was planned and executed stood in flagrant contradiction to the 162nd's main mission. The following describes and analyzes these principles.

The Mission

The 162nd's mission was to destroy the Egyptian 25th Brigade. This implied thwarting it, but thwarting does not imply destruction. Moreover, a mission of destruction manifests the universal rule of 80–20, that is, the destruction of 80 percent of the enemy force takes place during the first 20 percent of the entire battle time, whereas the destruction of the remaining 20 percent of the enemy force requires 80 percent of the remaining battle time. This rule was realized, more or less, in the battle against the Egyptian 25th. Within thirty minutes of the 217th Brigade's opening fire, Nir reported: "Many enemy tanks burning. Can't count them all. All enemy logistic units in flight." And, an hour after the 217th opened fire, he radioed: "We've lit too many bonfires to count." At this point, if not earlier, the 25th Brigade had already failed in its mission. The added value of the 162nd Division's product, in terms of thwarting the enemy's mission, was at this point zero, and, in terms of the Southern Command's main mission, the added value of the division's product one hour after the opening round of fire was definitely negative. At 1600, Adan updated Ben-Ari that many enemy tanks were ablaze but urged him on: "Keep going, keep going!"

The Method

The advantage of an ambush is that it is best suited to a cost-effective battle of annihilation, as Hannibal proved in his famous ambush of the Roman army near Lake Trasimene in 217 B.C. The terrain layout and the organization of Hannibal's ambush were similar to the 162nd's twenty-two centuries later. The major shortcoming of the ambush is that a critical element of the battle initiative—determining H-hour—is left to the enemy.

The battle began at 0800 October 17, when the commander of the 600th Brigade informed Adan that his lookouts at Hurva observed the 25th moving north. Adan immediately ordered Nir to deploy two battalions at Graphite and Yachfan area and prepare to meet the enemy as it approached from the south. From 0900 on, various forces opened fire on the Egyptians: the 183rd Battalion/252nd Division and an hour later Zelichover's platoon at Hurva. At 1330, heavier, more concentrated fire was poured on by a 14th Brigade force, and, soon after, the 217th entered the battle (Keren's second brigade was still plodding through the sand on its way to the fighting zone).

From the time the 25th started moving until the battle of annihilation began, seven or more hours passed, and the entire battle lasted ten hours! If the 162nd had not allowed the enemy so much initiative in the battle and kept the initiative for itself by adopting a more aggressive fighting method, it would have been able to cripple the 25th, thwart its mission, replenish, reorganize, and reach the bridge by the time it was standing and cross the canal in full force.

Economy of Force

In October 1973, the IDF's combat doctrine still included the principle of economy of force, which meant that each secondary mission would be allotted the minimum force needed to achieve it in order to enable the maximum concentration of strength for the decisive mission. In the battle with the 25th, this principle was thrown to the wind. It should be remembered that, in the Yom Kippur War, the battle against the 25th was not the first engagement in which significant Egyptian armor was wiped out by Israeli armor. For example, on October 9, an Egyptian armored brigade attacked the 600th Brigade, which was deployed at Hamadia. The 409th Battalion, which was holding positions on the back slope, lunged forward to its firing positions at the right moment and liquidated thirty-five to forty Egyptian tanks in nothing flat. On October 14, the 252nd Division's forces were operating with a reduced paratrooper battalion (the 202nd) and reduced tank battalion against the Egyptian 3rd Armored Brigade, which was in movement east of Wadi Mabrook, and knocked out fifty of its tanks. On the morning of October 17, the 198th Battalion/460th Brigade (attached to the 14th Brigade) had fourteen tanks deployed on Shik Road and came under repeated attack by a force of sixty tanks. It fought off all the attacks and destroyed forty-five Egyptian tanks (the 198th also had a company from the 599th Brigade attached to it but did not participate directly in the battle, being instead deployed toward Amir to secure the battalion's flank).

The battle against the 25th produced similar results but was fought with an entirely different proportion of forces, as table 1 illustrates.

Table 1. IDF Order of Battle against the 25th Brigade

Division	**Brigade**	**Battalion(s)**	**Number of Tanks**	**Initial Stage Only**	**All Stages**	**Final Stage Only**
143	14	79	10		X	
252	164	183	20	X		
143	600	410	4		X	
162	217	113,126	50, together		X	
II	II	142	20			X
Command Reserve	500	430	28		X	
	II	433	19		X	
Total			151			

Note: X indicates "present."

Approximately 150 Israeli tanks took part in the fighting (forty in some stages, 110 in all the stages). Eight battalions from five brigades of three divisions were involved. Given the 25th's estimated sixty tanks in the battle, the initial force ratio in tanks was close to 1:2 in the initial stages in favor of the IDF. This ratio quickly swelled in the IDF's favor as the battle progressed and the number of destroyed Egyptian tanks rose. Toward the end of the engagement, the ratio reached 1:12 in the IDF's favor, although at this stage it lost all meaning. Some observers claim that these data represent "a good example of the principle of optimizing the use of force," but the truth is that they serve as an example of a waste of force. All that was gained could have been achieved with a fraction of the total force that was employed (as the examples given above imply), and the rest of the force could have been diverted to the main mission of the Southern Command and the 162nd Division that day: getting across the Suez Canal as swiftly as possible.

> Who is wise? He who discerns what is about to come to pass.
> (Babylonian Talmud, Tamid Tractate)

In his book, Adan explained his division's long delay in reaching the bridgehead:

> While I was completely absorbed in directing the battle against the Egyptian 25th, Gaby [Amir, the commander of the 460th Brigade] sent me a message that Sharon's forces had not taken responsibility for the fighting opposite Tirtur and as a result his brigade was still engaged in battle and couldn't pull out Ehud [Barak's 100th Battalion] and Lapidot's [196th Battalion] [and have them] refuel and replenish. Gaby [Amir] complained that Amir Yaffe's 198th Battalion was replaced on the line . . . and had replenished . . . but Sharon wouldn't give it back [to the 460th Brigade]. . . . If Gaby's brigade was allowed to disengage from the enemy already at noon, as we agreed in the [sand dune] war council, it could have refueled and been ready to cross the bridge immediately. By the time Gaby Amir's brigade completed the crossing the rest of the division could have replenished [too] and been ready to move across. Unfortunately Sharon did not do his part. My repeated warnings to the Southern Command headquarters, even before the battle with the 25th Brigade, became more persistent after I left the battle, but to no avail. Now we saw the results. The bridge was ready and waiting, and there was no one to cross on it. (Adan 1979, 223)

After Adan singled out Sharon as the chief culprit in the 162nd's failure to reach the bridge on time, he added: "The main reason that the crossing was delayed was the need [to replenish the tanks] with fuel and ammunition. . . . Unfortunately, at 1745 [the replenishment] just began. The area was being shelled . . . and even though the shelling was ineffective it still posed a danger. We ignored it even but it slowed the pace and darkness also slowed us" (Adan 1979, 223).

A close look at the radio traffic transcripts reveals no complaint whatsoever on Amir's part about Sharon not releasing his battalions from the contact line. The only thing agreed on at the sand dune meeting was that Adan was to cross first and Sharon's division would replace the 162nd, which was operating in the Akavish area, but no actual orders were issued, nor were procedures or a timetable determined for executing the plan, as Adan charged. Only sometime between 1500 and 1740 did Elazar, Bar-Lev, and Gonen meet in the operations room at Um Hashiba and draw up Sharon's orders in the wake of the meeting, as the following exchange between Sharon and Uri Ben-Ari and Gonen attests. The conversation took place ten minutes before Dayan's arrival at the Southern Command, at which time he expressed amazement and anger on discovering that command's forces had not crossed yet:

Ben-Ari: Arik [Sharon], Uri [Ben-Ari] speaking. Regarding the orders, you have to release Gaby [Amir's 460th Brigade].
Sharon: What do you want me to do?
Ben-Ari: Relieve [the 460th Brigade] and replace it with someone else.
Sharon: I'm not keeping Gaby. I don't understand what it is that you want.
Gonen [intervenes]: The 460th is holding the contact line, keeping the Akavish Road open. If it leaves, Akavish will be blocked again.
Sharon: I'll bring in another unit in an hour.
Gonen: Can't you do it faster and issue the order immediately? I suggest you coordinate with the operation rooms and Bren [Adan] the exact task because Adan has to prepare them.
Sharon: Let me say something. The rafts are standing and no one's crossing on them.
Gonen: There's a bridge?. . . But they're waiting for you to relieve Gaby [Amir] and then he'll cross.
Sharon: That's what you're waiting for?
Gonen: Only that.
Sharon: Why didn't you tell me earlier? I could have replaced him earlier.
Gonen: I'm telling you now. Can you replace him now?
Sharon: I'll replace him in a few minutes.

Adan's complaints seem to echo the nasty conversation between Elazar and

Dayan when the latter arrived in Um Hashiba at 1730. To Dayan's exasperated taunt that the Southern Command's forces [i.e., the 162nd's] had not even started to cross despite the agreements and promises at the sand dune meeting, the CoGS found excuses, saying: "I ordered Adan to move and Sharon told me that he'd replace Adan in a few minutes." To this reply, Dayan, the responsible adult, impatiently and scornfully snapped: "Will replace, won't replace—just get to the bridge. The bridge is complete and ready." This was exactly the response to Adan's griping and evasions. Such excuses are unforgivable from Israeli generals as a rule, let alone in wartime when they should not expect their lame excuses to be accepted as sufficient and legitimate.

Furthermore, a transcript of the 162nd's operations radio network presents a different picture from Adan's account. A close look at the Adan-Amir conversation reveals that the main reason for the delay in the replenishment of Amir's battalions was the huge traffic jam on Akavish, which prevented contact between the supply units and the tanks. The following exchange between Adan, Tamari, and (Gabi) Amir illustrates this:

> Adan to Amir (1409): Your assignment is to refuel and rearm . . . as fast as you can.
>
> Adan to Tamari (1456): Are you making sure that [Amir] replenishes?
>
> Tamari to Adan: He's OK.
>
> Adan to Amir (1641): Replenish within sixty minutes. I intend to make the long haul with you.
>
> Amir to Adan: Impossible. . . . I have Amir [Yaffe, commander of the 198th Battalion], whose supply elements haven't reached him yet and [Ehud Barak's 100th Battalion] is still on the front in contact with the enemy and I haven't relieved him for replenishment.
>
> Adan to Amir: Is the contact serious?
>
> Amir to Adan: Not strong, but I can't take him out because the supply units are in a terrible traffic snarl in the rear.

This conversation seems to put the finger exactly where the problem lay in everything related to Amir's brigade's readiness to cross the canal. This was not the first or the last time in the Yom Kippur War that logistic blunders compromised, if not undermined, main operations. Against the background of Adan's grievances and accusations, his own admission speaks for itself: "The main reason the division's crossing was delayed was the need to refuel and rearm the tanks."

The need to replenish was not the ultimate reason for the 162nd's dithering. It was just the medium through which the real reason was revealed: the absence of logistic planning and preparation to ensure that the division could accomplish all missions with maximum success. The commander—and the commander alone—is responsible for the planning, and he cannot wiggle out of this responsibility. But, to aid him in fulfilling this function, he has a CoS with the rank of colonel, senior logistics staff officers, a logistics group headed by a full colonel presiding over a band of lieutenant colonels, and, if necessary for the success of the mission, even the deputy division commander. The sole function of these functionaries is to guarantee that the logistics of the division's operations are planned and taken care of according to the commander's instructions. The same holds true, mutatis mutandis, at the lower levels of command as well as at the levels above the division.

The battle with the 25th Brigade lacked effective (if any) logistical planning. The following snippets are from the 162nd's radio transmissions:

At 1715, toward the end of the battle, the commander of the 217th Brigade asked the commander of the 162nd Division: "What am I supposed to do next? You know I'm out of both [fuel and ammunition]. Can I reorganize where I was during the night?" Had the logistic planning been dealt with properly at the division, brigade, and battalion levels, this question would not have been asked.

At 1718, the 162nd's CoS, Colonel Ami Radian, said (it is not clear to whom): "We're looking for the logistical support units."

Ninety minutes after the battle, the following exchange took place between Adan and Nir:

> Adan: When will you be ready to cross?
> Nir: We're only beginning to assemble now . . .
> Adan: This is a catastrophe! [Adan finally realized what was happening.]
> Nir: Roger, we're doing the maximum. . . . I have serious problems assembling the men.

Gaby Amir, whom Adan was also pressing, replied to Adan just as Nir did: "Many problems in assembling the force."

The 162nd Division Crosses the Canal

Prior to Setting Out

At the end of the battle, the Southern Command urged Adan to hasten his division's reorganization and get it across the canal posthaste, replenished or not. This pressure was then conveyed to the brigade commanders as best it could be. The exchange between Gonen, his deputy, and Adan proceeded according to a set pattern. The commanding general demanded that the division commander move his forces immediately, even only part of them, without any further delay. He repeated the order, exhorted him, threatened sanctions, but all in vain for the simple reason that Adan's real problem was (as he admitted) the catastrophic tie-up in replenishing his brigades. Adan tried to parry Gonen's demands without admitting his logistic shortcomings by masking them with all kinds of demands, accusations, and excuses. One of the excuses that he repeated in his book is phrased in one instance as follows: "It wasn't a problem of quickly bringing tanks across, but bringing across formations prepared for a long-term war. . . . Replenishments were not the only preparations that were needed for the crossing. We had to organize and consolidate the force. I had to bring part of the artillery and small salvage units across with the brigades" (Adan 1979, 223).

No matter how much the commanding general of the Southern Command pressed Adan to cross immediately regardless of what would happen, the real problem, as stated, was not reorganization and traffic arrangements but the basic logistic snafu.

Another excuse—perhaps not exactly relevant—was the delay in releasing the 198th Battalion, which had replenished, and replacing it with the 184th Battalion at noon October 17. The 198th was kept at Lakekan in reserve under the command of the 14th Brigade. The transcripts from the Southern Command's radio frequencies and operational logs illustrate a dialogue of the deaf. The following is part of a slightly edited conversation between Gonen and Adan at 1745:

Gonen: Can you bring [Nir] in instead of the 460th Brigade?

Adan: Nir isn't ready yet. He hasn't finished replenishing. He just ended his armor-versus-armor battle. He needs to replenish after a whole day of fighting. The 460th is more prepared but two of its units haven't been relieved so they haven't replenished yet. They're now in contact [with the enemy]. They're not being replaced, why aren't they being relieved?

Gonen: Forget about this for now. You'll get these units back. In the meantime have Nir cross. Cross with the two units from the 460th that aren't in contact [with the enemy] and reorganize there [on the western bank]. I'll make sure that supplies reach the other side.

Adan: I'm not ready [yet].

Gonen: This is critical.

Adan: If it's that urgent, then my neighbor [Sharon] can release them.

Gonen: Drop it! You'll get them back later today. Cross as you are. . . . If you don't cross, they'll tell Sharon to. Cross immediately. Do you read me?

Adan: I understand. I'm completely out [of fuel and ammunition]. I have a suggestion. Half of the 460th is almost full. I'll begin sending it across.

Gonen: Take half of the 460th and cross. Take Nir as he is. Cross with him even if he's not full. Is that understood?

Adan had something to say about Gonen's tone: "His style infuriated me. I couldn't help thinking that Sharon should have been forced to release Amir at the designated time" (Adan 1979, 223).

At 1900, Adan and Gonen resumed their dialogue:

Gonen: When will Nir begin crossing?
Adan: Nir will cross with me first. [This was only an off-the-cuff answer, and things did not work out as Adan planned.]
Gonen: When will you begin?
Adan: I think in a half hour. I'll cross in another hour or an hour and a half. I'll be finished by midnight. [He would only just begin at midnight.]
Gonen: Try your damnedest to make it earlier.
Adan: [Tries to change the subject.] Look . . . I haven't exchanged a word with anyone. I still haven't planned what I'm going to do on the other side.
Gonen: For now just begin crossing. [Gonen is adamant.]

Forty minutes later, the following conversation took place between Gonen and Adan (Ezov 2011, 266):

Gonen: What's happening on the bridge?
Adan: I'm not there yet. I'll be there in a quarter of an hour.
Gonen: That's not good Bren!
Adan: That's how it is.
Gonen: That's not good. Get them moving even if they're not supplied and organized. Just bring them across.
Adan: Look, it doesn't work that way.
Gonen: No Bren, I'm not joking! I can't speak with you because this is over the radio. There's a reason.
Adan: There's a lot I can't tell you [over the radio]. People are taking the minimum with them. They're grabbing some food now because there won't be anything else for a whole day. They're gulping down a few drops of water. [He may have thought this would soften Gonen's heart of stone.]
Gonen: I don't know, I think that it's more important to get across. [Gonen doesn't buy Adan's supplications.]
Adan: OK. I wouldn't have told you if I didn't know that there are things I can't tell you.

Gonen: When will you be there?
Adan: Where?
Gonen: At the crossing site, Matzmed.
Adan: You're the one bringing me across. . . . I don't know where.
Gonen: First cross to the other side.
Adan: OK. . . . In another quarter of an hour we'll begin moving [apparently part of Amir's brigade]. Nir will move in another two hours. In another four to five hours the second half of the Amir's brigade will move.
Gonen: That isn't good.

At 2130, Adan finally realizes that he overdid it. He halts the replenishment and orders the units to prepare to go to Matzmed.

The 162nd Division Crosses the Canal

At 1600 October 17, construction on the Unifloat raft bridge was completed. As soon as the rafts entered the water and the bridge had begun, Egyptian artillery fire started landing in the Yard, a trickle of 160-millimeter mortar fire from the north, but a trickle that nevertheless took its toll in terms of casualties. Once the bridge was standing, access roads to it from the east were marked, and nighttime markers were put in place. An hour or two before the bridge was standing, Even reported to Sharon that he reckoned the bridge would be ready for traffic by 1600. Sharon conveyed this information to Dayan, Elazar, and the heads of the Southern Command. When the bridge was finally up, Even again reported that everything was ready for transferring masses of armor to the western bank. But, from 1600 to midnight, movement across was minimal despite repeated notifications. As the hours ticked by and the Egyptian fire intensified, soldiers and commanders of the bridging battalions, including Lieutenant Colonel Avi Zohar, the commander of the 630th Battalion, were hit by shrapnel. Zohar's deputy, Captain Yishai Dotan, replaced him. The 247th Paratrooper Brigade forces operating west of the bridge also came under artillery and mortar fire of similar intensity.

Shortly before 2215 (according to the operational radio transcript), Adan radioed to his subordinate commanders: "Hallelujah, we've just crossed!"

The more important question is why Adan crossed into Africa when his brigades were still in Asia (Sinai) and one of them was lumbering down the road to Matzmed and the second had not started to move. Adan says that he wanted to reconnoiter the ground in order to identify assembly areas for the impending attack at dawn. This is a most laudable task but not one that the division commander had to carry out and not under these circumstances. As far as we can fathom, Adan's intention to reconnoiter, if it existed, appears not to have been realized, and he was parked west of the bridge. By crossing the canal, Adan may have wanted to create, perhaps unawares, the impression of the start of his brigade's transfer to the western bank by anchoring his presence there before the crossing of the rest of the division. According to Dayan's *The Story of My Life* (1976) and Sharon's *Warrior* (1989), both Dayan and Sharon swallowed the bait, hook, line, and sinker and stated that the hour that the 162nd began to cross the canal was 2200 (Dayan)/2230 (Sharon).

To strengthen this conjecture, the following radio exchange at 2241 is instructive:

> Ben-Ari to Adan: An hour and a half has passed [since the last pestering]. What's happening?
>
> Adan to Ben-Ari: I'm in Egypt now. . . . My forces are behind me. (Adan 1979, 226)

From Adan's description of his adventures with the bridging tanks, he and his deputy both crossed the canal. The lonely hours that Adan, his deputy, and the FCP spent on the western bank until his first brigade crossed were undeniably a complete waste of valuable commander time. His division's most pressing task that night was to cross into Egypt proper without mishap; therefore, the division commander and his deputy should have been on the spot to oversee the operation. Adan should have been in the Yard that night. In reality, the officers who assumed responsibility for directly supervising the 162nd's crossing, tank by tank, were the deputy commander of Sharon's Division and his FCP officers.

The 460th Brigade Begins to Cross—and Breaks the Bridge

As the 162nd began rolling, and especially as it approached Lakekan, the shelling in the Yard increased. Just before the 460th Brigade entered the area, the artillery fire reached a level unprecedented in IDF history, falling in the Yard, on the water, and in the thickets adjacent to the western bank where the paratroopers of the 247th were assembled.

At 2300, Gabi Amir radioed Adan that the head of his brigade has reached Lakekan. Ten minutes later, he reported that his head is at the end of Nakhala. Since the western end of Nakhala Road abutted Matzmed, we can conclude that Amir meant the eastern edge of the road that branched from Lexicon. At around the same time, Nir reported that he was entering Akavish on his way west.

At 2345, Amir contacted Adan, who was parked a few hundred meters from him on the western bank, fuming: "Have somebody come and get me. We're practically blind here." Adan replied: "They're on the way. We just sent somebody. . . . The jeeps are behind you. Just follow them." These conversations exemplify our criticism of Adan's location.

Just before midnight, the division's first battalion (the 19th/460th Brigade, commanded by Zeyirah) reached the bridge and began crossing. The shelling had reached a crescendo, and the tank crews had closed hatches, against orders, and dashed west across the bridge, pedal to the floor. The third tank caused a rip in the bridge where it was moored to the western side. At 2400, Even informed Adan of the breakdown, explained the extent of damage and the repairs that had to be made, and suggested bringing the 460th's tanks across on the trusty Crocodiles. Even replied: "Send them north along the western embankment until they reach an opening. I've just sent someone to personally lead the 19th Battalion. Confirm that no contradictory orders are issued." As soon as the matter was settled, Adan, on the western bank, began nagging.

October 17–18, five minutes past midnight, the following exchange took place:

> Adan to Even: How much time will the repairs take?
> Even to Adan: Those working on it are incapacitated. All the senior officers are wounded.
> Adan to Even: That's not a reason not to continue the repair.
> Even to Adan: When I have more information, I'll inform you. Right now get them cross where I told you.
> Adan to Even: They're crossing. But I want to know how much time the repairs will take.

A few minutes later the exchange continued:

> Adan to Even: Are they working there?
> Even to Adan: Just now they've found where the problem is.
> Adan to Even: Are they working on it?
> Even to Adan: They will.
> Adan to Even: It has to be done with maximum speed. There are many forces here.
> Even to Adan: We are not playing around here.

And the nagging persisted:

> Adan to Even: What's happening in the Yard?

Even to Adan: There's a delay. Forget about crossing the bridge for now. Use the Crocs.
Adan to Even: Step on it and fix the bridge. There's a huge amount of forces here and they're causing a terrible delay. Do everything you can to get the bridge in working order.

Adan finally tries to do something practical:

Even to Adan: Does your column have a bridging tank?
Adan to Even: No, but there's one on the other [western] side not far from us.
Even to Adan: Excellent! Please send it to the bridge.
Adan to Even: I'm sending you the bridging tank.

Even describes the following events:

> The bridging tank never showed up, and we had to order Haim Erez [the commander of the 421st Brigade] to send another. While this was happening, I asked Adan to prepare his tankers to mount the Crocs very carefully since they'd already damaged one raft because of carelessness. My combat engineers and FCP were [busy] supervising the work on the bridge, leading Gabi Amir's tanks from the Yard's entrance to the breach in the embankment on the canal, and loading them onto the Crocodiles. The whole time we were exposed to incredibly concentrated artillery fire, yet we all seemed to ignore it.
>
> While I was dealing with the bridge repair, and because of this, I was in continuous radio contact with Adan and Gabi Amir, and my FCP officers were busy directing Amir's tanks to the loading points on the Crocodiles. The work was slow and difficult. Most of the tank crews were terrified and closed the hatches and mounted the Crocodiles hastily and incautiously. Be this as it may, the tank crossing proceeded slowly but surely to the western shore.
>
> At 0135, I informed Adan that the bridge was repaired or, to be more exact, patched up with a bridging tank's ramp and that we could bring the rest of Amir's brigade across. The tanks' movement on the bridge was slower now. I or one of my FCP officers would climb on each tank and instruct the commander to open the hatches, drive slowly on the bridge, not panic, not freak out, and turn on the lights as he approached the newly installed bridging tank's ramp on the torn-up western edge. The crossing operation was carefully monitored; one or maximum two tanks [were allowed] on the bridge at one time. The

> procedure was repeated for each tank, and all this took place under unimaginably heavy artillery fire . . . that the men and officers of the combat engineers, like my FCP officers, were totally exposed to.

Despite the slow movement on the bridge, the 460th completed its crossing at 0235. A quarter of an hour earlier, Colonel Nir, who was waiting at Lakekan with his brigade, received the green light to move to the Yard. At 0315, his tanks began the crossing. The procedure was the same. Enemy artillery fire finally tapered off. The learning curve had its effect, and the brigade's crossing took place smoothly and quickly. By 0500 October 18, the entire 217th Brigade was across the canal and after it came the self-propelled artillery and support units. At 0515, Adan's division, two tank brigades, some mobile artillery batteries, support units, and other forces were concentrated on the western bank.

Unfortunately, the Egyptian army in the area exploited the delay in the 162nd's organization before the crossing and deployed its force in concentration opposite it. Adan's division had no choice but to wage a time-consuming, costly breakthrough battle from the bridgehead into Egypt proper.

Two lessons can be drawn from all this mishmash and might be upgraded to the level of principles of war:

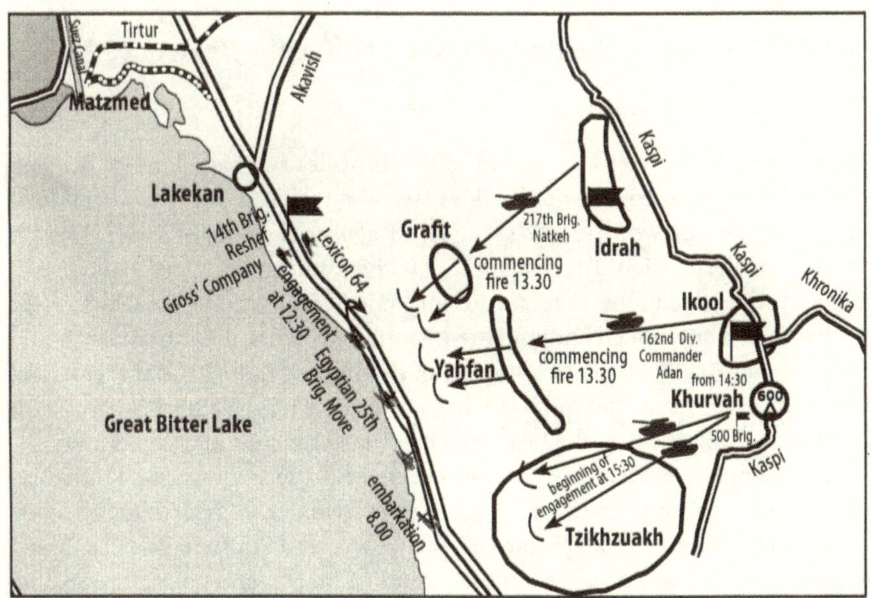

The Battle with the Egyptian 25th Brigade, October 17, 1220–1620 hours. Courtesy of Amiram Ezov.

1. Never try to bite off more than you can chew. It was beyond Adan's ability to conduct a battle of annihilation against the Egyptian 25th Brigade and at the same time secure his right to cross first. The CoGS erred in permitting him to take on both tasks, and the front commander should never have agreed (and, to make matters worse, he knew that it was a mistake from the beginning).
2. Indeed, the 25th Brigade was destroyed, but this is not to say that it failed to accomplish its mission. In the fifteen or sixteen hours that the 162nd wasted in trapping and eliminating most of it (according to the division's record, each Egyptian tank seems to have been knocked out more than once), and until the division completed the crossing, the Egyptians had sufficient time to gain an accurate picture of what was happening and concentrate their armor and infantry opposite the bridgehead. This concentration compromised the IDF's ability to force the Egyptian army to its knees "fast, hard, and elegantly," as Bar-Lev once famously said before he was tasked with having to make bold decisions that would result in either gain or loss. In sending the 25th north, the Egyptians may have sacrificed a pawn, but, knowingly or not, they went for the checkmate. Unfortunately for them, the IDF soldiers, tankers, infantrymen, artillerymen, combat engineers, and field officers spoiled the game.

October 18, 1973—the End of the Battle for the Bridgehead

Mopping Up Tirtur Road

The morning of October 18 found the 600th Brigade's two battalions (which had replaced the 460th Brigade on the line) spread out along Tirtur Road at Akavish 51. The area between Akavish and Tirtur appeared empty of the enemy. On orders from the division, Tuvia Raviv, the 600th's commander, instructed two battalions, the 409th and the 410th, to advance north to Tirtur. They reached Tirtur without being hit, though antitank fire was still directed at them from Amir and east of it. At 0700, Raviv sent a company of combat engineers to clear the road of mines. At 1100, visual and radio contact was made with the 88th Battalion/14th Brigade, which was still at the Lexicon-Tirtur Junction, four kilometers away.

After Raviv reported this, Sharon ordered him to harness the 410th Battalion to the roller bridge. The battalion commander, Major Yehuda Geller, received the order at 1100. Major Uzi Ben Yitzhak's 409th Battalion continued to advance west along an old train track route in the direction of point 185. The battalion began to incur heavy losses from mines, antitank missiles, and enemy aircraft and eventually stopped east of Amir.

The Capture of the Amir Stronghold

On the night of October 17–18, the 14th Brigade reorganized at Lakekan (excluding the 184th Battalion, which remained deployed on Shik Road) between Lexicon and Rosh Roads on the bank of the Suez Canal. The White Bear Amphibious Reconnaissance Battalion, comprising nine amphibious BTR 50 APCs and five amphibious PT 76 tanks (all war spoils), under the command of Major Yossi Yudovitch, joined the brigade in the afternoon of October 17 and, by evening, had secured the Lexicon-Tirtur and Lexicon-Nakhala Junction.

Because of the 600th's difficulty in seizing Amir, the 14th Brigade commander suggested to Sharon that his brigade attack the Chinese Farm (Amir) from west to east. The idea was accepted and the plan approved. The brigade received direct assistance from four artillery battalions. The 184th Battalion, which was deployed on Shik Road, and the 79th Battalion, which was deployed west and southwest of Amir, were assigned to secure the fighting zone from the north and advance north. The attack on the Chinese Farm began in the afternoon. The 424th Battalion advanced west and captured the "pumps building" (an outpost west of Amir). Next, the 88th Battalion turned north from its position at point 139 (south of the Chinese Farm) and attacked the farm's buildings, with the 424th Battalion supplying covering fire. The farm was captured in twenty minutes.

At 1400 October 18, the 79th and 184th Battalions launched an attack to the north, advancing three kilometers, inflicting heavy losses on the enemy, but also incurring casualties. The attack was halted owing to the losses and the depletion of fuel and ammunition. The 184th returned to Lakekan, arriving at 1600, and reorganized until October 20. The 79th stopped a few kilometers north of Shik Road and was replaced by the 88th Battalion in the evening. It then returned to Lakekan to reorganize.

Towing the Roller Bridge to the Canal

At 1100, the 410th Battalion reached the roller bridge, which was standing idle at Akavish 53, and hooked up to it. On Sharon's order, the deputy division commander took part of his FCP to the bridge to supervise its towing to point 95.5 on the canal, north of the Yard, where it would be launched.

All the officers taking part in the towing operation were present at Akavish 53 (many others were still in the crossing battle). Such a lineup was unprecedented in the IDF: Colonel Gur Menashe, the head combat engineer officer for the crossing; Lieutenant Colonel Fredo Raz, a field engineering R&D officer;

and Lieutenant Colonel Aharon Teneh, the Southern Command's chief engineering officer.

Roles and responsibilities were as follows:

- Overall command of the operation: the 143rd's deputy commander, Colonel Even.
- Command of the towing force and its security: the commander of the 410th Battalion, Major Geller.
- Technical responsibility: Colonel Menashe Gur and Lieutenant Colonel Raz.
- Navigation: Lieutenant Colonel Teneh.

The column for the bridge towing contained the following elements:

- The group of tanks harnessed to tow the bridge was under the direct command of the deputy commander of the 410th Battalion, Major Elkan.
- The bulldozer group, consisting of six bulldozer tanks and two civilian tractors, would prepare sections of the route by clearing it of obstacles. This group led the bridge column.
- To provide security, two tanks from K Company rode ahead of the bulldozer tanks, and two other tanks from the company escorted the column on the northern flank.
- Antiaircraft defense was provided by mobile antiaircraft cannon batteries that accompanied the column and warplanes that provided an air umbrella.

Navigational Snags

Negotiating the marshes between Akavish Road and the canal required precise navigation of the roller bridge on a fixed route. The Southern Command's engineering commander, Lieutenant Colonel Teneh, had reconnoitered the area before the war and discovered a route (along Tirtur Road) and even marked it with stakes and poles. When war erupted, navigation became critical. Since the Egyptians had occupied Tirtur Road and the vicinity until recently, it was necessary to tow the bridge to the launching site while operating under the assumption that Teneh's markers were no longer in place. For this reason, Teneh's presence was indispensable.

The column reorganized and moved west on a route parallel to and north of Tirtur. The movement proceeded smoothly but slowly because the route had to be cleared of junk and obstacles. The column came under desultory, weak shelling, and the number of casualties was minimal. Given the route's unsuitability to wheeled vehicles, Colonel Maoz and Teneh traveled by jeep on Tirtur to the Lexicon-Tirtur Junction and waited for the column. Scores of Israeli and Egyptian tanks and other armored combat vehicles—burned or abandoned—were accumulated at the junction.

At (about) 1600, six Egyptian fighter-bombers attacked this heap of burned combat vehicles and the bridge column east of the junction as well. Teneh ran for cover on an embankment by one of the farm's dry canals and was shot in the back by an Egyptian forward artillery team concealed in a water conduit in the canal. Colonel Maoz wiped out the team while two paratrooper medics, who were in the area from earlier fighting, provided covering fire. But the damage was done. A good man, an excellent officer, and a key player in the operation was dead. The column lost its navigator just as it approached the problematic area west of Lexicon.

When it reached the Akavish-Tirtur Junction and Even realized that Teneh was gone, he and the battalion commander navigated the column on foot, one step at a time, from the junction to kilometer 95.5, arriving there at 1800. The embankment had to be prepared for the bridge's entry into the water, but this activity was delayed until the forces on the western bank confirmed that the area was clean of the enemy.

At 2100 October 18, efforts were renewed to launch the bridge. At 0045 October 19, after sundry technical problems were solved, the bridge finally stood, and, at 0415, the tanks of the 14th Brigade began crossing on it into Egypt.

Thus ended the crossing battle.

Epilogue

On October 17, the assembling began on the "Austerity Bridge" (a term coined by Major Ya'akov Yerushalmi, of the chief of engineering headquarters) six kilometers southeast of the Tassa Junction, on Mavdil Road. This bridge consisted of a seventy-meter-long section of the bridge and five separate rafts. The next day, the bridge was towed to Matzmed. It arrived on October 19 and on the night of October 19–20 was launched in the water. Its assembly ended on the evening of October 20, but, at this stage, it could accommodate only wheeled vehicles. The following day, its construction was completed, and tanks and other armored combat vehicles could travel on it. The order was given to cease all traffic on the first Unifloat raft bridge, the one with the tank ramp patch, and commence work to return it to full operability.

On October 20, the Crocodile battalion was sent from the Yard to Lakekan with the only remaining Crocodile. Thus, the last remnant of the real heroes of the crossing battle—the Crocodiles—was removed from the bridgehead. If these secondhand pieces of equipment had been made of pure gold and studded with diamonds, their value would not have been one thousandth of a milligram of their value in the crossing battle and the defeat of the Egyptians.

10

Eight Days

October 18–25, 1973

October 18—Main Events

The 162nd Division

By midday October 17, when the Egyptian high command realized the gist and extent of the IDF move on the western bank, the Egyptian CoGS began assembling armor and infantry on the western side of the canal to contain the bridgehead. The reinforcements came from the Egyptian General Staff reserve in the Cairo area and the two armies on the front, including forces from the bridgeheads on the eastern bank.

According to the IDF's original plan, the 421st Brigade, which had been operating on the western bank since October 16, would seize the western edge of the bridgehead in the Havit Road area eight kilometers west of the canal. On the night of October 16–17, because of signs of superior Egyptian concentrations in the area, the brigade commander requested to withdraw his forces to a night park adjacent to the freshwater canal, four kilometers west of the Suez Canal. The division commander granted permission since Egyptian infantry and armor gained control of the area between the freshwater canal and Havit Road during the night.

At midnight October 17–18, the CoGS assigned the Southern Command the following missions for October 18:

- At dawn, the 162nd Division with its two tank brigades would be at the bridgehead west of the canal (the division's actual force that morning, in terms of tanks and artillery, was equivalent to a reinforced brigade and an artillery battalion).
- In the morning, the division would break through to the west and southwest in two armored efforts designed to engage in tank battles and at the same time avoid Egyptian infantry and antitank weapons.

Given the Southern Command's bitter experience in the last thirteen days, the second order sounds patently unrealistic and does not need to be discussed in detail. The division's fighting that day reflects the obscure thinking or muddled wording that led to the order. The CoGS ordered that another division effort—to be executed by the force crossing the canal that morning—would move north, clean out the artillery and SAM batteries in the area, proceed to expand the bridgehead northward, and create the basis for attacking Missouri with fire from the western bank. This was the lip service paid to Sharon and his division. At daybreak on October 18, the 162nd Division's 460th and 217th Brigades (together a force of 140 tanks) assembled on the western side of the bridgehead. The Southern Command's orders to the division commander, Major General Adan, reflected the CoGS's orders. Adan planned the brigades' advance in the following manner.

Colonel Nir (the commander of the 217th) would break through from the Bailey bridge on the freshwater canal in the Deversoir airfield area. From there, he would move west until he hit the Haifa road, move on it through the Abu-Sultan camps, capture Arel at the Havit-Haifa Junction seven kilometers west of the freshwater canal, and advance on Sakranut Road to the Maktzera compound some ten kilometers west-southwest of Arel.

Adan ordered Gabi Amir, the commander of the 460th Brigade, to move south on Test Road to the stone bridge near Mukhatat Abu Sultan, continue west on Sakranut Road and capture the Uri compound one kilometer west of the freshwater canal on Sakranut Road, and proceed to capture the Tzakh compound at the Havit-Sakranut Junction. From there, he would turn south and attain a toehold at the northern edges of the Geneifa Hills while leaving a detachment to protect the Fayed airfield.

At 0600 October 18, Adan gave the green light to break out of the bridgehead. "We expected an easy breakout from the freshwater canal and then armored fighting at the junction and open area, but," he rued, "this wasn't to be." Although the division had information that the Egyptians were rushing reinforcements to the crossing area from every direction, "they didn't appear to have arrived there yet." Why did Adan think that, and why did he think that the breakout from the bridgehead would be a stroll in the park? God only knows. At any rate, the fighting that began immediately with the 162nd Brigade's egress on its missions quickly slammed the division commander back to reality. Without going into details on the brigade's encounters with the enemy, let the following points be noted.

The 142nd Battalion/217th Brigade broke through on Haifa Road and captured the Arel compound on the Haifa-Havit Junction by 0700. Here, the brigade ran into trouble. Forces from Egyptian bases north of the Haifa Road blocked it and cut the 142nd off from the rest of the brigade at Arel. The brigade spent most of October 18 fighting the Egyptian blocking forces; these battles ended only when darkness fell. Assisting the brigade during the fighting were units from the 143rd Division: the 264th and 599th Battalions/421st Brigade engaged the Egyptian armor and artillery north of the brigade, and two paratrooper companies (one from the 247th Brigade and the other from Force Shmulik/14th Brigade). An Egyptian block near Arel was broken through only on the night of October 18–19. At nightfall, the brigade entered night parks near the Arel compound, which marked the 162nd Division's furthest advance west, about twelve kilometers from the freshwater canal.

The 460th Brigade failed to break through to Sakranut Road. A few hours later, having been reinforced by a company from a 247th Paratrooper Brigade, it managed to capture the Uri compound one kilometer west of the freshwater canal on Sakranut. At first, the brigade's attempt to advance west was blocked by an Egyptian tank battalion that was spotted south of the road that the brigade was advancing on. The 198th Tank Battalion removed this threat. But, as soon as the brigade tried to continue west, it was stopped by Egyptian infantry and armor deployed at the Tzakh compound on the Sakranut-Havit Junction about twelve kilometers west of the freshwater canal.

In the early afternoon, Adan decided to open Sakranut Road in a division attack on the Tzakh compound. His plan was simple: the 217th Brigade would be released for the attack by the 421st Brigade's movement toward the Gheshira compound (north of Arel on the Vardit-Havit Junction) and attack Tzakh from the north while the 460th Brigade attacked and pinned it down from the east. This attack was aborted the moment it began because of causalities incurred by the attacking forces, the 217th Brigade's concern over what was happening in its rear, and the brigade's critical lack of supplies.

Adan seems to have derived two conclusions from these mishaps:

- His armor force was too weak to accomplish what it set out to do.
- Air and artillery support was insufficient and had to be increased.

Thus, he demanded that the Southern Command return the 500th Brigade, the command's reserve force that was sitting idle on the eastern bank, to his division. He also suggested that he divert part of his force to raids on the SAM bases in his sector. The command approved his request at 1315. The 500th reached the bridgehead on the night of October 18–19, crossed the canal on the raft bridge and remaining Crocodiles (the roller bridge had not been launched yet), and entered the Deversoir airfield area, where it came under a lengthy and heavy barrage. The brigade arrived with only two of its battalions (the third battalion, the 429th, remained at Tziona on Talisman Road, east of the Canal).

That afternoon, the 217th Brigade sent Giora Kopel's 126th Battalion to the Arzel-Vada'ut Junction, about fourteen kilometers northwest of Arel, where it destroyed two SAM bases and returned to Arel on its last petrol fumes. Amir Yaffe's reduced (company-sized) 198th Battalion/460th Brigade knocked out a SAM base one kilometer northwest of the Fayed airfield but returned to its starting point without attacking the second SAM base because it ran out of fuel and ammunition.

In the evening, the division's brigades entered night parks. The 217th parked, as stated, in the Arel area; the 460th returned to the agricultural barrier (the narrow strip between the Suez Canal and the freshwater canal) except for one battalion that parked at Uri. From the point of view of the 162nd and the Southern Command this was a disappointing day. On the plus side, the 162nd could list the breakout from the freshwater canal area, the capture of the Uri and Arel compounds, and the destruction of three SAM bases. The last event turned out to be critical for the continuation of operations. On the minus side was the division's failure to accomplish that day's missions: the meager advance after the breakthrough from the bridgehead, the flaccid handling of the division attack on Tzakh, and the continuous logistic affliction that precluded the division's maximum exploitation of its strength.

The limited achievements of Adan's division stemmed directly from the way its battle against the Egyptian Army's 25th Brigade on October 17 was engendered, organized, and carried out, its failure to reorganize after that battle, and the Southern Command's conservatism and excessive caution in every stage of the battle for the bridgehead. The Southern Command failed to reinforce and exploit the battle success and mishandled its reserves. The first day of battle west of the canal ended with a whimper because of the paucity of forces allocated to the fighting, minimal and inefficient air and artillery support, and the defective logistic planning that was left uncorrected.

Above all, the 162nd's combat record of October 18 reflected a misidentification of the center of gravity of the Egyptian army on both banks of the canal, which resulted in an erroneous choice of the objectives that the division was supposed to attain. The division's objectives also reflected the myopia and misperception of the battle mainly on the part of the Southern Command and the General Staff. The division's efforts were characterized by obvious, conventional, and uninspired moves that lacked surprise, stratagem, and an indirect approach. The surprises in this day's fighting were provided by the Egyptians.

Finally, and without diminishing the bravery and sacrifice of the armor forces, the division's limited accomplishments owed much to the three paratrooper companies, which proved to be an invaluable factor in the day's battles.

The 143rd Division

The previous chapter described the 143rd Division's brigades' fighting on the eastern bank and the bridgehead on October 18. The (reduced) 421st Brigade and the (reduced) 247th Brigade were operating on the western bank. The 421st activity was initially limited because of the confusion over whom it was subordinate to. This continued until the Southern Command clarified that the brigade was subordinate to the 143rd but would assist the 162nd. After this was cleared up, the brigade deployed at Gheshira on the Vardit-Havit Junction.

Although the 247th Brigade, which included only two battalions, had suffered heavy losses from intense Egyptian shelling at the bridgehead, it nevertheless allotted two companies to assist the 162nd (Force Shmulik also allotted the division a paratrooper company) and spent most of the day fending off Egyptian attacks from the north. The brigade was unable to expand the bridgehead in its sector on the western bank.

The 252nd Division

On the morning of October 18, with the arrival of the first reports of Adan's difficulty in breaking through from the bridgehead, the defense minister realized that the division's resources were insufficient for its operations and certainly not at the pace expected. Dayan arrived at Um Hashiba in the morning and suggested that Gonen reinforce the command's forces on the western bank with elements from Kalman Magen's 252nd Division and bolster what remained of the 252nd Division on the eastern bank with forces from MARSHAL.

Gonen, who recognized a good idea when he heard one, received permission from the CoGS to send eighty of Magen's tanks, led by Magen, to the western bank. Also, the 500th Brigade was returned to Adan that day.

At 0930, Magen was ordered to organize two reduced brigades, forty tanks each, from his division, cross the canal with them, and join the fighting on the 162nd's western flank. Magen assembled his truncated division (whose number of tanks was smaller than that of a regular tank brigade) from the reduced 401st Brigade, under the command of Colonel Dan Shomron, and from the reduced 184th Brigade, under the command of Colonel Baruch Harel. The forces that were left east of the Canal—that is, those elements of the brigades that were not included in the new 252nd Division—together with the 875th Mechanized Brigade and other infantry and armor forces that had been sent to the division's sector from the MARSHAL and other sources were put under the command of the division CoS, Colonel Israel Granit, and continued to operate in the division's former sector in Sinai as "Force Granit." The commander of the mechanized brigade, Colonel Aryeh Dayan, was wounded on October 18 and replaced by the commander of the 164th Brigade, Colonel Avraham Baram. The splitting of Magen's division was completed by noon, and the split division began to cross the canal on the morning of the nineteenth.

"But where shall wisdom be found?" (Job 28:12)

Before noon October 18, while the front commander and his senior officers digested the first reports of Adan's difficulties in breaking through the freshwater canal and galloping west and south, the CoGS called a meeting to estimate the situation. General Tal, the deputy CoGS, pointed to the dwindling force ratio because of heavy IDF losses, expressed his deep concern that the IDF might not achieve a victory in this war, and suggested reviewing the war aims. In his opinion, the IDF's goal at this stage could, at best, be to restore its deterrence capabilities by a series of various operations.

The CoGS—who was apparently still unaware of the extent of IDF losses (and therefore could not fully assess their implications), still misunderstood the difficult nature of the fighting on the western bank, and probably still in a state of euphoria—refused to listen to this. Victory, as he saw it, stood above all else. The history and the lessons of the war and the Egyptians' military and political gains up until this point, the IDF's dismal situation, and the realistic expectation of the superpowers' intervention in the IDF's freedom of action—all of this was of no concern to him. In his view, the war aims, which even as they were being formulated were already unachievable, remained what they were:

- Preventing the enemy from making any military or political gain.
- Destroying as much of the enemy force as possible.
- Ending the war in a better military and political situation than that which existed before it erupted.

There is little to add here regarding the CoGS's lack of a sense of realism as reflected in his summary. Let us note only one fact. The entire discussion and the CoGS's instructions that appear in his summary had no impact whatsoever on what was happening in the field and were merely gratuitous verbiage, a kind of magic ritual whose subtext was: if we repeat the mantra enough times, perhaps something good will come of it, and, if not, then at least we will feel that we did something.

The Main Events of October 19

The CoGS's Instructions

On the morning of October 19, the CoGS reconvened the daily estimation-of-the-situation ritual. The discussion took place in the shadow of two facts that this time were taken into consideration:

- The difficulty in the fighting and the logistic problems on the western bank produced measly results compared to the overly optimistic expectations of the previous day.
- In light of the American assessment that the flow of the sand in the political hourglass had accelerated and a forced cease-fire was impending, Kissinger informed the Israeli ambassador to Washington, Simcha Dinitz, on the night of October 18–19 that what happened on the ground would determine the results of the war and that the IDF should stop sitting on its hands and concentrate more energy on the urgency of destroying the Egyptian army.

After this wake-up call, the CoGS discarded the anachronistic slogans of the day before and adopted what was obvious: attaining the war aims depended on what took place on the battlefield; every effort had to be made to maximize the dividends in the breakthrough sector. As noted, and as we shall soon see (e.g., on October 21), these statements, too, were revealed as sheer balderdash. In the General Staff Operations Branch's orders to the Southern Command—which were supposedly in accordance with the CoGS's summary—vacuity and ambiguity still reigned supreme.

As October 19 approached, the Southern Command was given the following tasks:

> Destroy the missile bases in the Southern Command's area of ops.
> Destroy the enemy forces south of the agricultural barrier.
> Destroy the enemy forces east and west of the canal in the crossing area.

Grandiose Ideas in the Southern Command

The planners in the Southern Command's headquarters agreed on the evening of October 18 that the command's forces would carry out the following missions on the western bank the next day.

The 162nd Division would break through to the south and southwest, bypass

Tzakh, attack Maktzera seven kilometers west of the Sakranut-Vada'ut Junction, and seize the southern edge of the Geneifa Hills. The 143rd Division would split: the deputy division commander would continue as bridgehead commander and receive Dani Matt's 247th Brigade and Raviv's 600th Brigade. The other part of the 143rd, which included the 421st and the 14th Brigades and infantry and reconnaissance forces under the direct command of Sharon, would operate on the western flank of Adan's division and reach Jebel Obeid. The 252nd Division would advance west in the direction of Maktzera, secure the bridges, and serve as a reserve for the forces operating in the southern effort.

At this point, the Southern Command would have a corps-sized force on the western bank made up of three armored divisions operating independently in the field and dependent on each other only by dint of the battle plan, which always tends to evaporate at the start of the battle. Amazingly, the Southern Command's brass did not conceive of establishing a corps FCP on the western bank to monitor the divisions' fighting closely, even though this corps was the IDF's main effort. Instead, they preferred to sit in the Um Hashiba room eighty kilometers from the theater of war and try to influence what was happening on the ground from there.

A straight line stretches from this questionable style of battle command to the Second Lebanon War (2006), when lower-level IDF commanders, such as brigade commanders, misconstrued their responsibility as leaders of combatants and instead directed their forces via electronic systems in operations rooms far in the rear. Cowardice was not the reason for the aberrant style of command on the part of the Southern Command's generals. The reason lay in their inexperience at high-level operational command, in combat leadership that had become rusty from not having been used over the years, and perhaps in their distaste of eating Spam out of a can and sleeping under the stars. Undoubtedly, it had not dawned on them that they too—major generals and lieutenant generals alike—were first and foremost soldiers (though not combat soldiers any more)!

No less interesting is the fact that the operational planning instantly dissolved when Sharon, who probably abhorred the idea of acting as a mere cover on Adan's flank, suggested that the Southern Command leave his division concentrated on both sides of the canal (under his command of course) and the command readily agreed. Furthermore, in his visionary acuity, the CoGS demanded that the Southern Command leave the 600th and 14th Brigades on the eastern side of the canal and expand the bridgehead by attacking Missouri.

Expansion of the corridor/bridgehead to the north quickly became code for the capture of Missouri. The obsession with taking Missouri should be seen against the feeling of a number of senior IDF generals who sensed that they would be called to pay for their bungling before and during the war but that, if they succeeded in turning back the wheels of time, the nation's wrath might be blunted and they might be exonerated since—as the saying goes—"all's well that ends well."

The Fighting of the 143rd Division

To recall, on October 18, the 600th Brigade had two main assignments. Its two battalions set out to mop up Tirtur Road in the morning. As soon as it was clear that enemy resistance was minimal and the roller bridge could be towed on the road, the 410th Battalion commander, Major Yehuda Geller, was ordered to hitch the battalion up to the bridge again and resume towing it to the canal. While the 410th was thus engaged, Uzi Ben Yitzhak's 409th Battalion moved directly west to Amir. On reaching point 185, the scene of the battalion's earlier fighting, several vehicles detonated mines and were hit with antitank fire, but the battalion continued its advance west to the eastern edge of the Amir compound, where it deployed defensively. In effect, the 409th was supposed to take control of the entire area between Lexicon and Hamadia. In the afternoon, the 14th Brigade attacked Amir from the west and southwest, capturing it. This enabled its 184th and 179th Battalions to deploy a kilometer or two north of Shik Road.

On the morning of October 18, Dayan visited the 143rd. Like Sharon, he too thought that the destruction of the Second Army was preferable to that of the Third Army and even pressed Sharon: "Take a tank force and go forward [i.e., to the north and northwest] and get rid of them [the Egyptians]. The more the better, and don't ask anyone for permission. You have a mandate to push north even as far as Kantara" (Bergman and Meltzer 2003, 281).

From this point on, all Sharon's moves were aimed at bringing the 14th Brigade to the western bank despite the intense opposition in the front's headquarters. The 79th Battalion was removed from the line in the afternoon and sent to reorganize. The 184th Battalion remained on the line. At midnight, October 18–19, the roller bridge was launched, and the battalion that had towed it, the 410th, replaced the 184th on the line. This exchange took place at dawn October 19 when the 410th left a company by the roller bridge's launching site for protection. The 184th also pulled out to reorganize at Lakekan and rejoined the brigade the next day.

In the morning, Sharon issued a warning order to the commander of the 14th Brigade to prepare to cross the canal. After the Southern Command agreed to Sharon's suggestion not to split his division and not to order it to advance south, he contacted Gonen at 1000 and requested that additional tanks from his division be allowed to cross to the western bank. Instead of giving a straightforward yes or no, Gonen replied: "Only if possible." But this satisfied Sharon. He interpreted Gonen's answer as permission and immediately ordered the 14th to cross the roller bridge and prepare for battle north of the bridgehead. Thus, at 1000, the 14th sent its armored combat vehicles across the canal on the roller bridge while the other vehicles used the raft bridge. The lesson to be learned here is unequivocal: orders must be worded in a way that leaves no room for interpretation; if an order is intentionally ambivalent, then it is not a bona fide order.

On October 19, the 14th Brigade consisted of the 79th Tank Battalion (seventeen tanks), the White Bear Amphibious Reconnaissance Battalion, the 424th (Shaked) Battalion (three infantry companies), and Force Shmulik (two companies of paratroopers) on the western bank. The 184th Battalion remained at Lakekan to reorganize. The brigade's first task was to capture the Orkha compound at the Nora-Vardit Junction. The brigade attacked the compound from the west, outflanking it while moving on Haifa and Havit Roads and east on Vardit. The attack began at 1430. The battle was bitter and underwent many fluctuations. It continued through the night and until the following morning, when the compound was finally captured and mopped up. On the morning of October 20, Natan Shunri's 582nd Antitank/Reconnaissance Battalion joined the brigade at Orkha.

The 421st Brigade advanced with two separate thrusts: one battalion reached the Nora-Havit Junction and destroyed two SAM bases north and northwest of the junction; the remaining force moved west on Vardit and deployed at point 37, five kilometers west of the Vardit-Havit Junction, thus arriving six to seven kilometers east of Arzel Road, the main Cairo-Ismailia desert axis. This compelled the Egyptians to close the road. The 421st's advance would seem to have pointed at one of the most promising courses of action leading to the surrender of the Second Army.

On October 19, the division received under its command Colonel Uzi Yairi's reduced 35th Paratrooper Brigade (the 890th Battalion, two companies of the 564th Battalion/247th Brigade, a company of combat engineers, and the squad leaders company of the 50th Battalion). The brigade crossed to the western bank on foot and advanced north to Serapeum.

The 162nd Division in Combat

The logistic problems remained Adan's nemesis on the morning of October 19. What was self-evident was revealed again: access roads and a bridgehead that were supposed to serve a multidivision task force should have been under the direct command of the task force's headquarters, that is, under the Southern

Command. Effective management of the roads and bridges, which included the prioritization of the traffic based on overarching operational considerations, had to be decided from the roads and bridgehead itself, not from Um Hashiba.

The 162nd Division's goal for this day was to attain what it had failed to the day before, but this time with the addition of the 500th Brigade and assistance from the reduced 252nd Division. Because of snags in replenishment, the 162nd's brigades were late in getting to their objectives, and their movement began in piecemeal fashion according to the pace of the replenishment.

As the 217th Brigade was moving west on Haifa Road toward Maktzera, its commander, Colonel Nir, met the commander of the 401st Brigade, Dan Shomron, who was also coming from Arel to Maktzera. The brigade commanders coordinated the attack on Maktzera: the 401st provided covering fire from the north while Nir's brigade attacked from the east. After overrunning the objective, Nir's brigade turned to the Sakranut-Vada'ut Junction ten kilometers southwest of Arel. As night approached, it entered a night park at Vitamin (point 47) six kilometers east of the Vitamin-Vada'ut Junction. In the course of the day, the brigade had driven almost twenty kilometers as the crow flies in a southerly direction.

On the morning of October 19, the 460th Brigade set out from Uri in a southwesterly direction. It passed east of Tazch, hit the missile bases north of the Fayed airfield and north of Jebel Shihabi (between the Uvda and Vitamin Roads), and parked for the night in the vicinity of the Vada'ut-Vitamin Junction. The brigade chalked up twenty kilometers in a southwesterly direction as the crow flies.

The 500th Brigade was supposed to move as a division reserve between the 217th and the 460th Brigades. Throughout the day, it engaged in encounters between Houshani and Maktzera, destroying six SAM bases on both sides of Vitamin Road, and entered night parks in the vicinity of the Vada'ut-Seria Junction. The brigade traveled twenty kilometers this day in a generally southwesterly direction.

The Fighting of the 252nd Division (Continued)

Kalman Magen's 252nd Division operated west of Adan's division. Its capture of the Tzakh compound on October 19 removed the blocking force on the Havit-Sakranut Junction, thus opening the key logistic road for Adan's division. After Tzakh and Maktzera were taken (the latter by the 217th Brigade with assistance from 401st), the 252nd received responsibility for the fighting in the western sector. Vada'ut Road and, in the east-west, Uvda Road were determined as the sector boundary between the 252nd and Adan's division. The 252nd forces replaced the 162nd in the Mitznefet and Sanson areas, and the 252nd captured the Fayed airfield the next day.

The Main Events of October 20

The CoGS took part in a meeting in Um Hashiba on the evening of October 19 in which the Southern Command's missions were formulated for the following day. On his return to Tel Aviv, he convened a preparatory discussion group that approved the orders decided on at Um Hashiba.

The 143rd Division would continue its advance north on both banks of the canal with the aim of reaching Bahariat el Timsah (Crocodile Lake). The 162nd Division would try to ascend Ras Geneifa, where it would destroy the SAM batteries and cut off the roads that linked Cairo to Suez, Asor, and Serge or at least make sure that they were within range of its artillery.

The 252nd would remain in the center of the area of operations as a reserve and a defense in case of an armored counterattack. The CoGS's summaries reflect the estimate that, on October 22 or 23, the superpowers would impose a cease-fire. Dayan had brought this likelihood (which indeed did come to pass) to Elazar's attention.

The Fighting of the 143rd Division (Continued)

The 600th Brigade's two battalions maintained their pressure on Missouri with the goal of expanding the bridgehead to the north. The 410th Battalion advanced to point 106, a kilometer and a half south of Usha Road (the 79th and 184th Battalions/14th Brigade had reached the road and withdrawn on the night of October 15–16). From this point, the 410th gained visual contact and fire control over the road.

The 421st Brigade expanded the division's control to the west and deployed on Vada'ut Road from Maktzera to the Vada'ut-Arzel Junction. Seizing this junction effectively blocked the desert road connecting Cairo to Ismailia. The 14th Brigade entered the agricultural barrier east from Orkha. The 79th Battalion captured the firing ramps at Teev A. The Shaked Battalion, operating to the north, captured SAM site 6521 and the firing ramp at Foxtrot A on the canal's 87th kilometer. As stated, Force Shmulik continued mopping up Serapeum village and its environs. The 184th Battalion (twenty-five tanks) joined the 14th Brigade in the morning. The 184th received the 88th Battalion, advanced on Havit Road north of Gheshira, and was tasked with capturing the bridges on the freshwater canal between Havit 29 and 27. The battalion took the bridges at Havit 29 but was stopped at SAM site 6620 two kilometers north of the Nora-Havit Junction.

The 35th Brigade received a large addition of reinforcements on October 20 and organized in four battalion frameworks: the 890th, the 469th Battalion/317th Reserve Paratrooper Brigade, which was brought to Sinai from the Golan Heights, the 48th Battalion/Jordan Valley Brigade, and a two-company force from the 564th Battalion/247th Brigade. As the brigade advanced north along Maseikha Road, it mopped up the agricultural barrier and ramps in its sector. By evening, it reached point 24 on Maseikha, ten kilometers north of the Nora-Vada'ut Junction.

The 247th Brigade focused on securing the bridgehead and capturing the areas that the 35th Brigade had evacuated when it advanced north.

Since the 143rd had begun fighting on the western bank, it managed to expand its hold on the agricultural barrier and west of it in a twelve- by eight-kilometer area mainly through infantry operations and to a lesser degree through joint infantry-armor warfare. Although its force on the western bank included no more than a hundred tanks, it had seven infantry battalions operating with the 274th, 35th, and 14th Brigades.

The Fighting of the 162nd Division

At dawn October 20, Adan designated the division's assignments for the day: blocking the Asor and Serge (Cairo-Ismailia) Roads, and if possible, capturing the city of Suez. The 460th and 500th Brigades left their night parks and moved east on Vitamin, Evra, and Seria Roads, halting on the eastern slopes of the hills. The 198th/460th's battalion reached the area above the Bulmus compound, two kilometers to the west, while the brigade's other forces, which were moving on Vitamin Road, halted at point 40. This day, the brigade's battalions covered fifteen to seventeen kilometers as the crow flies, in an easterly direction.

Keren's 500th Brigade moved east on Vitamin, turned southeast on Evra Road, and was blocked three kilometers west of Metsila, having covered twenty kilometers this day in an east-southeast straight line.

Nir's brigade also moved southeast on Seria Road to the Arish-Seria Junction, turned south on Arish, and proceeded to Asor Road and blocked both it and the Suez-Cairo railway line south of it, capturing SAM site 5121 on the way, south of the Arish-Asor Junction. Asor Road links up east to Havit and Test Roads and then to Tzidon (where the canal enters the Little Bitter Lake) and west to Cairo. The brigade covered eleven to twelve kilometers as the crow flies, in a southeasterly direction. The brigade settled into the night parks in the SAM site 5121 area. On the morning of October 20, the Southern Command ordered Adan to avoid dispersing his division but to focus on advancing east and reaching the Lituf area and Kabrit Peninsula. But, when the Southern Command realized the extent of the 217th's gains, it revised its instructions, and Nir was ordered to proceed south and block Serge Road too.

In his memoir, Adan summed up the division's fighting on October 20: "Another day passed in which the division advanced twenty kilometers south" (Adan 1979, 258). Another day did indeed pass, but the division most certainly did not advance twenty kilometers south. Most of its movement that day was east-southeast. At the end of the day, even the southernmost brigade (the 217th) was about thirty kilometers (in a direct line) south of its starting point, after it too traveled most of the way to its night park in an easterly-southeasterly direction.

The main point is that, in the three days since crossing the canal, the division fought hard and courageously and its gains were not inconsiderable, though nothing spectacular. In general, it failed to exploit its potential to the fullest or function with the necessary decisiveness, though this was not entirely its fault. A number of factors converged to prevent it from making full use of its potential.

The Logistics Ordeal

We have already noted that the Southern Command should have assumed direct responsibility for and exclusive authority over the regulation of traffic, prioritization, timetables, and control of movement on the roads to the bridgehead. Owing to the lack of understanding, inexperience and perhaps sheer lethargy, the command divested itself of all responsibility for administrating this rare and invaluable asset. As soon as the bridgehead was established, the problem of monitoring the traffic to and on the bridges metastasized. The 143rd's deputy commander and his FCP set up, organized, and operated the bridgehead and maintained its defense with supreme professionalism and efficiency. But it was not the responsibility of the 143rd's deputy commander or the division commander to prioritize the crossing of the reinforcements, weapons, and other means and the medical evacuation the Southern Command's formations. In other words, the bridgehead should have been at the Southern Command facility. The outcome of the command's failure to take responsibility for its most important and scarcest asset in the operations area—the access roads (on both sides of the canal) and the bridges on the canal—was the perpetual logistic ordeal of the command's formations on the western bank, which was exacerbated the further they moved from the bridgehead. The Southern Command's shirking of responsibility stemmed from a perception that saw nothing amiss in the absence of its FCP on the western bank. Added to this was the interminable heavy shelling of the bridgehead compound, which stymied the forces' movement, and the scandalous lack of professionalism at every level, including the

General Staff, in adopting alternative or complementary logistic means. Supplies, reinforcements, medical evacuation became major problems that limited the fighting potential of the command's formations. In addition to this omission, we have already seen where the division's logistic planning and performance were flawed to the point of failing it operationally.

Mission Glut

Adan's division was assigned three direct or indirect missions: the destruction of SAM bases, the maximum destruction of enemy forces, and the encirclement of the Third Army. The problem was that no one clarified the priority of its missions. Thus, it operated without a clear operational horizon but with an exaggerated degree of freedom of action and opportunism, with the result that it moved in every which direction to attack targets that otherwise might have been deemed unnecessary. It tried to seize as much as possible since the division commander still believed, as did the front commander when he formed his policy about letting large forces cross the canal before a bridge was in place that the sand in the hourglass was glued to the top of the glass. Finally, on October 20, and in light of Dayan's warning and Elazar's instructions, the Southern Command began focusing its attention on the mission that was supposed to have been the main goal of Operation Stouthearted Men—the encirclement, if not annihilation, of the Third Army—and ordered Adan accordingly.

The fighting on the western bank during these three days was characterized by an absence of the basic principles of war, first and foremost, defining a goal and sticking to it, concentrating and balancing forces and exploiting them to the fullest, and striving to surprise the enemy. The principle of security reigned supreme, keeping a large part of the command's force on the western bank as a reserve, whether openly or concealed. The indirect approach was glaringly missing.

One of the major factors that impaired the 162nd's fighting mettle was the shortage of crack infantry. Little more need be said about this weak point or the severe shortage of artillery and ammunition.

The Fighting of the 252nd Division (Continued)

The 401st Brigade deployed opposite Mitznefet and Bologna localities west of Vada'ut Road to protect Adan's operations. The 164th Brigade sent a detachment to capture the Fayed airfield and another to secure Vada'ut 48 (south of the Uvda-Vada'ut Junction). The 908th Battalion (infantry recruits) was transferred from the MARSHAL command to secure the captured airfield.

The Main Events of October 21

And in the pit* there is no water, but mire. (Jer. 38:6)

In the evening of October 20, the General Staff was aware that a cease-fire would take effect on October 22 or 23. The CoGS's decisions and priorities from October 22 on reflect his anxiety about public opinion and the IDF's and government's situation when the ax fell. These apprehensions led him to make an about-face in the military strategy that was to be adopted relative to his previous position. He now saw a canal crossing and fighting on the western bank as the key means for winning the war.

Employing the feeble excuse of needing to conserve strength, the CoGS issued orders that effective immediately the emphasis would be switched from capturing areas and encircling the Third Army on the western bank to destroying the Egyptian forces at the bridgeheads east of the canal. As noted, Elazar retained an abiding hope—and perhaps faith—that, if the IDF redeployed on the canal line and all the Egyptians disappeared from Sinai, then the Israeli government, the Jewish people, and history would remember only this happy ending and forgive him for botching the conduct of the IDF before and during the war and the terrible price that the nation paid on the road to the happy ending.

On the other hand, following the preparatory discussion group, the General Staff Operations Branch issued orders that ignored—in a manner rather characteristic of the General Staff's work—the CoGS's priorities and set forth the following missions for the Southern Command:

- Destroy SAM batteries with artillery fire.
- Attack and destroy the Egyptian army west of the canal while advancing south and north, beyond the agricultural barrier.
- Attack the enemy on the eastern bank in the north and south, and at the same time attack the Kantara area.
- Pursue the annihilation of the Egyptian army in the crossing area.

At midnight October 20–21, the Southern Command ordered the divisions—in light of the General Staff Operations Branch's orders (with modifications)—to carry out the following assignments:

- The 162nd Division would break through to the canal from east of Metzilla

* "The Pit" is the popular name of the IDF's high command subterranean headquarters.

and open Havit Road in the Fayed area, block Asor Road, and destroy SAM bases.

- The 252nd Division would remain where it was and, if necessary, assist the 162nd in destroying SAM bases.
- The 143rd Division was, contrary the General Staff Operations Branch's order, forbidden to cross the northern agricultural barrier and instead would attack and capture the Missouri compound. To accomplish this, it would be provided with massive air support.
- Force Tiger would, on instructions from the CoGS in what seemed an effort, albeit a secondary one, from north to south, put up a holding defense in its sector and apply light pressure to the southern edge of the force's sector—apparently integrated with the 143rd's attack.

The impression that this order leaves is that it did not fit the instructions of the CoGS's and the General Staff Operations Branch's orders and that it was designed primarily to prevent the 143rd Division from making any additional gain on the western bank and forcing it to attack Missouri—in effect, without substantial assistance from neighboring and other forces.

The Fighting of the 162nd Division (Continued)

At dawn, the division's brigades set out for another day of fighting. They soon encountered a stiff defense that was accompanied with vigorous infantry and armor counterattacks especially on Arish Road, which, it will be remembered, extended from north to south and crossed the Evra, Seria, Asor, and Serge Roads (the last was the Third Army's main logistics axis). The 217th Brigade had moved on Arish south the previous day, crossed Asor, and captured SAM site 5121, in the vicinity of which it deployed in night parks on the night of October 20–21. The Egyptian command probably perceived the IDF's advance south on this road all the way to Serge Road as a serious threat—and a stage in the encirclement of the Third Army. Arish Road was the expected axis of advance. Egyptian infantry and armor repeatedly attacked the 217th and kept it busy for most of the day. Thus, the brigade's advance south was slow and slight. The 500th Brigade, with its thirty tanks in two token battalions, tried a second time to descend the cliffs of the Geneifa Hills but was blocked on Agun Road west of Metzilla.

The 460th Brigade had been reinforced with the 429th Battalion/500th Brigade. The 429th, which the Southern Command ordered to remain on Talisman Road on the eastern bank, now joined the division. That evening, the 460th was reinforced with three companies from the 50th Airborne Infantry Battalion under the command of Yoram Yair (who had just arrived from the fighting on the Golan Heights) and the division's combat engineers battalion, which was tasked with clearing the mines from the roads that had been opened and with diverting the freshwater canal to the Great Bitter Lake in order to prevent the water from reaching the Third Army. The brigade's success in opening the Havit-Vitamin Road enabled the logistic support echelons to reach the division's units. By nightfall, the brigade's battalions were in Havit 49 two to three kilometers southeast of the junction.

Bar-Lev and Yigal Allon (a former general, former commander of the Palmach, former superior officer of Elazar, Bar-Lev, and Adan, and currently a member of Golda Meir's security cabinet) arrived at Adan's FCP at noon. Differences of opinion erupted between the front commander and the division commander regarding the direction of the division's movement. Bar-Lev opposed the 162nd's advance south to Serge and demanded that Adan advance east on Asor Road and then south on the roads along the Bitter Lakes, and have these movements converge on the point where the canal enters the Little Bitter Lake. Adan felt that deployment on Serge Road was a no less important move, one that would contribute significantly to the encirclement of the Third Army. The operational concept behind Bar-Lev's move defies understanding. Adan's approach appeared—and indeed proved to be—capable of producing a considerable strategic gain. The challenge in fully understanding the disputants stems from the Southern Command's absence of a clearly defined goal in the fighting on the western bank.

The Fighting of the 252nd Division (Continued)

As a rule, the division remained in its positions opposite Mitznefet. The 401st Brigade deployed south of Mitznefet, where it engaged the enemy and, according to its account, destroyed eighteen tanks. The 164th Brigade attacked two SAM bases from the south and north of Mitznefet and waged armor-versus-armor battles west of the compound.

Blood and Sand at Missouri—the 143rd Division's Fighting

As morning dawned, the 35th and 14 Brigades, with the addition of the 48th Airborne Battalion and a company of officer cadets, continued their slow advance through the thick vegetation of the agricultural barrier. In the discussions between the division and the Southern Command, it became clear to Sharon that the command was giving priority to operational activity on the eastern bank. Earlier, Gonen had allowed Sharon to decide on this matter according to the best of his judgment: "Determine your priorities, and take Ismailia or Missouri; I'm more interested in Missouri." But, after Elazar's irate intervention, Gonen's liberal approach became an explicit order to capture Missouri.

All Sharon's efforts to convince his superiors that an attack on Missouri would fail at a heavy cost to the IDF and that it was preferable to advance on the western bank to the northern agricultural barrier were in vain. Their only result was that the front commander flew to Sharon's FCP to deliver to him in person the order to capture Missouri. Moreover, the 143rd was forbidden to advance north of point 24 on Maseikha (opposite Usha on the western bank). The Southern Command's operational concept envisioned attacking the Second Army bridgehead along its narrow dimension east of the canal from both ends simultaneously: 143rd Division would attack Missouri from the south, and Force Tiger would take Hamutal from the north and reach the canal in the Mifras area, about one kilometer north of the Usha-Rosh Junction. As H-hour (1300) approached, the IAF would repeatedly bomb and strafe Missouri.

To minimize the damage that the attack was likely to cause his division, Sharon employed only the 600th Brigade with its forty tanks organized in two reduced battalions. The 409th Battalion, which was deployed south and southwest of Missouri, and the 410th Battalion would advance cautiously between Missouri and the canal and reach the Mifras area. The 14th Brigade would cover the 600th's move with tank fire from the ramps on the western bank, three and a half to four kilometers from the western edge of the Missouri compound. The artillery had seven hundred shells at its disposal for supporting fire. The commander of Force Tiger, Brigadier General Sasson Yitzhaki, assigned the capture of Hamutal to Colonel Yoel Gonen, the commander of the 274th Brigade, who conveyed the task to a reduced battalion force randomly code-named "Force Lazy."

The commander of the 600th Brigade, Colonel Tuvia Raviv, and the division commander were aware that the attack had no chance of succeeding and that the losses would be high, owing especially to the small number of attacking forces and the critical mistakes in its composition. But Raviv was duty bound to obey orders. His plan was simple. His two battalions would attack Missouri from their current positions: the 409th would attack from its location to the north and the 410th from its location to the northeast.

The Battle and Its Collapse

H-hour was pushed back to 1515 because of delays in the air attack. After a few bombing and strafing runs by the IAF, the ground attack commenced. The 409th Battalion attacked from the southeast, engaged Egyptian armor, hit twenty tanks, but was stopped at a minefield, from which point it continued to engage the enemy and came under Egyptian antitank fire from Missouri and the direction of Televizia. The 410th attacked from Usha to the northwest and encountered tank and antitank fire from the compound and from the west. Only four of the battalion's initial twenty-six tanks emerged unscathed. The battalion lost over fifty men (killed, wounded, captured, and missing). At the end of the day, the 600th was left with only nineteen operable tanks out of the forty-one it started the battle with. Twenty-four soldiers were killed, including eight officers, and nothing had been gained. The brigade withdrew two kilometers south.

Force Lazy's two reduced tank companies and armored infantry company reached Hamutal from the east and attacked to the west after clashing with a large number of Egyptian infantry on the way. While it advanced, some of its APCs were hit with antitank rockets and mines, and, when the force reached the high ground at the western edge of the compound that evening, it came under heavy artillery fire and had to pull back to the eastern part of Hamutal.

Assessment of the Attack on Missouri

The failure of the Missouri attack did not come as a surprise to the division's commanders, and it probably was not a surprise to the front commanders either. The main factors contributing to the 143rd Division's stinging failure were the paucity of attacking forces and their flawed composition, the meager support available to them, and the Egyptians' firm and effective resistance, which undermined the CoGS's rosy expectations. The results of the battle were foreseeable and inevitable, and there is no need to analyze them. But there is value in discussing two issues that go to the heart of generalship at the highest level: why did the CoGS and the southern front commanders initiate the battle in the first place, and how can Sharon's and Raviv's agreement to it be explained?

Why Did the CoGS and Front Commanders Instigate the Battle of Missouri?

Immediately after the battle, accusations were made—directly and indirectly—about the extraneous and unacceptable motives that led to the battle for Missouri. The CoGS and the commander of the front claimed that the corridor east of the canal was narrow and perilous and that it therefore had to be urgently expanded by capturing Missouri. Sharon's assertion that the order to attack was a mistake on both generalship and intelligence grounds was a cry in the wilderness. During this period, Elazar's and Bar-Lev's explanation for taking Missouri became a kind of code word that identified expanding and stabilizing the corridor with the capture of Missouri, regardless of what the real reasons for attempting its capture were.

Sharon explained the Southern Command's pressure to capture Missouri as its misreading of the battle—a blunder that characterized its battle conduct during the entire war. Later, he elaborated on the command's performance in the war:

> It was generalship of the worst kind. But I am afraid it was more than just bad generalship. . . . I knew that Bar-Lev and Elazar considered this proposal self-serving on my part. . . . To this day I cannot free myself from the feeling that one of the reasons they were pressing me to attack the Sixteenth and Twenty-First Divisions on the east side of the canal was not because they considered the corridor too narrow but because they wanted to keep my troops on the eastern side. They would allow me to proceed north, but they did not want me to have sufficient forces to do it effectively. These are hard things to say. But my strong impression then was that the antagonisms of years between myself and those in command (Bar-Lev and Elazar), augmented now by political considerations, played a considerable role in the military decisions that were made at the time. (Sharon 1989, 330)

The years that have passed since Sharon wrote this harsh indictment have not blunted the acerbity of this feeling. Although his testimony is not objective, it should not detract from his superb ability to identify precisely where the truth lay. Another observer who is also perhaps not objective but who is without doubt experienced and perceptive and also sensitive has this to say about Sharon's superiors' battle conduct: "As an observant bystander, again I couldn't say if the orders issued to Sharon stemmed from an ulterior operational need or from the wish to teach him a lesson" (Baron 1992, 226).

Dayan said as much, and there is no denying the defense minister's ability to recognize despicable motives. It will be remembered that, after Sharon's request on the night of October 21–22, Dayan scuttled the Southern Command's plans to renew the attack on Missouri. On the morning of the twenty-second, Dayan went to Sharon's FCP and was updated on the previous day's events. From there, seething and disconsolate, he arrived at Um Hashiba, convened the Southern Command senior commanders, excluding Bar-Lev, who had wisely flown off that morning to Tel Aviv, and said to those present: "You ordered [Sharon] to take Missouri. This is a scandal. . . . This headquarters has a gut reaction against anything that Sharon suggests" (Schiff 1974, 226).

Gonen, who usually kept his mouth shut in the presence of the higher and mightier (see Adan 1979, 116), now deviated from this prudent policy and responded: "[But] Sharon's waging a private war." Dayan, with rare patience, lectured him and the rest of the officers: "Let me make one thing clear to you; the word is out that political elements have infiltrated [the Southern Command headquarters]." At the conclusion of the meeting, Dayan returned to Tel Aviv and did not visit Um Hashiba again. He seems to have finally realized that there was no one worth talking to or anything worth talking about there.

The view that the attack on Missouri stemmed from political considerations and the personal motives of those issuing the order—and not from operational exigency—is supported by related events. As stated, the operational need to expand and stabilize the corridor on the eastern bank to the bridgehead was the pretext for the order to attack Missouri and the single string the CoGS and the commander of the Southern Command strummed until the moment of truth came, that is, the moment the generals of the General Staff and the Southern Command realized that a cease-fire was imminent. We have already noted that Elazar was bitterly disappointed with the scant gains on the western bank up—in terms of defeating the Egyptian army—and thought that the only way to salvage his military and public skin was to brush off the Second Army from the eastern bank in the little time that remained until the cease-fire took effect by seizing Missouri and perhaps a larger area in the army's sector.

On the day before and on the morning of the battle, in all the discussions, talks, instructions, and other verbiage that were supposed to lead to the capture of Missouri, not once did Elazar mention the widening and securing of the corridor. It will be remembered that, in the expanded preparatory CoGS discussion group that was held at midnight October 20–21, Elazar changed his position regarding the Southern Command's main effort and ordered it to focus on the Egyptian bridgeheads east of the canal (by which he meant Missouri). In effect, he wanted to wipe them from the face of the earth: "If we can concentrate the effort only on the [Egyptian] expeditionary force in Sinai, . . . I'm all for it since that way [we can create] a situation in which the canal is the cease-fire line." This was the same convoluted prewar idea of preventing the enemy from any gain and thus "renew our days as of old" (Lam. 5:21).

Hanoch Bartov (1978, 298–99) relates that, on the morning of October 21, the CoGS was furious that the attack on Missouri was not under way and that Gonen was bellyaching that the air force's bombing of Missouri was ineffective and answered him angrily over the phone: "According to all the information . . . the 16th Division has been annihilated, left without almost any tanks, the commanders have lost control over their troops and are just waiting for a good excuse to withdraw. They've informed the [Egyptian] high command that their situation is perilous—yet [we] don't attack them!" In reading the CoGS's optimistic intelligence assessments, we may ask: If the enemy was in a situation so deplorable, why was there such fear that it would have the strength and will to attack the IDF's narrow bridgehead? The logical answer is that this likelihood did not concern the CoGS; he simply wanted Missouri taken as quickly as possible, and he explained to Gonen that the operation would be as easy as pie.

On the night of October 21–22, after the disastrous results of the attack on Missouri were known, Gonen ordered Sharon to resume the attack on Missouri and reinforce the remnants of his forces on the eastern bank with the 14th Brigade, which was operating on the western bank. Sharon, livid, contacted Dayan and entreated him to countermand the order. Dayan, who was well aware of what had happened at Missouri, sought the CoGS and, not finding him, turned to the deputy CoGS, General Tal, and demanded that he clarify with the Southern Command what they were thinking about this time and cancel the order. Tal contacted the Southern Command, listened to Gonen's explanation, and was not convinced. He informed the CoGS of Dayan's demands and the result of his inquiries with the Southern Command. Elazar, who undoubtedly was also alarmed about the results of the battle, agreed to order the Southern Command to abort the attack. He explained to Tal that he had agreed to call it off because it was a waste of time and effort: "Nibbling another kilometer from the Egyptian perimeter won't change much now." We can understand from this particular wording of the acceptance of fate that Elazar's (personal) goal would probably have been realized only by the complete capture of Missouri because, if the expansion and stabilization of the corridor had truly been a most crucial matter as far as he was concerned, then every additional kilometer "nibbl[ed] off" Missouri would have been of the utmost importance to him.

Furthermore, on October 21, after Sharon protested to Gonen a second time that the order to attack Missouri was a catastrophe in the making, Bar-Lev flew to Sharon's FCP to issue the order to him in person. Sharon tried to convince Bar-Lev that attacking Missouri was nothing but banging one's head against a wall and that it would be wiser to pursue the attack in the Ismailia area and encircle the Second Army. Bar-Lev admitted that Ismailia was indeed an important target, but he also explained his main consideration: "We're close to a cease-fire, and this kind of a bridgehead [as Missouri on the eastern bank] isn't good for us."

In other words, there was no concrete military reason for the attack. The Egyptians' hold on the eastern bank simply wasn't "good for us." As to who "us" was and why it was not "good," Bar-Lev was silent and did not elaborate; there was no need to.

The decision to attack Missouri was not supported by any political consideration. Such considerations, whatever the case, are not the concern of the CoGS and certainly not in the job description of his subordinates. Assessments of political matters or political information are conveyed to the military leadership by the representative from the political level (the defense minister) whose job it is to advise the military high command on the implications of such assessments or provide information on the army's goals, targets, priorities, and expected accomplishments. Indeed, both at the General Staff and at the Southern Command, there was much talk about the imminent political events, but all this was only a bunch of hooey. On the night of October 21–22, when Dayan (the political level) spoke with Tal (the military level) about the attack on Missouri, not only did he not mention the capture of the compound for political needs, but he also even asked the deputy CoGS with open displeasure: "What do you want from Missouri?" (Schiff 1974, 218).

Can Sharon's and Raviv's Agreeing to Attack Missouri Be Explained?

When Sharon returned to civilian life, he expressed his regret and remorse for not daring to disobey the senseless order to attack Missouri, especially since he correctly estimated the losses that would be incurred. Sixteen years after the war, he wrote:

> Among all the tragic mistakes and all the grim fighting of the Yom Kippur War, it was the attack on Missouri that weighed most heavily on me. I had ordered Tuvia's brigade into battle even though I knew for a fact that many of those solders were going to their deaths for nothing. It was something I should never have done, regardless of my orders. I knew instinctively at the time that it was wrong for me to have obeyed. And later, on reflection, I became sure morally and legally too I should not have obeyed. In an interview I gave to the newspaper *Ma'ariv* on January 25, 1974, I said exactly that. . . . I should have disobeyed and accepted a court-martial for my disobedience. (Sharon 1989, 330–31)

It is impossible not to agree with this assessment. The Agranat Commission, which also had to tackle this issue, following Sharon's testimony regarding October 8, found that, from the point of view of military law and discipline, his position was completely correct. "But," Sharon added, "all the justification in the world did not change the fact that was done, that those lives were sacrificed, and that I shared the responsibility for it" (1989, 333).

This was the second time that Sharon faced so dramatic a dilemma. The first time was on October 8 when—despite his understanding of the precariousness of the situation in the field and his gut feeling—he obeyed Gonen's command to abandon his positions in the Second Army's sector and took his entire division south. Then, as later, he regretted having carried out his superior's command. Unfortunately, then as later, his self-reproach came too late for many of his men. Then, as later, he declined to reveal why he agreed to obey the orders rather than the dictates of his conscience. The first time one could have tried to explain what may have motivated him to obey; the second time, there was no acceptable explanation for his conduct, and no admission of guilt and remorse can cover up the omission.

Sun Tzu has said: There are roads that are not to be traveled on, armies that should not be attacked, cities that should not be laid siege to, positions that cannot be captured, and orders of the sovereign that should not be obeyed.

The Main Events of October 22

And after the fire a still small voice. (1 Kings 19:12)

Anticipating the expected Security Council meeting to ratify the American-Soviet formula for a cease-fire in the Middle East, the Israeli government decided already before dawn to accede fully to the resolution. Indeed, at 0700 October 22, Security Council Resolution 338 stated that a cease-fire would become effective that day at 1852. Neither the superpowers (who initiated it) nor the Security Council (which ratified it) made any arrangements to enforce it.

The Fighting of the 143rd Division (Continued)

The 143rd's mission was to secure the western flank of the area of operations on the western bank from the Fayed airfield (which the IAF was already operating) and to the north. The 421st Brigade was assigned the task and deployed the 599th Battalion at Mitznefet 2 (in the southern part of the compound), point 48 on Uvda Road, SAM site 5914, Sakranut 46, and SAM sites 6115 and 6214. The 264th Battalion was sent to the Vardit-Arzel Junction, opposite the northern agricultural barrier (southwest of the Abu Suweir airfield) on Vada'ut Road, SAM site 6615, and the Arzel 33 area.

At 1000, the 14th Brigade began the advance north with the 184th Battalion (reinforced with paratroopers) moving on Havit Road and the rest of the brigade, with the brigade commander and the 35th Brigade, moving in the agricultural barrier. The advance proceeded slowly because of continuous engagements with the Egyptian 150th Paratrooper Brigade. The fighting was over by 1930, but the division's forces were still unable to make it across the northern freshwater canal and come in behind Ismailia. As the cease-fire took effect, units of the 14th and 35th Brigades found themselves on a line extending from Nefeesha (one kilometer south of the Snir compound) southeast to the canal, opposite Mifras. The 247th Brigade advanced to the area that the 35th Brigade had evacuated in its advance north and was now spread out six or seven kilometers north of the bridgehead. The 600th Brigade, which had been saved by the skin of its teeth from the second attack on Missouri, gingerly attempted to advance north but lost two tanks to mines. It also lost four men in the air force bombing.

The heavy artillery fire on the bridgehead continued without respite. A quarter of an hour before the cease-fire was about to take effect, the Egyptians let loose with the largest artillery barrage of the war (as was their wont, from time immemorial, before a lull or cease-fire). The forces at the bridgehead, although entrenched and secured, nevertheless sustained heavy causalities, including those in the Yard, those already on the western bank, and many in Adan's main headquarters as it was crossing Yard en route to Africa. A Scud missile landed east of the Yard and blasted a wide crater, killing seven soldiers from the 600th Brigade's maintenance unit.

The Fighting of the 162nd Division (Continued)

The commander of the 162nd Division assigned his brigades the following missions for October 22:

- The 460th Brigade would dispatch a force south on Havit Road to break through the enemy's defenses at point 49. A second force would move on Evra Road, enter Agun Road, attack the enemy's defenses on Havit, and open the road from south to north. The brigade would clean out the Egyptian army camps in its sector as well as parts of the agricultural barrier.
- The 500th Brigade would also move on Asor and Seria Roads, its first objective being the Odeida compound at the Asor-Akal Junction, and from there it would proceed east to the canal.
- The 217th Brigade was to advance south on Arish Road, join Serge Road, advance east to the Serge-Akal Junction, and from there move on Akal in order to assist the 500th Brigade.

The plan underwent several modifications during the day, but its general parameters remained intact, except for a major change in the 217th's missions that the front commander ordered despite the division commander's misgivings. At noon, Bar-Lev ordered Adan to alter the 217th's plans to move south on Arish and then east on Serge and instead have it move east in the 500th's tracks on

Asor and Re-ee Roads. The brigade changed its direction at 1330, reached the Havit-Pakh Junction, and seized the Shalufa Height, east of the agricultural barrier, covering over twenty kilometers east that afternoon!

The 460th Brigade advanced on two routes. Two battalions moved out and attacked Havit from north to south; two others took trackless routes between the hills, moving north to south, and turning east to the Akal-Agun Junction, from which point they intended to descend to the plain.

The 500th Brigade moved east on the Asor, Havit, and Pakh Roads with the aim of reaching the water in the "Sidon" area (the code name for the southern point of the Little Bitter Lake, where the canal enters it) and seizing control of the firing ramps. At the Pakh-Test Junction, it encountered enemy resistance and drove northwest two or three kilometers to a night park, where it again encountered the enemy. After fighting its way out while taking losses, it reached the Test-Ktav Junction, continued south, and entered a night park two kilometers north of the Havit-Pakh Junction.

As evening fell, the 162nd Division entered night parks in the area between the agricultural barrier in the east, the hills in the west, the Akal-Havit Junction in the northwest down to Luka, and Mina in the Shalufa area in the southeast. Most of the division's forces covered much territory that day, but the majority of them, except for the 460th Brigade, had moved east. The division's main accomplishment was cleaning out another section of Havit Road. Other key missions, such as cutting off the Third Army's main supply route, completing the mop-up of the agricultural barrier, and moving south to the waterline in order to encircle the Third Army, were not achieved. In the five days of fighting, beginning with the crossing of the canal and ending on the evening of October 22, the brigade covered over one hundred kilometers, but its overall advance south was not more than forty to forty-five kilometers. The troops fought courageously and selflessly. Although the 162nd undoubtedly made important gains, the main goal—the destruction or at the least encirclement of the Third Army—was not accomplished, though this was not solely the division's fault.

The Fighting of the 252nd Division (Continued)

The 252nd Division left the 401st Brigade with only twenty-five tanks in the Jebel el Hatib area south of Mitznefet to secure the fighting area to the west. The 164th Brigade now numbered thirty-five tanks (five of its tanks—"Force Kohel"—were attached to the 460th Brigade). The division was scheduled to receive Ran Sarig's 179th Brigade (and its thirty tanks), which was transferred from the Northern Command, but, before it arrived, the 164th embarked on a long drive from Mitznefet on the Evra and Asor Roads to Arish Road, where it turned south, captured the Avit compound four kilometers east of Arish, set up a defensive position in the direction of the Bologna complex, continued south, arriving close to Serge Road (north of point 101), where it left a company-size force, and entered a night park two kilometers west of the Asor-Arish Junction.

At daybreak October 22, Ran Sarig's 179th Brigade crossed the canal, drove south to join up with the division, and continued its drive, now east, on Evra and Seria Roads. About twenty of the brigade's tanks, with the brigade commander, moved on Asor, reached the Akal-Havit Junction in the evening, and deployed defensively. The ten remaining tanks moved east on Evra, missed the turn, and joined the 460th Brigade in its night park.

A Moment of Silence—the Cease-Fire That Wasn't

The General Staff's order instructing compliance with the government's decision to honor the cease-fire reached the Southern Command at 0815. The cease-fire was scheduled to go into effect at 1900; however, the order contained both an official, written section and unofficial, oral guidelines. The written section instructed the Southern Command to be on the alert for Egyptian encroachments of the cease-fire: "Fire on enemy aircraft flying over IDF forces; thwart infiltration into areas held by the IDF; and in general, proceed freely for as long as necessary wherever the Egyptians violate the cease-fire." The CoGS orally instructed the front commander that all Southern Command forces that were still in operational movement when the cease-fire went into effect would be permitted to complete their movement as long as they did not encounter resistance.

We have already noted that the cease-fire resolution that the Soviet Union and the United States agreed to and the Security Council ratified lacked any arrangements for overseeing its enforcement or preventing its violation. In the absence of such mechanisms, the military and political reality left a wide gap open for the immediate renewal of fire by the hostile sides, both of whom abhorred the cease-fire. Israel's political and military levels had to break off their efforts before accomplishing many of their objectives. The Egyptian forces, which had been struggling to reduce the threat to the Third Army at all levels, continued fighting only when the initiatives were local or with tacit direction from Third Army headquarters. In addition, the unofficial oral guidelines of Sadat and his cohorts on the General Staff were directed toward minimizing the IDF's gains as much as possible.

When the cease-fire took effect, the IDF still had not achieved the objectives it had fought bloody battles for since the night of October 15. The reason for this can be summed up in two words: *failed generalship,* especially at the General Staff and the Southern Command level, but also at the 162nd Division level. Elhanan Oren (2004) discusses this in detail, but his main points can be condensed as follows:

- Goals, objectives, and operational priorities at the General Staff and front level were muddled, groundless, sometimes missing, and frequently fluctuating from one end to the other.
- A command and control system that was ineffective and essentially worthless and ignored or even ran counter to the basic principles of generalship.
- Logistics problems and shortcomings were flagrant from the General Staff level down.
- The was a flagrant disregard—born out of downright ignorance, incompetence, and inexperience—of the essential principles of war (such as mass, offensive, surprise, and indirect approach), which were replaced them with a powerful tendency to crown hesitancy, excessive apprehensiveness, and "seeing the shadow of the mountains as if they were men" (Judg. 9:36) as dominant principles of war.
- Troops strength and fighting spirit were wasted on sterile and disastrous operations (e.g., the battle for Missouri), mostly owing to extraneous considerations.

Nevertheless, in the five days preceding the cease-fire, the foundations were laid for continuing the operations to destroy or at least encircle the Third Army. Had they been realized, they would have resulted in a collapse that would have been intolerable to Sadat and his regime. As the cease-fire was going into effect, the IDF could have prepared for the continuation of the fighting, if it was called for, on the following gains.

The Southern Command's forces on the western bank needed only one more move to complete the encirclement of the Third Army; from there, the final step to totally crushing it was extremely short. The Second Army, too, although not in a situation as critical as the Third Army's, nevertheless also faced encirclement or even annihilation.

The Egyptian SAM layout south of the northern agricultural barrier was destroyed for all practical purposes. The IAF was using the Fayed airfield on the western bank. The IAF had freedom of the air, and the conditions had been created for its participation in the IDF's moves against the Third Army, both operationally (e.g., crushing the Third Army) and logistically (ferrying in supplies, reinforcements, and medical evacuation teams). The IAF's freedom in the sky in the central and southern theaters, even if not absolute, amplified the danger facing the Second Army.

The bridgehead had expanded geographically; its very existence, reliability, and potential output were now based on three bridges. It was functioning efficiently and could be seen as a crucial force multiplier.

Adan's and Kalman's divisions had been greatly reinforced in the last few days. The recently arrived forces on the western bank included two brigades. Kalman's division received the 179th Brigade, under the command of Ran Sarig, which had been transferred from the Northern Command; the 11th Brigade, under the command of Colonel Aharon Peled from Force Tiger, was due to arrive; and reconnaissance and airborne battalions were being called in from wherever possible.

Despite the losses and intense fatigue, the morale of the men and their commanders in the Southern Command was high.

Between the Two Cease-Fires: October 23–24

If it weren't for the last minute, nothing would get done. (attributed to Benjamin Franklin)

The Fighting Continues: October 23

The cease-fire took effect before the Israeli government, the General Staff, and southern front headquarters had achieved their goals. In the five days of fighting since the 162nd crossed the canal, not a single gain had been made that could have contributed to a decisive victory. At best, necessary conditions had been established for winning the war by surrounding or destroying the Third Army. One thing was certain: winning the war did not require that the Second Army be defeated or even dislodged from the eastern bank. Destroying the Third Army would be sufficient, and, in effect, the threat of encirclement was enough to break the will to fight of the highest level of Egyptian leadership—President Sadat and his war minister (the CoGS had collapsed a few days earlier).

The frustration of Israel's political and military leadership—with full cooperation from the Egyptian side—eventually led to a resumption of the fighting and a drastic change in the final results even before the ink was dry on Security Council Resolution 338. It could not have been otherwise. Israel's decision-making levels were determined to prevent a situation in which the IDF troops and the country's citizens felt that the drawn-out, costly fighting, the tremendous strain on the economy, and, above all, the outrageous price in Israeli lives had all been in vain. Added to this were two factors that we have already mentioned.

In the southern agricultural barrier, on the road to the city of Suez, Egyptian and Israeli forces were extensively enmeshed. Such a situation was conducive to a violation of the cease-fire by both Egyptian and Israeli troops in the area.

Furthermore, the Egyptian top brass had probably ordered the ground forces to block any IDF effort to make last-minute gains the moment the cease-fire went into effect and in the same breath instructed them to attack wherever possible and advantageous, without strictly adhering to the timing of the cease-fire. This was designed to improve the Egyptians' situation in the sector and the bargaining position in the final cease-fire that would surely come. In other words, the IDF and the Egyptians had the same incentive, if not with the same decisiveness, to resume the fighting.

Strangely, and perhaps intentionally, the superpower agreement and the Security Council resolution lacked mechanisms for monitoring and enforcing the cease-fire. Under these circumstances, it was only natural that the war would flare up again. As in every war, the Egyptians knew how to rekindle it, but they erred in their estimation of how it would end. On this issue, the IDF's estimates were more realistic, but not entirely so. Optimism and military and logistic incompetence still reigned supreme and confounded operations to the point of compromising the IDF's moves on the southern front.

But the IDF's goal was finally clear: the destruction or forced surrender of the Third Army or at least the creation of conditions for it by encirclement and cutting off the supply lines from Egypt. This goal underscored, for the first time perhaps, the basic strategic mistake in the war planning of the Egyptians. They had deployed for defense with a deep and wide water obstacle in their immediate rear and constructed two bridgeheads without planning for rapidly joining them together, without depth, and without mutual assistance.

The 162nd and 252nd Divisions renewed their attacks on the morning of October 23. Kalman's division, recently reinforced with tanks and paratroopers, left its blocking positions on the western bank on Serge (Suez-Cairo) Road and completed the envelopment of the Third Army by capturing the city of Adabiya and its port, about eight kilometers south of the city of Suez. Adan's Division was ordered to mop up the southern agricultural barrier and military camps and facilities along the Bitter Lakes and in general tie down the Third Army's forces while the 252nd Division carried out a deep flanking maneuver toward Adabiya.

At noon, Adan pulled the 500th and 460th Brigades out of the agricultural barrier and sent them to attack south in the direction of the city and Gulf of Suez. The 217th Brigade and the infantry forces ("Force Dovik") attached to the division continued mopping up the agricultural barrier and the camps. The 500th moved into night parks on Evra Road, several kilometers north of Serge. At the end of the day, the 460th Brigade deployed in four battalion night parks where Marpek Road intersected Serge Road in the north up to the northern end of the Mashber area, southwest of the city of Suez (on Pulkhan Road). The 217th

Brigade entered night parks on the western edge of the agricultural barrier, from SAM site 5228 in the north to approximately five kilometers north of the Havit-Serge Junction. The city of Suez was thus surrounded from the north, west, and southwest by the 162nd's brigades.

Kalman's division was supposed to be replaced in the western part of the area of operations by armor and infantry reinforcements, but their arrival was, of course, delayed for the usual reasons, such as an unrealistic time estimate for their arrival, the time needed for them to deploy on the line, and the time needed by the division to get organized and move to the target. Finally, by nightfall, the division was ready for movement on Serge Road west. At the conclusion of the 162nd's settling into its parking areas, the 252nd Division, which included the 401st and 179th Brigades, set out at 2035. After more delays, the division arrived at the town of Adabiya, seizing Ras Adabiya south of it and eventually the port of Adabiya. Vessels of the Israeli Red Sea Flotilla arrived at this port on the morning of the twenty-fourth.

The 252nd's control of Adabiya and its port, and its blocking of Serge Road kilometer 101 marked the completion of the Third Army's encirclement that day. Indications appeared that the army was disintegrating, especially given the number of prisoners the IDF's took that day.

Toward midnight, the Security Council ratified Resolution 339, which was merely a repeat of the previous resolution, but this time with monitoring and enforcement arrangements. The implementation of the resolution was assigned to the Finnish General Siilasvuo, the commander of the UN forces in the Middle East. At sunrise October 24, Siilasvuo informed Dayan that the Egyptians were prepared for a cease-fire at 0700. The IDF's gains on October 23 had broken the Egyptian leadership's will to fight on and achieved the decisive victory.

"This is not the way, neither is this the city" (2 Kings 6:19)

Before the second cease-fire went into effect at 0700 under UN supervision, the defense minister, the CoGS, and front headquarters wanted to capture the city of Suez. Adan's division was assigned the job. At 0130 October 24, Ben-Ari instructed Adan to take Suez "on the condition that it would not turn into a Stalingrad" (i.e., if it could be taken easily). The operational rationale behind the order was that this would block the Third Army's water, mop up the division's area of operations, and seize the Egyptian firing ramps facing the eastern bank.

Adan's plan called for the 460th Brigade to gain control of the coastal strip and industrial zone in the southern part of the city. The 500th Brigade, reinforced with a reduced paratrooper company of eighty men under the command of Lieutenant Colonel Ya'akov Hisdai, would capture the city's center and its port (Port Ibrahim) to the south. The 240 paratroopers arrived for the battle in APCs, half-tracks, and buses. The attack was scheduled to take place after a heavy air bombardment that would last until 0700, when, as stated, the cease-fire would take effect.

The Battle in the City of Suez

At 0520, Adan transmitted the attack order to the brigade commanders. Problems arose even before the brigades began the breakthrough into the city. The air force's mountain of a massive bombing gave birth to a little bombing molehill: In the half-hour window between the dissipation of the morning fog, which prevented any bombing, and the point at which the cease-fire would go into effect, only four quartets of fighter-bombers dropped their ordnance. "Indeed a rather pathetic preparatory bombing," Adan remarked.

Three hours after receiving the order, the 460th Brigade began the breakthrough into the city and advanced as planned. The 500th Brigade began its movement from the north, encountered enemy forces, and was delayed in its deployment area at the Havit-Serge Junction because of difficulties linking up with its paratroopers. At 1015, it commenced the breakthrough into the city on Serge Road from the northwest to the southeast, according to the brigade commander's plan. Leading the attack was Nahum Zaken's 433rd Battalion, followed by the paratrooper force, with two tank battalions providing covering fire at this stage and joining the breakthrough force later. The breakthrough was implemented à la Moshe Dayan's 89th Mobile Commando Battalion in Operation Dani in the 1948 War of Independence, which broke through the city of Lydda with Dayan leading the battalion down the main street firing its weapons in every direction, thus crushing, as the myth goes, the townspeople's will to fight.

However, this time, the story was entirely different. When the head of the armored column reached the Serge-Eitza (Arba'in) Junction, the breakthrough forces came under murderous antitank and light weapons fire. The tank battalion was mauled but managed to extricate itself forward to the gulf coast. The infantry was cut off from the armor, and the 564th Paratrooper Battalion, which arrived on its own at the junction, also encountered the same fire. Incurring many losses, including the wounding of its commander, the battalion abandoned its vehicles and put up a defense in a police station abutting the junction. The wounded and remaining fighters concentrated there and in two other buildings. Lieutenant David Amit, one of the company commanders, took charge of the battalion and organized the building's defense. "Force Hisdai," which had been following the 564th Battalion and absorbing some its remnants, was also hit. It abandoned its vehicles and organized, with the wounded, in a number of buildings close to where it had come under fire. The brigade's reconnaissance unit, at the end of the column, was severely hit, but, since it had been traveling in APCs, it managed to withdraw to the rear.

Like the events on the night of October 16–17, when the 890th Battalion set out to mop up the area between Tirtur and Akavish, the battle of the city of Suez suddenly metamorphosed into a rescue and evacuation operation. The brigade's forces were scattered along Serge. The paratroopers were besieged and fighting for their lives and protecting the wounded and the bodies of their dead comrades. One-third of the paratrooper force was hit. The attempts of the division and brigade commanders to carry out the mission and capture the city vaporized in the face of the Egyptians' vigorous resistance. In the afternoon, the division commander abandoned the effort to take the city and focused, with the 500th's commander, on extricating the trapped infantry and evacuating the casualties.

In the evening, Zaken's battalion and the 86th Armored Infantry Battalion attached to it withdrew to the west along the coast, followed by the 460th Brigade's retreating battalions. At 1600, the 484th Reconnaissance Battalion, under the command of Major Haim ("Ivan") Oren, reached the trapped Force Hisdai and extracted some of the wounded in empty APCs from the 500th Brigade's reconnaissance company.

During the night, the 564th Battalion and the rest of Force Hisdai managed to get out on foot and link up with the 162nd's forces west of the city of Suez. Adan later offered a very instructive story about this event:

> Yossi's ninety men, among them twenty-three wounded, were besieged in the city center, 4 km from our lines. Lieutenant Dudu [David Amit], who had assumed command, saw no possibility of getting out because he was so deep in the city. He thought it would be far simpler to wait for daylight to be extricated by an armored force. Aryeh [Colonel Keren] tried to convince him to move out on his own, but his efforts dragged on and on and nearly broke down altogether. Finally, with great unwillingness, he agreed and said they would try to slip out of the city toward our lines in small groups. However Aryeh rejected, asserting they must make the attempt as one group that could both carry the wounded and defend itself, fighting its way out if attacked. Now Colonel Hisdai took the microphone to carry on with the persuasion efforts. He himself had just made it out a short time before and was acquainted with Dudu; their conversation was fruitful and resulted in the drawing up of a plan for organizing the force and for a route of escape.
>
> In the meantime, Gonen contacted Dudu directly and was told

> that he was being called on to move out on his own, whereas he would rather wait until the following day so as to be rescued by an armored column. Dudu explained his difficulties to Gonen, and Gonen accepted his point of view. Now Aryeh called me to explain that after hours he had managed to convince Dudu to pull out, and then Gonen had intervened and spoiled the whole matter. I contacted Gonen and made it clear that we well understood Dudu's apprehension and were well aware of how complex this extraction effort would be. I went on to ask Gonen whether he was aware of the rescue efforts that had been made during the day and of their cost in blood. Gonen now changed his mind, called Dudu again, and—with the aid of an aerial photo—tried to pinpoint his location and guide him home in an exit route. But Dudu had no such map, and Gonen's explanation seemed to him complicated and abstract. Meanwhile, battalion commander Yossi had regained consciousness and after hearing Dudu's report said he favored moving out by night, Aryeh's unequivocal order to commence the pullout within ten minutes provided the final impetus. (Adan 1979, 420–21)

An unambiguous order from Keren to Lieutenant Amit did the trick. Amit organized his force, loaded the seriously wounded on stretchers, under covering artillery fire pulled out the entire force as a single body with the walking wounded, and reached safe haven before morning. The most interesting question of the whole story is what motivated General Gonen to speak directly—over the heads of Adan and Keren—with Lieutenant Amit and personally instruct him in carrying out the extraction?

End of Story—in the Meantime

Throughout October 25 until the UN observers arrived in Suez, the 500th and 460th Brigades renewed their struggle to take the city. With the support of direct tank, artillery, and half-track antiaircraft fire, they chewed away at the western and northern parts of the city. In the end, at an intolerably heavy price of 80 killed and 120 wounded, they achieved nothing. On the contrary, the battle's added value, in terms of political and military gain for Israel, was expressly negative and detracted from the IDF's achievements up until that day.

Comments on the Battle for the City of Suez

We will spare the reader a rehash of the shortcomings, blunders, and mishaps at the various levels, from the defense minister and the CoGS, through the

Southern Command and the 162nd Division, to the lower levels that led to the intolerable scandal known as the Battle for the city of Suez. The failings at all levels have been described and analyzed to the point of exhaustion, their lessons derived and some of them—we would like to believe—applied, especially on the personal level. Nevertheless, a few points in this tragic saga still require illumination.

Whose Decision Was It to Launch the Battle?

It will be remembered that, on the night of October 23–24, Brigadier General Ben-Ari told the commander of the 162nd that his mission for the next day was capturing the city of Suez "on the condition that it would not turn into a Stalingrad." That is, if it could be accomplished cheaply, then do it; if not, then don't. Adan claims that he interpreted this wording to mean that the Southern Command was ordering him to capture the city but that if, in the course of the action, it became too hard a nut to crack, then his superiors were prepared to abort the mission. This, at any rate, was how he understood the order. In the same context, he notes: "In the spirit of what [Ben-Ari] told him and in light [of these and other signs] he assumed [yes, thus!] that the city could be captured without getting bogged down in an intractable battle" (Adan 1979, 302).

The issue before us is not one of semantics but one that gets to the roots of generalship. What Ben-Ari said cannot be construed as a military command. It is very difficult to see how his wording reflects the assumption that capturing the city of Suez could be accomplished without getting caught up in a bloody battle. He merely recommended that, as the man on the spot, Adan check whether the capture of the city could be done cheaply or at a high cost, and, accordingly, this is how his words should be construed. It was left to Adan to decide whether to go for it or to give up on it.

Neither the Southern Command nor the 162nd Division had any information on the enemy's strength and deployment in the city. How was it possible to assess whether the city of Suez would be like Stalingrad or Smallville, Kansas, without these data?

The only basis for Adan's estimation of the situation was the *assumption*—as he calls it, or *belief*, if you prefer—that capturing the city would be a walk in the park. He claims that the Southern Command also assumed as such, but no evidence exists for this claim, and, at any rate, it is irrelevant. Adan also attributes his assumption, or gut feeling, to the so-called signs of the Third Army's collapse and its men and officers' loss of fighting spirit. He forgot or overlooked the lessons of this war in everything related to the Egyptians' fighting spirit and combat proficiency, especially when their back was against the wall.

There is no getting away from the fact that, despite the one-of-the-guys camaraderie of Ben-Ari's words to Adan, the decision to capture Suez was in the end Adan's alone. And, like that of the night of October 16–17, when the 890th Battalion was sent on its mission impossible and suffered heavy losses, this time, too, the decision was made without demonstrating the operational need and carefully weighing the expected profit and loss.

Adan summed up the issue thus: "Today I regret that I was assigned the mission and that I accepted it" (Adan 1979, 302). Unfortunately, even as he wrote this expression of remorse, he still did not realize—or refused to admit—that no mission had actually been assigned and that he should have expressed any objection to carrying out any mission only to himself.

"Haste is from the devil" (Arabic saying)

One of the factors contributing to the failure in Suez was the haste with which all the preparations for the attack were made. The 162nd Division commander, however, proudly explained that he solved all the problems "with the fighting spirit that characterized the division throughout the war": "Obstacles naturally abound. But if we make an effort, we can overcome them!"

This is undeniably the right spirit, but it is not the point. Adan admits: "I believe that the capture of Suez contributed nothing to the encirclement [of the Third Army]." On this he is correct, but the following questions arise:

1. If the capture of the city did not appear vital, and if the Southern Command left the so-called order to capture it to the division commander's discretion, why the panic? Why was the battle fought? Who was the interested party?
2. When did it become clear to the division commander that taking the city was unnecessary? Was he aware of it when he decided to capture it or after he gave thought to the matter following the mess he had created?

Throughout the short and steep chain of command from the defense minister to the division commander, there was no one who did not want the city of Suez captured. Some had an operational explanation for this desire. Dayan, for example, stated: "If the city were taken, it would also lead to the surrender of the Third Army, despite American intervention. The Egyptian defeat would be greater" (1976, 684). (Later, he tried to show the political advantages that would result.) In hindsight, Adan rightly agrees that the city's capture was of no importance to the encirclement of the Third Army. However, he finds operational justification for the move: "The capture would have strengthened our

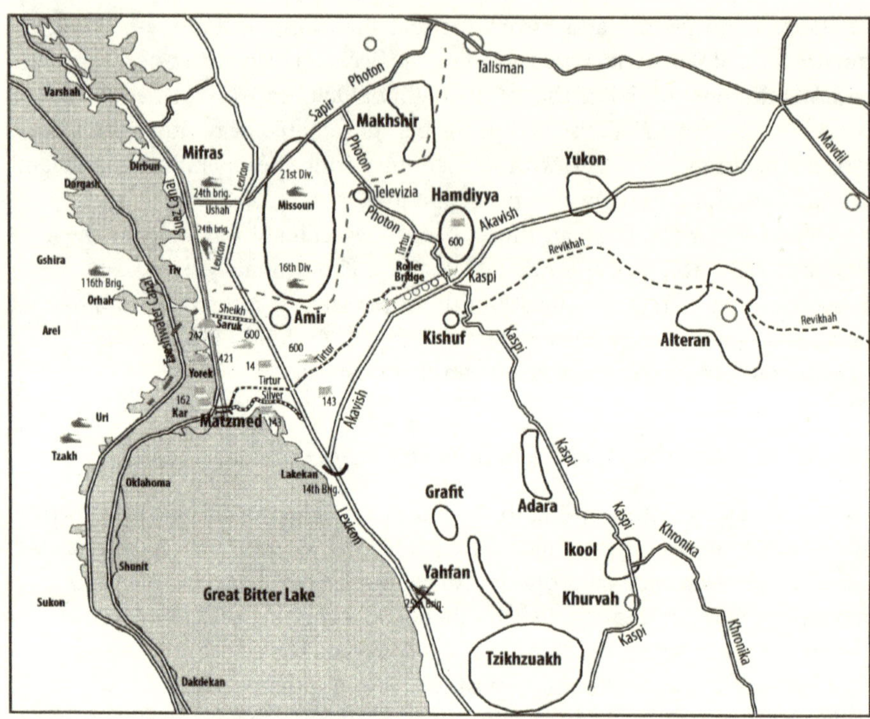

Situation picture, morning October 18. Courtesy of Amiram Ezov.

control along the entire Suez Canal in my sector, and increased the cutoff of the water sources to that part of the Third Army on the eastern bank" (Adan 1979, 304). The Southern Command recommended this move to its superiors and subordinates, reasoning that the water supply to the Third Army would be severed, the division's area of operations would be mopped up, and the firing ramps aimed at the eastern bank would be seized. The CoGS thought whatever he thought.

These operational and political arguments are only attempts to justify a wrongdoing. First and foremost, personal motives underlay them. Dayan, Elazar, and Gonen wanted to wash over the mistakes that they made on the eve of and during the war as much as possible. Adan, too, had myriad personal motives for wanting to glorify himself with the laurels of the victor of Suez.

The capture of Suez would be the cherry on the frosting. However, washing his hands of the matter, Dayan wrote: "The attempt to take the City of Suez failed. This was an error of the commanders" (1976, 684).

Adan and the Paratroopers

One of the factors that led to the fiasco in Suez was, according to the commander of the 162nd Division, this: "The weak spot in the fighting forces was the infantry. . . . The infantry battalions were not equipped or trained for armored warfare. . . . None of their equipment, vehicles, or training was designated for armored warfare. . . . Put simply, they were not the right force for the situation" (Adan 1979, 304). The inherent flaw in Adan's diagnosis is that armored warfare was not the issue; urban warfare was. Crack infantry, supported by tanks and artillery, is best suited for this type of warfare. The problem is that three hundred infantrymen were insufficient to capture this city. An entire brigade was needed, if not two. It will be remembered that, after the 162nd's failure to employ the 890th Battalion properly on the night of October 16–17, the deputy division commander, Brigadier General Dov Tamari, tongue-lashed the paratroopers in approximately the same way as the division commander did this time. Tamari was already a senior commander when he served as Adan's deputy, but not a top-level commander yet. Adan was.

Until the outbreak of the war, Adan had, ex officio, a seat among the wise paladins who made up the IDF's General Staff for over three years, and by dint of this position he bore (with his commander and colleagues) the responsibility for the infantry's shortcomings that he later lamented. Given his position as a member of the General Staff, he knew, or was supposed to know, that the infantry available to him was not good enough to capture a city the size of Suez because it was thoroughly deficient in everything he said later regarding fighting spirit, training, equipment, and suitability. Why, then, did he send these troops into a battle whose fatal results he should have foreseen? The weak point in the attempt to capture the city stemmed not from the infantry's shortcomings but primarily from the lack of intelligence on the enemy in the city, the lack of a combat doctrine and training, armor's inexperience in urban warfare in coordination with infantry and artillery, the serious shortage of paratroopers for carrying out the mission, and the half-baked planning. Obviously, this was an attempt at a land grab triggered by the imminent cease-fire, but a large city cannot be captured, just as a well-defended compound cannot be overrun as though it were a meeting engagement.

In conclusion, Adan's decision to capture the city of Suez by the method that he chose was an uncalculated risk, that is, an out-and-out gamble. The risks that he knew, or should have assessed, before committing his troops to battle were greater, in terms of almost certain loss, than the gains that might have been achieved had the city been taken. If the city had been captured, the gain would have been virtual. The price, even if the city were conquered, would have been real and high, as should be expected in a built-up area organized for defense. Under these circumstances, a general must forgo the prestige of so trivial a military gain at such an exorbitant cost.

11

"Better Is the End of a Thing Than the Beginning Thereof" (Eccles. 7:8)

War Aims

Much of contemporary academic writing on national security issues deals with the clarification of terms that until now seemed clear. A vast number of books and articles have been written on the nature of war compared to the character of war, what sets victory apart from triumph, what is the very meaning of victory, and so forth. All this being nothing but semantics in the guise of analysis, and even though we will not get involved in such issues in this chapter, we still cannot ignore their subject matter. Accordingly, we will tackle the outcome of the Yom Kippur War from Israel's point of view as well as that of the Arab coalition against which it fought.

By its nature, war is waged to achieve goals. The results of a war can be formulated as the degree to which the war aims are achieved. This definition may be considered equivalent to that of *victory*, and, by implication, it also floats the concept of defeat. Essentially, victory is a continuum that has as one extremity "a huge victory, unlike any other ever," and as the other "the worst of all defeats," and in between these extremities one can define or encounter a practically infinite number of possible war outcomes, less rewarding than the unimaginably ultimate great victory, yet not so futile and bloody as the greatest catastrophe ever. In other words, the result of war cannot be conceived as a dichotomy.

War aims ought to be formulated and attain validity outside the military establishment. There is no such thing as *the army's war aims*. Only the state—the army's sovereign—has war aims.

War aims can be looked at from myriad angles. Here, four will suffice:

1. Genuine, authentic aims that represent comprehensive, long-term national interests versus spurious aims that represent other interests (personal, sectoral, and so forth).
2. Achievable versus illusory aims. This classification is connected to, but not identical with, the previous one.

3. War aims that were formulated and presented to the nation before the war and underlie it versus fake war aims, fabricated after the war ended and meant to justify its results.
4. Known and formally announced war aims versus latent (usually the real) ones.

Israel's War Aims Prior to the 1973 War

Approximately half a year before the Yom Kippur War, the Israeli government approved the aim of the coming war. As far as is known, it was formulated by the deputy CoGS, Major General Israel Tal, and his assistant for strategic planning, Brigadier General Avraham ("Abrasha") Tamir. The CoGS endorsed it, the defense minister followed suit (after introducing minor revisions), and Prime Minister Golda Meir gave it her stamp of approval. The official war aim in October 1973 was as follows: "To deny the enemy any military gain by inflicting on him a military defeat based on the maximum destruction of his forces and military infrastructure. Achieving this goal ought to provide Israel with significant military advantages for several years as regards the balance of forces and on the cease-fire lines as well." This war aim included the following:

1. "To deny the enemy any military gain by inflicting on him a military defeat." The two parts of this sentence, as in verse in a biblical psalm, express the same idea, but here it is still unclear what the idea is. Did it mean denying the enemy any gain, from the minute war broke out and during every single minute during which it went on—as the Israeli military leadership had conceived since the Six-Day War—or did it mean just ending the war without the enemy having gained anything? At any rate, if this war aim was meant in the first sense, it was pure lunacy.
2. Causing the enemy a military defeat "based on the maximum destruction of his forces and military infrastructure." "Destruction of his forces" is not and never was anything but an empty slogan whose partial accomplishment in any previous war brought no benefit to Israel, considering its long-range interests.
3. "Achieving this goal ought to provide Israel with significant military advantages for several years." Here is where the cat is let out of the bag. Israel consciously gave up on the desire to exploit the war (which was bound to come) to impose its true long-term aims on the enemy. Inspired by the IDF, the political level approved a war aim that was based on false assumptions that abandoned the long run, expressed unjustified despair and fatalism, and crystallized them into the foundations for defeat.

How did so sterile and negative a war aim sprout in Israel's flowerbed? In 1996, General Tal published his book *National Security* with the ancient cliché *Few against the Many* as its subtitle. The following excerpts are from this book:

> The limitations of force that influence Israel's national goals and that are contained in the absence of any likelihood of forcing the Arabs to end the conflict and reconcile themselves to Israel's existence by means of a military decision, are clear: the option for a total victory in the conflict by means of military victory is possible for one side alone—the side of the many. The quantitative balance of forces precludes Israel's winning a decisive final victory by military means. While the adverse option—its decisive defeat by the Arabs—is firm and valid. (49)

> Israel can and will win many wars and this ability is a vital condition for its existence, but it will never be able to dictate its will to the Arab and Muslim world by means of military victory. . . . The Arabs possess a quantitative superiority in manpower, resources, material, geographic space, and potential allies. . . . A critical asymmetric relationship exists between Israel and the Arab states: Israel's victories, no matter how many, will only guarantee its existence but will not achieve other national goals. (50)

Tal's book was published twenty-three years after Israel had defeated Egypt and forced it to beg, on its knees, for a cease-fire and later, in the same posture, to offer Israel peace. We will not bother to elaborate here on Tal's thesis and its assumptions and systematically demonstrate where he went wrong. Forty years of peace with the major powers of the Middle East (excluding a few flare-ups with nonstate players that Israel seems to have initiated) is enough to brand Tal's far-fetched analysis and ensuing conclusion an enormous mistake. We have introduced these excerpts from Tal's book because it is an odd but instructive example of the thinking prevailing a generation ago, which was predicated on David Ben-Gurion's understanding, in his day and with his military, rather untrained mind, of Israel's situation.

Israel's Real War Aim Prior to the Yom Kippur War

In 1955, Ben-Gurion stated simply and sagaciously that "peace is Israel's ultimate goal" (Wald 1987, 222), although it is not clear whether he meant formal peace or a situation resembling peace in which Israel would be free for generations from the shadow of periodic wars. Peace was Israel's true goal, and, from the establishment of the state until the 1970s, reaching it meant that Israel had to remove Egypt from the cycle of war. Its grand military strategy was to attain this one goal.

The Arab states in the Middle East in the 1970s were and remain military dictatorships whose main driving force has always been personal and regime survival. This phenomenon is the Achilles heel of their strategy. To ensure Israel's existence and destiny, its military strategy was and still is to create a clear and unconditional threat to the survival of the dictatorships and regimes in the main confrontational states. Any other view is a misperception.

The rebellions and putsches in the Middle East as we enter the second decade of the twenty-first century are likely to overturn this thesis. In our opinion, what is happening in Tunisia, Egypt, Syria, Yemen, and Libya is not so much regime change as dictator change. After the euphoria cools, the dust settles, and the mobs calm down, these states will find themselves under new, perhaps even more autocratic regimes, some more masked, others less. The regimes of the Middle Eastern and North African states will continue to constitute the source of their own vulnerability.

Egyptian War Aims Prior to the Ramadan War

The Overt Goal

According to the accounts of Sadat and Major General Abdel Ghani el-Gamasy, the Egyptian head of the General Staff branch and the CoGS during the Yom Kippur War, Sadat sent his war minister a tortuous harangue on October 1, 1973, entitled "Directive to the Supreme Commander of the Armed Forces, War Minister Ahmed Ismail Ali." Part of the directive stated: "The strategic objective that I am assigning to the armed forces of Egypt and that I take full political responsibility for is to undermine Israel's security doctrine by executing a military action according to the armed forces' capabilities with the aim of inflicting the highest number of casualties on the enemy and convincing him that the continued occupation of our land will exact an intolerable price from him and that therefore his security doctrine . . . is not an invulnerable iron defense shield" (Sadat 1978).

According to the same accounts, on October 5, Sadat sent a second strategic directive to Field Marshal Ismail Ali in which he clarified the first directive regarding the war's aims. The Egyptian armed forces would:

1. Shatter the political and military status quo.
2. Cause maximum damage to IDF's personnel, weapons, and equipment.
3. Liberate the occupied lands in successive stages according to the develop-

ments in the war and the actual and potential combat power of the Egyptian army.

The first two tasks were the by-products of the implementation of the third task, although a contradiction may have existed between the third task and the second. Nevertheless, the first task could, in an emergency, such as a military debacle, serve alone as a virtual gain that would be packaged as "smashing the political and military status quo . . . and Israeli security doctrine" (Sadat 1978) and marketed to the Arab nation.

Sadat believed that the third task was the real and declared intention of the war. Its wording clearly indicates that the long-range goal was to recapture the entire Sinai Peninsula and Gaza Strip (in stages), but much obscurity still shrouds this since, on other occasions, Sadat and other officials declared that their intention was to expel Israel not only from all Egyptian territory but also, in the spirit of Nasser, from the other Arab lands (read: Palestine) that were conquered in 1967. The goal was "the return of our lands occupied since 1967 and finding a way to restore the legitimate rights of the Palestinian people" (Avi Shai 1975). On October 22, Sadat announced his agreement to a cease-fire on the basis of Security Council Resolution 242 and only vaguely referred to the Palestinian issue, more giving it lip service than stipulating its importance. A day or two later, as the threat to the Third Army mounted, Egypt concentrated solely on the return of its occupied lands.

The Hidden Aim

For almost two decades, Sadat had served as Gamal Abdel Nasser's ultimate yes-man, and, even after he was appointed president, following Nasser's death in 1970, his image as a national leader failed to take wing and soar. In his autobiography, Sadat discloses his real attitude toward Nasser. Alongside his qualified adulation and a token nod to the Nasserites, he reveals his resentment toward and blatant criticism of Nasser and his legacy, his burning jealousy of the late president's leadership in the Arab world and Nasser's uncanny knack for converting ignominious defeat into virtual victory time after time.

This attitude drove Sadat to initiate a military move against Israel that would not end in a humiliating defeat but prove to the world that he was an outstanding strategist, unlike Nasser the serial loser. In our opinion, this was Sadat's hidden yet primary war aim. We are not alone in thinking this: "Sadat was impatient. He did not want a long war. . . . He wanted to cross the canal, raise the Egyptian flag in Sinai, and immediately end hostilities" (Shazly quoted in Barnea and Perry 2003).

Overwhelming Defeat of the Enemy? Victory?

In a field weak in analysis, the intellectual vacuum is filled with material obsessed with definitions, categorization, and casuistry. In the last generations, the hot subject in the scholastic discourse on national security has been the definition of the meaning of victory and the overwhelming defeat of the enemy and the analysis of the differences between them. The following excerpt from Zigdon (2008) illustrates the utter confusion and mental and professional sterility on this subject:

> The overwhelming defeat of the enemy is an objective concept, whereas victory is subjective. Be this as it may, when one side overwhelms the enemy, the other side finds it difficult to claim a victory. . . . This is why the overwhelming defeat of the enemy is the military achievement needed to gain unconditional victory in war. . . . Therefore when we ask if military force . . . was applied efficiently in a war, we must examine [its contribution] to achieving the overwhelming defeat of the enemy or at the very least to making gains that enable it to claim that victory was achieved.

To correctly assess this excerpt, readers should compare the statement "the overwhelming defeat of the enemy is the military achievement needed to gain unconditional victory in war" with "victory is the military accomplishment needed in war to achieve the overwhelming defeat of the enemy" and decide for themselves which of the two assertions is more correct.

So Who Won?

The Yom Kippur War ended on October 24, 1973, when Israel was forced to muzzle its guns (Egypt had done so for other reasons a few days earlier). This was the beginning of the end. The finale came in two stages: Sadat's journey to Jerusalem and his speech in the Knesset on November 20, 1977, and the Egypt-Israel Peace Treaty on March 26, 1979.

From the day the cease-fire went into effect on October 24, 1973, until today, one school of thought in Israel claims that Israel lost the Yom Kippur War because it failed to attain the goals in pursuit of which it went to war. For example, the title of a 2003 article by the journalist Amir Oren is "Comparing the Aims with the Results, Israel Failed in '73 and Its Achievements Were Only Partial." Oren claimed: "The Arab armies were battered but not defeated." In our opinion, the opposite is true. The Arab armies, especially Egypt's, were defeated but not battered. Egypt was decisively defeated, Syria indirectly so because of the overwhelming Egyptian defeat.

Colonel (Res.) Ya'akov Hisdai (1980) came to the conclusion in that "it is impossible to call the results of the Yom Kippur War a 'victory,' and to our dismay we have to admit that the results were closer to a 'failure.'" Hisdai realized that Israel's war aims were wholly impractical, but he nevertheless found a way to compare them to the war's results. His conclusion is based mainly on the impact of the war's results on Israeli society, the country's disintegration, and so forth. We will not analyze the problems inherent in this article, but we will note that blaming negative processes in Israeli society on the Yom Kippur War expresses the logical fallacy that was discussed in chapter 8: post hoc, ergo propter hoc; if event B took place after event A did, then B happened because of A.

It was Sadat who initiated the cease-fire when he perceived with growing apprehension that, unless a cease-fire went into effect immediately, a large chunk of the Third Army in Sinai would be surrounded and vulnerable to annihilation and that the fate of the Second Army could soon be the same. Even Israel's only partial implementation of these threats would have triggered a shock wave that would have brought an end to Sadat's political career and probably to his life and regime as well. Since Sadat lacked Nasser's charisma, he had no chance of surviving a military downfall. If his army was defeated, his name would be blackened forever in the Arab world in particular and in world history in general. He quickly sensed that any Arab army that went to war with Israel in the foreseeable future would be trounced no matter what the initial conditions were and that no excuse, like the one that Sadat sold to Assad at the time, would convince otherwise.

The moment that this insight crystallized in Sadat's mind and the minds of his colleagues within the army and outside it was the moment that Israel removed Egypt from the circle of war. Since then, despite the basic pessimistic assumptions held by Ben-Gurion, Tal, and others, the land has been, as the book of Judges has it, "quiet for forty years." The main lesson is that for every enemy keyhole a strategic key exists. Israel, without realizing it, chanced on the right key. From Israel's point of view, the Yom Kippur War ended in a magnificent victory.

The Egyptian president needed another four years to realize that he could not take by force what Israel had taken from his country in 1967. The only way to return the rest of Egypt's captured lands was to purchase them, ostensibly from Israel, but actually from the United States. The deal with the Americans was simple and included formal peace with Israel. It was completed in 1979 when Egypt replaced the Soviet Union with the United States as its patron, signed a peace treaty with Israel, and recovered all the territorial assets—to the last grain of sand—that it lost in the 1967 debacle. Thus, Egypt attained the declared goal for which it had gone to war in 1973. Sadat also achieved the hidden parallel goal: his and his regime's survival. From Egypt's point of view, the Ramadan War culminated in a brilliant victory.

Both Egypt and Israel ended the war in 1973 believing, justifiably, that a great victory had been won. In our opinion, this rare, if not sui generis, result was made possible because each side fought to achieve a different goal, although both goals were to a degree connected. Israel strove to remove Egypt from the circle of war; Egypt went to war to restore the economic and territorial assets it lost in 1967.

The argument is made that, because of these different goals, the same results could have been reached through negotiations in 1971. We believe that this is a false claim, primarily because of Sadat's insistence on fighting to attain his personal goals. Sadat's rejectionism was expressed in his demand that Israel withdraw from all the territories it captured in June 1967. Israel, too, seems to have viewed war as desirable and its results advantageous. Before the war, Israeli leaders and military chiefs ignorantly and arrogantly assumed that, if hostilities broke out, the IDF would swiftly clobber the Egyptians and thus strengthen Israel's deterrence and extend the status quo. Then came the Yom Kippur War, which taught both sides the facts of life.

Appendix A

Main Secondary Senior Commanders and Staff Officers

Unit	Type of Unit	Name of Officer	Rank of Officer	Role of Officer
143rd Division	headquarters and staff	Ariel Sharon	major general	division commander
		Jacob Even	colonel/brigadier general	deputy division commander
		Gideon Altshuler	colonel	CoS
		Aharon Tal	lieutenant colonel	General Staff officer
		Yehoshua Sagi	colonel	intelligence officer
		Hillel Carmeli	lieutenant colonel	communications officer
		Zion Masuri	lieutenant colonel	supply officer
		Dr. Ya'akov Adler	lieutenant colonel	division medical officer
		Baruch Dileon	lieutenant colonel	division engineering officer, KIA
421st Brigade	tank	Haim Erez	colonel	brigade commander
600th Brigade	tank	Tuvia Raviv	colonel	brigade commander
875th Brigade	armored infantry	Aryeh Dayan	colonel	brigade commander
14th Brigade	tank	Amnon Reshef	colonel	brigade commander
247th Brigade	paratroopers	Danny Matt	colonel	brigade commander
35th Brigade	paratroopers	Uzi Yairi	colonel	brigade commander
87th Reconnaissance Battalion	tank	Bentzi Carmeli, Yoav Brom	lieutenant colonels	battalion commanders, both KIA
214th Artillery Group	artillery	Ya'akov Aknin	colonel	artillery group commander
812nd Supply Group	812	Moshe Zapler	lieutenant colonel	group commander
504th Medical Battalion	medical corps	Dr. Yehezkel Kishon	lieutenant colonel	battalion commander

Note: KIA = killed in action.

Appendix B

The Bridgehead Compound

The 143rd Division captured, built, and operated the bridgehead on the Suez Canal from October 16 until the IDF evacuated the Canal Zone half a year later. The bridgehead was an unparalleled operational phenomenon in IDF history. Forty years later, it remains a unique experience in the IDF.

While myth would have it to be so, the bridgehead was not seized in bitter breakthrough battles. The 247th Paratrooper Brigade captured it in a daring move without bloodshed on the night of October 15–16 thanks to Colonel Amnon Reshef's 14th Tank Brigade's long and grueling battle with the Egyptian Second Army west of the Missouri and Amir (Chinese Farm) compounds.

On the other hand, the assembly of the bridges on the canal, which began on October 17, was conducted under heavy, well-coordinated artillery fire that was of a degree unprecedented in IDF history and that continued with the same intensity until the cease-fire went into effect a week later. The artillery fire landed on the combat engineers and other forces on the eastern side of the bridgehead and on the paratroopers on the western side, exacting an exorbitant price in dead and wounded.

Despite the murderous fire, all the soldiers manning the bridgehead, officers and other ranks alike, performed, fully exposed to this fire, courageously and with utter self-sacrifice, thus making this bridgehead the most crucial and important factor in overthrowing the Egyptian army.

The Bridgehead Compound Mission, Location, and Organization

The bridgehead can be seen as a defined compound with a specific mission that operated within the framework of the 143rd Division, under the command of the deputy division commander, Colonel (later Major General) Jacob Even. Even's appointment as bridgehead commander was made by the division commander, Major General Ariel Sharon, and unquestioningly supported by the front commander, Lieutenant General Haim Bar-Lev.

The bridgehead's status as a military compound was determined by its having a specific mission, located in a defined area that it dominated, and by its being manned by military units that functioned in its area and under Even's command. Given the number of units operating the compound and their strength, the bridgehead functioned as a military formation in its own right.

The Compound's Area

The bridgehead compound included the following areas:

1. The Yard was the area bounded by the northern Matzmed and the southern Matzmed strongholds, by the Israeli embankment on the western bank of the Suez Canal in the west, and by the Israeli embankment, at the average distance of two hundred meters east of the canal, in the east. It was the heart of the compound, where all activity connected with its mission was concentrated. The access roads from Lexicon can also be seen as part of the compound.
2. A partly wooded area of fifteen square kilometers immediately west of the canal was occupied by the 247th Brigade.
3. On the night of October 18–19, the roller bridge was unrolled on canal kilometer 95.5, north of northern Matzmed. Colonel Menashe Gur, of the headquarters of the IDF's chief of engineering, commanded this area with his staff, with a tank company from the 600th Brigade and paratrooper platoon for security.

The Bridgehead's Mission

The bridgehead's sole mission was to ensure the free flow of and control the two-way traffic between the banks of the canal. The following tasks were derived from this mission:

1. Constructing additional bridges according to the division commander's orders.
2. Operating the Crocodile rafts to carry traffic to and from the banks.
3. Maintaining the infrastructure (bridges, rafts, and inner roads)
4. Maintaining traffic control, discipline, and policing in the Yard, on the bridges, the rafts, and the rubber boats, and regulating the traffic among the bridges themselves and between them and the other crossing means.
5. Actively securing the Yard and bridges from attack and fire from land, air, and sea (the Great Bitter Lake).
6. Minimizing losses at the bridgehead through passive defense (entrenchments, conduct during shelling, protective gear, and so forth).
7. Setting up and maintaining the infrastructure for the initial treatment

and evacuation of the wounded; confining, guarding, and evacuating the prisoners.

The Bridgehead Forces

From a functional point of view, the forces at the bridgehead can be classified as follows:

1. Command and control elements.
2. Designated forces such as engineering battalions.
3. The division's artillery, the 247th Brigade in its entirety, and the IAF's fighters, i.e., security forces in *general support.*
4. Battalion aid stations.
5. Administration.

Engineering Forces Operating in the Compound (October 16–24)

The 630th Bridging Battalion

The 630th Battalion reached the Yard with its own rafts and two from the 605th Bridging Battalion in the early hours of October 17, and most of the battalion evacuated the compound on October 19. Only a few officers and the replacement battalion commander, Captain Yishai Dotan (the battalion commander, Lieutenant Colonel Avi Zohar, was wounded on October 18), remained. The battalion's assignments were as follows:

- Conveying the 247th Brigade to the western bank in rubber boats.
- Constructing and maintaining a Unifloat raft bridge.
- Operating heavy engineering equipment.

The 605th Bridging Battalion

The 605th Battalion, under the command of Moshe Leshem, arrived in the Yard on October 18 and remained there until the end of the war. At a certain point, Captain Dotan was appointed commander of the 605th Battalion and given charge of all the engineering forces in the compound. The battalion's tasks were as follows:

- Maintaining the raft bridge and building a so-called austerity bridge.
- Operating heavy engineering equipment.

The 634th Crocodile Battalion

The battalion, under the command of Lieutenant Colonel Yigal Yaniv, pulled into the Yard on the morning of October 16. On October 19, the battalion was left with only one raft since the rest had been damaged by the shelling and rendered inoperable. On October 20, most of the battalion moved out the Yard, and its evacuation was completed the next day. The battalion's tasks were as follows:

- Assembling and operating the Crocodile rafts.
- Conveying the wounded and providing first aid; guarding and caring for the prisoners of war in an improvised barbed-wire yard (both minor roles).

The Roller Bridge Force

For the roller bridge force, see the description of the compound offered above.

The 229th Division Engineering Battalion

This battalion, under the command of Lieutenant Colonel Nisim Ben Shushan, operated in the division's entire sector. Its heavy mechanical engineering equipment units prepared the roads to the Yard and the roller bridge. The heavy earthwork equipment company was parked in the Yard. Ten bulldozer tanks from the 606th Engineering Battalion were attached to the bridging battalions and the roller bridge.

Defense and Security Forces at the Bridgehead

Antiaircraft Defense

Antiaircraft defense in the Yard and the part of the compound west of the canal was provided by two mobile antiaircraft artillery battalions under the command of Major Nisan Elad. In the initial stages of the crossing battle, most of the force was used to protect the roller bridge, and a small part of it was allocated for the defense of the Yard (October 16). The next day, half the forces defended the Yard, and half remained at the roller bridge. On October 18, most of the antiaircraft force was concentrated in the Yard and only one battalion deployed at Lakekan to protect the supply battalion. On October 19, the battalion was divided among the Yard, the woods on the western side of the bridgehead, the roller bridge, and the supply battalion at Lakekan.

Ground Defense

Ground defense of the Yard was provided by the following:

- An improvised, reduced paratrooper battalion/247th Brigade, under the command of Lieutenant Colonel Yossi Fradkin, deployed between the woods west of the Yard and the Bitter Lake shore. A reduced company was positioned on the embankments surrounding the Yard, and a reduced platoon was deployed near the roller bridge. Teams from this force were supposed to be posted by the bridges for close protection when warnings of impending Egyptian commando attacks were issued.
- Three partly operable tanks with their crews that Colonel Even managed to scrape up were placed in position ready for action against attacks coming from the Bitter Lake. One of the tanks was also used to anchor the western edge of the raft bridge.
- The antiaircraft batteries deployed on the Yard's embankment were assigned, as a secondary mission, protecting against ground targets.

Close protection of the bridges was carried out by patrols of paratroopers and combat engineers, some on the bridge and others in boats. Protection against floating mines, naval commandos, and underwater sabotage was assigned to a team from the 707th Defensive Divers Unit under the command of Lieutenant Colonel Sela. The unit also helped maintain the bridges.

In the first days of the crossing battle, the Yard served as a collection point and aid station for the wounded prior to their evacuation. Lieutenant Colonel Dr. Yechezkel Kishon, the commander of the 504th Medical Battalion, organized the battalion aid station. During the first two days (October 16–17), the Crocodile Battalion's aid station operated in the Yard.

The forward evacuation system consisted of medical stations in the Yard and Lakekan. Beginning on October 18, the engineering battalions' collection stations and two platoons of the forward medical company/504th Medical Battalion operated in the Yard. A number of evacuation tanks, APCs, and stretchers from the Crocodile Battalion were in the "Yard." Later, medical units from the 252nd Division reinforced the medical evacuation layout and came under the command of the 504th Medical Battalion.

In the beginning of the crossing battle, the wounded from the western bank were evacuated to the Yard in rubber boats, lifted onto stretchers from the Crocodile Battalion (often under fire and by improvised means, such as a bulldozer shovel), given first aid, and taken to Lakekan in an armored evacuation vehicle.

Traffic Policing and Discipline

The bridgehead headquarters determined the traffic arrangements and vehicle discipline at the bridgehead and the Yard. This included the following:

- Priority in entering the Yard.
- Movement on the bridges: direction and proper conduct in approaching, mounting, and exiting them.
- Vehicle disciple in the Yard and preventing overcrowding.
- Regulating the movement between the bridges (including the roller bridge).

A network of traffic control points was organized at the entrances and exits to the Yard to supervise these arrangements. The points were interlinked and connected to the FCP by a special network and manned by officers of the 812th Division Supply Group and military police from the division's military police companies. Until the points were set up, traffic in the Yard was under the direct control of the FCP officers, who were assisted by the officers and men of the combat engineering battalion.

Firefighting

Passive defense in the Yard was attended to by a civil defense fire truck manned by an officer and four civil defense soldiers (three of whom were senior citizens and quickly replaced).

The Operational Conditions during Bridgehead Activity

The forces at the bridgehead worked until the cease-fire under increasingly heavy artillery fire as the construction of the raft bridge approached completion, in the afternoon of October 17. During this period, over one hundred men were killed and several hundred wounded by artillery fire and occasional air attacks.

The compound was targeted by cannons, heavy mortars, and 240-millimeter Katyusha rocket launchers mostly from the north on both sides of the canal. Three Egyptian artillery groups seem to have been actively engaged in blasting away at the compound. Especially lethal Katyusha barrages fell on the bridgehead for about ten minutes beginning at 1845 on October 22. Sixty soldiers were hit, twelve of them killed. Among the wounded were the Crocodile Battalion commander, Lieutenant Colonel Yaniv, and the commander of the

630th Bridging Battalion, Lieutenant Colonel Avi Zohar. Among the dead were the division's chief of engineering, Lieutenant Colonel Baruch Dileon (on the eighteenth), and Major Yehuda Hudeda, the deputy commander of the 605th Bridging Battalion (on the twenty-second). A Scud missile was also fired at the bridgehead but missed.

Air attacks commenced at noon October 16 with two sorties, in the second of which two Migs were shot down by antiaircraft fire from the bridgehead. The next afternoon, the compound was attacked by Migs and Mirage aircraft, and dogfights took place above it. The heaviest air attacks on the Yard occurred on October 17 and 18. Throughout all of October 18, the Yard was bombed and strafed by jet fighters and attack helicopters. Antiaircraft fire from the compound knocked down six planes and one helicopter. On October 19, eight Mig-21s attacked the raft bridge with rockets, napalm, and strafing, killing one Israeli and wounding ten, including Colonel Dov Karni from the Southern Command and Lieutenant Colonel Leshem, the commander of the 605th Battalion. One enemy aircraft was shot down by antiaircraft fire from the compound. Egyptian helicopters tried to bomb the bridge with napalm barrels and explosive charges. Several helicopters were destroyed, as stated, by bridgehead antiaircraft fire, some of them plunging into the water, and others crashing on the ground west of the bridgehead.

Overseeing Activity and Routine at the Bridgehead

The Command and Control Layout

Colonel Jacob Even oversaw operations at the bridgehead. His FCP functioned both as a headquarters and staff. The FCP comprised two senior assistants, Colonel Simcha Maoz and Lieutenant Colonel Amos Ne'eman, the operations officer (Captain Ilan Oko), and the communications officer (Lieutenant Moshe Shapira). The FCP had a command APC, a radio-telephone system carrying half-tracks, and a command jeep.

To attain effective control over all the forces in the Yard, Colonel Even appointed five subordinate commanders as follows:

- Lieutenant Colonel Fradkin, the commander of the paratrooper battalion, was given command of all the security forces.
- The commander of the 605th Battalion was to command all combat engineers in the Yard.
- The commander of one of the antiaircraft battalions was given command of air defense.

- Lieutenant Colonel Sela was given command of the naval defensive divers unit.
- Colonel Menashe Gur was in charge of the roller bridge area.

Meetings with these commanders were held almost immediately in the FCP to coordinate operations and routine in the compound.

Since the bridgehead was a vital installation on the access roads under the Southern Command's control (at least since the completion of the bridge's construction and the crossing of the 162nd Division to the western bank), the Southern Command set up a number of supervisory arrangements. On October 19, Brigadier General (Res.) Avnon arrived at the Yard and announced that he had been put in charge of the movement of all the forces in the Southern Command's rear. Even's FCP began packing and prepared to move out on the assumption that General Avnon would take control. In a personal exchange with Colonel Even, Bar-Lev insisted that the 143rd Division and Even in particular continue to oversee all action at the bridgehead. Thus, Even continued in his role as bridgehead commander until the end of the war. As traffic on the bridges increased on October 18, a second senior officer from Southern the Command, Colonel (Res.) Uri Bar-Ratzon, was appointed to coordinate movement on the roads. Communications were established between the bridgehead's FCP and Bar-Ratzon's FCP at the Nakhala Junction; traffic to the bridges was regulated according to the density of movement on the roads and the intensity of shelling falling on them and the bridgehead.

Administration

Administrative issues at the bridgehead included the following:

- Supplying food, gas, fortification equipment, clothes, underwear, and protective vests for the units at the compound.
- Evacuating the dead and wounded.
- Treating and evacuating the enemy prisoners of war.

The compound commander was responsible for drumming up solutions to administrative matters, while his FCP, as stated, served as his staff. In solving these problems, Even received the backing of the division's main headquarters and the administrative elements of the combat engineer, paratrooper, and antiaircraft battalions in the compound. Throughout the whole period, the 143rd Division's main headquarters, situated in Tassa under the command of the division's CoS, Colonel Gideon Altshuler, assisted bridgehead staff in overcoming administrative obstacles. To accomplish this, the division's supply group was called into action. Given the conditions at the bridgehead, the response of the main headquarters and the logistics group was prompt, smooth, and superbly efficient.

Traffic and Transportation

The major activity at the bridgehead revolved around its mission: traffic and transportation between the banks. The bridgehead headquarters was responsible for the following tasks:

<bulleted list>

- Supervising the traffic that passed through the traffic control points at the bridgehead's entrances and exits.
- Controlling the volume of transportation on the bridges. The bridgehead headquarters determined when a bridge would close for repairs or overhaul (the policy was to ensure that at least one raft bridge would always be available for the movement of all types of armored vehicles). This policy permitted the shutting down of the first bridge for repair and renovation only on October 21. The bridgehead headquarters assumed the heavy responsibility of postponing and permitting maintenance repairs (again, we emphasize the essence of command in finding the proper balance between risks).
- Determining the travel lanes on the bridge. Beginning on October 20, the bridgehead headquarters operated three bridges: the raft bridge (the southernmost bridge), the austerity bridge (to the north but still in the Yard), and the roller bridge (two kilometers north of the point where the Suez Canal egresses from the Great Bitter Lake). Once the two Yard bridges were standing, it was decided that each would be one-directional. The raft bridge was designated for movement to the west and the austerity bridge for movement to the east. The roller bridge was kept for the conveyance of armored combat vehicles only.
- Initiating the paving and preparation of roads to and from the compound. The division's 229th Engineering Battalion performed this task.

Evacuation of Wounded, Dead, and Prisoners

The bridgehead headquarters took responsibility for the evacuation of the bodies of IDF soldiers who fell on the western bank and were collected in the Yard. The swift evacuation out of deep respect for the dead and the prevention of sacrilege was a painful topic on the headquarters' agenda. We should note the vigorous and effective intervention of Major General (Res.) Rabbi Shlomo Goren (the former IDF chief rabbi) during his visit to the division. Colonel Even spoke with him in the Yard, and representatives from the military rabbinate soon arrived and assumed responsibility for the IDF bodies. The rabbinate personnel performed their work under fire.

A prisoner enclosure, marked by barbed wire concertina, was improvised in the Yard and a system devised for guarding the prisoners, whose evacuation to the rear of the bridgehead headquarters was continuously dealt with. Toward the end of the war, the division logistics group was given charge of prisoner evacuation.

Evacuation of the wounded was carried out by the battalion aid stations at the Yard. The bridgehead headquarters was regularly required to solve various problems related to this, such as providing medical evacuation vehicles, medical supplies, and so forth.

Appendix C

Biographical and Career Highlights

Moshe Dayan: Lieutenant General, Minister of Defense

Early Years

Moshe Dayan was born on May 20, 1915, in Deganiya Aleph, the first kibbutz in Palestine, at that time a remote part of the Ottoman Empire. As a toddler, he moved with his parents to Nahallal, the first moshav (cooperative village) in Palestine.

At the age of fourteen he joined the Hagganah, the Jewish self-defense organization (*hagganah* is Hebrew for *defense*). Ten years later, he joined the British-organized, Jewish-manned Auxiliary Rural Police Patrols. One of the figures that inspired the formation of his military persona was the English intelligence officer and guerrilla leader Captain Orde Charles Wingate.[1]

In 1939, Dayan and forty-three of his men were arrested and tried by the British on illegal weapons charge and sentenced to ten-year terms in prison. After about a year and a half, the group was set free owing to pressure from Jewish leaders and also from the British military in the Middle East, who needed those motivated and loyal men for their thorough familiarity with the lay of the land in Palestine, Lebanon, Syria, and Transjordan. Dayan, with a few of his colleagues in the budding PALMACH,[2] were attached to commando and reconnaissance groups that were formed by the British forces in the Middle East as they were preparing to oust the Vichy[3] forces from Syria and Lebanon.

The Trademark Eye Patch

On June 7, 1941, a small Australian reconnaissance unit led by Dayan as its scout and navigator crossed the Palestine-Lebanon border and captured two bridges on the Litani River and a French police post. At some point, Dayan went up the station roof to scan the area. As he was holding his binoculars to his eyes, a French sniper hit the binoculars, sending shattered metal and glass straight into his left eye. The eye was gone and its socket so damaged that could not accommodate a glass eye. The only device that could be used to cover the cavity was an eye patch. Notwithstanding the worldwide military stardom appeal that the eye patch had conferred on Dayan, the naked cavity beneath it was for him a source of constant, excruciating pain and bother. He just hated it.

The War of Independence

In the War of Independence (1948–1949), Dayan's first major appointment was as commander of the 89th Commando Battalion. Leading his unit, he had demonstrated those traits that would eventually propel him to the position of CoGS of the IDF: oodles of leadership, charisma, courage, boldness, and toughness and extraordinary intelligence.

In less than two months, David Ben-Gurion, the legendary prime minister and minister of defense of the newly born state of Israel, deeply impressed with Dayan, appointed him to command the Jerusalem area of operations. Several months later, Lieutenant Colonel[4] Dayan held, ex officio, a series of talks with senior officers of the Jordanian Arab Legion and with King Abdallah himself, leading eventually to a cease-fire on the Jerusalem front. Following his success there, Dayan took part in the armistice talks that were held in Rhodes and later headed the Israeli delegations to the Mixed Armistice Commissions that were set up to supervise the armistice.

Senior Officer of the IDF

In 1949, at the age of thirty-four, Dayan was made a major general[5] and appointed commanding general of the Southern Command, charged with defending Israel's borders with Egypt (including the Gaza Strip) and southern Jordan. At that time, Israel's most urgent and alarming problem was the massive infiltration of Bedouin tribes and Palestinian civilians into the Negev and other parts of Israel. General Dayan implemented a harsh and merciless military policy against this menace, involving cross-border punitive raids aimed at Arab towns and village and, later, against Egyptian and Jordanian army posts, and employing the IAF as well as artillery and armored infantry against the intruding Bedouins. In his words, collective punishment was "not justified or moral, but effective."

CoGS

Toward the end of 1953, at the age of thirty-nine, Dayan became CoGS, with the rank of lieutenant general. As such, he continued even more energetically to pursue the policy of cross-border retaliatory raids on military installations.

He set up the 101st Commando Unit, manned by several dozens of the ablest fighters of the IDF and headed by Major (Res.) Ariel Sharon, whom he called back to service.

As CoGS, Dayan acted quickly and decisively to revitalize the IDF and pull it out of the lethargy and incompetence that pervaded it after the War of Independence by bringing to the combat units quality manpower, improving training, increasing and modernizing the air force and armor elements of the IDF, and, above all, instilling in the IDF a fighting spirit, the so called élan. This he achieved by merging the fighting 101st Unit with the only paratrooper battalion of the IDF, the 890th, until then a spit-and-polish, practically idle unit, appointing Sharon its commander and his 101st paladins to key positions in the battalion, and sending the revamped battalion on a long and bloody series of cross-border raids. In no time, this battalion turned into the proverbial Pillar of Fire lighting the path to combat excellence for the IDF.

The Sinai Campaign

In 1956, worried by a huge arms deal between the Soviet bloc and Egypt, Israel joined hands with France and England, who had an account to settle with Egypt over the nationalization of the Suez Canal. Together, these three powers planned to attack Egypt, topple its regime, retake the canal, and destroy the newly armed Egyptian army. In accordance with their plan, IDF infantry and armor, spearheaded by Sharon's parachute brigade, invaded the Sinai Peninsula, and, in five days, the IDF captured it all—the Gaza Strip included. The architect of this feat was Dayan, who, true to nature, also personally led the forces in the field. Bowing to US pressure and open Soviet threats, the IDF evacuated Sinai in March 1957.

A Lull in Action

Having in 1958 retired from active service at the end of the usual five-year stint as CoGS, Dayan joined the then ruling party, Ben-Gurion's MAPAI, and became a government minister. This phase ended in 1964, owing to MAPAI's penchant for patricide, causing Ben-Gurion and his supporters to go into political exile. In 1966, Dayan traveled to Vietnam for a two-month stint there as a superreporter for the Israeli daily *Ma'ariv.*

The Six-Day War

As a result of a series miscalculations on the part of both Israel and Egypt, these two old enemies found themselves in May 1967 poised for another round of the

Sinai fracas. Under heavy public pressure and a vocal General Staff, the hesitant prime minister, Levi Eshkoll, was forced to add Dayan to his cabinet and make him minister of defense. The nation was elated, and the army regained its self-assurance and morale. Soon enough, war broke out; in six days, the armed forces of Egypt, Jordan, and Syria were thoroughly beaten: Israel extended its territory to three time its original size, to include the Sinai Peninsula and the Gaza Strip, the Western Bank, and the Golan Heights. Dayan reaped most of the glory and remained in office for the next seven years.

The October 1973 War

As minister of defense, Dayan was, on the one hand, admired and trusted by the public and as a rule also by the army; on the other hand, however, his position in Golda Meir's government was far from strong, owing to her political tendencies and personal likes and dislikes. As a result, he was at times forced to swallow major appointments in the army that were rammed down his throat by Meir and her cronies, such as the 1972 appointment of General David Elazar as CoGS.

Since 1970, Egypt's Sadat had been planning to attack Israel, together with Syria. When the surprise blow fell, Israel was caught militarily unprepared, disorganized, and disoriented. A great deal of the blame for that fell directly on Dayan's shoulders. By misconstruing the signs of the impending assault, too conveniently trusting the army brass, unwilling to take necessary steps without Meir's express consent, and too often losing his fighting nerve, Dayan significantly hampered Israel's ability to cope effectively and decisively with the initially worsening situation. He came out of this war denuded of his popularity, the subject of popular displeasure and scorn. He did not last long in office.

Epilogue

In the 1977 elections, the ruling MAPAI lost its thirty-year dominance of Israel's politics. The Likkud Party, led by Menachem Begin, took over. Aware of his extraordinary mental and personal abilities and the absence of a figure of a similar caliber in his party, Begin invited Dayan to become foreign minister in his government. Dayan accepted and became the moving force in bringing about the 1978 peace treaty with Egypt (the Camp David Accords).

In 1979, Dayan resigned his post, and, two years later, on October 16, 1981, he died of a heart attack at the age of sixty-six.

Moshe Dayan was an unusually brave warrior, tremendously charismatic, brilliant, a realist to the core, and devoid of any illusions and, at the same time, a true lover of the Jewish people, their history, their legacy, their Bible, and their land.

Ariel Sharon: Major General, Commander, 143rd Tank Division

Early Years

Ariel Sharon was born on February 26, 1928, in the moshav Kfar Malal, in British-mandate Palestine. His parents were constantly at odds with the other members of the moshav, who practically ostracized them, a situation that no doubt had its impact on the formation of Sharon's personality and behavior.

In 1945, Sharon joined the Hagganah; two years later, he enlisted in the Jewish-manned Auxiliary Rural Police Patrol. In the War of Independence (1948–1949), as a platoon leader he took part in the notoriously bloody battle of Latrun, where he was badly wounded; were it not for one of his soldiers happening to stumble on him bleeding to death and carrying him for miles on his back all the way to base, he would have perished then and there. This incident too had an indelible effect on his attitudes and values as a warrior.

After the war, Sharon stayed in the army, serving as a reconnaissance company commander, followed by a stint in 1951 as the intelligence officer of the Central Command and later of the Northern Command. In 1952, he left the army to study history and Middle Eastern culture at the University of Jerusalem.

Unit 101

In 1953, on Ben-Gurion's order, Sharon returned to active service, was made a major and instructed to set up a clandestine commando unit to carry out retaliatory, cross-border raids in response to increasing Palestinian terrorist attacks launched from Egypt and Jordan. Sharon formed Unit 101, manning it with a few dozen superlative warriors and scouts he gleaned from various IDF units. The extraordinary achievements of this tiny, tough, trigger-happy unit induced the CoGS, Dayan, to merge it with the disappointing 890th Paratrooper Battalion. Sharon was made battalion commander, and his 101st men were appointed to key positions in the battalion.

In no time, the battalion found itself fighting terrorist infiltration intensively and successfully, inspiring the IDF with its élan and fighting fame.

The Suez War (1956)

In 1956, England, France, and Israel joined together, each for its own reasons, in order to attack Egypt and topple its dictator, Gamal Abdel Nasser. This strange coalition's operation started with the—October 29, 1956, jump of the 890th Battalion—by this time part of Sharon's 202nd Parachute Brigade—near the eastern entrance to the Mitla Pass, about forty miles east of the Suez Canal. On October 31, disregarding orders, Sharon got the 890th involved in a fierce battle with Egyptian troops in the pass. The 890th incurred some 160 casualties, 40 of them killed in action. It did not help that 260 Egyptian soldiers also died in the clash: Sharon drew the ire of his superiors and many of his subordinates as well, and his career was brought to a halt. Fortunately for him, Ben-Gurion kept his infatuation with him and pressed the IDF to rehabilitate the erring warrior, and, indeed, when Itzhak Rabin took office as CoGS in 1964, he brought Sharon in from the cold and eventually (in February 1967) made the thirty-one-year-old Sharon a major general.

The Six-Day War (June 1967)

The Six-Day War found Sharon at the head of the ad hoc 38th Division, tasked with the destruction of the vast, division-sized Egyptian Abou Agheila fortified complex (some twenty miles west of the Egypt-Israel border). He planned a far-from-simple night battle, involving infantry, armor, artillery, combat engineers, and helicopter-borne paratroopers and carried it out with clockwork precision. This battle was later thoroughly studied by many armies, notably the US Army Training and Doctrine Command.

Commanding General of the Southern Command

In 1969, Sharon was appointed commanding general of the Southern Command. One of his missions was to put an end to the growing terrorist activity in the Gaza Strip. He approached this task with his typical determination, methodicalness, ruthlessness, and originality. This operation went on for more than two years, at the end of which time the Gaza Strip was totally pacified and stayed so for the next fifteen years. Similar steps, with similar results, were taken against the Bedouins of Northern Sinai—whose living depended on smuggling weapons to the terrorists in Gaza Strip.

The Controversy over the Defense of Sinai

In 1968, General Chaim Barlev replaced Rabin as CoGS; one of his more important—and fateful—decisions was to set up along the Sinai bank of the Suez Canal a line of some thirty fortified strongholds (the so-called Ma'ozim) as a major component in the defenses of the Canal. Two of the most experienced and able generals of the IDF, Israel Tal and Ariel Sharon, opposed this concept as being too static and far from effective. Instead, they pressed for an aggressive, mobile, armored defensive posture, using the ground as a means, not as an object to be defended.

Barlev moved to separate those two from active service. General Tal was banished to a certain position at the Ministry of Defense, but the attempt push Sharon out was aborted by an irate party boss, the strongman of the ruling party (MAPAI), who understood that ousting the popular, potentially politically powerful Sharon would send him into the open arms of the Likkud opposition and gave Barlev a dressing down for his shortsightedness in this regard. Nevertheless, having completed his term as the commander of the Southern Command, and realizing that further promotion (his life's dream was to become CoGS) was not in the cards, Sharon retired in August 1973 and, as a reserve officer, was appointed commander of the 143rd Tank Division. A young, newly promoted, rather inexperienced, and highly controversial general, Shmuel Gonen, stepped into the huge shoes Sharon had left. Sharon himself became the moving force in bringing the Likkud ("Unity") party into being.

The October 1973 War

On the morning of October 6, Sharon's 143rd Tank Division got the call-up order. Several hours later, at about 1400 Middle East time, the armies of Egypt and Syria invaded the territories held by Israel since the Six-Day War. The 143rd was sent down to the Suez Canal theater; from the beginning, Sharon pressed for an offensive strategy, with the crossing of the canal as its central idea. In the meanwhile, Sharon, who had already as a rather low-ranking commander had serious trouble functioning as a subordinate, now developed an attitude of disrespectful distrust toward General Gonen, his superior, especially after the latter's abject failure to run the show in the first stage of the war, and probably also toward Gonen's replacement, Lieutenant General Bar-Lev, and Lieutenant General Elazar, the CoGS, for the same reasons. But, because he was the best field general Israel had ever produced, any attempt to dismiss him was doomed from the start. The idea of crossing the canal took root; Sharon's 143rd Division was ordered to carry out its crucial stages: approaching the point selected for the bridgehead, capturing it and the opposite bank as well, bringing in the bridging equipment, building the bridges over the canal, organizing and running the bridgehead, opening and widening the roads leading to it, clearing them of the enemy, constructing whatever was required, and taking part in operations west of the canal, all under the heaviest artillery fire ever recorded in the military history of Israel. Of all IDF's generals before and after, only Sharon could be trusted with such a gigantic task, and he carried it out with flying colors, thus practically winning the war for Israel. His men—soldiers and officers alike—admired him and trusted him unboundedly and would have followed him through hell or high water to wherever he had a mind to lead them.

Prime Minister

In February 1974, Sharon exchanged his fatigues for a politician's suit. For several years, he served as a member of the Knesset and as a minister in Likkud governments. As minister of defense, he was instrumental in launching the First Lebanon War (on June 6, 1982) and running it. While Beirut was under Israeli occupation, the Phalangists (the Christian militia) entered, with Israel's consent, the Palestinian refugee camps of Sabra and Shatila and massacred there close to a thousand people. An Israeli board of inquiry (the Cohen Committee) found Sharon personally responsible for this atrocity and recommended removing him from office. By government decision, a recalcitrant Sharon had to leave his post but not his position as a member of the government.

On May 1999, Sharon was elected chairman of the Likkud Party, and, two years later, having trounced Ehud Barak in the general elections, he became prime minister of Israel. He is considered to have been second only to Ben-Gurion as regards personal and political power, popularity, acumen, ability, and results.

On January 4, 2006, after five stormy years in office, Sharon suffered a devastating stroke that sent him into an eight-year coma; he died in 2014.

Arik Sharon was a great warrior, a great fighting general, a similarly great strategist, a great prime minister, a great Israeli, a lover of life, and an avid pantophagos.

David Elazar: Lieutenant General, CoGS

Early Years

David ("Dado") Elazar was born on August 27, 1925, in Sarajevo (now the capital of Bosnia and Herzegovina). In 1945, he came to British-mandate Palestine and settled in the kibbutz Ein Shemer.

Military Career

In 1946, Elazar joined the PALMACH. A year later, he became a squad leader, and, in the beginning of 1948, he was made a platoon leader. As a member of PALMACH, he fought in many battles that took place in Jerusalem and around it. In no time, he was made a company commander and almost immediately thereafter a battalion commander.

Elazar stayed in the army. In 1955, he was appointed commander of the 12th

Infantry Brigade, with the rank of colonel. In the Suez War of 1956, his brigade was employed in the Gaza Strip, mainly hunting down Feda'eens (Palestinian guerrillas and infiltrators).

After the war, Elazar transferred to the armored corps, becoming its commander. Promoted to major general, he was appointed general commander of the Northern Command in 1964. In the Six-Day War, his command's forces captured parts of the West Bank and the Golan Heights.

The October 1973 War and After

In August 1972, Elazar was appointed CoGS. In the October 1973 war, his performance revealed his inadequacy in preparing the armed forces and conducting the war. The Agranat Commission[6] found him lacking in these respects and recommended terminating him as CoGS.

Elazar resigned his position and immediately retired. On April 15, 1976, at the age of fifty-one, he died of a heart attack.

Chaim Bar-Lev: Member of the Knesset, Government Minister, Lieutenant General, Former CoGS, Commander of the Southern Command

Early Days

Born in 1924 in Vienna, Chaim Bar-Lev grew up in Zagreb (Yugoslavia) and came to British-mandate Palestine in 1938 alone. Four years later, he joined PALMACH and became a platoon leader, rising quickly to command, at twenty-three, a battalion. In 1952, he became CoS of the Northern Command and, two years later, assumed command of the 5th ("Giv'ati") Infantry Brigade.

In the Suez War of 1956, Bar-Lev commanded the 27th Armored Reserve Brigade, which operated in the Gaza Strip and northern Sinai. This, incidentally, was the last time he directly commanded a formation of any size in war.

In mid-1957, Bar-Lev was appointed commander of the armor corps and, about a year later, was promoted to major general. Between 1961 and 1964, he studied business administration at Columbia University; returning to active service in 1964, he was appointed CoGS Operations Branch. In 1967, he became deputy to the CoGS (Rabin), a position he held during the Six-Day War.

Later Days

In 1968, Bar-Lev was appointed CoGS and promoted to lieutenant general.

After four years in office, he retired to become a prominent member of the ruling party at that time, MAPAI.

As the October 1973 broke out, Bar-Lev, an officer in the reserves, was called up for active service as commander of the Southern Command, replacing its failing commander, General Gonen. After the war, he resumed his political career.

On May 7, 1994, at the age of seventy, Bar-Lev died.

As a senior commander, Bar-Lev's strengths were his steadiness, calmness, assertiveness, toughness, and risk aversion. Lack of updated experience, lack of charisma, and mediocrity negatively balanced the picture.

Shmuel Gonen: Major General, Commander of the Southern Command

Shmuel ("Gorodish") Gonen was born in Vilnius (now in Lithuania) in 1930 and came to Palestine three years later. At the age of fourteen, he joined the Hagganah, and, as a PALMACH soldier in the War of Independence, he was wounded five times in the battles for Jerusalem.

After the war, Gonen transferred to the budding armor corps, became an officer, and steadily rose up the command ladder. In the 1956 Suez War, he commanded a company and was awarded the IDF's second highest decoration for valor. In the Six-Day War (June 1967), he led the prestigious 7th Tank Brigade westward, through a series of bloody battles, all the way from the Gaza Strip to the Suez Canal.

In 1972, Gonen was promoted to major general and, a year later, was appointed general commander of the Southern Command. In the October 1973 War, his performance as commander of the theater proved way below par. Both Elazar and Dayan realized that he was not fit for his position and dismissed him then and there—for all practical purposes. After the war, the Agranat Commission found him unfit for high command.[7]

Abraham Adan: Major General, Commander of the 162nd Tank Division

Born in 1926 in the kibbutz Kfar Ghiladi, in British-mandate Palestine, and raised in Tel Aviv, Abraham ("Bren") Adan joined the PALMACH at the age of seventeen. There, for some reason, he earned the sobriquet "Bren" (the British light machine gun of those days) by which he would be known for the rest of his life.

In the War of Independence, he was a company commander in the Negev Brigade, which fought against the Egyptian expeditionary force in southern

Israel. His company was the first to reach Umm Rashrash (today's Eilat), at the tip of the Akaba Gulf of the Red Sea.

After the war, Adan transferred to the armored corps. In the 1956 Suez War, he commanded a tank battalion (the 82nd) and saw action in Sinai. A year later, he completed an advanced course at the Armor School of the US Army. After returning, he commanded the 7th Armored Brigade and the IDF Armor School. In the Six-Day War, he served as deputy commander of the 31st Tank Division, which fought in Central Sinai. In 1969, he was promoted to major general and made commander of the armored corps.

In the October 1973 War, Adan commanded the 162nd Tank Division, which operated in the central sector of the Suez Canal area of operations and, after crossing the canal, was instrumental in encircling the Egyptian Third Army, a move that brought Egypt's Sadat to sue frantically for a cease-fire.

As a rule, Adan's record in that war was judged to be far from anything to boast about; the fact that his career withered away in its wake, instead of blooming, supports this claim.

Adan died on September 28, 2012, at the age of eighty-six.

Seven Years Later: General Even Meets President Anwar Sadat

In 1980, Prime Minister Menachem Begin's office received an invitation for Major General Ariel Sharon and Major General Jacob Even to accompany President Yitzhak Navon during his state visit to Egypt, an event that marked the signing of the Egyptian-Israeli peace agreement. At the time, General Sharon was serving as a minister in the Israeli government and was unable to accept the invitation. General Even, who was commander of the National Defense College, was appointed to the team that provided military aid for President Navon.

The group arrived in Cairo on October 26, 1980, to receive a gracious welcome from President Anwar Sadat. General Even was impressed by the president's warm handshake and the meticulous planning and successful execution of the event. On October 29, at a formal dinner hosted by President Sadat at Abdin Palace, Even dined at the Egyptian Military High Command's table with Minister of Defense Ahmed Badawi, and the officials in attendance discussed the war in an open and friendly manner. Even talked about his role as General Sharon's deputy and his command of the Suez Canal crossing operation, and at one point, Minister Badawi asked Even what he would enjoy doing if he could spend a free day in Egypt. Even replied that he would like to meet with BG Abdalla Omran, an old friend from the UK RCDS, and to visit the Egyptian National Defense College to have a look at Egypt's 1973 war plans, particularly the canal crossing operation.

General Even's requests were granted. He met with BG Omran at his home and visited the college for a day.

The following day, Even joined President Navon's delegation for a tour of President Sadat's native village. During the tour, Sadat asked Even how the Israeli troops had managed to cross the canal despite the barrage of heavy artillery fire from the Egyptian forces. Even replied, "We passed through the fire." Sadat puffed on his pipe with a sharp expression. When the group parted ways at the end of the state visit, Even regarded Sadat as a charismatic leader who looked at the world with courage and practicality.

Notes

1. A major general in the British army during World War II who served in the India-Burma theater, he was killed in a plane crash in 1944.

2. PALMACH is an acronym for Plugot Mahatz (Hebrew for "Assault Companies"), the semimobilized units of the Jewish Hagganah organization.

3. Vichy, the part of conquered France that the victorious Germans left ostensibly independent during World War II, had a sort of control of its overseas assets as well as its colonial army and navy units. The capital of that puppet state was the town of Vichy.

4. Immediately on being formed, the new IDF did not have ranks equivalent to full colonel and brigadier-general. Thus, a lieutenant colonel would command either a battalion or a brigade, and, at the same time, another brigade could have a major general as its commander.

5. He rose straight from colonel (that rank was added in 1950) to major general since, at that time, the IDF still did not have the equivalent of a brigadier general. That rank (*tat-aluf*) was introduced about a year and a half later.

6. The Agranat Commission, named after its chairman, Chief Justice Agranat, was formed on November 21, 1973, to investigate what caused and who was responsible for the initial snafu on the part of the IDF. It released its interim report, containing recommendations regarding the CoGS and a few others, on April 1, 1974. An abridged version of that report was published in Hebrew by Amm Oved of Tel Aviv in 1975.

7. The Agranat Commission's third (and last) report, as submitted to the government on January 30, 1975.

Bibliography

The Yom Kippur War

Egyptian Sources

Gamasy, Field Marshal Mohamed Abdel Ghani el-. *The October War.* Translated by Gillian Potter et al. Cairo: American University in Cairo Press, 1993.

Sadat, Anwar el-. *In Search of Identity: An Autobiography.* New York: Harper & Row, 1978.

Shazly, Lieutenant General Saad el-. *The Crossing of the Suez.* San Francisco: American Mideast Research, 1980.

Other Sources

Bar Siman-Tov, Ya'acov. *The Israeli-Egyptian War of Attrition, 1969–1970.* New York: Columbia University Press, 1980.

Bell, J. Bowyer. "National Character and Military Strategy: The Egyptian Experience, October 1973." *Parameters* (US Army War College) 5, no. 1 (1975): 6–16.

Bolia, Robert S. "Overreliance on Technology in Wartime: The Yom Kippur War as a Case Study." *Parameters* (US Army War College) 43, no. 2 (Summer 2004): 46–56.

Gal, Reuven. *A Portrait of the Israeli Soldier.* New York: Greenwood, 1986.

Hussein, Hamid. "The Fourth Round—a Critical Review of the 1973 Arab-Israeli War." *Defence Journal,* November 2002. www.defencejournal.com/2002/nov/4th-round.htm.

Kissinger, Henry. *Years of Upheaval.* Boston: Little, Brown, 1982.

Machiavelli, Nicolo. *Discourses on Livy.* Mineola, NY: Dover, 2007.

Sharon, Major General Ariel. *Warrior.* New York: Simon & Schuster, 1989.

Vegetius (Flavius Vegetius Renatus). *De re militari.* http://www.sonshi.com/vegetius.html.

River Crossing and Bridgeheads

Combined Arms Breaching Operations. Field Manual 90-13-1. Washington, DC: US Department of the Army, 1991.

Laurie, Clayton D. *Anzio Beachhead.* Washington, DC: US War Department, Historical Division, 1949. Reprinted as CMH 100-10 (Washington, DC: US Army Center of Military History, 1989).

Lazenby, J. F. *Hannibal's War: A Military History of the Second Punic War.* 1978. Norman: University of Oklahoma Press, 1998.

River-Crossing Operations. Field Manual 90-13; Marine Corps Warfighting Publication 3-17.1. Washington, DC: US Department of the Army, 1998.

Generalship

Ambrose, Stephen E. "Eisenhower's Generalship." *Parameters* (US Army War College) 40, no. 4 (Winter 2010–2011): 90–98.

Bradley, General of the Army Omar N. "On Leadership." *Parameters* (US Army War College) 11, no. 3 (September 1981): 2–7.

Clausewitz, General Karl von. *On War.* Abridged and edited by Colonel Harry G. Summers under the title *War, Politics and Power.* Washington, DC: Regency Gateway, 1997.

———. *On War.* The Project Gutenberg E-Book of *On War.* Released February 25, 2005.

Fuller, Major General J. F. C. *Generalship—Its Diseases and Their Cure.* Reprint, Harrisburg, PA: Military Service Publishing Co., 1936.

———. *The Conduct of War.* London: Eyre & Spottiswoode, 1961.

Gelb, Norman. *Ike and Monty: Generals at War.* New York: William Morrow, 1994.

Jomini, Antoine-Henri, Baron de. *The Art of War.* 1838. Mineola, NY: Dover, 2007.

Meigs, General Montgomery C. "Generalship: Qualities, Instincts, and Character." *Parameters* (US Army War College) 32, no. 2 (Summer 2001): 4–17.

Saxe, Marshal Maurice de. *Reveries on the Art of War.* 1757. Translated and edited by Brigadier General Thomas R. Phillips. Mineola, NY: Dover, 2007.

Sun Tzu. *The Art of War.* Translated and with an introduction by Samuel B. Griffith. With a preface by B. H. Liddel-Hart. Oxford: Oxford University Press, 1963.

Thompson, Henry L. *The Stress Effect: Why Smart Leaders Make Dumb Decisions—and What to Do about it.* Hoboken, NJ: Jossey-Bass, 2010.

Tuchman, Barbara. "Generalship." *Parameters* (US Army War College) 2, no. 2 (Spring 1972): 2–11.

———. "An Inquiry into the Persistence of Unwisdom in Government." *Parameters* (US Army War College) 10, no. 1 (March 1980): 2–9.

Wavell, General Archibald, and General John Dill. *Generals and Generalship.* New York: Macmillan, 1941.

Yingling, Lieutenant Colonel Paul, US Army. "A Failure in Generalship." *Armed Forces Journal,* May 1, 2007. armedforcesjournal.com/a-failure-in-generalship.

Risk

Chisolm, Donald. "The Risk of Optimism in the Conduct of War." *Parameters* (US Army War College) 33, no. 4 (Winter 2003–2004): 114–31.

Kahneman, Daniel, and Amos Tversky. "Prospect Theory: An Analysis of Decision under Risk." *Econometrica* 47, no. 2 (March 1979): 263–92.

Risk Management. FM-100-14. Washington, DC: US Department of the Army, 1998.

Risk Management—Principles and Guidelines. ISO 31000:2009. Geneva: International Organization for Standardization, 2009.

Other Topics

Adan, Avraham. *On the Banks of the Suez: An Israeli General's Personal Account of the Yom Kippur War* (in Hebrew). Jerusalem: Edanim, 1979.

Arie, Braun. *Moshe Dayan in the Yom Kippur War* (in Hebrew). Tel Aviv: Idanim, 1992.

Asher, Colonel Danny. "The Egyptian Plans for the Yom Kippur War" (in Hebrew). *Maarachot,* November 1978.

Barnea, Nahum, and Smadar Perry. *Yedioth Ahronoth,* holiday supplement, October 5, 2003.

Baron, Brigadier General Aryeh. *Moshe Dayan in the Yom Kippur War* (in Hebrew). Tel Aviv: Idanim/Yedioth Ahronoth, 1992.

Bartholomees, J. Boone. "Theory of Victory." *Parameters* (US Army War College) 38, no. 2 (Summer 2008): 25–36.

Bartov, Hanoch. *Dado* (in Hebrew). Vol. 2. Tel Aviv: Sifriat Maariv, 1978.

Bergman, Ronen, and Gil Meltzer. *Real Time* (in Hebrew). Tel Aviv: Yedioth Ahronoth/Sifrei Hemed, 2003.

Crane, Conrad C. "Beware of Boldness." *Parameters* (US Army War College) 36, no. 2 (Summer 2006): 88–97.

Dayan, Moshe. *Milestones* (in Hebrew). Jerusalem: Idanim; Tel Aviv: Dvir, 1976.

———. *The Story of My Life* (in Hebrew). Tel Aviv: Yedioth Ahronoth, 1976.

Drori, Zeev. *Ma'ariv,* April 30, 2004.

Duggan, William. *Coup d'Oeil: Strategic Intuition in Army Planning.* Carlisle, PA: Strategic Studies Institute, US Army War College, November 2005.

Echevarria, Antulio J., II. "The Trouble with History." *Parameters* (US Army War College) 35, no. 2 (Summer 2005): 78–90.

Edwards, A. F. W. *Likelihood.* Baltimore: Johns Hopkins University Press, 1992.

Eilon, Colonel Avraham. "Why Was October 14, 1973, Omitted from the History in Sadat's Book?" (in Hebrew). *Maarachot,* November 1978.

Eitan, Zeev. "The Battle Next to the Bitter Lakes" (in Hebrew). *Maarachot,* November–December 1974.

Ezov, Amiram. *Crossing* (in Hebrew). Kinneret: Zemora-Bitan, 2011.

Golan, Lieutenant Colonel Shimon. "October 12, 1973—the CoGS's and the Political Level's Positions: The Canal Crossing and the Need for a Cease-Fire" (in Hebrew). *Maarachot,* November–December 1978.

———. "In the Shadow of the Surprise: The High Command in the Yom Kippur War" (in Hebrew). *Maarachot,* December 2005.

Gray, Colin S. *Defining and Achieving Decisive Victory.* Carlisle, PA: Strategic Studies Institute, US Army War College, April 2002.

Guy, Carmit. *Bar-Lev* (in Hebrew). Tel Aviv: Am Oved, 1988.

Haber, Eithan. "Not for the Protocol" (in Hebrew). *Yedioth Ahronoth,* October 17, 2010, 21.

Hisdai, Colonel Ya'akov. *Maarachot,* August 1980.

Izzo, Lieutenant Colonel Lawrence L. "The Center of Gravity Is Not an Achilles Heel." *Military Review,* January 1988, 72–77.

Kissinger, Henry. *Years of Upheaval.* Boston: Little, Brown, 1982.

Oren, Amir. "Comparing the Aims with the Results, Israel Failed in '73, and Its Achievements Were Only Partial" (in Hebrew). *Haaretz,* March 12, 2003.

Oren, Lieutenant Colonel Elhanan. *A History of the Yom Kippur War* (in Hebrew). Tel Aviv: IDF History Branch, December 2004.

M——, Lieutenant Colonel. "The Egyptian Army's Operational Halt in the Yom Kippur War" (in Hebrew). *Maarachot,* November–December 1992.

Peled, Major General Binyamin. *Days of Reckoning* (in Hebrew). Ben Shemen: Modan, 2004.

Segev, Tom. *Haaretz* (Tel Aviv), weekly supplement, March 3, 2010.

Sneh, Efraim. *Ma'ariv,* April 30, 2004.

Tal, Major General Israel. *National Security: Few against the Many* (in Hebrew). Tel Aviv: Dvir, 1996.

Wald, Colonel Dr. Emanuel. *The Curse of the Broken Vessels* (in Hebrew). Jerusalem: Schoken, 1987.

Zamir, Zvi. *Eyes-Wide-Open* (in Hebrew). Or Yehuda: Kineret, Beitan, 2011.

Index

Note: Italicized page numbers indicate illustrations.

www.ingramcontent.com/pod-product-compliance
Lightning Source LLC
LaVergne TN
LVHW050148080826
844660LV00002B/119
9780813169552